Teaching Young Children
in Multicultural Classrooms
Issues, Concepts, and
Strategies

Teaching Young Children in Multicultural Classrooms
Issues, Concepts, and Strategies

Wilma Robles de Meléndez, PhD
Nova Southeastern University

Vesna Ostertag, EdD
Nova Southeastern University

Contributed by
Johanne Peck, PhD
Nova Southeastern University

Delmar Publishers

 **International Thomson Publishing**

Albany • Bonn • Boston • Cincinnati • Detroit • London • Madrid
Melbourne • Mexico City • New York • Pacific Grove • Paris • San Francisco
Singapore • Tokyo • Toronto • Washington

NOTICE TO THE READER

Cover Design: joanne beckmann design

Delmar Staff
Acquisitions Editor: Jay Whitney
Associate Editor: Erin O'Connor Traylor
Production Editor: Marah Bellegarde
Editorial Assistant: Glenna Stanfield

COPYRIGHT © 1997
By Delmar Publishers
a division of International Thomson Publishing Inc.

The ITP logo is a trademark under license.

Printed in the United States of America

For more information, contact:

Delmar Publishers
3 Columbia Circle, Box 15015
Albany, New York 12212-5015

International Thomson Publishing Europe
Berkshire House
168-173 High Holborn
London, WC1V 7AA
England

Thomas Nelson Australia
102 Dodds Street
South Melbourne, 3205
Victoria, Australia

Nelson Canada
1120 Birchmount Road
Scarborough, Ontario
Canada, M1K 5G4

International Thomson Editores
Campos Eliseos 385, Piso 7
Col Polanco
11560 Mexico D F Mexico

International Thomson Publishing GmbH
Konigswinterer Strasse 418
53227 Bonn
Germany

International Thomson Publishing Asia
221 Henderson Road
#05-10 Henderson Building
Singapore 0315

International Thomson Publishing—Japan
Hirakawacho Kyowa Building, 3F
2-2-1 Hirakawacho
Chiyoda-ku, Tokyo 102
Japan

1 2 3 4 5 6 7 8 9 10 XXX 02 01 00 99 98 97 96

Library of Congress Cataloging-in-Publication Data

De Meléndez, Wilma Robles.
    Teaching young children in multicultural classrooms : issues,
concepts, and strategies / Wilma Robles de Meléndez. Vesna Ostertag
;   contributed by Johanne Peck.
      p.   cm.
    Includes bibliographical references.
    ISBN 0-8273-7275-2
    1. Multicultural education—United States.   2. Early childhood
education—United States—Curricula.   3. Minorities—Education
(Early childhood)—United States.   I. Ostertag, Vesna.   II. Peck,
Johanne T.   III. Title.
LC1099.3.D4   1997
370. 19'6—dc20   96-23105
                                                      CIP

To my family, from whom I learned that we are all equal. To my husband Sal with whom I share my life and my dreams.

W. R. M.

To the children of Bosnia: Muslims, Serbs, and Croats alike, who are the most recent victims of ignorance and prejudice. May the future heal your wounds with love and universal understanding.

V. O.

Preface

Introduction

We are as proud of being Americans as we are of our own cultural heritages. We also feel proud when we hear and see that so many people still consider our country the bastion of freedom and hope. This pride is diminished, however, whenever we witness prejudice, discrimination, and unfairness against some members of our society. Much has been written and said about what makes some people have wrong ideas about others. Undoubtedly, much more will be said about this topic as we enter the 21st century. Instead of engaging in philosophical and theoretical discussions about such injustices, we, as educators, believe we need to look for practical solutions that can effectively address the challenge of living in a pluralistic society. That solution is found in education. Our belief that people can learn to see the sameness in all has led us to the writing of this book. Envisioning empowering classrooms where our young children will find themselves and their cultures validated is the dream that sustains this work. Because we believe early childhood teachers are the cornerstone of educational success, we dedicate this work as a source of ideas that will allow them to create such classrooms for all children.

Purpose and Organization of the Book

The purpose of this book is to provide a plan for early childhood professionals for development and teaching of a multicultural curriculum.

The authors envision this work to be particularly useful as a resource for classroom teachers of young children, as a resource for inservice programs in multicultural education, and as an undergraduate textbook for a course dealing with teaching for diversity.

The book is organized in three parts. Part I deals with social foundations and theory of multicultural instruction. It contains the current historical perspectives of multiculturalism, future trends, and the social, psychological developmental influences that affect young children. Part II explores the past and current issues and directions of multicultural education. It explores the historical background and different approaches to teaching for diversity. Part III provides resources in the form of guidelines and ideas for classroom implementation. Several actual multicultural instruments, curriculum plans, and classroom techniques are presented.

The book balances theory and practice, which makes it suitable for the several purposes mentioned earlier. The theoretical component is necessary for several reasons. *First*, the authors believe it is good practice to base the recommendations and conclusions on a sound scholarly knowledge base and proven practices. *Second*, it is necessary for teachers to understand the principles and theories that underlie practices related to multicultural education in order to know how to implement them properly. *Third*, the theoretical background provides a framework for multiculturalism that makes it fit into the larger context of teaching and learning. The practical aspect of the book is a consequence of the authors' strong commitment to practitioners in the field of early childhood education and to the commitment of bonding theory and practice.

There are four types of activities provided throughout the book: "In action . . . ," "Snapshots," "Focus on classroom practices," and "Things to Do." They are intended to provide exercises, promote discussions, and present practical ideas. Each *In action* activity is accompanied with questions and other information related to the material discussed in the body of the chapter. *Snapshots* are used to present events or excerpts from literature related to the information in the chapter. *Focus on classroom practices* offers examples of activities and suggestions for classroom application of the theoretical concepts discussed in each chapter. The activities at the end of the chapter, *Things to Do,* provide additional practice for individuals and groups.

All the activities are designed to be explored in the broad context of our society, in their relationship to the teachers' personal frame of reference, and in connection with classroom practices. Readers are encouraged to make adaptations to the activities and other material at any time.

We have also chosen Barbara, the kindergarten teacher, to go on our multicultural journey. We believe that she is a typical teacher with whom many of the readers will identify. Her joys and dilemmas are familiar. As Barbara resolved her problems, we hope so will you.

Each chapter also contains a reference list and a children's literature corner. The references provide additional sources of study and the children's books can be brought into the classroom for immediate implementation of the principles and practices presented in each chapter. The *Appendix* section includes a detailed children's literature list as well as information about classroom resources.

A Final Word From the Authors

We chose to write about education for diversity not only because we believe in its importance to education and to the future of our country, but also for very personal reasons. Both of us are "newcomers" to America. Both have experienced, together with our families, the tribulations and sometimes painful adjustments of starting a new life in a strange new land. Many of the experiences we wrote about in the book have personal significance. We know from first hand what it is to be different.

We have also experienced diversity as American residents of other countries like the U.S. Virgin Islands, Puerto Rico, Spain, Germany, India, and the former country of Yugoslavia. Our travels have taken us to many other interesting places as well. These experiences have enriched us and given us multicultural and global perspectives that we wish to share through this book with our fellow educators and other readers. Join us on our journey!

Wilma Robles de Meléndez
Vesna Ostertag

Acknowledgments

No work is ever accomplished without the help of family members, colleagues, and friends. We would like to thank in particular our colleague and a significant contributor to this work, Dr. Johanne Peck, the Director of the Nova Southeastern University (NSU) Graduate Teacher Education Program (GTEP) for the many hours of editing and her many valuable suggestions that enhanced this work. Our thanks go to our colleague Professor Audrey Henry for her assistance in researching the resources for this book. Her contributions to the listings of children's literature were especially valuable. Our gratitude also goes to NSU staff members Ada Christy and Kim Nicely for their help.

We are also thankful to our graduate students majoring in early childhood education who through the years generously shared their ideas and experiences with us. Their dilemmas and concerns were greatly responsible for the direction and focus of this book.

We also would like to acknowledge the support and collaboration of the Delmar staff: Glenna Stanfield, Erin O'Connor, and Marah Bellegarde. A very special thank you (¡Muchas, muchas gracias!) to our editor, Jay Whitney, who from the very beginning believed and supported this work.

A very special thank you (¡Gracias mil!) goes to our families who stayed at our side through the many long hours, during holidays, and weekends giving us encouragement and providing suggestions that helped shape this work.

The authors would like to extend their appreciation to the reviewers enlisted through Delmar for their constructive criticism and helpful suggestions. They include:

Audrey Byrd
Guilford Technical Community College
Greensboro, North Carolina

Kathleen Fite
Southwest Texas State University
San Marcos, Texas

Maureen Gillette
College of St. Rose
Albany, New York

Karen Liu
Indiana State University
Terre Haute, Indiana

Lyn Miller-Lachmann
Editor-in-Chief
Multicultural Review
Ballston Spa, New York

Delia Richards
Prince George's Community College
Largo, Maryland

Jackie Schmidt
University of Alaska
Palmer, Alaska

Barbara Wierserbs
Kingsborough Community College
Brooklyn, New York

Wilma Robles de Meléndez
Vesna Ostertag

Contents

Preface   *vii*
Acknowledgments   *ix*

PART I   **Foundations for Multicultural Education in Today's Early Childhood Classrooms**   **1**

CHAPTER 1   *Facing the Reality of Diversity: The Intricate Nature of Our Society*   *3*

The United States—A Nation of Contrasts   4
School—The Arena of Diversity and Action   4
How Did We Become a Culturally Diverse Society?   6
A Nation of Immigrants   8
A Call for Action   33
Points to Remember   37
Things to Do   38
Children's Literature Corner   39
References   39

CHAPTER 2   *The Nature of Culture, the Nature of People*   *43*

Culture, the Magic Web of Life   44
Planning to Take Action   70
Things to Do   71
Children's Literature Corner   71
References   72

CHAPTER 3   *Families in Our Classrooms: Many Ways, Many Voices*   *75*

Families, a Constant in Our Changing Society   76
What Is a Family?   76
The Family Structure: Who Is in the Family?   86
The Family, the Most Important Element in Our Lives   94
The Power of the Family   96

Families, the Essence of Social Life   104
Things to Do   106
Children's Literature Corner   106
References   106

CHAPTER 4   *Who Is the Child? Developmental Characteristics of*
Young Children   109

Looking at Children: So Alike and Yet So Different   110
Development: The Process of Becoming   110
Socialization: Learning to Be with Others, Learning to Be Ourselves   123
Social Learning Happens All Around Us   126
Discovering That You Are Not Like Me   129
Prosocial Skills: A Basis for Equity   141
Knowing the Child   142
Things to Do   143
Children's Literature Corner   143
References   143

PART II   **Exploring the Roots of Multicultural Education:**
Issues and Directions   145

CHAPTER 5   *Everything Started When . . . Tracing the Beginnings of*
Multicultural Education   147

Setting the Stage   148
Early Efforts Toward Equality in Education   152
The Road to Multicultural Education   164
The Birth of Multicultural Education   168
Things to Do   175
Children's Literature Corner   175
References   176

CHAPTER 6   *Approaches to Multicultural Education: Ways and Designs*
for Classroom Implementation   179

Time for Decisions   180
Exploring Models and Approaches   181
Models of Multicultural Education   182
Reflecting on the Approaches for Multicultural Education   204
Things to Do   205
Children's Literature Corner   206
References   206

P A R T   I I I   **Into Action: Implementing a Pluricultural Program for Children   207**

CHAPTER 7   *The Classroom, Where Words Become Action   209*

Reaffirming the Decision to Teach Multiculturally   210
Where Do We Start?   210
Exploring Our Teaching Environment   213
Assessing Curriculum Programs   219
Discovering the Reality of Our Programs   226
Designing Multicultural Assessment Tools   232
Things to Do   237
Children's Literature Corner   238
References   238

CHAPTER 8   *Preparing to Bring Ideas into Action   241*

A Time for Ideas: Planning for Multicultural Teaching   242
Planning and Organizing: The Critical Steps   243
What Is Planning? Do We Need to Plan?   244
Setting Directions: A Curriculum Design of Our Choice   249
Making Decisions: What Barbara Did   249
Focus on the Environment   252
Putting Everything Together   263
Selecting the Content for Multicultural Teaching   266
What Is the Next Step?   271
Things to Do   271
Children's Literature Corner   271
References   271

CHAPTER 9   *Activities and Resources for Multicultural Teaching: A World of Possibilities!   273*

Building a Classroom for Our Multicultural Society   274
A Classroom for Teaching About Diversity   278
Guidelines for a Multicultural Classroom Environment   280
Preparing to Design Activities for the Classroom   299
Planning for Multiple Perspective Learning   299
The Stage Is Set!   313
Things to Do   316
Children's Literature Corner   316
References   317

CHAPTER 10 *A World of Resources: Involving Parents, Friends, and the Community*   *319*

Working Together: The Essence of a Child's Success   320
Involving Everyone in the Family   323
At Home: Where the Self Begins, Where We Become   328
The School Neighborhood and the Community   339
Communication: The Road to Positive Relationships   341
Ideas for Planning Activities with Families   349
What Lies Ahead?   353
Before We End, a Word to the Reader   353
Things to Do   353
Organizations and Advocates for Parents and Families   354
Children's Literature Corner   354
References   355

APPENDICES

A   List of Multicultural Children's Books   357
B   Web of Possibilities Using Multicultural Literature   363
C   Developing Multicultural Awareness: Sample Activities   365
D   Sample Lesson Plan Using "The Black Snowman"   369
E   Sample Lesson Plan Using the Bredekamp and Rosegrant Model (1992)   371
F   Patterns for Persona Dolls   375
G   Learning About Islands   377
H   Island Stick Puppets   379
I   Planning for Cultural Diversity: Developing a Class Profile   381
J   Creating the Multicultural Environment: Resources for the Classroom   383
K   Checklist for Diversity in Early Childhood Education and Care (SECA)   389

Glossary   *393*
Index   *396*

> "We are preparing children to lead rewarding, productive lives in a world that always has been, and surely always will be, diverse."
>
> Janet Brown McCracken (1993)

PART I

Foundations for Multicultural Education in Today's Early Childhood Classrooms

Let's Meet Barbara!

Barbara, an experienced kindergarten teacher, decided to take a summer workshop in multicultural education in order to renew her certification. Having taught for seven years, Barbara was not seriously expecting to learn anything new. The course sounded like an easy, fun way to pick up three credits and maybe get some new handouts. Besides, she had lots of experience with cultural diversity. She thought of Etienne, the slender boy with bright big eyes who often mumbled to himself in Creole; Lavanya, the quietest girl with the loveliest smile who did not have many friends; and little Caroline, who went to live with her grandparents after her family lost their home because her father was laid off. "They all came from different cultures, but they did as well as could be expected this year," Barbara reassured herself.

The workshop proved to be full of surprises. On the way home after the last class, new ideas still whirling in her head, Barbara thought, "I never really knew much about diversity! I have to do things differently to help all the children in my class. I could have done so much more for Etienne, Lavanya, and Caroline if I had known all this last year. But it's not too late for my new class. I already know I will have six children with different ethnic backgrounds."

Barbara also remembered something important the instructor said. "You will be a good teacher only if you give each of your students an equal opportunity. To do that you must adjust your teaching to include the cultural backgrounds of your students." Barbara could still vividly remember the heated discussion that followed. Both experienced and beginning teachers took offense to this statement until they began to analyze their teaching. Practically everyone in the class had a different concept of culture, and no one considered the children's cultures in their planning. For the first time, Barbara began to suspect that she was not the kind of teacher she thought she was.

Writing in the journal, started during the workshop, Barbara entered the following: "I need to do something. I have to make my classroom the kind of social and cultural laboratory the professor described. But, I still don't know enough about different cultures and the influence of culture on children. Perhaps I can get more information at the library. The instructor said that one course will not make me into a multicultural teacher, that there were many things I had to do on my own. Well, I've made a decision. Starting this year all my students will matter. All will be accepted as they are. I want to be their best teacher."

Barbara

Join us as we follow Barbara on her journey!

"He met many people along the way. He shook hands with black men, with yellow men and red men."

Allen Say (1994)

CHAPTER 1

Facing the Reality of Diversity: The Intricate Nature of Our Society

In this chapter we will:

- define cultural diversity
- explain why our country is described as multicultural
- establish the implications of demographic changes in American society
- establish why early childhood teachers need to be aware of cultural diversity issues

Key concepts:

- cultural diversity
- multicultural society
- demographic changes
- immigration
- non-European Americans

❖ The United States—A Nation of Contrasts

Nothing in this world reflects diversity more than nature. The landscape of our planet Earth is an intricate mix of shapes, forms, and colors each with its own identity and spirit, separate, and yet a piece of a whole. The land we live in probably best reflects this notion. The landscape of America, a quilt woven of dramatically different terrains, is populated by people equally unique and diverse. Glancing over the entire country from the Pacific to the Atlantic, we envision a land where many different environments co-exist: warm deserts, snowcapped mountains, golden plains, green valleys, lush marshlands, sandy beaches, and bustling cities. All are different yet one: America. No less than its geography, the people who inhabit America are also an example of nature's diversity. Much like its eclectic landscape, America's people mirror the diversity of the world. In small country towns and large cities alike, we find numerous examples of world cultures. Whether they wear a sari, attend a mosque, speak Tagalog, Hmong, or French Creole, members of different cultures have changed the semblance of our social landscape.

We are quickly learning about the rest of the world as we live and interact with individuals from other cultures in our communities, schools, and places of work. Not being immigrants or children of immigrants, many of us find ourselves in the midst of a new environment that challenges our American life style and our values. The new pluralism also evokes a myriad of emotions and prompts actions never experienced before (Greene 1993). There have always been newcomers whose English we did not understand very well. However, the pluralism we encounter today is somehow different. It has an urgency about it, it demands soul-searching and acceptance of unknown concepts, philosophies,

and ways of life. It is this sense of urgency that demands from all educators and in particular from early childhood educators a commitment to redesign and reformulate teaching practices. Education is the key to a strong nation. One of the goals of education is to make people discover and build upon their own strengths. As we transform our educational perspectives through a framework of cultural responsiveness, we will set the foundation for the United States of the twenty-first century.

The presence of culturally diverse groups has brought American people in contact with ways different from the traditional (Baruth & Manning 1992). What decades ago would have caught the eye, today appears customary. Nowhere else is this more apparent than at the community level. It is there that most of us recognize to what extent pluralism permeates our world. Diversity makes itself known through the fascinating contrasts that bring a new vitality to our surroundings. For example, American food often takes a back seat to flavorful pizza and spicy burritos, the Latin beat can be heard on radio stations just as often as American rock 'n' roll, sari clad women shop next to women in jeans, and a Vietnamese language newspaper can be found next to the English ones at the neighborhood newspaper stand. School grounds echo with different languages of children trying to communicate. Community centers all over the country are filled with newly arrived immigrants trying to learn the language of their newly adopted homeland. Many of today's immigrants, however, remain cloistered in their communities, clinging to their language and culture, unaware of the mainstream world.

❖ School—The Arena of Diversity and Action

The word "arena" conjures visions of early Christians fighting for their lives. It evokes violent vi-

Like this Eastern European family in Chicago (circa 1925), many Europeans migrated to the United States during the early part of the 20th century. In search of a better life, they left behind their homelands to make this country their new home. Do you find any similarities between them and today's immigrant families?

sions of combat, prisoners, and other impressions associated with war. But, an ancient arena today can also be a place of tranquility and wisdom, or a place where beauty and grace are found. Why is it that educators often refer to the classroom as an arena? This epithet embodies many characteristics of today's classrooms. Unfortunately, thousands of our classrooms are often warlike. It is also a fact that wisdom and excellence are still much valued there. Classrooms are also places

Throughout the entire history of our country, children of immigrants have learned about their new home culture through school. This group of first graders from 1928 shared many things in common, but one in particular characterized them: They were all born in different countries and spoke languages different from English. Can you imagine the challenges they faced?

Educators at all levels realize that diversity has entered the schools. We recognize its effects on our way of thinking, and we know its force through the new laws and regulations that mandate innovative strategies and skills. Early childhood professionals know diversity through the joyous shouting of exotic words heard on the school playgrounds and through the tears of frustration that accompany conquests of new ground. The account of the first day of school depicted in Snapshot 1.1 is fictitious; however, today's teachers can easily relate to it.

That the ethnographic composition of American students has changed dramatically in the last two decades is a well-known fact. More and more schools are housing students with nontraditional cultural backgrounds (Adler 1993). A visit to any classroom, like the one described in Snapshot 1.1, would probably show the same or similar degree of cultural variety in many places in our country. The presence of different cultural groups varies from one geographical area to another. For example, Hispanics are found in greater numbers in South Florida and California; cities like Chicago and Seattle include large populations of Asian Indians and Vietnamese; and Alaska, Arizona, and New Mexico contain large contingents of Native Americans. Even states like Vermont and Maine, traditionally known for being populated by predominantly European Americans, participate in today's national diversity (Hodgkinson 1993).

❖ How Did We Become a Culturally Diverse Society?

Culture and diversity are terms that have become a part of today's educational jargon. Although this will be further explained in Chapter 2, let us briefly explore what they signify. We will begin with *culture*, a very hard term to define, for social scientists have not yet agreed on one single definition. Some define culture as a collection of

where beauty and creativity can be witnessed at the most unexpected moments. Like arenas, classrooms can be tranquil sanctuaries that nurture the spirit of the young. It is in the classroom that the battle of breaking cultural barriers will take place.

IN ACTION . . .   *What Is Diversity?*

Sometimes we are not fully aware of the diversity around us. To find out if diversity is a part of your community and your life, list all those things/details about other cultural groups that you have observed in your community. Find out how much you know about individuals from other cultures, their backgrounds, ways of life, etc.

- ▌ What role do these individuals play in your life?
- ▌ How has their presence changed your community?
- ▌ What are some important things you learned from them?
- ▌ What do you think they know about you?

beliefs, attitudes, habits, values, and practices a human group uses to form a view of reality (Shade & New 1993). This means that every cultural group like Filipinos, Koreans, and Jamaicans, for example, will interpret life events (marriage, death, child rearing, and others) according to the cultural frameworks they have established. These sets of ideas are accumulated and formed through time. They represent recognized and accepted frames of reference of a cultural group. Such frameworks are owned by every cultural group and are transmitted through

generations. At the classroom level, this means that young children from different cultures view our world in very heterogeneous ways. This is especially true of children of newly arrived immigrants. This also implies that as teachers we may have different ways of interpreting life than the children we teach. This divergence of ideas is how we encounter diversity in the classroom. This is also what makes teaching today's young children exciting and challenging.

Like the kindergarten teacher in Snapshot 1.1 who had children of six different cultural origins,

---

Snapshot 1.1
Teacher's Notes on the First Day of School

"Today I finally met my class. Twenty-three vivacious kids! When they handed me their list of names, I never imagined what I would find. As I talked with the children and some of their parents, I realized I have a mini United Nations in my classroom. Seven children are from Central America (Guatemala and Nicaragua), four are Jamaican, one is Haitian, two just came from Puerto Rico, one is Bahamian, and the rest are African American, like me. I've decided to make this year their best school year. I want to be their best teacher, but I don't think it will be easy."

many classrooms are exciting mosaics of cultural diversity. They are a natural extension of a new America where groups of many different origins and extractions have come together to form a *culturally diverse, multicultural,* or *pluralistic society* (Baruth & Manning 1992; Martorella 1994).

Diversity denotes contrasts, variations, or divergences from the ways of the mainstream or majority culture. When diversity is used in reference to human beings, we find that there are many elements involved in this concept. These meanings will be explored in Chapter 2 where we will focus on the connotation of *cultural origin* or *descent.*

Cultural diversity has not only transformed the composition of our population, it has also enriched the character of American life. The various groups have brought much knowledge about other parts of the world in forms of languages, traditions, customs, and folklore. This diversity is displayed in the classroom in countless ways: the various snacks children bring to school, the words and phrases they use, the ideas about families and social relationships they express, the special holidays they celebrate, and even the fashions they prefer. The classroom is a very polychromatic place that can be considered a microcosm of the new society. This polychromatic quality makes the United States exciting and special. This is also why American society is described as culturally

diverse. A culturally diverse society is one where different cultures exist, socially interact, and yet remain visible in their own context.

❖ A Nation of Immigrants

To answer how, why, and when the United States acquired this multicultural personality, we need to look back in history. The United States of America has traditionally been defined as a nation of immigrants. Nieto (1992) points out: "Immigration is not a phenomenon of the past. In fact, the experience of immigration is still fresh in the minds of a great many people in our country. It is an experience that begins anew every day that planes land, ships reach our shores, and people make their way on foot to our borders." (pp. xxiv–xxv)

The United States has also been described as a land where dreams for a better and more equitable life become a reality. Like the characters in the book *How many days to America* (Bunting 1988), the oppressed and the dreamers of the world, who are longing to find the land where all are equal, are still arriving by the thousands. Since the days of the first settlements, this part of North America has represented the pathway to liberty, justice, and opportunity. The chronicles of

---

WORKING GLOSSARY

▮ **Multiculturalism**—"a philosophical position and movement that assumes that the gender, ethnic, racial, and cultural diversity of a pluralistic society should be reflected in all of the institutionalized structures of educational institutions, including the staff, the norms, and values, the curriculum, and the student body" (Banks & Banks 1993, p. 359).

▮ **Cultural Pluralism**—a social state based on the premise that all newcomers have a right to maintain their languages and cultures while combining with others to form a new society reflective of all our differences (Nieto 1992, p. 307).

FOCUS ON CLASSROOM PRACTICES

LEARNING THAT WE ARE ALIKE AND DIFFERENT

Our present American society has sometimes been described as a wonderful tossed salad. This same metaphor probably describes children in most classrooms. As children begin to notice human diversity, it is just as important to guide them to discover how alike they are. You can begin with an activity like paper plate self-portraits. You will need a paper plate for each child, a set of cutouts of the different parts of the face, glue, and yarn for the hair and for hanging the "portraits." To highlight differences of facial traits, cutouts should include a variety of facial features like different eye colors and different shapes of noses, mouths, and ears that resemble the traits of your students. Including face parts different from those of the children in the group can be used as starters for later discussions. Distribute the materials, making sure that you have provided enough cutouts. To work on their portraits, have children work in pairs or in groups of four. This could be an introductory activity of a thematic unit, "Who We Are." After finishing their portraits, the children can talk about themselves. Emphasize similarities. Follow up with a rhyme like the following:

We are so alike!
(Have children face each other to point at face parts as they are named.)
Eyes I have and so do you.
I have a nose and so do you.
You and I also have a mouth to say HELLO!
And ears we also have.
Wow! We are so alike and how! (Showing surprise)

You can also have them play "Simon says." Here they would stand up as Simon asks: "Stand up if you have green eyes, if you have a long nose, etc." You may want to include other body parts to further stress similarities.

Teachers may want to share stories like *All the Colors We Are* by Katie Kissinger (1994 Redleaf Press) and *All the Colors of the Race* by Arnold Adoff (1982 Lothrop, Lee, and Shepard Books).

American history are full of vivid accounts of people who left their countries seduced by a land where freedom and respect for the individual are among the core principles (Banks & Banks 1993). The journey that began with the seventeenth century Mayflower Pilgrims, that still continues today, helped establish the distinctive trait of this country: cultural plurality.

European immigrants settled this country in the seventeenth and eighteenth centuries. Native

FOCUS ON CLASSROOM PRACTICES

LEADING CHILDREN TO DISCOVER DIVERSITY

At the core of diversity one finds the issue of human differences. Learning to live with diversity means helping children to recognize its value and its presence in our lives. To help children discover that we all hold distinctive traits, teachers can help them create a "Me Bag." This could be a part of the activities conducted at the beginning of the school year. This activity is based on the belief that because we all bring to our societies a unique bag of cultural characteristics, we are all special. It is also intended to help children see differences as a normal or logical part of daily life. This activity starts by the teacher's preparation of the "Me Bag" to be shared with the children.

Preparing a teacher's "ME BAG":
(You will need one large brown bag for each child.) Write your name on it and draw or paste your picture on the outside. Then, depending on the age level you teach, put inside the bag objects, drawings, or words that would define you as unique.

For example, you may want to include items about hobbies, pets, languages, music, favorite colors, flowers, etc. The bag can be introduced through an informal chat about yourself. As you talk, share the items with the class. Let children comment freely. Then ask the children to prepare their own "Me Bags." Distribute the brown bags and ask them to begin putting inside their bags at least three things that tell about them. Plan to have children present their bags. Their presentations can lead to the preparation of charts like "Facts about us." For example, charts could describe games, activities, colors, foods, and other things they like. Finding out things they have in common as well as those where they differ can be the topic of many interesting discussions. Either in small groups or with the whole class, the teacher can lead children in answering the following questions:

▌ What did we learn about our class? Tell me something you discovered about two of your friends.

▌ What things in common or those not in common did we discover about our classmates?

▌ In what ways are we all alike? Why?

▌ Tell me something that makes you special.

Bags can be displayed and kept as an ongoing activity. Other details can be added through the year. Teachers can follow up by adding books to the literacy center to reinforce the characteristics of diversity found among the children in the class.

IN ACTION . . . *Diversity in Your Life*

Perhaps you have not yet discerned how diversity touches your life. To find out, let us do a personal inventory. You will need a pad of self-stick notes, pencil, and a piece of paper. Make five columns on the piece of paper. Label the first four columns as things you *use, wear, eat,* and *read.* Label the fifth column *cultures.* Now, using the "stickies," write names of things you consider a part of your world that come from cultures other than your own. Once you have finished your cultural search, place the stickies in the appropriate columns. Fill in the names of cultures from which they originate.

▌ What have you learned about diversity in your life?

▌ What are the implications of your findings?

▌ Can you draw some conclusions about diversity?

Americans, as well as Africans and people of the Caribbean brought over as slave laborers, were the other significant population groups during that time. Historically, the beginning of today's American multicultures is found in the social interaction patterns that emerged among these groups. Because these interactions were largely based on discriminatory distinctions among people based on their race and the color of their skin, the seeds of unfairness and inequality were planted in the early days of this nation. Long years of persecution of the African Americans, the systematic eradication of the Native Americans, and later the disenfranchisement of the large numbers of Mexican Americans hampered the efforts of unification among peoples destined to share this land.

The First Immigrants

Early English settlers established unprecedented power to shape the culture of this land in the early years of the seventeenth century. Their values and social ethics defined a system of discrimination and persecution that still remains with us today. It first began with the early settlers' discrimination and systematic eradication of the East Coast Indian tribes. This was the beginning of one of the longest, most tragic and shameful chapters in our history.

WORKING GLOSSARY

▌ **Immigrants**—individuals from a country or a nation who settle in another country for various reasons. For example, Jamaicans came from their native country to establish themselves in the USA.

▌ **Migrants**—individuals who relocate to a different geographical region of one country or cross borders of other countries on a regular basis for a specific reason. For example, farm workers move seasonally from one state to another to pick oranges.

An elementary class of the 1950s resembles many of today's classrooms: More than half of these students were recent newcomers or children of first generation immigrant parents. Is it true that history repeats itself?

Having established themselves in Virginia, many of the first settlers were not fit to survive in the New World wilderness. They needed (and got) the help of the Native Americans to survive. However, soon the colonists were no longer satisfied with just food and provisions. They wanted the Indians' land, cattle, homes, and their trade. The early settlers' need for land was suddenly intensified by the tobacco trade that was beginning to flourish with Europe. The tobacco agriculture stimulated not only land expansion but also immigration. During the "Great Migration" of 1618–1623, the colony in Virginia grew from 400 to 4,500 people. This influx of people into the New World intensified the fight against the Native Americans and contributed to the settlers' violent theft of their lands and other possessions.

In order to justify the violence against the Indians, the English invented a myth of the "savage." They never recognized the realities of the Indian culture such as their highly developed agricultural system and their sophisticated building and craft skills. Instead, they invented the image of the bloodthirsty savage heathens naturally incapable of civilization (Takaki 1993). The systematic eradication and persecution of Native Americans that began with the English in the seventeenth century was modeled by the future generations of Americans who extended it across America for the next three centuries. This system of violent destruction rooted in discrimination resulted in the annihilation of entire Indian nations. The residual effects of this catastrophic tragedy cannot be estimated by sociologists and historians.

We can say, however, that the tragic history of the Native Americans has greatly impacted the conditions of their descendants today.

The second most significant societal change in the seventeenth century was the beginning of slavery of African Americans. Takaki (1993) indicates that the first 20 blacks brought to Virginia came as indentured servants and not as slaves. In the early days of Virginia, most workers were white indentured servants, many of whom were captured by English soldiers for sale in the New World. Coming mainly from England, Germany, and Ireland, these individuals were at the bottom of the social hierarchy. They were soon joined by increasing numbers of blacks from Africa and the Caribbean islands. At first there were no legal social differences ascribed to white and black groups. By 1660, however, slavery of blacks was institutionalized, setting a pattern of life of African Americans for centuries to come. Much of the reason was economic. With the rise of the cotton industry in the South, the white landowning elite needed a cheap source of labor to sustain the economy. The blacks filled that role because the supply of white indentured servants from Europe was drastically reduced. Therefore, the slave trade with Africa became a lucrative enterprise for those looking to get rich.

Justifying slavery morally was done in much the same way as justifying the eradication of Indians. Blacks were depicted as child-like heathen not in control of their emotions and impulses. The fact that they were not Christian originally separated them from the whites as well. This notion did not remain long, however, as many blacks adopted Christianity. The color of their skin soon became the most important element of discrimination.

Slavery was not invented by the Virginians. It existed in the West Indies. Therefore, it was considered a legitimate practice in the New World. It was also not instituted throughout the rest of the colonies, such as the New England settlements, largely because of different economies and the religious differences between the Puritans and the Virginians.

The beginning of slavery in the seventeenth century marked the start of violent persecution and segregation of African Americans that formally ended with the Emancipation Proclamation in 1864. This was the act that allowed the slaves to finally throw off the chains of bondage. Unfortunately, this legislation did not end the injustices committed by America's mainstream culture against this group. Partial equality came piecemeal through hard work, sacrifice, and even bloodshed. Over 130 years later African Americans still find themselves engaged in the battle for equality.

During the eighteenth and nineteenth centuries the United States matured and grew as a nation. Independence from England was won. Political stability was achieved as wars were waged against external enemies as well as the natives of this land. The great Western Expansion concluded with the United States reaching "from sea to shining sea." The Civil War that ravaged the country ended slavery and preserved the union. Economic, social, and political reforms following the post Civil War years initiated the new era in America. This age also marked the beginning of a new kind of diversity that intensified the kaleidoscope nature of this country and presented new challenges.

The great waves of immigration began with the Irish as early as the 1850s. Most settled in the large cities where they later made great strides in business and politics. On the West Coast the Chinese were arriving at the same time. Some came as economic immigrants looking for a better life, while many more came to join the 49ers in their quest for California's gold. By 1870, there were 63,000 Chinese living mostly in California (77%), the West, and the Southwest (Takaki 1993). The construction of the Central Pacific Railroad, completed in 1869, was largely a Chinese achievement.

The Mexicans came to build the Texas and Mexican railroad in the 1880s. Earlier, many Mexicans worked in the gold mines in California and in the copper mines in Arizona. They were employed as general laborers and were always paid less than their Anglo counterparts. Many of these laborers were migrants who never settled permanently in states where they worked. Others found themselves strangers in their own land after the annexation of Texas and California by the United States.

At the time of the Civil War, 35% of all African Americans lived in slavery in the South (Takaki 1993). They constituted the essential labor force in the agriculture of tobacco, cotton, hemp, rice, and sugar. The social conditions and treatment of the African Americans varied with the dispositions of their owners. Few were ruled by kindness; many were subjected to daily violence; all were required to work long and hard with no guarantees of any kind.

The Western Expansion brought about the building of the railroads and a growing number of settlers. Along with this came a cry for removal of the Indians from the Great Plains, the Rockies, the Black Hills, and other ancient homelands. The Choctaws of Mississippi and the Cherokees of Georgia were dispossessed of their lands as early as 1830. The Great Plains Indians—the Cheyenne, Kiowa, Arapaho, Sioux, and the Pawnees—were soon to follow with the completion of the railroad. Some went down fighting like the proud Pawnees while others, like the more pacifist Cherokees, suffered through the "Trail of Tears" that eradicated one fourth of their nation. By the end of the nineteenth century, Native Americans were confined to a system of reservations administered by the federal government.

The New Immigrants

By the end of the nineteenth century, America had entered into an unprecedented age of industrialization and progress. This age produced the industrial giants, entrepreneurs, and philanthropists like Carnegie, Morgan, Vanderbilt, Cermak, Dupont, Rockefeller, and others. It was also an era of great immigration waves beginning in

---

Snapshot 1.2
The Routine of a Slave

"The hands are required to be in the cotton field as soon as it is light in the morning, and, with the exception of ten or fifteen minutes, which is given to them at noon to swallow their allowance of cold bacon, they are not permitted to be a moment idle until it is too dark to see, and when the moon is full, they often labor till the middle of the night." After they left the fields they had more work to do. "Each one must attend to his respective chores. One feeds the mules, another the swine—another cuts the wood and so forth; besides the packing (of cotton) is all done by candlelight. Finally, at late hour, they reach the quarters, sleepy and overcome with the long day's toil."

Source: Northrop, S. (1993). Twelve years a slave. In R. Takaki (ed.). *A different mirror* (p. 111). New York: Little, Brown & Company.

the 1880s. The newcomers inspired a new backlash of nativism that led to many discriminatory practices. Among the most notable were the resurgence of anti-Catholicism, the exclusion of the Chinese who came to build the Central Pacific Railroad, and the segregation of the Japanese Americans who were seen as a threat after Japan won the Sino-Japanese War in 1895 and the Russo-Japanese War in 1905. African Americans were still excluded from unions, most businesses, education, and political endeavors (Clark & Remini 1975).

The first great wave of immigrants during the twentieth century occurred between 1905 and 1915 when various economic and political events in Europe caused ten million people to seek refuge in America (Borestein, Oct. 30, 1994). These were mostly economic immigrants, people who primarily came to America in search of a better life. Approximately 2 million Italians and 1.5 million Russians, many of them Jews avoiding persecution, came to the large cities on the East Coast. The new immigrants comprised 3% of the labor force.

The majority of European immigrants came to America as common people. Settling in cities where there were jobs and where they could live with their own kind in places like little Italies, Bohemias, and Germantowns, they worked hard and eked out a living. In many cases the common laborer earned $1.50 a day and paid $4.00 or $5.00 for room and board per week (Clark & Remini 1975, p. 352). Women, who usually worked in sweatshops, earned even less. Most immigrants lived in the slums in rundown tenements without heat and running water. Working conditions were just as deplorable. Hazardous working conditions caused many accidents where many were maimed for life, even killed.

Part of the new American labor force consisted of children. They were largely children of the poor and of immigrant families who were not able to partake in the national prosperity experienced at the turn of the twentieth century. Even

---

IN ACTION . . . *Portrait of America*

This is a description of New Rochelle, a suburb of New York City, in 1906 in Doctorow's *Ragtime*. This description eerily reaches into the present, whether or not we ride the trolley.

Teddy Roosevelt was President. The popularity customarily gathered in great numbers either out of doors for parades, public concerts, fish fries, political picnics, social outings, indoor meeting halls, vaudeville theaters, operas, or ballrooms. There seemed to be no end to entertainment that did not involve great swarms of people. Trains and steamers and trolleys moved them from one place to another. That was the style: that was the way people lived. Women were stouter then. They visited the fleet carrying white parasols. Everyone wore white in summer. There was a lot of sexual fainting. There were no Negroes. There were no immigrants.

▌ What can you say about this America?

▌ Are some corners of our country (or our minds) still like that?

▌ Write a paragraph about your community emulating Doctorow's style.

Source: Doctorow 1975 (pp. 3–4).

FOCUS ON CLASSROOM PRACTICES

TEACHING CHILDREN ABOUT IMMIGRANTS

Stories are powerful learning sources for young children for sharing the experiences of *immigrants*. Two of our recommendations include *Friends from the other side* by Gloria Anzaldua (1993, CA: Children's Press) and *The story of Ana* by Ely Vázquez (1985, CA: Hope Publishers). In the first book, children will enjoy learning about Prietita, the girl who decides to help Joaquín and his mother as they come to our country. Based on current facts, it is a good way to develop awareness and a sense of empathy toward today's immigrants and their struggles. The second book tells the story of a Salvadorean girl who comes to the USA.

---

though the laws regulating child labor existed for the prior 50 years, hundreds of thousands of children worked long shifts each day in hazardous jobs. It was not until 1938 that the Fair Labor Standards Act established national minimum standards for child labor that were accompanied by methods of enforcement.

Laws Limiting Immigration

The first national limits on immigration in form of a quota system, imposed in 1924, were known as the National Origins Act. The quotas limited the total number of immigrants per year to 150,000. Quotas for each nationality group were 2% of the total members of that nationality residing in the United States according to the 1890 census. Western European aliens were exempt and classified as "nonquota" immigrants (Wood 1994). The main purpose of this system was to preserve the original racial and ethnic composition of the United States by preventing the poor and the illiterate from the eastern, middle, and southern European countries, Russia, and Asia from coming in and becoming a social and economic burden to the American society. The system gave an enormous advantage to the British, the Germans, and

other Western Europeans whose ancestors were among the pioneers who settled this country.

The law was changed in 1952 with the passing of the McCarren-Walter Act that repealed the quota system and instead gave preference to skilled workers in fields experiencing shortages in the United States, reunification of families, and protection of the domestic labor force (Frost 1994). This system was also biased in favor of the Western Europeans whose immigration numbers continued to be unrestricted.

In 1965, as a result of many political changes in the world, the increasing intensity of the Cold War, Castro's rise to power, and the Vietnam War, Congress passed an immigration law that was based on a humanitarian notion of "reunification of families." The law abolished the national origins system and the major restrictions against the Asiatic countries. The Western Hemisphere was also subject for the first time to an overall annual quota of 120,000. A seven-category system was created with preference given to reunification of families and to individuals with needed talents or skills.

Many immigrants who arrived in the 1960s and the early 1970s were political dissidents, artists, intellectuals, and entrepreneurs from the

IN ACTION . . .   *Immigrant Families in Pennsylvania in 1900*

August's rich heat baked the First Ward relentlessly, one hot, clear-skied day after another. Kracha, sprawled on a bed that grew sticky with his sweat, gasped for air and in wakeful sleep kept confusing the buzzing of flies with sounds from the mill. Freight trains shook the house with the rhythmic double thump of their trucks of a cocked joint some thirty feet from his pillow; cinders rattled against the window, smoke and dust sifted through the curtains. Anna, suffering from prickly heat whimpered endlessly in the kitchen.

More stupefied than rested, it was almost with a sense of relief that he heard Elena start up the stairs to call him, to tell him it was time to go to work. The two boarders who were also working night turn that week had already left when Kracha stepped out of the house. Elena followed him, wiping her hands on her apron. She asked a child playing near by if she'd seen Alice and the child said no, she hadn't, but Mary was over by the stables.

Elena lifted her head and yelled, and down by the soap factory and the stables a dark-dressed, black-stockinged figure stopped running. Her voice reached them as from a great distance,

"What do you want?"
"Go to the store."
"I can't go now. Make Alice go."
"Come here!"
"I can't. I'm it."
"Stop yelling your lungs out," Kracha said. "What does she mean, she is it?"
"Some game they play."

Beside them the house was a row of windows and doorways stretching off on either side in diminishing perspectives, washtubs hanging beside every other door.

From within came the common household sounds, men and women talking, babies crying. The barren, filled-in ground on which the house stood seemed lifted above the river by its sheer drop to the water's edge where the company had built up the bank by pouring molten slag. The hill on the other side of the river was a dusty green. A rowboat was crossing from the direction of Kenny's Grove. Over to the right, past the comparatively new wire works, the sun was sliding toward the hills back of Homestead. The smoke and dust there would turn it into an enormous crimson disk.

Source: Thomas, B. (1976). *Out of this furnace* (pp. 49–50). Pittsburgh, PA. The University of Pittsburgh Press.

FOCUS ON CLASSROOM PRACTICES

LEARNING ABOUT WHERE OUR FAMILIES CAME FROM

Children can enjoy discovering where their families came from while also learning to value their family roots. As part of a thematic unit on the family, you may want to have children investigate the places where their parents and grandparents were born. This is also a way to involve their parents. Children can be introduced to the activity by reading Patricia Polacco's *The keeping quilt* (1988, Simon & Schuster) or Allen Say's *Grandfather's journey* (1994, Houghton Mifflin). Both stories take children to meet people who, like their own families, came as immigrants. Using a world map or a world globe, show where these characters came from. Talk about the hardships of the trip and discuss their reasons for coming to our country. Also talk about the families they built and how they became a part of a community. At this point, have the children identify where their families came from. Using a wall world map, you may want to begin by pointing to where your own family came from. Begin a family roots class project. If possible, share with the class something from your ancestors like a family heirloom. This will serve to peek the children's interest in learning about their own roots. A simple form will help children to obtain the information about their ancestors from their parents. Lead the class in creating the interview form by asking: Why do we want to learn about our family roots? Where can we get that information? What questions do we need to ask?

> *Where did my family come from?*
> *My father came from_____*
> *and my mother came from_____.*
> *My grandfather came from_____.*
> *My grandmother came from_____.*

Questions need to be adapted according to the family configurations in your classroom.

To avoid misinterpretations of the purposes of this activity, forms can be sent home with a letter explaining to the parents and family members that the intention is simply to enhance the child's sense of identity and pride in his/her roots. Findings can be displayed on a world map where the countries of origin of the children's families would be highlighted. With primary children, individual maps can also be prepared. The information on the students' countries of origin can be used to design year-round activities focused on those areas.

Genealogy Projects:

You may want to continue exploring the family roots of the children if they seem interested. As a continuation, you can lead the class in learning additional details about the history of their families. Projects on genealogy, the study of family history, can be a great way to develop pride in our own roots. They are also a fascinating medium for children to

Focus on classroom practices **continued**

learn about things in the past. A helpful resource to begin organizing a class project is *Roots for kids*, a genealogy guide for young people by Susan Provost Beller (1989 Betterway Publications). Intended for upper elementary students, it provides ideas and guidelines that can be easily adapted for the early childhood classroom. For more specific directions and suggestions, contact:

National Genealogical Society, 4527 17th Street, North Arlington, VA 22207.

Eastern European communist countries, from Asia, and from Cuba. (It should be noted that this law was applied very selectively in the 1980s, granting immigrants from the communist countries legal entry while opponents to the right-wing dictatorships of countries like Guatemala and El Salvador were forced to enter illegally.) Under the kinship system, newly arrived refugees did not need to have any job skills, education, or means of support. The "reunification" law brought 10 million immigrants to this country who are closely and distantly related to the first newcomers (Borestein, Oct. 30, 1994). It is the second and third generations of those originally allowed into the United States who are changing the makeup of the American society.

The second highest wave of immigrants occurred in the 1980s when the latest waves of Asians, Latin Americans, people from the Caribbean nations, and people from the countries of the Middle East arrived in this country. Another amendment in the immigration law, which broadened the definition of "refugee," further increased the numbers of those admitted. Between 1985 and 1994, almost 10 million people came to the United States: 2.7 million came from Mexico, one million from the countries in the Caribbean, one million from Europe, and approximately 5 million came from other parts of the world. The majority of them were unskilled, illiterate, poor,

FIGURE 1.1 Distribution of Immigrants from 1983–1992

Texas—835,703	New York—1,300,476
California—3,158,927	Florida—587,766

Source: Borestein, *Sun Sentinel*, Oct. 30, 1994.

and of non-European origin. Many of the new arrivals entered this country illegally. The United States Department of Immigration and Naturalization estimates the number of illegal aliens to be approximately 3.4 million (Borestein, Oct. 30, 1994). Four states—California, New York, Texas, and Florida—took in most of the immigrants (Figures 1.1 and 1.2). The new arrivals settled in large cities where the job markets are believed to be better.

FIGURE 1.2 Current Immigrant Populations in Key States

California—6,454,000	New York—2,852,000
Florida—1,663,000	Texas—2,138,000

Source: Borestein, *Sun Sentinel*, Oct. 30, 1994.

IN ACTION . . . *Immigrants*

Have you ever wondered why people become immigrants? If you know individuals who were born in another country, ask them what brought them to the United States. If you have parents or relatives who were born in another country, interview them to find out what brought them here. Write down their answers and examine them.
What did you learn?

▮ What attracts people to this country?

▮ How do you feel about the people you interviewed?

▮ How do you feel about your country?

▮ What is the history of immigrants in your family?

▮ How are the stories of different immigrants you interviewed the same or different?

▮ Would you ever consider immigrating to another country? Why or why not?

The United States Census Bureau projects that by the year 2050, there will be 392 million people in the United States, up from 258 million in 1994. Hispanics will be the fastest growing population rising from 9.7% to 22.5%. They are expected to surpass the African Americans as the largest minority in this country by 2010. During the same time, non-Hispanic white population will decline from 74.4% to 52.4%. Native Americans will double from 1.9 million to 3.7 million (Borestein, Oct. 30, 1994).

Immigration: Key to the Growing Cultural Diversity

The features of contemporary American society have changed a great deal. A look at people in towns and cities everywhere attests to that. No longer can we say that one set of specific physical characteristics fits a profile of a typical American. In fact, we have become a showcase of all possible human traits!

The American population used to be defined as being mainly of white European and, to some ex-

tent, of African origin. The findings of the 1990s census show a drastically changed demographic picture. The population of European descent is losing its predominance. According to the 1990 census (Figure 1.3), the American society is now formed by two main cultural groups: those of *European American* descent and those of *non-European American* origin (Hodgkinson 1993). Essentially this means that the non-European Americans account for the growing cultural diversity now found in the United States. Who, then, are the non-European Americans?

Using the geographical area of origin as a descriptor, American society is actually formed by six main non-European American groups.

Educators should note that the geographic labels are used for the purpose of bureaucratic expediency and that they do not signify cultural homogeneity. The use of these labels is discouraged because the members of each of the non-European and European groups are different and distinct and should be recognized as such. For example, Asian Americans, like Koreans, are very distinct from the Vietnamese; black Haitians have

FOCUS ON CLASSROOM PRACTICES

CAN WE TEACH CHILDREN ABOUT IMMIGRATION?

For most young children, *immigration* is a difficult concept to understand. Even for many of those who are immigrants themselves the term will not be familiar at all. Others, either because of first-hand experiences or from the comments by adults, might hold a negative perception of immigration. However, as we move into responsive teaching, this concept becomes a part of the ideas we want children to learn. The option here is to transform the topic into aspects more familiar to children. Brainstorming what immigration means would probably yield the following words: movement of people, moving from one country to another, coming from another part of the world, etc. We find that *moving* is the common denominator for today's children, which makes it a good concept for study.

Teachers can build a thematic unit based on the idea of moving. There are many possibilities in terms of how to develop it with your class.

One kindergarten teacher developed her ideas after her group was moved into another part of the school building. Through the story of "Carmencita," a character created by the teacher, who had left behind everything she had when her family came to our country, the class began talking about what it means to move. Asking who knew what moving was like led to an interesting conversation. The children shared how they felt and why they felt sad or happy after moving. A list titled *We can move to* included things like: "we move into a bigger house"; "we move to another bedroom"; "we move to an apartment"; "we move to our grandparents' house"; "we move to another development"; "we move to a new city"; and, of course, "we move to a different classroom." The activity led the class to prepare a big book they titled "Places we move to."

After reading and discussing *The Conversation Club* by Diane Stanley (1983, Macmillan), where a newcomer, Peter Fieldmouse, is welcomed to the neighborhood, the class decided to prepare a welcoming plan for children and adults. Needless to say that with new students arriving frequently, the plan was used almost immediately.

---

a history much different from Africans living in Ghana; and the heritage of Hispanics like Mexicans differs greatly from the past of the Brazilians. The same is true of the European groups like the Poles, Swedes, Greeks, and Italians, who all have distinct languages, customs, and histories.

WORKING GLOSSARY

■ **Non-European Americans**—a broad category that includes all those who are, or whose ancestors were originally, from any part of the world other than Europe.

FIGURE 1.3 Main cultural groups

European Americans		Non-European Americans

Form by all those born or descending from Europeans. For example:

- English
- Scottish
- Irish
- Spaniards
- French
- Portuguese
- Italians
- Greeks
- Scandinavians
- Eastern Europeans

American ethnic groups

Native Americans

All the indigenous groups in the continental U.S. and Alaska. Represent all the groups belonging to the Indian Nations.

All those ethnic groups with origins other than Europeans to include:

- Hispanics
- African Americans
- Pacific Islanders
- Asian Americans
- Caribbean Islanders
- Middle Easterners

We all belong to the United States!

Source: U.S. Bureau of the Census.

Asian Americans

Koreans, Vietnamese, Khmer, and Hmong make up the four major ethnic groups of **Asian Americans** who immigrated to the United States in the last two decades (Cetron & Davies 1989). In the 1990s we are experiencing the arrivals of large contingents of Filipinos and Indians, as well. Koreans, along with the previous generations of Japanese Americans, represent the elite of Asian Americans. They are for the most part refugees and the children of refugees who fled the communist regime of South Korea in the 1950s. They number roughly about 1.5 million. Hard working

and well educated, the Koreans easily entered the entrepreneurial American society by quickly becoming self-employed. In 1989, they owned 85% of green grocery business in New York City, and 300 stores in Atlanta along with most liquor and convenience stores in Los Angeles (Cetron & Davies 1989, p. 26).

The **Vietnamese** have been a significant success story in this country. They came over to the United States in two major waves. The first occurred after the fall of Saigon in 1975 and in the late 1970s when the communist government of Vietnam expelled the ethnic Chinese. The people who left in the

1970s represented the elite of the Vietnamese society. Most were college graduates who spoke English. They established themselves quickly on the West Coast of the United States as leaders in the electronics and computer industries, real estate, markets, and other small businesses.

The second wave of "boatpeople" who arrived in the 1980s faced different challenges. Many were poor and illiterate, and lacked the command of the English language. With many still emotionally marked as a result of the Vietnam War, the arduous voyages out of Vietnam, or years of living in refugee camps, they have fought to succeed in this country.

The **Khmer** of Kampuchea (Cambodia), like the Vietnamese, lived the horror of war. These people survived the deaths of their families and the destruction of their country by the Khmer Rouge and the Heng Samrin regime put in place by Vietnamese communist government. The largest settlements are in California where as many as 7 out of 10 were on welfare in the late 1980s (Cetron & Davies 1989). Struggling still with the shadow and the pain of the war, they are beginning to build a future for themselves in our country.

The semi-nomadic **Hmong** originating from the jungles of Southeast Asia also settled in California. Skillful scouts trained by the United States Central Intelligence Agency (CIA) to fight the communist Patet Lao forces, many of them fled with the help of the Americans at the end of the Vietnam War to avoid persecution by the communist government. The Hmong still live in one of the most closely knit clan societies known. Largely illiterate and totally unprepared for the challenges of a modern technological society, many are on welfare while some have committed suicide. However, being an agricultural people, many are leaving the urban settings and seeking a better life in Minnesota, Nebraska, and North Carolina where they are settling into farming communities. For many Hmong the future is beginning to look brighter for the first time.

Hispanics

The term "Hispanic" encompasses an enormous range of people and cultures. It is " . . . an umbrella term for anyone of Spanish or Portuguese descent, in or outside the United States" (Wood 1994, p. 20). Hispanics are expected to become America's largest minority group by the end of this century. They will account for 40% of the United States population growth in the 1990s (Wood 1994). By far the most successful have been the Cuban Americans who make up about 5% of the total Hispanic population. There are, however, great social and economic differences even within this group. The early immigrants who fled Castro's regime and arrived in Florida in the 1960s represented Cuba's social, economic, and intellectual elite. They are largely responsible for making Miami an important commercial center and a "Gateway to South America." Cetron and Davies (1989) report that among the Cubans, 30% of the men are self-employed, many of them very affluent and politically influential. Unlike most immigrant groups, Cuban Americans are fiercely Republican. They are also largely responsible for the passage of the family "reunification" act of 1965.

A second group of Cuban Americans arrived in the 1980 Mariel boatlift. With many coming from poor families, they are still struggling to succeed. More recently, the Cuban rafters who arrived on the Florida coasts constitute the newest group of immigrants from this Caribbean island.

Mexicans comprise two thirds of the total Hispanic population. The largest concentration, 12 million, are found in California, Texas, and the Southwest. More than 60% of the heads of household came directly from Mexico. More than 70% are under age 35. Mexican immigrants have on the average six years of schooling (Cetron & Davies 1989, p. 28). They also have the highest number of illegal aliens of all groups combined.

The case of Puerto Ricans is different. The Caribbean island of Puerto Rico became part of

Hispanics are currently the fastest growing group of non-European Americans.

Snapshot 1.3
Early Settlers

"Once California belonged to Mexico and its land to Mexicans and a horde of tattered feverish Americans poured in. And such was their hunger for land that they took the land . . . and they guarded with guns the land they had stolen . . . Then, with time, the squatters were no longer squatters, but owners."

Source: Steinbeck, J. (1975). *Grapes of wrath.*

the United States in 1898. Puerto Ricans are American citizens by birth who are free to live anywhere in the United States and its territories. Over one third of Puerto Ricans live in the mainland United States. They account for 14% of the total Hispanic population of this country. It is estimated that a total of 43% of Puerto Rican families are headed by women. The average income of a Puerto Rican family is even lower than the Mexican Americans' annual family income.

The fastest growing Hispanic group settling in this country comes from countries of Central America other than Mexico, and from South America. They make up 20% of the total Hispanic population. For example, by 1989, 500,000 came from El Salvador. There are also Hispanics from the Caribbean countries. It is estimated that approximately 300,000 from the Dominican Republic settled in New York City alone. It is difficult to determine the exact number of immigrants from Central America and the Caribbean because many of them entered this country illegally.

Unfortunately, with the exception of some Cuban Americans, many Hispanics are still struggling for success. One of the reasons may be that they tend to cling to their culture far more strongly than any other group. According to Cetron and Davies (1989), only 26% are fluent in English. They indicate that of the estimated 30 million, 70% live in just four states: California, Florida, New

Puerto Ricans are American citizens with Hispano-Caribbean roots.

York, and Texas. The birthrate among Hispanics is twice the birthrate of African Americans and quadruple that of whites. Six in ten Hispanics fall into the modest or low-income categories. Cetron and Davies (1989) project that there will be 70 million Hispanics in the United States by 2015. Others estimate they will become the largest American minority at the end of the century.

Native Americans

Native Americans represent the indigenous inhabitants of the United States. Long before any immigrants came, many Native American nations and tribes already called this territory their homeland. Native Americans are a pluralistic society that should not be viewed as a homogeneous group. The history and customs of different nations and tribes are unique and should be studied and presented as individual cultures.

The end of the nineteenth century brought about the confinement of Native Americans to designated reservations, many of which were useless patches of wasteland. In addition to having to create a living in these new places, Native Americans were subjected to concerted government efforts to assimilate into the mainstream culture. One of the assimilation efforts by the federal government included relocating young members of tribes to the cities, often in urban ghettos where they were not allowed to live by each other (Lynch & Hanson 1992, p. 95). These kinds of efforts met with great resistance and caused additional clashes. Today, the violent resistance to assimilation has eased somewhat and has been replaced with a cultural revival and an adoption of some political and entrepreneurial models from the mainstream culture.

A true number of American Indians is not known, however. Frost (1994) reports that the 1990 census counted 1.8 million, a 38% leap from 1.4 million in 1980. Four states with the largest Indian population are Oklahoma, California, Arizona, and New Mexico.

As was mentioned earlier in this chapter, Native Americans have suffered irreparable harm by the government and by the white settlers. The damage that was done to their culture and heritage has caused many problems for the current generations. Having survived the centuries of persecution and genocide, the Native Americans are trying to reclaim their place in our society. They have many obstacles to overcome like poverty, alcoholism, and unemployment. Many young and talented members of the tribes and Indian nations are leaving the reservations for urban areas where they are trying their hand at small business. Gambling and tourism are also being pursued as reservation-based enterprises. Most Native Americans are in the low income bracket.

Middle Easterners

People from the Middle East came to the United States in the late nineteenth century. Christian traders from the Ottoman Empire were probably the first ones who arrived in the United States in 1875 (Lynch & Hanson 1992). In the period between 1890 and 1930, large groups of Armenians fled the Turkish persecution and some came to the United States. After the Armenian exodus, there was no large scale immigration from the Middle East until the two major Israeli Wars in 1967 and 1973 and the continued Lebanese conflict, which started in 1975 (Lynch & Hanson 1992). Other political events led to additional migrations of Iranians, Iraqis, and Afghans. The Iranian revolution in 1978 and the Iran-Iraq war between 1980 and 1988 brought a continuous flow of Iranian immigrants to the United States. They constitute the largest group, approximately 400,000, of Middle Easterners in this country. More recently, the Persian Gulf War brought Kuwaiti refugees to this country.

The immigrants from the Middle Eastern countries are concentrated mainly in large cities. Those

Many Middle Eastern families came to our country in the early 1980s as a result of many political and religious unrests in their world.

who arrived prior to 1980 are generally educated members of the professional class who possessed good command of English prior to coming to this country. Those arriving in this country after 1980 seemed to have less education although most have at least a high school diploma and some knowledge of English (Lynch & Hanson 1992, p. 327). Differences exist among the various Middle Eastern groups and even more so between the urban and the rural contingents of each group. They are also among the least studied minority groups in the United States. The data about their problems and future trends are very limited.

African Americans

Historically, African Americans were the only group who did not originally come to our country as immigrants. Removed against their desire from their homeland by the unscrupulous human traffickers of colonial times, they were brought to the New World as slaves. This led to the institutionalized inhumane treatment rooted in violence and injustice, which they endured for centuries. The system was replaced in the post Civil War Era by discrimination and racism sanctioned by legislation.

After the abolition of slavery in 1864, the newly freed slaves created a paradox for the nation

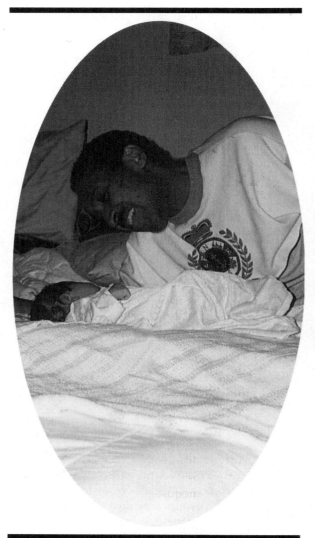

African American families are characterized by strong family ties. Children are nurtured by many different family members.

committed to the principle of justice and equality, and yet rooted in hatred of the dark-skinned people whom they perceived as a threat to the American way of life. As a result of this strange social dichotomy, during the years following the Civil War, racial hatred produced many contradictory social initiatives that altered the fabric of American society for the next hundred years. The founding of the Klu Klux Klan in 1866 for the purpose of committing atrocities against the African Americans; the Black Codes enacted in 1865–1866 to disenfranchise them; and the Supreme Court decision Plessy vs. Fergusson in 1896 that established "the separate but equal" doctrine were all designed to deny African Americans their rightful place in society (Lynch & Hanson 1992, p. 125).

During the twentieth century, racism and discrimination kept the African Americans segregated from the whites in schools, factories, businesses, housing, public facilities, and services. "Jim Crow" laws, which took the form of literacy tests, "white primaries," poll taxes, and "grandfather" clauses were all enacted to prevent African Americans from exercising their right to vote. Not being able to exercise this right prevented African Americans from participating in the greatest era of progress in American history. It was not until World War II, when the military desegregated and the landmark case of Brown vs. the Board of Education in 1954 abolished school segregation, that things began to change (Lynch & Hanson 1992).

The late 1950s and 1960s mark the greatest years of social change in recent American history. The Civil Rights Movement became the focus of American society largely as a result of the leadership of African American organizations like the National Association for the Advancement of Colored People (NAACP), the Urban League, and the Southern Christian Leadership Conference and individuals like Dr. Martin Luther King, Jr., Rosa Parks, Thurgood Marshall, and others. The sit-ins, freedom rides, peace demonstrations, and violence associated with African Americans attempting to gain admission to formerly all white institutions provided the nation with a renewed look at the depth of hatred and racism. Many battles were won during those years like the Civil Rights Act and Equal Opportunity Act of 1964 and the Voting Rights Act of 1965. Much money was poured by the federal government into social programs intended to assist the poor and the disadvantaged during the 1960s and 1970s. These initiatives and services gave the government the right to interfere in cases of discrimination within the individual states, without which many cases involving African Americans could not be settled (Lynch & Hanson 1992, p. 124).

During the decades of the 1980s and 1990s, African Americans have suffered some setbacks in the equal opportunity arena as a result of the more conservative forces in the federal government and society at large. Recently there has been a resurgence in racism and hatred against African Americans as seen through the rise of various white supremacist groups and militias. The initiatives to abolish the equal opportunity quotas in employment provide additional evidence that more setbacks can be expected.

Presently, African Americans represent 12.5% of the total population, according to the 1990 United States Census (Hacker 1992). At the time of the first census in 1790, African Americans were in highest proportion to the rest of the population. Each succeeding decade until 1940 they declined in percentages as a result of the growing numbers of white immigrants. The census projections indicate that with the high influx of immigrants in the next two decades, African Americans may become the second largest majority, surpassed by the Hispanics by the end of this century. African Americans differ from many minorities in the country in one very significant way. They are classified by race. This has resulted in segregating African Americans not only from the mainstream culture, but from most other minority groups as well. This fundamental distinction has literally prevented millions of people from claiming their share in major life's endeavors. Although released from bondage more than a century ago, African

Americans are still struggling to gain their lawful place in American society. According to Hacker (1992), being black in America still bears the marks of slavery. The recollections of the past reinforce old stereotypes about the character and the capacities of the blacks.

The presence of the blacks in American society has also created a paradox: a commitment to universal justice and equality, and unequal de facto treatment. This condition has resulted in many negative societal trends that currently impact the whole country. Lynch and Hanson (1992, p. 129) identify several of these problematic trends African Americans are experiencing.

1. Death from nutritional deficiency among infants is more than ten times that of white children.
2. Infant mortality is twice as high as among the whites.
3. Homicide is the leading cause of death for young adult African Americans under 25.
4. Almost 43% of children of African American families live in homes in which the father is absent.
5. 67% of the households are poor.

In spite of some of these statistics, African Americans have kept their faith and their sense of family and community. Many are doing well and thriving, with increasing numbers completing their education and entering the professions. However, major inequities in income, health, and quality of life continue to exist.

Unfortunately, the future for African Americans does not look particularly bright in the next century. This is partly true because large societal institutions are not currently meeting the needs of this group. We can only hope that the African Americans' incredible resiliency, the desire to improve their fortune, and their sense of pride will further facilitate their progress. The Million Men March to Washington in October 1995 had among its many purposes to remind the country of the African Americans' continued fight for equality.

Pacific Islanders

Two Pacific Island groups with the highest population in the United States are the Hawaiians and the Samoans. They, like many other colonized people, experienced many changes as a result of Western cultures. Samoa was occupied by the Dutch in 1722 and Christianized by the missionaries by the 1830s. Throughout the twentieth century, the United States, England, and Germany asserted power over this small nation. In 1900 Samoa was partitioned into two parts, one of which, American Samoa, still remains a U.S. territory in 1996. The majority of American Samoans came to this country for economic reasons and settled in ethnic enclaves in California. The transfer of this group was also facilitated through the transfer of navy base personnel. Samoans in America have been acculturated to a lesser extent than the Hawaiians whose association with America has closer ties.

Hawaiians first came in touch with the Europeans through the explorer Captain James Cook in 1778. Throughout the nineteenth century, visitors from the United States, England, Germany, Spain, Portugal, and other countries influenced massive changes not only in religious practices, but also in the political and socioeconomic practices of native Hawaiian people (Lynch & Hanson 1992, p. 302). The Westerners had a devastating effect on the decline of the population of purebred Hawaiians, largely attributed to diseases for which the natives had no immunity. Hawaiians are very proactively engaged in preserving their culture, especially in their native islands where they are in the minority.

Pondering What We Have Examined

The information regarding the non-European Americans reveals the extent of the new plural-ism and demonstrates recent immigration patterns in the United States. However, we cannot neglect the fact that European Americans, from 37 European countries speaking ten different languages, helped settle this continent and created this country. They are the original creators of the pluralism that has always been a part of the United States.

The arrival of people representing all the continents has resulted in the change of the immigrant profile from the traditional European to the more global one (Díaz 1992). This shift in the population has also affected our lifestyle. Aside from being numbers in immigration records, the new immigrants have brought along their own ways of life, which have created new dimensions in our collective existence.

We have learned that some areas of our country are characterized by a higher degree of non-European American population than others. For instance, cities like Miami, Los Angeles, Chicago, New York, or El Paso stand out because of their culturally different populations. We have seen that several states across the nation, like Arizona, Florida, California, Hawaii, and Texas, possess a higher percentage of non-European Americans.

Perhaps your state is not included among the highly demographically diverse. However, one revealing fact about current population patterns is that diversity has been brought to those areas traditionally not diverse. In an analysis of American demographics, Hodgkinson (1993) found that, "only ten states now have a youth population that is not European American that is less than 10 percent" (p. 11). The conclusions are obvious: we are all faced with various degrees of diversity and we are *all* a part of it.

We have seen that cultural diversity is not a new phenomenon for the United States. Pluralism already existed at the time of this country's founding when American society consisted of Europeans, indigenous groups of Native Americans, and Africans brought in bondage since the

IN ACTION . . .   *Who Are the Non-European Americans?*

Identify the non-European American groups found in your community. Identify the students in your classroom who belong to these groups. Assess your knowledge of these groups by writing down on a piece of paper all the facts you know about their cultures. After you complete your list, verify your findings by contacting members of those cultures and find out how factual or stereotypical your knowledge is.

▌ What can you say about your level of knowledge of your community and your students?

▌ How did you acquire your knowledge of other cultures?

▌ How would you rate your knowledge of other cultures?

▌ What new things did you learn?

▌ How can this kind of information help you as an educator?

Plan to incorporate two things you learned about each of the cultures present in your classroom into your lesson plans.

IN ACTION . . .   *The Pot of Pluralism*

Chinese Hawaiian poet Wing Tek Lum has a new vision of today's United States. As you read this poem, consider how this view differs from the idea of a melting pot.

My dream of America
is like *da bin louth*
with people of all persuasions and tastes
sitting down around a common pot
chopsticks and basket scoop here and there
some cooking squid and others beef
some tofu and watercress
all in one broth
like a stew that really isn't
as each one chooses what he wishes to eat
only that the pot and the fire are shared
and the sweet soup
spooned out at the end of the meal.

Reprinted by permission from the author.

early seventeenth century. Learning to live together, learning to accept and recognize the sameness in all was not a simple task then, or now. As in all social processes, differences in ideas and perceptions resulted in clashes. Incidents related to cultural divergences abound in the pages of American history. Today, dealing with cultural diversity remains a challenge for our country that civic and professional organizations, like the National Association of the Education of Young Children (NAEYC), Association for Supervision and Curriculum Development (ASCD), Southern Early Childhood Association (SECA), and National Council for the Social Studies (NCSS), work to overcome. There is a pressing need for early childhood educators to be aware of these past and present efforts (Neugebauer 1994) in order to assist children in acquiring ways to deal with the challenges of our continuously growing pluralistic world.

The United States: A Kaleidoscope of People

Have you ever spent time at any of our major airports? If you have, you probably saw a kaleidoscope of people just like the teacher did in Snapshot 1.5 when she traveled through the Miami International Airport.

Similar scenarios are being played all over America. Our communities, schools, and places of work have come to reflect the new cultural environment. Everything we know about the demographic patterns in America indicates that diversity is here to stay. We also need to realize that even though the non-European cultural groups are playing an increasingly more dominant role, the groups of European origin will continue to be an important influence on the development of the country in the twenty-first century. Aside from both being part of the American demogra-

---

Snapshot 1.4
A View of the World

"When I came to catch my flight, I never thought that I would have such a remarkable experience. The hour and a half that I had to spend because of a flight delay, showed me the real face of America. Everything started when I decided to have a second cup of coffee. I went to the coffee bar in one of the concourses where they serve the best "cortadito" (espresso with milk) and "pastelitos" (guava and cheese pastries). A smiling Cuban lady served me the aromatic coffee. While sipping it, I saw an airport employee greeting a friend just returning from his hometown in Nicaragua. At the same time, several Haitians chatted while also sipping coffee. Two Colombians joined the group in front of the coffee stand. I noticed two Indian ladies, who wore the prettiest saris, chatting about their children. I finally made the line to board my flight where I heard a father call his child in very distinct Arabic. As we flew out, a thought came to my mind: my country is not just a country, it's a world in itself, a world that I see in my classroom."

Source: Rosales 1992 (p. 9).

phy, both groups share another common characteristic: heterogeneity. (See Figure 1.4a and b.)

Terms are useful in identifying a specific quality or shared characteristics. There are times, however, when a term can oversimplify the meaning or hide the magnitude of it. Earlier we warned against using geographical terminology in connection with individual non-European American and European American cultural groups.

Recently, a group of early childhood graduate students were informally asked to web what the terms non-European Americans and European Americans stand for. Their responses showed a wide range of ideas (Robles de Meléndez 1994). In most cases, some cultural groups like the Pacific Is-

landers and the Middle Easterners were not included, while all failed to identify the European Americans as being a diverse group in itself. What are the implications of these responses? Mainly one: early childhood educators must possess accurate knowledge about various cultural groups if they are to design developmentally appropriate programs that are sensitive and responsive to the world of today's children.

❖ A Call for Action

Now more than ever, educators of young children recognize that the new complex diversity

FIGURE 1.4a Who are the European Americans? What else would you add?

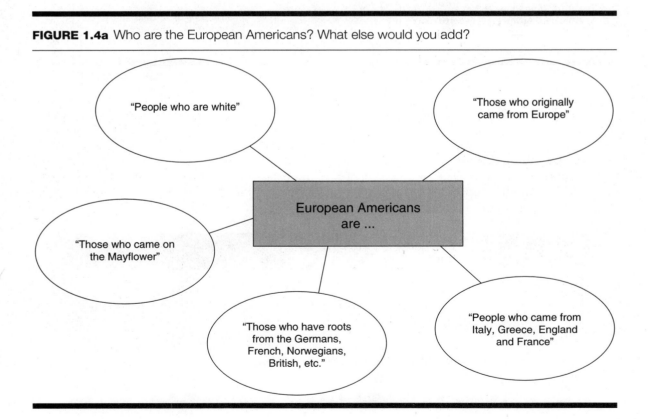

"People who are white"

"Those who originally came from Europe"

European Americans are ...

"Those who came on the Mayflower"

"Those who have roots from the Germans, French, Norwegians, British, etc."

"People who came from Italy, Greece, England and France"

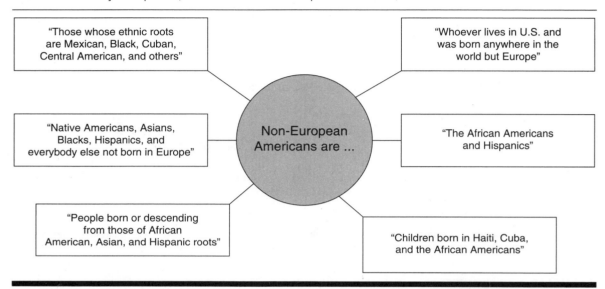

FIGURE 1.4b In your opinion, who are the non-European Americans?

"Those whose ethnic roots are Mexican, Black, Cuban, Central American, and others"

"Whoever lives in U.S. and was born anywhere in the world but Europe"

Non-European Americans are ...

"Native Americans, Asians, Blacks, Hispanics, and everybody else not born in Europe"

"The African Americans and Hispanics"

"People born or descending from those of African American, Asian, and Hispanic roots"

"Children born in Haiti, Cuba, and the African Americans"

mandates programs that positively affect the learning processes and social adjustments of all school children. As early childhood educators, we know that providing children with developmentally appropriate practices (DAP) is at the core of our profession (Bredekamp 1987). Today, for pro-

grams to be truly appropriate, they must become sensitive to the children's cultures. The National Association for the Education of Young Children (NAEYC) acknowledges in its code of ethics the importance of culture as an element of quality programs for children. Sections II and IV of the

IN ACTION . . . *The New Americans*

What are your concepts of European Americans and of non-European Americans? To find out, simply web what those two terms represent to you. Web each term separately. Then, compare your webs with those on pages 33–34.

▌ What did you find?

▌ Were any groups similar/different from yours?

▌ Why do you think that happened?

Code of Ethical Conduct and Statement of Commitment (Feeney & Kipnis 1992) read as follows:

Section II

1.2.3-To respect the dignity of each family and its culture, customs, and beliefs (p. 6)

Section IV

1.4.2-To provide the community with high-quality services (p. 10)

Early childhood educators know that nothing opens more doors to understanding children than understanding them in the "context of their family, culture and society" (Feeney & Kipnis 1992, p. 3). To create responsive environments, like the teacher in Snapshot 1.1 wants to create, early childhood educators cannot isolate activities from the social and cultural framework of the child. Educational designs that are based on the principles of child development recognize the undeniable influence culture has on the child (Berger 1993).

Early childhood professionals must be cognizant of the cultural transformations American society has experienced and will continue to experience. This state of socio-cultural flux will affect the physical and social environment of all children. More precisely, the increased growth of the non-European American population, as demographers have predicted, will produce a very different social climate for children living in the United States in the twenty-first century (U.S. Bureau of the Census 1991).

Research has shown that the way a young child learns to view and respond to the social world depends on the cultural values held in the immediate surroundings (Bandura 1977; Bronfenbrenner 1979; Whiting & Edwards 1988; Zigler & Finn Stevenson 1993). Culture, thus, plays a crucial role in the development of the child. If we are to

Like all children, these Jamaican descendants hope to find teachers who will responsively meet their needs.

IN ACTION . . .   *Becoming a Multicultural Early Childhood Educator*

Becoming a multicultural early childhood educator is a process. However, there are steps you can begin taking now. One of those is to examine the ideas and views on multiculturalism of leading early childhood professionals. You may want to begin by reading *White teacher* by Vivian Gussin Paley (1979). Paley, an experienced kindergarten teacher who has taught in the South and the Midwest, shares her struggles as she learned how to teach culturally diverse children. As you read, you may want to reflect on your own experiences as a student and a teacher in a culturally diverse society. Another good introductory reading is Olivia Saracho and Bernard Spodek's *The multicultural experience in early childhood education* (1983, National Association for the Education of Young Children). This book provides an overview of what multicultural education entails when teaching young children in today's diverse classrooms.

consider that the society of the next century is to be characterized by a higher degree of diversity, this unquestionably describes an environment where children will find a multiplicity of cultural values. As early childhood educators we must ask ourselves the following questions: "Are we preparing children to live in this new reality? Are we aware that today's preschoolers, kindergartners, and primary grade students will live their adult lives in a new era very different from ours? And, what are we doing about it?"

Issues raised by these questions constitute a call for action for early childhood professionals. We need to prepare ourselves to serve children in consonance with reality. This is not only a need but a mandate if we are to teach children in genuinely developmentally appropriate ways (Mallory & New 1994). It is no longer satisfactory to just display pictures of groups different from the mainstream culture, or to assign a week to celebrate multiculturalism, practices still found in many places. Nor is it acceptable to decide what students should learn, without regard for the new socio-cultural realities.

Education is a process of guiding and preparing a child to succeed in life. Given the social reality of the very near future, education of the young will have to encompass skills and knowledge to navigate in this new pluralistic world. This will include learning to live effectively and productively in a society where diversity is a major factor. The success formula for future generations will include a solid foundation in cultural knowledge of many non-European American groups. The social skills and tools to interact effectively with these groups will be an essential part of everyday life and ultimately the key to survival in the twenty-first century.

One out of three children in 2010 in the United States will be a non-European American (U.S. Bureau of Census 1992). The difference between successful and unsuccessful individuals, at that time, may be the ability to interact effectively with people of various cultures. Early childhood professionals must lay the foundation by offering all children appropriate educational programs that will enable them to become successful individuals in this multicultural environment. This position is supported by Louise Derman-Sparks and the Anti Bias Curriculum (A.B.C.) Task Force—developed (Derman-Sparks 1989) through the movement for anti-bias approach to teaching and

IN ACTION . . . *Becoming a Multicultural Early Childhood Educator*

As you answer the call for multicultural education, you may want to learn about existing programs in your community. Because its origin comes from the need to serve culturally different children, you may want to contact the local Head Start program. Call for an interview with its coordinator and ask about its approach toward multiculturalism. A visit to any of the classrooms could be arranged where you could get first-hand experience with Head Start's services. Your community probably has other programs for the culturally diverse child. A call to the division of Child Services at your local Department of Human Resources and Services will let you know about other programs. For example, some areas have designed programs for migrant children, low-income families, or for the chronically ill. Based on your interests, you may want to plan an interview with the program coordinator.

learning—and by other well-known advocates of multicultural education like James Banks (1994), Hilda Hernandez (1989), and Sonia Nieto (1992).

James S. Banks, the leading scholar in the field of multiculturalism, defines the aim of education for diversity as a way of keeping and maintaining the spirit and the essence of the American *unum* (Banks 1994; NCSS 1992). This idea of the *American unum*, literally where all are one, where everyone is equally important, is a reminder of the goals and purposes that define our country, the champion of democracy and equality for all individuals. The authors of this book also believe that the only way to achieve and preserve the idea of *e pluribus unum* begins with the child. Recognizing the vital role early childhood educators play in the development of children, it can be said that the future of our society rests in their hands.

Teaching young children today is especially exciting because they reflect our multicultural society. We house the people of the world in our classrooms! Yates (1988) says that by the year 2000 one-third of school-age children will be African American, Asian American, and particularly, Hispanic American. Our challenge is clear: We need

to prepare ourselves to serve the child in more than just one way. Early childhood educators have always successfully met challenges. That is why we know that we will also be able to face the challenge of teaching children in our culturally diverse American community. As we face our challenge, there are questions we need to answer: Are we ready to offer children what they need? Have we achieved a level of awareness and knowledge that enables us to design responsive programs? To answer these questions, we will continue exploring other dimensions of our social diversity in the next chapter.

❖ Points to Remember

▌ The American society of today is characterized by being ethnically and culturally diverse.

▌ The United States has always been defined as a nation of human and natural diversity. The very beginnings of our country are founded in the many people who came in search of a better future.

▌ Everyone in the United States to some extent has participated in the immigrant experience.

Snapshot 1.5
Why Has Cultural Diversity Become So Noticeable?

You probably have asked yourself why today we seem to notice diversity more than ever. One of the reasons is that there is a recognized core or mainstream culture in the United States. This culture evolved out of the ideas and ways brought by the people who settled in this land as well as from the interaction of these early immigrants with the Native American groups (Banks 1993). Ideas like equality, individualism, and opportunities for all individuals, as stated in the Declaration of Independence, are basic values that form the American society. These ideas became the recognized beliefs of the American *mainstream* or *overarching culture*. All those who came to this country were expected to follow and adhere to the ideals of the mainstream culture. People were presumed to "melt in." Now, we are changing from a melting pot to a pluralistic society. People are encouraged to preserve their cultural identities while following the ideals and principles of the American culture. Today we accept the premise that there is more than one way to interpret reality in the United States. This is the essence of American diversity.

- The 1960s–1990s have been characterized by the increased number of people who immigrated to this country. This has produced a diversification of the ethnic composition in the United States.
- Today's American society is a reflection of the world's ethnic groups. Our country is comprised of people of European ancestry and of people of six different non-European backgrounds.
- Changes in our demographic makeup have directly impacted education, and in particular that of young children.
- Early childhood educators wanting to teach children in a developmental and responsive manner must address the cultural needs of the child.

❖ **Things to Do . . .**

1. Discovering the cultural composition of your neighborhood and of the community of your school helps us to gain a practical awareness about the people we live with. Begin by making a list of the cultures present in both environments, your neighborhood and your school. Then, take a field trip and list all the things that reflect diversity (signs, buildings, decorations, etc.). What did you find? Highlight those cultures you feel you need to learn more about. Your school or community library is a good place to continue your search.

2. Are you aware of your own culture? To appreciate cultural diversity we must first know ourselves. Get a stack of index cards. On one of the index cards, write the name of the cultural group you think you belong to. Next, find out where (geographical area) that cultural group originates and write it on another card. Use the other cards to describe the things you do that underline your being part of that cultural group. Examine your results and see what you discovered about yourself that you were not aware of before.

3. Get together with two or three colleagues and discuss your backgrounds. Identify the historical event that brought the members of your family or you to the United States. Then, using a sheet of paper create lists of social, economic, and political events that caused their or your immigration. Discuss what may have happened if they or you never left. How has your and their life changed as a result of coming to the United States? List the positive and negative elements of the experience.

4. Take action in your classroom by examining your present curriculum for diversity. Highlight those activities and concepts that focus on pluralism.

5. This book will take you on a journey where you will find ways to develop an appropriate multicultural environment for young children. Begin a diary of your experiences. You may want to get a small notebook where you can record your thoughts and experiences. To begin your diary, enter your comments to these questions:
   - What do I want for children as a person and as a teacher?
   - What can I do for the culturally different child?

6. Write a description of your community in 2050. While writing, think about what the architecture, recreation, schools, churches, and people may be like. What about language, technology, transportation, etc.?

❖ Children's Literature Corner

We believe that stories have the power to bring life issues into the world of the child in ways that sometimes adults could not do. Throughout the book we will share book titles we consider appropriate to develop not only children's awareness about the value of diversity but that will also help in empowering them to live in a culturally diverse society.

Adoff, A. (1973). *Black is brown is tan*. New York: Harper & Row.

Arnold, C. (1992). *The ancient cliffdwellers of Mesa Verde*. New York: Clarion Books.

Berry, J. (1991). *A jeeman and his son*. New York: HarperCollins.

Bunting, E. (1988). *How many days to America. A thanksgiving story*. New York: Clarion Books.

Hamilton, V. (1988). *In the beginning. Creation stories from around the world*. New York: Harcourt Brace Jovanovich.

Manjo, N. (1970). *The drinking gourd*. Englewood Cliffs, NJ: Harper & Row.

Say, A. (1994). *Grandfather's journey*. Boston, MA: Houghton Mifflin.

Yep, L. (1977). *Child of the owl*. Englewood Cliffs, NJ: Harper & Row.

❖ References

Adler, S. (1993). *Multicultural communication skills in the classroom*. Needham Heights, MA: Allyn & Bacon.

Bandura, A. (1977). *Social learning theory*. Englewood Cliffs, NJ: Prentice Hall.

Banks, J. (1993). Multicultural education for freedom's sake. In *Reflecting diversity. Multicultural guidelines for educational publishing professionals.* New York: Macmillan/McGraw-Hill.

Banks, J., & Banks, C. (eds.). (1993). *Multicultural education: Issues and perspectives* (2nd ed.). Needham Heights, MA: Allyn & Bacon.

Banks, J. (1994). Transforming the mainstream curriculum. *Educational Leadership* 8:4–8.

Baruth, L., & Manning, M. L. (1992). *Multicultural education of children and adolescents.* Needham Heights, MA: Allyn & Bacon.

Bennett, L. (1994). 10 most dramatic events in African-American history. In J. A. Kromkowski (ed.), *Race and ethnic relations. Annual Editions 94/95.* Guilford, CT: Dushkin.

Berger, K. (1993). *The developing person through childhood and adolescence.* New York: Worth.

Borestein, S. (1994). America by the numbers. *Sun Sentinel.* Fort Lauderdale, FL. Oct. 30, 1994. 5S.

Bredekamp, S. (ed.) (1987). *Developmentally appropriate practice in early childhood programs serving children ages from birth through age eight.* (exp. ed.). Washington, DC: National Association for the Education of Young Children.

Bronfenbrenner, U. (1979). *The ecology of human development: Experiments by nature and design.* Cambridge, MA: Harvard University Press.

Bunting, E. (1988). *How many days to America.* New York: Clarion.

Cetron, M., & Davies, O. (1989). *American renaissance. Our lives at the turn of the 21st century.* New York: St. Martin's Press.

Clark, J. I., & Remini, R. V. (1975). *We the People.* Beverly Hills, CA: Glencoe Press.

Derman-Sparks, L., & the A.B.C. Task Force. (1989). *Anti-bias curriculum: Tools for empowering young children.* Washington, DC: National Association for the Education of Young Children.

Díaz, C. (1992). The next millenium: A multicultural imperative for education. In C. Díaz (ed.), *Multicultural education for the 21st century.* Washington, DC: National Education Association.

Doctorow, E. L. (1975). *Ragtime.* New York: Alfred Knopf.

Feeney, S., & Kipnis, K. (1992). *Code of ethical conduct & statement of commitment. Guidelines for responsible behavior in early childhood education.* (Brochure #503). Washington, DC: National Association for the Education of Young Children.

Frost, D. (1994). American Indians in the 1990s. In J. A. Kromkowski (ed.), *Race and ethnic relations. Annual Editions 94/95.* Guilford, CT: Dushkin.

Greene, M. (1993). The passions of pluralism. In T. Perry & J. Fraser (eds.) *Freedom's plow.* New York: Routledge.

Hacker, A. (1992). *Two nations black and white, separate, hostile, unequal.* New York: Ballentine Books.

Hernandez, H. (1989). *Multicultural education: A teacher's guide to content and process.* New York: Merrill.

Hodgkinson, H. (1993). A demographic look at tomorrow. In *Reflecting diversity. Multicultural guidelines for educational publishing professionals.* New York: Macmillan/McGraw-Hill.

Lynch, E. W., & Hanson, M. J. (1992). *Developing cross-cultural competence. A guide for working with young children and their families.* Baltimore, MD: Paul Brookes.

Mallory, B., & New, R. (1994). *Diversity and developmentally appropriate practices.* New York: Teacher's College Press.

Martorella, P. H. (1994). *Social studies for elementary school children.* New York: Merrill.

McCracken, J. B. (1993). *Valuing diversity: The primary years.* Washington, DC: National Association for the Education of Young Children.

National Council for the Social Studies. (1992). Guidelines for multicultural teaching. *Social Education* 56, 3:(pp. 274–294).

Neugebauer, B. (1994). *Alike and different. Exploring our humanity with children.* (rev. ed.). Washington, DC: National Association for the Education of Young Children.

Nieto, S. (1992). *Affirming diversity. The sociopolitical context of multicultural education.* New York: Longman.

Northrop, S. (1993). Twelve years a slave. In R. Takaki (ed.), *A different mirror.* New York: Little, Brown & Co.

Robles de Meléndez, W. (1994). Activities for the graduate course. *Planning the multicultural environment. Summer.* Fort Lauderdale, FL: Nova Southeastern University.

Rosales, L. (1992). *Listen to the heart. Impressions and memories of a teacher.* Unpublished manuscript.

Say, A. (1994). *Grandfather's journey.* Boston, MA: Houghton Mifflin.

Shade, B., & New, C. (1993). Cultural influences on learning: Teaching implications. In J. Banks & C. McGee Banks (eds). *Multicultural education. Issues and perspectives.* (2nd ed.). Boston, MA: Allyn & Bacon.

Takaki, R. (1993). *A different mirror.* New York: Little, Brown & Co.

Thomas, B. (1976). *Out of the furnace.* Pittsburgh, PA: The University of Pittsburgh Press.

Whiting, B., & Edwards, C. P. (1988). *Children of different worlds: The formation of social behavior.* Cambridge, MA: Harvard University Press.

Wood, D. B. (1994). U.S. Hispanics: To be or not to be. In J. A. Kromkowski (ed.), *Race and Ethnic Relations. Annual Editions 94/95.* Guilford, CT: Dushkin.

Yates, J. (1988). Demography as its affects special education. In A. Ortiz and B. Ramírez (eds.), *Schools and the culturally diverse exceptional student: Promises and future directions.* Reston, VA: Council for Exceptional Children.

Zigler, E., & Finn Stevenson, M. (1993). *Children in a changing world. Development and social issues.* Pacific Grove, CA: Brooks/Cole.

"There is not one aspect of human life that is not touched and altered by culture."

Edward T. Hall (1976)

CHAPTER 2

The Nature of Culture, the Nature of People

In this chapter we will:
- define culture
- establish how culture shapes our lives
- identify what areas of life are influenced by culture
- describe how children reflect their culture in the classroom

Key concepts:
- culture
- cultural values
- cultural identity
- cultural diversity
- socialization

IN ACTION . . .   *What Is Your Idea of Culture?*

Before reading any further, let us explore your ideas about culture. Take a piece of paper and fold it in three parts. Title each part as follows: "My ideas about culture," "formal definitions," and "things in common." Fill in the first column by writing all the ideas you believe define culture. As you read through this chapter, complete the rest of the columns. We will get back to this activity later.

❖ Culture, the Magic Web of Life

Have you ever asked yourself why you are the way you are? Why you act the way you act? Why you believe in what you believe? Why you speak the language you speak? Why you eat what you eat? The answer is: culture, the determining factor in everything we do, say, believe, and are.

The concept of culture has been a focus of discussions among social scientists, educators, philosophers, and people in general for generations. Many learned and famous people have searched hard and debated long trying to define the meaning of culture. No one seems to be able to agree on one definition. There is, however, one fact that everybody acknowledges: We all have a culture.

Culture is a part of an individual because it is a part of every society (Geertz 1973). No one can claim to be exempt from having a culture. Despite the fact that many Americans say they have no culture, every individual lives according to the patterns of a given culture. This condition is inherent to human nature. Whether aware of it or not, "everybody has a culture" (Nieto 1992, p. 16). Individuals begin to assimilate culture from birth. As early childhood educators, you have probably noticed the different ways your students interpret events and reality in the classroom. This may be even more evident at times when your interpretations diverge from the children's. These variations are largely rooted in cultural distinctions.

The Need for Guideposts: What Culture Does for Human Beings

Imagine a world with no rules. Think about how it would be if there were no directions to guide our existence; no principles to tell us what is right or wrong; no frames of reference to give us clues as we confront things never encountered before. Those are the problems we would face if there were no culture.

Culture provides a framework for our lives. It is the paradigm humans use to guide their be-

WORKING GLOSSARY

▌ **Culture**—the way of life of a social group, including all of its materials and nonmaterial products that are transmitted from one generation to the next (Dickinson & Leming 1990, p. 16).

Culture is defined by the sharing of values, beliefs, and traditions among people.

are shared. This participant status is what entitles the child to learn the ways of the group. Learning them is what makes the child a member of a group. These "ways of the group" are what we call culture. As social human beings, we all belong to a group and all groups have culture.

Social scientists—sociologists, anthropologists, psychologists—believe that culture demarcates all manners people use to interact in the context of society. Culture is needed by humans if they are to survive in a social group. Bruner (1990) affirms that, "the divide in human evolution was crossed when culture became the major factor in giving form to the minds of those living under its sway (pp. 11–12)." One thing becomes clear: As humans strive for survival, the need for an organizing pattern becomes a necessity. This is what makes culture a thing shared by all social groups.

Freire (1970) defines culture as encompassing all that is done by people. According to Spradley and McCurdy (1972/1988, p. 8), it is "the knowledge people use to generate and interpret social behavior." Elaborating on the concept, Hernandez (1989, p. 20) says that culture refers to "the complex processes of human social interaction and symbolic communication." Others, like Arvizu, Snyder, and Espinosa (cited by Hernandez 1989), describe culture as being an instrument people use as they struggle to survive in a social group. The definition that will be used throughout this book identifies culture as the ways and manners people use to see, perceive, represent, interpret, and assign value and meaning (Figure 2.1) to the reality they live or experience (Banks 1992, 1993; Kroeber & Kluckhuhn 1952; Lynch & Hanson 1992; Nieto 1992).

Looking at Life Through Our Cultures

"Todo es del color del cristal con que se mira." (Everything depends on the color of the glass you look through.)

Pedro Calderón de la Barca
(La vida es sueño, 16th century)

havior, find meaning in events, interpret the past, and set aspirations. From very early in life, we learn to follow and apply the recognized guidelines of our society, sometimes without even being consciously aware of them. A child discovers what is acceptable behavior through daily interaction with others, observation, and modeling. Psychologist Jerome Bruner (1990) says that when the child enters into a group, the child does so as a participant of a public process where meanings

IN ACTION . . . *Exploring Culture*

One of the ways to "see" proof that we all have and respond within a cultural framework is to find two persons and ask them what they think is the right way to celebrate a wedding. Write their answers and compare them with your own.

▌ Were they in agreement with each other?

▌ Were you in agreement with them? Why?

Culture is a glass prism through which we look at life. Culture, like a prism, has many facets. It is important that the early childhood educator gains an awareness of these various facets to be able to explain the behavior and manners of children in the classroom.

▌ *Culture defines the accepted behaviors, roles, interpretations, and expectations of a social group.* Every social group has norms and principles that reflect agreed meanings. For example, in the Nepalese society it is accepted "to pop in and stare at the strange [Westerner] at great length, without thinking twice about it" (Murray 1993, p. 35).

▌ *Culture is present in visible, tangible ways.* It also exists in abstract ways, not physically perceived by the eye. For example, we see the sari dress of an Indian woman and a child's toy truck and recognize them for what they are. However, we do not know why the Indian woman is smiling, or why the child is

hugging the toy. These reactions are rooted in inner feelings that are not readily visible.

▌ *Culture offers stable patterns to guide human behavior.* While being stable, however, culture is also dynamic. It is constantly responding to the various influences in the surroundings, affecting changes whenever necessary. An example of this is seen in the concept of a child. Today, a child is considered an individual with unique characteristics and rights, whereas in the past, the child was not valued as a person (Roopnarine & Johnson 1993).

▌ *Culture is acquired through interactions with the environment.* A major setting where this occurs is the school. Consider as an example what Mead (1975) found among the Manus of New Guinea. She found that the education of six-year-old Manus children included mastering swimming and canoeing, skills usually associated with older children, because those skills are essential for survival in the Manu society.

▌ *We begin learning the patterns and shared meanings of the group we belong to from birth.* This knowledge increases and changes as we grow and develop. Think about how a five-year-old interprets a birthday party and compare it with the reactions of a two-year-old. Compare the ideas held about single parents in the 1950s with those of today.

FIGURE 2.1 The dimensions of culture

Through culture we . . .

SEE   PERCEIVE   INTERPRET   REPRESENT

SYMBOLIZE   VALUE   ASSIGN MEANING

■ *Culture influences different aspects of life* (Banks 1988). Nothing escapes the power of culture. Notice, for example, how you dress yourself, how you decide what appeals to you as beautiful in contrast to what you label as not beautiful.

■ *There are also cultural differences among people of the same culture.* For instance, the views and practices concerning childrearing held by urban parents probably differ from the views held by parents in rural areas.

■ *Culture gives people identity.* The sharing of ideas, values, and practices gives humans a sense of being a part of an entity. However, there are various factors that make people feel as individuals within a group. Having a gender, age, religion, and family background are the basic factors that provide a sense of identity. Additional traits that define one's unique persona are derived from cultural sources.

The Two Worlds of Culture

The influence of culture is so powerful that it covers every aspect of behavior. As Hall (1976) says:

> There is not one aspect of life that is *not touched and altered* by culture. This also means personality, how people dress themselves (including shows of emotions), the way they think, how they move, how problems are solved, how their cities are planned and laid out, how transportation systems function, as well as how economic and government systems are put together and function (pp. 16–17) (emphasis added).

Following Hall, we realize that culture can be exhibited in visible (i.e., our body movements, our gestures; the physical distribution of our cities) and invisible ways (i.e., how we think, how we solve problems). This premise suggests another relevant feature of culture, the dual way in which we exhibit its influences and effects. An example of cultural visibility is demonstrated in different artifacts that we associate with given cultures, such as typical dress or architectural style. There are also things that remain invisible to the eye, but which are perceived through actions. Examples of the invisible culture may be seen in emotional reactions to events such as death and in ideas about how to welcome guests into one's home.

Whether visible or not, culture provides patterns to interpret life. We use them every day. Like the skin that covers our bodies and gives us our individual identity, culture is always with us (Lynch & Hanson 1992). As a classroom educator, you have probably found that there are times when you can easily identify the cultural patterns followed by your students; there are other times when you have probably been unable to do so. This occurs because culture presents itself in ways that are either materially or nonmaterially expressed (Figure 2.2) (Hernandez 1989).

There are two important dimensions that define how culture influences people's lives. One is the dimension called *overt* or material, while the second is described as the *covert* or nonmaterial. In the overt culture, people display their ideas through things that are concrete, visible. Examples of the overt culture are found in the ways people dress, speak, the foods they prefer, and even the way they decorate their homes (Hernandez 1989). The covert, the nonmaterial, is more difficult to identify because it assumes forms invisible to the eye. You come in contact with the covert in the context of behavior. That is when attitudes, fears, and values surface, all of which are rooted in various cultures.

Differences in values and customs are readily visible in the most familiar settings. The incident described in Snapshot 2.1 exhibits a cultural misunderstanding that can occur anywhere.

The material and the nonmaterial sides of culture are constantly working together. You and your children display them in the classroom through your actions and interactions. Usually,

FOCUS ON CLASSROOM PRACTICES

DISCOVERING THE CULTURES OF CHILDREN

We begin to acquire the ways of those we live and interact with since birth. We learn about the culture of others and ourselves as we interact with people. Because every individual's environment has a culture of its own, we come in contact with many different cultural patterns. Perhaps the best place to see these differences is in the classroom. You probably have noticed already that the children you teach have unique ways. This is easier to see in the context of their interactions when they begin to share their thoughts and feelings.

We want you to do a simple exercise to help you "see" the many cultures that characterize your children. Begin by selecting a story to share with the children. Select, for instance, any of Verna Aardeema's stories or any of the Jafta's books by Hugh Lewin. If you want, bring in an issue for them to ponder and react to. Before sharing the story or issue, write down what *in your opinion* is the central message, point, or morale of the story. Then, share the story or the issue and ask the children to offer their interpretations. Here is where the fun part begins. As you listen to their comments, see how many different ideas are given. Compare their answers with your own. You will find that your students, despite their young age, have an exciting variety of views. Charting their comments is another thing to do. It will give you additional opportunities to learn how their answers reflect their cultures. This beginning experience will make you aware of two important facts: (1) everyone has a culture and (2) culture influences our views.

FIGURE 2.2 Cultural levels

Material Culture	Nonmaterial Culture
▌dress	▌ideas
▌works of art	▌beliefs
▌utensils	▌fears
▌tools	▌emotions
▌food	▌values
▌language	

Can you think about ways in which the material and nonmaterial cultures are exhibited in the classroom?

---

we can easily note differences in others when they are at the overt level and, to a lesser extent, if they are at the covert level. Also, we can more easily observe differences in others, while we often fail to detect our own patterns of divergence. This is the result of our own culture being so embedded in us that we forget it exists. It also happens because we consider our ways as the most appropriate formula for responding to the environment. To further understand how culture is seen in our classrooms, let us look at the findings of a kindergarten teacher who took a cultural inventory of her children. As you read "Culture in Action" (Figure 2.3), highlight the similarities between her findings and yours.

The influence of culture in our lives is such that it will define even what we own (material culture) and do (nonmaterial culture). Can you identify how material and nonmaterial cultures influence the women in this illustration?

After reading how culture comes into action, think about the following: How many of these instances reflect culture at the material and at the nonmaterial level? How many additional ways can you identify in which your students display their cultures?

Hernandez (1989) warns that we must become more attentive to the students' cultures if we want

WORKING GLOSSARY

▮ **Material Culture**—those overt or tangible aspects that are easily observed in a culture. They include ways of decoration, what people eat, manners, and what they wear.

▮ **Nonmaterial Culture**—represents those things not overtly seen but discovered through interaction with people of a specific culture. Nonmaterial aspects include ideas, values, ethics, beliefs, and behaviors.

Snapshot 2.1
"An Indecent Practice"

Ms. Allen believed that her day-care center was the best facility for young children. Every effort had been made to follow developmentally appropriate practices. Recently opened in a suburban area, the center was enthusiastically received by the parents in the community. The children seemed very happy. The staff, hand-picked by Ms. Allen, was excellent.

One morning, Ms. Allen was surprised to get a call from a very irate Mrs. Garcia who informed her that she was moving her four-year-old daughter to another school. Only a week before, Ms. Allen had personally registered the bright-eyed child and had a pleasant conversation with Mrs. Garcia who seemed very impressed by the school. Ms. Allen could not understand the reason for the parent's sudden anger or her actions.

After getting off the phone, the very puzzled Ms. Allen asked if anyone in the office was aware of an incident involving the Garcia girl. Her secretary informed her that the child's mother called the day before and complained that in her child's classroom they were doing things that were indecent, "especially for a girl." But, the secretary had been so busy this morning that she forgot to mention the conversation to Ms. Allen. "This can't be true," said Ms. Allen and went to see the teacher in order to learn more before calling back Mrs. Garcia.

Ms. Morton, the teacher, told Ms. Allen that Mrs. Garcia visited her daughter's classroom the day before and saw the children's bathrooms and that made her "very irate." Ms. Morton tried to explain that the absence of doors was a safety measure. Despite her efforts to elaborate further, Mrs. Garcia took her child and left very annoyed. "I really don't know why," Ms. Morton said. Ms. Allen thought for a moment and said, "I do, I do."

---

to truly respond to their needs. It can prove to be a disadvantage for the child if we fail to use our aptitude to perceive his or her needs and end up designing activities that do not respond to the child's value structure. For instance, recognizing what certain words or contexts connote for some children will help us interpret the behavior they exhibit. Consider, for instance, the experience of the day-care center director in Snapshot 2.1. Without a doubt, the bathroom facility was designed to provide for the safety of the children in the center; however, from the parent's perspective, not having a door to provide for her daughter's privacy was a violation of her cultural principles, both at the overt and covert levels. Gaining an awareness about the interplay of various cultural

FIGURE 2.3 Culture in action

In the classroom my students express their cultures by:

▌ sharing their fears
▌ using oral expressions unique to their family
▌ sharing their likes and dislikes
▌ expressing their preferences
▌ discussing their views about various events
▌ bringing pictures of their families and discussing them
▌ playing in the classroom and on the playground
▌ arguing with another child and expressing their feelings
▌ discussing holidays and special events

worlds gives the early childhood educator an opportunity to create environments sensitive to children and to their realities.

Patterns of Life

"Who are you?" said the caterpillar. . . . Alice replied rather shyly, "I hardly know, sir, just at present—at least I know who I was when I got up this morning, but I think I must have been changed several times since then."

Alice's Adventures in Wonderland. L. B. Carrol (1987, p. 41)

You probably would have answered like Alice if you found yourself in her wonderland. When Alice went through the mirror, she left behind the rules and roles that gave meaning to her life and she entered a world of unfamiliar ways. Like Alice, we have encountered similar experiences. For instance, how many times have you been in a place where you could not understand what the others were doing or saying? It is only when something familiar is said or done that it makes sense.

Everything we do responds to the patterns set and accepted by the group we belong to. In social groups, everyone knows and follows the frame of reference that serves to organize their experiences. It is this pattern that gives meaning and direction to our actions and behaviors. This is what we call the essential role of culture. Spradley and McCurdy (1972/1988) point out that "like the system of rules that defines a game of football or hockey, agreed-on cultural definitions enable people to coordinate their behavior and make sense of their shared experiences" (pp. 59–60).

Experiences reflect how the members of a group use their frames of reference or scripts. These frameworks are made up of:

▌ values
▌ beliefs
▌ shared meanings and interpretations
▌ rules

It would be difficult to explain when and why the social patterns of a group were established. The origins are found in the events experienced long ago by elders who, in turn, decided ways and ascribed meanings. Recognizing the need to perpetuate their ways, each generation took the responsibility of delivering the message from one generation to the next. How we came to learn and follow them is a result of the social environment in which we were born and live.

People of Every Culture Behave According to Their Cultural Schema

Underlying our behavior lies a set of complex ideas that individuals in our particular group use "to generate and interpret social behavior" (Spradley & McCurdy 1972/1988, p. 8). These are rules, values, beliefs, and principles that, when followed, provide coherence and integrity to human existence. Each of these structures or schemes is known to the members of the group. Despite how unusual rules might look to an outsider, for its members they are logical. In fact,

CELEBRATIONS, ONE OF CULTURE'S UNIVERSAL TRAITS

There are many common elements shared by different cultures. Perhaps one of the most characteristic ones is the need to celebrate. Celebrations can happen for a variety of reasons. They can also be observed through a multiplicity of ways, all understood and shared by those who belong to the cultural group. In simple terms, celebrations are happenings that people observe because of the significance they have in their lives. When celebrations are observed by an entire religious group or when they hold national relevance, they become holidays. For the early childhood teacher who wants to discover more about the culture of her/his students, learning about the what's and why's of celebrations opens another door to cultural understanding. In the classroom, you may want to explore the celebrations observed by children and their families. Begin by brainstorming with children what a celebration is. A good storybook to use is *Celebrations: Birthday Celebrations Around the World* (Feldman 1996). Information about the holidays and celebrations families observe can be obtained by sending home a letter with these two questions:

▋ *What are the three most important celebrations or special days for your family?*

▋ *What are the holidays your family observes?*

Take time to analyze the answers. They will give you not only a glimpse of their cultures but also of what families consider important. With the information gathered, engage the class in creating a mural depicting the holidays and special days they celebrate. You may want to involve students in a further exploration of the topic. Actually, this can become the target of an interesting thematic unit. To help you build a thematic unit, here are some essential points that will help you focus on the cultural aspects:

What Constitutes Cultural Aspects in Holidays and Celebrations

1. Meanings: *Why is it observed?*
   a. religious
   b. personal
   c. national or patriotic
2. Ways in which it is observed: *How is it observed? What do people do?*
   a. When does it take place? (Time, season, dates)
   b. What do people do? (External or physical aspects)
      1. colors and symbols
      2. decorations
      3. traditions (like gift-giving, food, music)
3. People involved: *Who participates?*
   a. adults; children
   b. all
4. Places, locations: *Where do activities takes place?*
   a. home
   b. community
   c. school

when practiced, they grant a sense of identity to the collective group (Hernandez 1989). Cultural schemes are used to define the behavior parameters as well as the needs and aspirations of the group. Practices are also based on the particular interpretations that the group has made of life events. For instance, this is what Milo, the character in *The Phantom Tollbooth,* discovers during his encounter with a magical child.

> Milo turned around and found himself staring at two very neatly polished brown shoes, for standing directly in front of him . . . was another boy just about his age, whose feet were easily three feet above the ground . . .
>
> "Well," said the boy, "in my family everyone is born in the air, with his head at exactly the height it's going to be when he's an adult, and then we all grow toward the ground."
>
> [Milo said] "In my family we all start on the ground and grow up, and we never know how far until we actually get there" (Juster 1961, p. 151).

"What a silly system," was the child's reaction to what Milo considered a logical growing style, probably the same comment you would have made had you been part of the boy's culture group. Trying to see the rules, beliefs, and values of other cultures while using the mirror of our own will not always prove effective. Each culture needs to be observed and understood from the view of its actors. More precisely, the ideas of different cultures cannot be fully equated (Spradley & McCurdy 1972/1988). For example, individuality, prized in American culture, is not equally important in other cultures. Lynch and Hanson (1992) remark that in traditional Asian cultures, social orientation is focused on the collective

"we" rather than on the individual. Awareness of values and visions of others contributes to our appreciation of diversity.

Practices in early childhood classrooms are influenced by cultural beliefs and values. Lewis (1991) reports how the view about responsibility varies in Japanese schools and how it influences classroom practices in nursery school. During her study, Lewis observed how five-year-olds were given responsibility at an age when, in the American context, the child is still guided by teachers. As their "brother's keepers," Japanese children were granted the authority to control the behavior of their peers and were held accountable for chores and tasks expected to be carried out by the group. Sanctions for activities or routines not followed emerged from the peers and not the teacher, for she was to remain as a conflict-free benevolent figure (Lewis 1991).

Examples of differences in the interpretation of reality abound. Each of them reveals what is logical and correct in a particular culture. Knowledge of these interpretations helps the early childhood educator establish positive interactions and avoid misinterpretations. Take, for example, the extended use of baby language commonly employed by Hispanics in their communication with young children. This practice is not encouraged in the American culture because the members of this group believe that adult language should be used from infancy. Another illustration pertains to visiting Native American families for the first time. It is advisable for a guest to ask for a place to sit, rather than assume any place is acceptable (Joe & Malach 1992). Although special practices might differ from ours,

WORKING GLOSSARY

▮ **Cultural Schema**—information that defines how to behave in a particular culture. Information in schemes represents the way the particular cultural group interprets reality.

Can you describe the cultural schema of these young Eastern European women who arrived in the United States at the turn of the 20th century?

IN ACTION . . .   *Becoming Ethnographers (I)*

Social scientists dedicated to describing cultures are called ethnographers. Like them, you can also become an ethnographer. The basic responsibility of an ethnographer is learning how to observe in order to produce precise descriptions of a specific culture. The tasks in this activity will help you understand how a society learns to deal with reality. They will also help you sharpen your understanding of the behavior children exhibit in the classroom.

First, you must choose a setting in which to conduct your observations. This will become your cultural scenario. Choosing a scenario within your own culture is usually the best way to start. Possible settings to choose from are a sports stadium, a beauty shop, a restaurant, or even your own school faculty lounge.

Try to select a setting where you can have easy access or where you can make several observations. Take your time in choosing the setting. We will continue this activity later.

Source: Adapted from Spradley, J., & McCurdy, D. (1972/1988). *The cultural experience. Enthnography in complex society.* Chicago: Waveland Press, Inc.

we must always remember that they are a part of what gives members of a particular culture a sense of identity.

A Sense of Identity: Being a Part of the Group

"In our society, elementary school children learn far more than reading, writing, and arithmetic. Some of the mere aspects of their knowledge are never taught in a systematic way. They are acquired as part of their culture through interaction with teachers and peers."

J. Spradley and D. McCurdy (1972/1988, p. 155)

Have you ever stopped to consider what prompts you to say "I am . . . "? Are you aware of what saying what you are means? Ask a five-year-old what she is and see how quickly she states her identity. Even if the answer is, "I am a girl," that child is establishing herself as a member of a group. This sense of identification reveals an awareness of a group in which the individual participates and discloses another trait of culture: a sense of identity.

Cultural identity is determined by many factors. In fact, we belong to many more groups than we may be aware of. Every individual's identity is based upon the elements in Figure 2.4 (Banks 1992; Gollnick & Chinn 1990).

Each cultural element conveys a specific pattern; collectively they set clear expectations and behaviors for those who exhibit them, whereby

FIGURE 2.4 Elements of cultural identity

▌ ethnic or national origin	▌ geographical region
▌ family	▌ language
▌ religion	▌ age
▌ gender	▌ socioeconomic level
▌ educational background	▌ job or occupation

creating subcultures. For example, when we see ourselves as members of a family, we understand that in that context we are expected to assume specific roles, adopt special responsibilities, perform assigned tasks, and, in general, interact and behave in preagreed ways. The influence of the family is such that it anchors us in this mini culture. This, then, becomes a micro culture.

Environment is another powerful source that molds and shapes us as members of micro cultures. For example, we understand that inhabitants of Vietnam may embody special cultural characteristics resulting from their geographical location. Garza and Lipton (cited by Hernandez 1989) state that because individuals are defined by more than just one cultural influence, "everyone is multicultural to varying degrees with [the] specific characteristics of each individual being unique" (p. 25).

The interplay of all these variables—age, family, ethnicity, religion, socioeconomic status, gender, religion—is what makes us who we are. For instance, imagine the life of a middle-class European American six-year-old female, born in Nevada and living in an urban area in the state of Washington. Compare her to a girl of the same age and descent living in a middle-class family in urban Connecticut. Will they both possess the same cultural identity? Are they both going to see things in the same manner? We might be tempted to affirm that they will both exhibit similar behavior patterns. It is more likely that both girls will show differences, despite the fact that they are of the same gender, age, and social status, as a result of having different families and being unique individuals. What are the implications? This basically indicates the need to be cautious when defining a person's culture. It also reminds us of the role of developmental appropriateness, for it indicates that although all children have common patterns, they are to be seen as individual human beings (Bredekamp 1987; Bredekamp & Rosegrant 1992). All characteristics

IN ACTION . . . *Becoming Ethnographers (II)*

In the first part of this exercise you were asked to choose a setting to conduct your ethnographic study. Now, we will proceed with the next steps.

Suppose you chose a sports event like a football game and you wanted to find out how people behave during a tailgate party. You will have to collect data. First, you will need to identify individuals who will provide you with information. You will gather your data directly from them without the use of formal surveys or interviews. Before you begin, you need to know that three tasks are involved in the information collecting process: *observing, participating, and talking to the participants.* This is what makes ethnographic studies so much fun!

Continuing with our activity, select a person or two you think will be willing to provide you with the data you need. Tell what your purposes are. The next step? With eyes wide and attentive ears, join the party! But, remember to observe carefully.

If you want, take a small pad (sticky notes are particularly good) and take notes of what you find particularly important. To conclude your ethnographic experience, you will need to examine what you gathered. This will give you the opportunity to discover the cultural meanings attached to what you observed. We recommend you engage in some brainstorming or do some webbing to help you identify how a group interprets reality, which in this case was a sports event. Write at the top of a piece of paper the event observed. Then, begin to brainstorm the possible categories or related areas in which you can group your observations. In the case of a sports event, possible categories would include: players, spectators, vendors, people's behaviors, symbols or paraphernalia used, rituals, etc. As you identify categories, you will begin to see how the event reflects the existence of a set of organized patterns. You will also see how they all fit together. In fact, you have already identified two of the characteristics of culture: *patterns* and *inclusiveness.*

Continue to brainstorm further one of the categories to see what behaviors give meaning to a sports setting for this particular cultural group. Take, for example, the behavior of the spectators. You will probably find out that despite the eccentric and weird character of the various actions, these behaviors are accepted as normal by the group. They are accepted because the group members understand what the behaviors represent and mean. Once you arrive at this conclusion, you will see that you will have discovered the greatest truth about cultures: that they define and entail meanings shared by those who belong to it. No one, then, has the right to question or label the culture of others as illogical or absurd. Reality is not the same for all of us.

of a person need to be considered before establishing who she or he is. It also reminds us that ethnic origin, the element most commonly used in identifying an individual, is *not* the only factor to consider when describing a person's cultural identity.

A Myriad of Cultural Identities: The Essence of Cultural Diversity

Many factors make us what we are. A cultural identity, as we have seen already, is based on numerous elements, each having varying degrees of influence on one's individuality. We have also seen that ethnic or cultural descent is not the only element that defines a cultural orientation. Because of the effects of many other elements or subcultures, we recognize that we are all different. We might share some similar traits, like the culture of origin, or religion, but we probably have values that diverge to various degree from those of others. You as an individual represent a myriad of ideas and influences all blended into who *you* are. They are your unique experiences and will not be like those of others. As you constructed your reality, you processed every bit of it according to your own mental schemes (De Vries & Kohlberg 1987). If, as an early child educator, you find that your ideas about education or about parenting differ from those of your colleagues, it is because you are the sum of your particular experiences. This is an example of diversity on a personal level.

Diversity is found in every single individual because each of us is a composite of cultures. Diversity has also become a very fashionable term, usually applied to define our social mosaic. It has become an accepted truth that the American soci-ety is the most complex reflection of cultural identities. It is a social reality spawned of the multitude of different nationalities and ideologies representative of the immigrant nature of this nation. Today, we freely use the term "cultural diversity" whenever we talk about the cultural spectrum found through our communities. However, when we analyze how the concept "cultural diversity" is used, we discover it has been narrowed down to just a few elements that define it.

We asked a group of early childhood graduate students to give us their opinion of what the term "cultural diversity" meant to them and found out the following:

- people from other countries who now live in the United States
- people who speak a language other than English
- children who are of a different race
- those born in other countries
- people with a culture different from mine

IN ACTION . . . *What Is Your Identity?*

Could you name the things that make you what you are? To find out, you will need a pair of scissors, construction paper in eight different colors, and a piece of white paper. Place the white paper on a desk or table and write your name across the top. Using the color construction papers, assign cultural elements that define cultural identity to each one. Now, reflect carefully on those factors as they pertain to your identity. Establish which one has the most impact in determining who you are. Do the same with the rest of the elements. As you decide their levels of impact, cut the papers in triangles proportional to the priorities they represent. Arrange the triangles in a circular form on the white paper. This is a representation of what you believe defines your identity.

- What are the reasons for your choices?
- Do this exercise with other members of your family and discuss the results.

Snapshot 2.2
Another Way to Define Our Cultural Identity

Did you know that you are actually a member of many intermingling cultures?

According to Vontress (1976), every individual is a member of at least five different cultures. Of these five, one is shared by all human beings; others are particular to the individual.

Universal—All human beings are alike in their needs and rights.

Ecological—The place where humans live on the earth determines the way they will respond and relate to their natural environment.

National—Depending on the country where they were born, individuals will have characteristics that identify them (language, world views, etc.).

Regional—Based on the region where humans live, they will develop area-specific cultures.

Racio-Ethnic—All people have distinct racial and ethnic characteristics.

Source: Adapted from Baruth, L. G., & Manning, M. L. (1992). *Multicultural education of children and adolescents.* Needham Heights, MA: Allyn & Bacon.

Cultural diversity entails many more factors than a place of origin (where you or your parents were born or came from) or language. It is necessary to define diversity in an operational way because there is confusion about what it really means.

Diversity, as observed in the social context, contains a variety of social factors that exert an influence, either singly or interactively, on the individual's behavior. These social factors are nationality, race/ethnicity, religion, social class, gender, exceptionality, and age (Figure 2.5). Knowledge of the factors that confirm the individual can enable educators to better understand behavior and to determine needs (Banks & Banks 1993; McCracken 1993; Derman-Sparks 1989). In the early childhood classroom, it becomes crucial for teachers to be aware of the presence and influence of these factors because they serve as a basis for designing a truly developmentally appropriate program. How to respond to those variables in the context of our classroom is presented in the third part of this book.

Banks & Banks (1993) describes the elements of diversity as socially constructed categories. They are ideas or representations of physical or social traits an individual might possess. For instance, social class is a category very hard to define concretely, for it entails areas that are exclusive to those said to belong to it. Today, many of the attributes ascribed in the past to lower classes like single parenthood or substance abuse problems, are found in other social groups (Banks & Banks 1993). Caution must be exercised by educators when determining what makes a child culturally diverse because of the difficulty in establishing

FOCUS ON CLASSROOM PRACTICES

CHILDREN'S LITERATURE ABOUT CULTURAL DIVERSITY

One of the principles early childhood teachers believe in is the need to respond to the child's identity. Because diversity is the best characterizing descriptor of today's society, we know that diversity will be found and reflected through every child. We also know that one of the ways in which we build a positive cultural identity is by recognizing that we are accepted and acknowledged for who we are. For the child, the classroom is one of the most powerful tools for influencing the development of a positive self-perception. An initial step in responding to and reaffirming the children's diversity is to review the stories commonly shared in the classroom. As you learn about the cultural identities of your students, you can also begin to make an appraisal of what you share during storytelling. Check your resources to ensure they reflect a wide range of aspects of diversity.

Using the checklist described here, identify the titles of resources according to the category of diversity. Those categories where no titles were checked, as well as those where less than three were found, will indicate areas for improvement.

Checklist

Please check if there are titles about each of the different categories of diversity:

Category	Yes	No	If yes, how many?
1. Ethnicity			
2. Religion			
3. Nationality			
4. Social class			
5. Gender issues			
6. Exceptionality			
7. Age			

Comments:
Action:

FIGURE 2.5 Elements of diversity

Nationality	Refers to country where you were born or from where parents came.
Race/ethnic	Defines the cultural traditions that serve to shape the individual's identity.
Religion	Refers to the religious affiliations and the freedom to exercise any faith as defined in the First Amendment of the Constitution.
Social class	Determined by income, education, occupation, lifestyles, and values typically held by a group.
Gender	Defines the behavior socially accepted and assigned to females and males. Includes role expectations.
Exceptionality	Defines the child with any disability or who is gifted.
Age	Defines the social expectations for behavior established by society for individuals of different age groups. They vary according to the individual's main cultural influence.

Understanding diversity requires an awareness of many different elements. This figure can serve as a barometer for assessing the levels of diversity in our classrooms.

Even though they share a common Hispanic background, these children are diverse in their own ways. Teachers need to be aware of using only one variable when addressing children's needs.

strict, objective parameters to define who possesses what factor.

Cultural Diversity Defines the American Way

Some still contend that we are not diverse. They claim that we are simply Americans. Others say that cultural diversity will endanger the future of the nation. Comments reflecting such resistance are commonly found because some people are still unclear about the significance of diversity.

Diversity has been the common denominator of our nation since its inception. As we studied in Chapter 1, people from many different countries came to forge the nation we feel so proud of. Decades ago when the founders—the poor, the idealists, and the persecuted of the world—came to this part of North America, they faced many physical and social adjustments. One of their major tasks was to become Americans. This process required the newcomers to blend into a common culture. This common framework, defined as the core or mainstream culture, evolved from the cultures brought over first by the early English and later by the German settlers. This mainstream culture is still the nucleus of the American lifestyle. Those who developed it, traded their individual cultural identities in the process of Americanization. They "melted" not knowing that they could become one and keep their own heritage. The concept of the United states as a "melting pot" where everyone becomes a mainstream kind of American has changed because the new immigrants have proven that it is possible to be productive members of society and maintain their own cultural heritage. It is possible because pluralism has become a part of the American *unum*.

Being a classroom teacher requires understanding the significance of the new social directions caused by diversity. More than ever before, professionals must understand the effects of the process on early childhood practices. There is an added responsibility to adapt our curriculum to new socialization patterns. The new diversity demands that early childhood professionals acquire respect for the various cultures of children and teach in an atmosphere of mutual respect.

Snapshot 2.3
America, the Melting Pot

Israel Zangwill, twentieth century writer, political activist, and founder of the Zionist movement, used the phrase "melting pot" in one of his plays. The term is still used today to define the socialization trend now substituted by pluralism. In his 1908 melodrama, he wrote the following dialogue for one of his characters:

"America is God's crucible, the great Melting-Pot where all races of Europe are melting and re-forming . . . Germans and Frenchmen, Irishmen and Englishmen, Jews and Russians—into the crucible with you all! God is making the American!"

Source: Morganthau, T. (1994). America: Still a melting pot? In J. A. Kromkowski (ed.). *Race and ethnic relations. Annual Editions 94/95* (p. 16). Guilford, CT: Dushkin.

The classrooms of our nation are settings where the country's future is being forged. Preparation for the real world in our society now entails giving our children the skills needed to interact with others. This has special meaning in an increasingly diverse society. "Education ought to illuminate what is happening in the self of each child" (Novak 1994, p. 174). Inclusion and infusion of realities of our society will prove to be the key elements, as an early childhood professional strives to create the best environment for a child. Teaching the whole child must include considerations toward the child's cultural background.

Talking About Race and Ethnicity

There are probably no two concepts that are more misunderstood than race and ethnicity. Both tend to be included in discussions about culture. What relevance do they have to culture? What is the meaning of each term?

What is Ethnicity?

Central to the idea of culture is the concept of ethnicity. According to Allport (1958), ethnicity is defined by three factors: (1) nationality, (2) ancestry, and (3) religious affiliation. A member of an ethnic group might portray a combination of these characteristics or might actually possess all of them (Figure 2.6). Theodorson and Theodorson (cited by Bullivant 1993) describe ethnic groups as those existing as part of a larger social group and which have a common cultural tradition and a clear sense of identity. Ethnicity, thus, becomes the set of features that historically has characterized a particular subgroup in the con-

FIGURE 2.6 Are there any other elements or characteristics that define membership in an ethnic group?

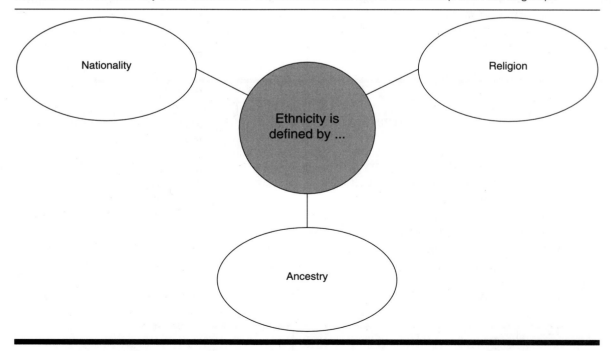

FIGURE 2.6 continued

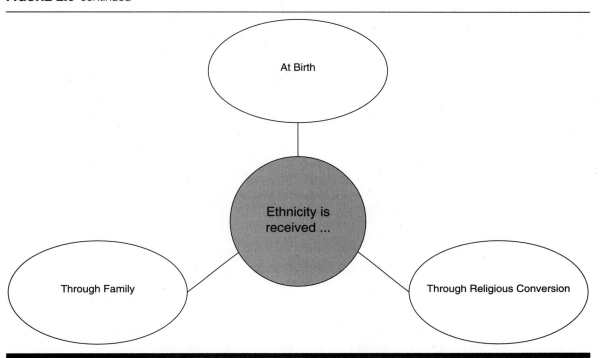

text of a larger dominant culture (McGoldrick 1993). At the personal level, ethnicity becomes the sense an individual has of having a commonality or community [which is] derived from networks of family experiences (Feinstein 1974, cited by McGoldrick 1993). The family plays an instrumental role in a person's acquisition and development of a sense of ethnicity, serving as the initial source and reinforcer of ethnic characterizations. The impact of ethnicity on people is such that it identifies them within the spectrum of a society. Some of the examples of ethnic groups found in the American society are the Amish, the African Americans, and the Jews. These three ethnic groups are good examples for they represent the differences one can find when defining ethnicity. While the Amish have all three basic elements of diversity (religion, ancestry, nationality), and the African Americans possess two (ancestry, nationality), the Jews, affiliated through their common religious tradition, only have one. Regardless of what element establishes the character of being an ethnic group, we all belong to one.

Baruth and Manning (1992) add another interesting dimension to the concept of ethnicity: the role of self-perception and of outsiders' perception about the individual. They assert that ethnicity is a "dynamic and complex concept [that] refers to how members of a group *perceive themselves,* and how, in turn, *they are perceived by others"* (emphasis added) (p. 11).

Subjective perception can lead to very distorted views about individuals and social groups. In fact, it reminds us of the child who perceives breaking apart a brand new toy as an exploration, while the parent may interpret the action as misbehavior. Or, recognizing that practicing hand movements with a marker on a living room wall has a different meaning to the child than to an adult. When subjective perception is applied to ethnicity, we find that we do not agree with how others see us. For example, you might see yourself as part of an ethnic group, and yet, people might not consider you as part of it. The same can happen when people see you as part of an ethnicity that *you do not* perceive yourself being a part of.

Divergences in ethnic perception commonly occur in connection with non-European American groups. Examples of this involve people from the Caribbean region as well as Hispanics. During graduate courses on multiculturalism, the authors of this book have found repeatedly how non-European American students differ in their ethnic perceptions of themselves from those assigned to them by the mainstream society. More specifically, the authors found that a student born in Barbados was shocked to find herself defined as "black," when in her country she was not classified that way. She found that her ethnicity was being designated by the color of her skin, rather than by her ethnic heritage. Similarly, it was traumatic for light-colored Hispanics to be denied the designation of "white" because of their heritage. One student commented that for her it was particularly disappointing to find how her color was more commonly used to describe her while her nationality was given a second place. One of the authors of this book remembers witnessing how a dark-skin teacher, born in Trinidad, was once questioned by her colleagues when she refused to identify herself as an African American. Using solely the parameter of color, the teacher's colleagues were unable to acknowledge her Caribbean ethnicity. Similar misconceptions are common among Asian Americans whose ethnicities are usually compounded into one, Oriental, a very abstract and misleading term.

Race, a Controversial Concept

Race is a subject that has been used to establish differences that led to unfair separation of human beings in American society. The term "race" has been synonymous with color and whenever color is the sole attribute used to define an individual, it can become a dangerous tool. Banks (1988)

IN ACTION . . .   *Can You Define Your Ethnicity?*

Clarity about our own roots is critical when trying to understand and teach children from various cultures. Let us try to establish your ethnic affiliation. Ask yourself the following questions:

▌ How do I define myself?

▌ How do I know that I belong to that group?

▌ How did I receive my ethnic identity?

▌ How do other people consider me? Are they in agreement with my view?

▌ What things do I do that identify me as part of that group?

Snapshot 2.4
Factors Influencing Intensity of Ethnic Feelings

Perhaps you have wondered why all the people in a same group do not show the same intensity of ethnic traits. According to McGoldrick (1993), that is due to the following factors:

▮ *Reasons for immigration*—what they were seeking when they left their countries

▮ *Length of time since immigration and the effects of generational acculturation*—how long has it been since they left and to what extent have the families become part of the mainstream

▮ *Place of residence*—if they live or lived in an ethnic neighborhood

▮ *Order of migration*—whether one person migrated alone or with the family

▮ *Socioeconomic status*—the upward mobility capability of the individual; education

▮ *Political and religious ties*—if the individual maintains such ties to the ethnic group

▮ *Language*—what languages are spoken by the individual

▮ *Interracial marriages*—extent of intermarriage with other ethnicities

▮ *Personal attitudes*—how the individual feels about his/her ethnic group

Source: McGoldrick, M. (1993). Ethnicity, cultural diversity, and normality. In F. Walsh (ed.). *Normal family processes* (p. 341). New York: The Guilford Press.

---

warns that nothing has had a more destructive effect on humankind than ideas about races. Montague affirms it is, in fact, "man's most dangerous myth" (cited by Baruth & Manning 1992, p. 10). Recently, the term "people of color" has been coined to depict the non-European groups. Nieto (1992) states her disagreement with this terminology because of the misleading connotation given to color. The authors of this book also agree that "people of color" emphasizes only one irrelevant characteristic of a cultural group. Many others, including the authors of this book, prefer the more inclusive term "culturally diverse."

Race is defined as the phenotypical characteristics that designate a group. It basically refers to the biological features common to a human group. Different from ethnicity, racial characteristics are something that individuals cannot easily change (Bullivant 1993). They are transmitted from one individual to another.

The concept of race has its origins in anthropology where it was used to describe physical characteristics (eyes, skin color, size of head, etc.) of people (Hernandez 1989). It was from this anthropological perspective that scientists identified humans by racial groups. But today, even in the scientific sphere it proves difficult to categorize human beings by such closed attributes. With the high incidence of interracial marriages, it definitely becomes challenging to apply strict descriptors to define the children of diversity. Just think how you would define some of the children in your classroom who are a combination of many racial groups. Take the case of a three-year-old living on the East Coast, whose father is Italian American and whose mother is half Asian and half African American. Racially it would be a hard task to label the child. One would need to get a formula to determine the physical racial proportions, which at the end would yield no significant information about the child as an individual. Unfortunately, we still find people who persist in the use of race labels. Applied as a social descriptor of people, race turns into a misleading concept. The pronounced emphasis on a physical aspect like color helps to create inaccurate images of people, for it ignores the social and traditional heritage embedded by culture in every individual.

Perhaps the ideas presented by Gollnick and Chinn (1990) will clarify the social implications and the meaning of race.

▌ *Race as a concept still carries a strong social meaning in our country as well as in many other societies.* This is despite the extensive movement of people from one geographical region to another and the incidence of interracial marriages.

▌ *The concept of race contributes very little to cultural understanding.* Race seldom correlates with cultural groups defined by nationality, language, or religion. The racial identity of people does not necessarily correspond to their nationality.

▌ *The persistent use of racial, ethnic, and language categories in public and governmental documents provokes more confusion about the American population.* The use of racial and ethnic indicators has proven to be not always effective when trying to assign individuals to a category. An individual could belong to several categories at the same time, thus, it is hard to have totally inclusive categories.

Prejudice and Racism, the Plagues of the Past and the Present

Any discussion about race and ethnicity would be incomplete if we were not to acknowledge the presence of prejudice and racism in American society. Unfortunately, neither is a stranger to our country. American history is full of instances where people were victims of unfair treatment because they were different.

Prejudice has caused more destruction in the world than any war. It is the essence of racism and

---

IN ACTION . . .   *All the Colors We Are*

The story of how we get our skin color is a book written by Katie Kissinger (1994) to tell children about differences in skin color. Read the following citation and see how she addresses this difficult concept.

"The skin color we are born with comes from our parents, ancestors, and where they lived a long time ago. Do you think your ancestors came from a very warm, sunny place, or a cooler place with less sunshine? Dark skin, light skin, and skin with freckles, are all caused by our ancestors, the sun, and the melanin" (pp. 26–28).

▌ What do you think about her approach? Is it developmentally appropriate?

IN ACTION . . . *What Accounts for Our Views about Others?*

Many times people hold prejudiced views about others because they ignore who they really are. As you read the following quote from Seelye (1993), consider how you would have reacted in that situation and its implications for multicultural education.

"Sometimes just having a strange-sounding name is enough to incur disdain. A study of American attitudes towards 58 ethnic groups included the fictitious 'Wisians.' Although 61% of the respondents said they didn't know enough about them to rank them, the other 39% went ahead and gave them a low rating." (reported in *Time magazine*, Jan. [sic] 20, 1992, p. 20)

Source: Seelye 1993 (p. 39).

---

bigotry. Prejudice is based on holding negative views about others not supported by solid evidence. The dislikes manifested by those who are prejudiced are based on poor or inadequate knowledge.

Sometimes those who hold prejudices are not aware of their own feelings, states Kehoe as cited by Hernandez (1989). Dislikes of others are often demonstrated through attitudes and nonverbal ways. Victims of prejudice have been subjected to subtle covert ways as a condescending smile or a mocking look that wounds and often permanently stigmatizes them. Kehoe (cited by Hernandez 1989) in an analysis of prejudice, found key points that alert educators to its sources. Some of Kehoe's findings are included in Snapshot 2.5.

Sadly, prejudice has proven not to be a stranger in our schools. As early as 1884, Marie, an American-born child of Chinese migrants Joseph and Mary McGladery Tape, was denied enrollment at the Spring Valley Primary School in San Francisco. Decades later, nine-year-old Martha Lum, an Asian American in Bolivar County, Mississippi, was denied entrance to the school for whites and required to attend the school for "colored" children. Her case reached the U.S. Supreme Court where in 1927 the judge reaffirmed the right to segregate facilities. This was the status quo in American schools until 1954, when the ruling in Brown vs. the Board of Education (Topeka, Kansas) declared segregation unfair (Okihiro 1994). However, prejudice still prevails in our society. Use of racial slurs and hate crimes are only the more overt forms of prejudice. The subtle ones, for instance the patronizing ways in which culturally diverse parents are often treated, are as damaging and offensive as the more tangible ones. Eradicating prejudice from our country is a goal some describe as too ambitious. However, it is the one we who have embraced multicultural education struggle for every day.

Stereotypes

"Our stereotypical views of others perpetuate racism, blame the victims, and often reflect unresolved views we have of ourselves."

Clyde Ford (1994, p. 39)

One of the most damaging ways prejudice is expressed is in the form of stereotypes. A stereotype is an oversimplified, generalized image describing all individuals in a group as having the same characteristics in appearance, in behavior, and in beliefs. While there may be a germ of truth in a stereotype, the image usually represents "a gross distortion, or an exaggeration of the truth, and has offensive, dehumanizing implications"

Snapshot 2.5
Facts about Prejudice

▮ Individual differences in temperament cannot be attributed to race.

▮ Prejudice and stereotypes are learned, not innate. They are learned in the family and in school without conscious intent.

▮ Generally, individuals do not realize how prejudiced they are.

▮ Those prejudiced against one ethnic group are likely to be prejudiced against others.

▮ Individuals who are not directly competing with minority group members tend to be less prejudiced toward them.

▮ As a group's character becomes more distinctive, a consensus develops regarding stereotypes associated with that group.

▮ Stereotypes resist change. However, social and economic conditions especially of the kind that modify relations among groups can alter stereotypes.

▮ Prejudice is a predictor of discriminatory behavior.

▮ There is considerable agreement within a society about specific stereotypes assigned to particular groups.

Source: Kehoe, J. (1984). In H. Hernandez (1989). *Multicultural education: a teacher's guide to content and process.* New York: Merrill.

(Council on Interracial Books for Children in Saracho and Spodek 1983, p. 91). The effects of being stereotyped are damaging to the individual and to those who witness it. As found by Kehoe (cited by Hernandez 1989), stereotypes are learned usually in the context of the family and, unfortunately, in schools. Actions to prevent and stop stereotyping are the responsibility of all educators, particularly during the early years because of the inherent vulnerability of young learners. Developing an anti-bias curriculum, like the one developed by the staff at Pacific Oaks College in California, is a good way to start (Derman-Sparks 1992). Familiarizing young children with action-oriented multicultural activities that promote understanding and tolerance is not only recommended but essential.

Racism is often a crime many reject but refuse to stop. It continues to be a "prevailing social practice" (Derman-Sparks 1989, p. 31). Hernandez (1989) states that racism is found in those individuals exhibiting behaviors and actions that reflect (a) the conviction that physical, psychological, and intellectual characteristics are inherited and distributed differently among humans and (b) the belief of being racially superior to other racial groups. Throughout history, many individuals and groups have been victimized

---

FIGURE 2.7 Ford's steps to reduce our stereotypical views. How can you use them to prevent use of stereotypes in your classroom?

---

1. Begin by acknowledging the stereotypical views you have about other ethnicities or groups. Make a list of those you identified.

2. Read your list and verbalize them. Say them out loud: "I believe (ethnic group or others) to be _____.

3. Write how you felt when you heard yourself verbalizing those views.

4. Discover why you hold that belief. Transpose each view by saying, "This belief about _____ comes from an attitude I have about myself." Take time to reflect on the reason behind the concept held about others. Discover what is the idea about yourself that you are using to see and evaluate the behavior and ways of others. For example, because you are a workaholic, you might believe that other ethnic groups are lazy, not realizing that other groups might hold a different interpretation about work.

5. Describe how it feels to realize that your stereotypes stem from your beliefs about yourself. Make the decision to change those beliefs about others.

Source: Ford 1994 (pp. 40–41).

as a result of these tenets. The latest are among the recently arrived non-European Americans (Derman-Sparks 1989).

As we strive to offer children an education that will empower them to become successful members of society, early childhood educators must realize that the key to *unum* is in their hands. Prejudice and racism must be eradicated in order for America to enter strong and triumphant into the new century. Old ideas about superiority of some racial and ethnic groups have poisoned the minds of many and must be abandoned. As an early childhood educator, we remind you that change begins with the child. The battles to eliminate prejudice and racism are to be won in your classrooms, and you as teachers are the champions we look to (Figure 2.7).

Stability and Change, the Rhythm of Culture

All cultures have shared meanings that give direction to the group (Bowman 1992). Your classroom is the place children come to explore and discover how to live in their social environment.

The playground is another place children express their views of the world that they have so far acquired. We say "so far" because these views are not static. Being a dynamic process, culture evolves and changes with time. This process affects our personal perceptions and beliefs about people and environments. Like the human organism, which experiences changes in order to assume new functions, culture also evolves as the environment changes (Swick 1987).

Your classroom reflects cultural changes in many ways. For example, educational theories of early childhood practices evolved from being teacher-centered to being child-centered. If you had been teaching in the 1950s or 1960s, your classroom would have included more academic materials and activities. A higher number of large group experiences would have dominated your teaching. Children would have probably been found doing many "pencil and paper" exercises while you would have been delivering more information for them "to learn." You, also, would have looked different. Most likely, your school dress code would not have included sneakers and today's informal, casual clothing. Because our

IN ACTION . . .   *That Was Me . . . Before!*

We all have changed some of our ideas, sometimes without being aware of it. In order to find some of the ways in which you have been a part of this process, let us visit your closet! Yes, that is right. If there is anything that can depict the trends of our society, that is, of culture, it is in the fashions we wear. Search through your clothes and find any outfit you stopped using quite some time ago, in fact, the older the outfit, the better. Now ask yourself why you stopped wearing it and if you think you will wear it again.

▮ Give yourself two reasons you "forgot" that outfit.

▮ Examine your own answers and discuss them with a friend.

cultural values have experienced modifications, we now have a very different picture of how the early childhood classroom should be.

Change is a positive characteristic of all cultures. It is through change that a group keeps itself alive. Comparing culture to the human organism, we find that in the same manner that the body affects modifications when faced with new circumstances, culture similarly adapts itself to new pressures. This capacity to adapt itself grants culture the ability to respond to reality. Actually, this mechanism of change is as active as the one in our bodies. It is imperative that as teachers we keep ourselves abreast of current social transformations that take place in society. This will allow us to respond and provide for the needs of children.

❖ Planning to Take Action

Your classroom is a reflection of our social mosaic. The children you teach bring to the classroom the ideas and experiences that characterize the United States as it approaches the twenty-first century. One of the things the children reflect is the diversity of visions found in our communities. As they interact in their social environments—the family, the classroom, the neighborhood, the commu-

nity—they learn that not all individuals are alike. For example, they will discover that what makes a person happy might be different from their ideas of happiness. They will notice that not all people like to wear the same kind of clothes as they do, or that other people have a hair texture smoother or curlier than theirs. They will learn that they have ideas of their own and that others see the world differently. While holding their own views, children—and you as a teacher—come to discover that there are other ways to see and interpret reality. Sometimes we will agree with others' interpretations, sometimes we will disagree. Not everyone looks at life through the same glasses!

Preparing ourselves to serve children who live in a diverse country requires much initiative and imagination. Becoming effective teachers of young children in a multicultural world begins with the following steps:

▮ First, discover and clarify your own cultural viewpoints. Begin by ascertaining your own beliefs, values, and practices. It is impossible to appreciate other cultures when you are not clear about your own. The search for your roots can begin by talking to your relatives and family. Examine official records that document your and your family's birthplace, marriages, travels, and other significant events. Analyze your responses to the activities presented in the section "In action" throughout this chapter. They are intended to help you clarify ideas about your own cultural identity.

■ Learn to be more culturally competent. Examine the cultures represented in the community where you live and those in your school. See what cultural groups are there that you know very little about, or that you would like to learn more about. One way to decide on your choices is to think about those cultures commonly found in your classroom. Remember, we are all learning more about the cultures in this country. Do not feel bad if you lack knowledge about some of them!

■ Do an honest examination of the stereotypes about other groups that you have in the classroom or that you have encountered. Do a self-inventory to find out what you know about any stereotypes associated with those groups. You will be surprised to find that they are probably based on very inconsequential and unfair facts.

■ Read about people from other cultures. The reference list in this book is a starting point.

■ Consider the importance that principles of development have on planning and designing classroom experiences. Along with that, learn to recognize and appreciate the influence of the family in the child's overall development. These two points will be examined in Chapters 3 and 4.

❖ Things to Do . . .

1. Based on the definition of culture presented in this chapter, observe the children in your classroom and make a list of examples of culture. Classify them as overt or covert.

2. Contact teachers from a school known for its cultural diversity. Interview 2–3 teachers to find out how they respond to the needs of their students.

3. Learning about your roots is important in understanding others. Find out how your family or your ancestors came to this country. Are there any stories in your family that narrate their arrival?

4. Can you name the material cultural items that you carry with you (for instance, in your bag, pockets) or that you have inherited? What is their significance?

5. Many people claim to be "color blind." Discuss the topic with a European American and a non-European American. List similarities and differences of their perceptions on a piece of paper. Then, check those that coincide with your beliefs. What did you find out about yourself? Record the findings in the journal you are keeping while reading this book.

6. Select a cultural group in your community that has been the object of prejudice. Examine the causes for the prejudice and name ways you would propose to stop it.

❖ Children's Literature Corner

Branderburg, F. (1978). *Six new students.* New York: Greenwillow Books.

Esbensen, B. (1988). *The star maiden.* New York: Little, Brown & Co.

Garcia, R. (1987). *My aunt Otilia's spirits.* Chicago: Children's Press.

Hamilton, V. (1993). *Many thousand gone. African-Americans from slavery to freedom.* New York: Alfred Knopf.

Kissinger, K. (1994). *All the colors we are. The story of how we get our skin color/Todos los colores de nuestra piel. La historia de por qué tenemos diferentes colores de piel.* St. Paul, MN: Redleaf Press.

Kroll, V. (1993). *Africa. Brothers and sisters.* New York: Four Winds.

Levine, E. (1989). *I hate English!* New York: Scholastic Books.

Pluckrose, H. (1988). *Look at faces.* London, England: Franklin Watts.

Sans Souci, R. (1992). *Sukey and the mermaid.* New York: Four Winds.

❖ References

Allport, G. (1958). *The nature of prejudice.* Garden City, NJ: Doubleday.

Banks, J. (1988). *Multicultural education* (2nd ed.). Newton, MA: Allyn & Bacon.

Banks, J. (1992, November/December). Reducing prejudice in children. Guidelines from research. *Social studies and the young learner* (pp. 3–5).

Banks, J., & Banks, C. (1993). *Multicultural education. Issues and perspectives.* (2nd ed.). Needham Heights, MA: Allyn & Bacon.

Baruth, L. G., & Manning, M. L. (1992). *Multicultural education of children and adolescents.* Needham Heights, MA: Allyn & Bacon.

Bowman, B. (1992). Reaching potentials of minority children through developmentally and culturally appropriate programs. In S. Bredekamp & T. Rosegrant (eds.). *Reaching potential: Appropriate curriculum and assessment for young children.* Vol. I. pp. 128–136. Washington, DC: National Association for the Education of Young Children.

Bredekamp, S. (ed.) (1987). *Developmentally appropriate practice in early childhood programs serving children birth through age 8.* Washington, DC: National Association for the Education of Young Children.

Bredekamp, S., & Rosegrant, T. (1992). Reaching potentials: Appropriate curriculum and assessment for young children. Washington, DC: National Association for the Education of Young Children.

Bruner, J. (1990). *Acts of meaning.* Cambridge, MA: Harvard University Press.

Bullivant, B. (1993). Culture: Its nature and meaning for educators. In J. Banks & C. Banks. *Multicultural education. Issues and perspectives* (2nd ed.). Boston, MA: Allyn & Bacon.

Carroll, L. B. (1989). *Alice's adventures in wonderland.* New York: Philomel Books.

Derman-Sparks, L., & A.B.C. Task Force. (1989). *The anti-bias curriculum: Tools for empowering children.* Washington, DC: National Association for the Education of Young Children.

Derman-Sparks, L. (1992). Reaching potential through antibias, multicultural curriculum. In S. Bredekamp & T. Rosegrant (eds.). *Reaching potential: Appropriate curriculum assessment for young children.* Vol. 1 (pp. 114–128). Washington, DC: National Association for the Education of Young Children.

DeVries, R., & Kohlberg, L. (1987). *Constructivist early education: Overview and comparison with other programs.* Washington, DC: National Association for the Education of Young Children.

Dickinson, G. & Leming, A. (1990). *Understanding families: Diversity, continuity, and change.* Boston, MA: Allyn & Bacon.

Ford, C. (1994). *We can all get along. 50 steps you can take to help end racism.* New York: Dell Trade Paperback.

Freire (1970). *Pedagogía del oprimido.* [Pedagogy of the oppressed]. Mexico, DF, Mexico: Siglo Veintiuno.

Geertz, C. (1973). *The interpretation of cultures.* New York: Basic Books.

Gollnick, D. M., & Chinn, P. C. (1990). *Multicultural education in a pluralistic society* (3rd ed.). New York: Merrill.

Hall, E. T. (1976). *The silent language.* New York: Fawcett.

Hernandez, H. (1989). *Multicultural education: A teacher's guide to content and process.* New York: Merrill.

Joe, J., & Malach, F. (1992). Families with Native American roots. In E. Lynch & M. J. Hanson (eds.). *Developing cross-cultural competence. A guide for working with young children and their families.* (pp. 89–120). Baltimore, MD: Paul Brooks.

Kissinger, K. (1994). *All the colors we are. The story of how we get our skin color/Todos los colores de nuestra piel.*

La historia de por qué tenemos diferentes colores de piel. St. Paul, MN: Redleaf Press.

Kroeber, A., & Kluckhorn, C. (1952). *Culture: A critical review of concepts and definitions.* Papers of the Peabody Museum of American Archeology and Ethnology. Vol. 47. No. 1. Cambridge, MA: Harvard University Press.

Lewis, C. (1991). Nursery schools: The transition from home to school. In B. Finkelstein, A. Imamura, & J. Tobin (eds.). *Transcending stereotypes. Discovering Japanese culture and education.* (pp. 109–118). Yarmouth, ME: Intercultural Press.

Lynch, E. W., & Hanson, M.J. (1992). Developing cross cultural competence. A guide for working with young children and their families. Baltimore, MD: Paul Brookes.

McCracken, J. (1993). *Valuing diversity: The primary years.* Washington, DC: National Association for the Education of Young Children.

McGoldrick, M. (1993). Ethnicity, cultural diversity, and normality. In F. Walsh (ed.). *Normal family processes.* New York: The Guilford Press.

Mead, M. (1975). *Growing up in New Guinea.* New York: Morrow.

Morganthau, T. (1994). America: Still a melting pot? In J. A. Kromkowski (ed.). *Race and ethnic relations. Annual Editions 94/95.* (pp. 210–215). Guilford, CT: Dushkin.

Murray, G. (1993). The inner side of experiential learning. In T. Gochenour (ed.). *Beyond experience. The experiential approach to cross-cultural education* (rev. ed.). Yarmouth, ME: Intercultural Press.

Nieto, S. (1992). *Affirming diversity. The sociopolitical context of multicultural education.* New York: Longman.

Novak, M. (1994). The new ethnicity. In J. A. Kromkowski (ed.). *Race and ethnic relations. Annual Editions 94/95.* (pp. 169–174). Guilford, CT: Dushkin.

Okihiro, G. (1994). The victimization of Asians in America. In J. A. Kromkowski. (ed.). *Race and ethnic relations. Annual Editions 94/95.* (pp. 114–122). Guilford, CT: Dushkin.

Roopnarine, J. L., & Johnson, J. E. (1993). *Approaches to childhood education* (2nd ed.). New York: Merrill.

Saracho, O., and Spodek, B. (eds.). (1983). *Understanding the multicultural experience in early childhood education.* Washington, DC: National Association for the Education of Young Children.

Seelye, H. N. (1993). *Teaching culture. Strategies for intercultural communication.* Lincolnwood, IL: National Textbook Company.

Spradley, J., & McCurdy, D. (1972/1988). *The cultural experience. Ethnography in complex society.* Chicago: Waveland Press.

Swick, K. (1987). *Reading on multicultural learning in early childhood education.* Little Rock, AR: Southern Association of Children Under Six.

Vontress, C. (1976). Counseling the racial minorities. In G. Belkin (ed.). *Counseling: Direction in theory and practice* (pp. 277–290). Belmont, CA: Wadsworth.

"No matter the size,
No matter the name,
One thing in families
Is always the same . . .
LOVE, LOVE, LOVE!"

The Kindergarten Children of Westfield School
Sacramento, California (1995)

CHAPTER 3

Families in Our Classrooms: Many Ways, Many Voices

In this chapter we will:

▮ define "family"
▮ describe the existing variety of family structures
▮ discuss the characteristics of families across cultures
▮ determine the role of families in the transmission of culture

Key concepts:

▮ family
▮ culture
▮ family configurations

❖ Families, a Constant in Our Changing Society

"Call it a clan, call it a network, call it a tribe, call it a family. Whatever you call it, whoever you are, you need one."

Jane Howard (1978)

As we approach the threshold of the new millennium, we recognize that the everpresent process of change causes very few things to remain the same. Fortunately, one of the few constants in the cycle of life is "the family," an essential unit of society. It continues to be a fundamental force in creating and perpetuating humankind, in spite of the many changes it has experienced. The family is still the basic channel for learning about human nature because of its essential role in transmitting culture. This notion is particularly important in multicultural early childhood education, where learning about the families of young children is the best way to discover the diversity of views that form our students.

Through this chapter, we want to tour the world of the family with special emphasis on those characteristics that make them alike and yet so different. As we examine the nature, the composition, and the role of families in culture, we will learn about ourselves and about the children in our classrooms.

❖ What Is a Family?

We need to begin by asking ourselves what a family is—a difficult question particularly in the light of today's society. You probably have read and heard people say that families are no longer what they used to be; that today's families are too different and complex; and even that the family no longer exists. The reality is that families have evolved along with our society. The traditional family unit has changed so much and assumed so many different formulas that even the United Na-

tions prefers using the plural term, *families* and not *family,* in order to more accurately describe the current nature of this social unit (United Nations 1994).

Diversity, the Ever Existing Character of Families

Because of today's social changes and because of diverse perceptions regarding family roles, trying to find just one pattern to define and to fit the family is impossible. The fact is that even though families and their roles have changed recently, they have always been diverse (Walsh 1993). Talking about the normal family, Froma Walsh reminds us of the ever existing diversity of the family:

"A sociohistorical perspective reveals that it was our illusion of a singular model of the normal family— as both average and ideal—that blinded us to this diversity and the potential for healthy functioning in a variety of family arrangements" (1993, p. 60).

We need not travel far to be able to state with certainty that diversity of family configurations is one of the essential characteristics of families. Our classrooms present the most vivid example of this.

While it is generally acknowledged that the concept of the traditional family has changed, it is encouraging to confirm that the family as an institution continues to exist. We can say with certainty that "the concept of the family is perhaps the most basic one in social life" (United Nations 1994). From this general acknowledgment we can attempt to describe the family as being a basic social and human unit instrumental for individual and social survival. How the literature defines the family will be explored in the next section.

Defining the Family: What the Literature Says

Social researchers have always considered the family an important and basic societal concept.

Families come in all shapes and sizes.

Throughout generations the coming together of two individuals perpetuates the foundation of society.

IN ACTION . . .   *Who Is in Your Family?*

As teachers of young children, it is important for us to know ourselves. So, before continuing, we ask you to describe your family. Consider whether your family fits the traditional or the non-traditional model. To facilitate your description, use the following prompts.

My family is comprised of. . . .
I think my family is traditional/nontraditional because. . . .

Today, there is such interest in families that they have become the focus of study across many other disciplines. Numerous ideas defining the family have been proposed over time, as researchers attempted to define the meaning of families. One thing they all agree upon is the fact that today it is very difficult to establish only one definition. By examining what several social scientists have observed, we will get a better idea of what a family is.

According to Garbarino and Abramovitz (1992), families, "'the headquarters for human development,' are the most basic and enduring of social institutions" (p. 71). They also express the dual perspective found in the family: "as a small group of people sharing love, intimacy, and responsibility for children; and, as a social institution that serves and reflects the American macrosystem" (p. 71). In Reiss and Keller's opinion (cited by Garbarino & Abramovitz 1992a), the family becomes an instrument of human society where the most essential function is the socialization of the young. According to Keller, "the family means many things to many people, but in its essence it refers to those socially patterned ideals and practices concerned with biological and cultural survival of the species" (p. 73).

Urie Bronfenbrenner's theory (1979) places the family at the core of influences for individuals. Based on Bronfenbrenner's ecological theory, the family is the main source of influence within the microsystem which describes the network of first-hand social experiences individuals confront across cultures. According to this theory, families are the heart of the process of becoming what each of us is. Serving as interpreters and mediators between the individual and the society, families teach individuals how to be family members and how to become members of the immediate sociocultural environs (Figure 3.1). Being cognizant of the incredible task and powerful influence that families have on children helps educators realize the need to design closer collaborations with families.

FIGURE 3.1 Like a filter, the family serves as a mediator between the individual and those forces in the environment.

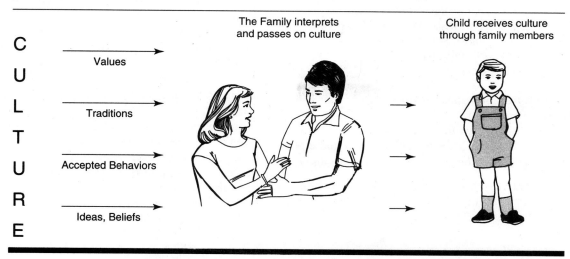

The Family interprets and passes on culture

Child receives culture through family members

C
U
L
T
U
R
E

Values

Traditions

Accepted Behaviors

Ideas, Beliefs

Children Define the Family

In our search to gain better understanding of young children's perceptions of families, we asked some of our graduate students to ask their children to define the family. In order to elicit more information, the children were asked to draw their families prior to being questioned. Questions like: "Is this your family?", "Who is in your family?" and "Can you tell me what you like best about your family?" were asked. The array of answers was fascinating mainly because they highlighted what children perceive as meaningful. They also shed light on the differences found across cultures. As you read the children's answers, remember that their ages ranged from four through six.

What Is a Family?

- "Me, Mommy, grandma."
- "Papi y el *baby*, mami y yo." [Daddy, and the baby, mommy, and me.]
- "Cuando papi y todos vamos a pasear," [When daddy and everybody go out.]
- "My sister, my dad, my mommy, and Melissa." [pointing to the drawing of her family]
- "We are happy because we live together. We like to laugh."
- [Pointing to his drawing] "This is dad, and mommy, and me and Kessie (his doggie)."
- "People that live together."
- [Pointing to the drawing] "Mommy, Tylor* (the child), Eric* (mother's boyfriend)."
- "We go to church and to the park. And mommy buys ice cream."

Can There Be Consensus as to What Is a Family?

One of the best ways to define the family is expressed by Gina and Mercer Mayer (1992) in their story *This is my family:*

> This is my family. Each of us is different, but we love each other a lot. I think that's what a family is all about. (n.p.)

———
*The real names were changed.

As a social institution, and despite diversity, all families are alike in the roles, tasks, and functions they perform. Let us explore what makes our families alike.

What Are the Functions and the Roles of the Family?

Society needs families essentially to prepare the young to become constructive members. This is accomplished through the transference of expectations, social responsibilities, and behaviors to the future generations of adults. All families share these basic social responsibilities even though cultures define the ways those functions are performed. Social researchers have defined these functions as being both basic and complex tasks. There are divergent opinions regarding the ways these specific responsibilities are carried out by families. As we describe each of them, remember that they are activities expected of *all* families, but that the way they are performed may be very different as a result of the family's culture.

According to Epstein, Bishop, Ryan, Miller, and Gabor (1993), there are three basic task areas or *functions* families perform: basic, developmental, and hazardous. A common denominator among the three tasks is the implicit support the family provides in the context of each task.

1. *Basic Tasks:* Include provision of basic needs such as food, shelter, financial stability, and transportation.
2. *Developmental Tasks:* Encompass all the situations and issues taking place as the family is instituted. They describe all the interactional processes among family members. Included here are the interactions among spouses; the beginning of parenting; the relations with children during infancy, adolescence and adulthood; and the incorporation of other family members.

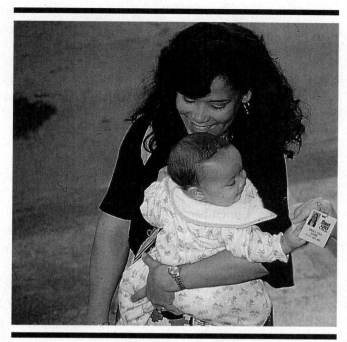

The role of the family in preparing an individual to become a part of society begins at birth.

3. *Hazardous Tasks:* Describe the ways the family handles crises. For instance, it defines how the family copes with family illnesses, accidents, moving, loss of income, and death (Epstein et al. 1993, p. 141).

There are other social researchers who assign even more functions to the family. Seven basic functions based on the needs of the family are identified by Barber, Turnbull, Behr, and Kerns (cited by Zeitlin & Williamson 1994):

1. *economic*—covering the financial needs of the family, maintaining the family safe and economically stable.

2. *domestic/health care*—providing basic needs like food, health care, safety, and protection.

3. *recreation*—planning and establishing time to share and enjoy together.

4. *socialization*—fostering an atmosphere of positive interpersonal relationships; modeling ways to interact in a social group.

5. *self-definition*—creating a sense of belonging for all the family members (feeling one "is part of the family"); fostering a positive self-identity and self-image; valuing fairly each family member.

6. *affection*—providing nurturance, love, and support for all members.

7. *educational/vocational*—promoting pride in own culture; transmitting values, ideals, and traditions; encouraging and supporting school work (Zeitlin & Williamson 1994, p. 47).

This is a project that could also contribute to increase participation of families and the classroom. It also gives teachers another opportunity to learn about the specific family cultures in their classrooms. For the children, learning what their classmates eat and the ingredients used will provide another window into how alike and different they are.

Family Roles

Roles are another common denominator of families. Family roles "are defined as the repetitive patterns of behavior by which family members fulfill family functions" (Epstein et al. 1993, p. 147). From the literature, we have identified four roles played by families (Epstein et al. 1993; Curran 1983; Commission on Children 1991; Garbarino 1992).

Families are expected to:

1. Provide basic resources (shelter, food, clothing, health care, and financial support).
2. Provide nurturance and support to their members (establishing a warm and reassuring emotional environment where family members find themselves being supported during crises and whenever needed).
3. Serve as role models for their younger members (offering positive social models where children learn the ways of their group; modeling basic interactional skills, and teaching children what are their roles and responsibilities in a social group).

4. Transmit the values and beliefs of their cultural group (serving as vehicles for cultural and spiritual teaching and learning).

In our efforts to understand the meaning of the family, we asked a group of early childhood educators representing several ethnic groups (European American, African American, Afro-Caribbean, and Hispanic) to define the basic tasks and responsibilities of the family. We have included their answers, which express their opinions. As you read them, think about other descriptors or details that you may want to add to this list.

Families are a group of people who . . .

❚ provide love and nurturance to their members.

❚ keep people together.

❚ meet the basic needs of their members.

❚ provide role models for their younger members.

❚ support each other in *any* and *all* circumstances.

❚ transmit values and beliefs to their members.

❚ teach their members respect toward others.

❚ model problem-solving skills to their members.

❚ model how to live in a social group.

❚ create a sense of pride about their own cultural heritage to their members. Establish a sense of cultural identity.

IN ACTION . . .   *Define Your Family*

Considering the characteristic family tasks and roles discussed in this chapter, define your own family. Share your definition with your colleagues.

Snapshot 3.1
Children's Views of the Family

A group of early childhood teachers in Florida and Las Vegas asked their students to tell them about their families. Their findings proved very interesting. Through their responses, children ages 4–6 described the family in terms of the functions and roles they perceived. Essentially two main roles were elicited from their responses.

▌ One, nurturance and a sense of a warm environment ("My family loves me." "My mommy is always with me." "Nana reads me stories.")

▌ Second, provision of basic needs ("Daddy buys me food." "We play together." "Mi familia cocina [My family cooks]." "Grandpa bought me these [pointing toward his sneakers]." "Mom makes me potatoes.")

Although their responses are characteristic of the still egocentric child, they reflect an early perception of what being a part of a family means.

▌ create an invisible but strong bond among their members (Robles de Meléndez 1995).

Still other elements need to be considered as we define the families of the children we teach. In the next section we will consider the variations in family configurations.

Culture, What Rules Our Lives

Culture establishes meanings shared and understood by those who respond to it (Spradley & McCurdy 1972). Because each of us lives and responds to our own cultural patterns, our interpretations of how to perform a specific function vary. In the American pluricultural context, this means realizing that what one holds as an expectation might diverge from that of others. This is the paradigm and challenge of living in a multicultural society. Working with families of different cultural backgrounds affords teachers an opportunity to experience the variety of interpretations given to social roles and functions. Even the simplest task is viewed differently when examined crossculturally. Melvin Konner (1991) punctuates that what is valued as necessary for social survival in a group will become an expected task for their families to perform. Take, for instance, the function of education, one that we as teachers expect families to carry out. It is true that valuing education represents a shared task among all cultures. However, not all cultures will expect children to acquire the same kind of knowledge because their concepts of education differ. While Americans expect children to master the "3 R's," families from other cultures like the Baka and the iKung believe that learning their tribal history and mastering tool making and tool-use are most important because they are related to their survival (Konner 1991). This example is remote from our realities; however, it points out that each cultural group assigns expectations that respond to its own needs and circumstances.

Diversity in Childrearing Practices

Childrearing, an essential function and role of families, is an area where differences in ideas and practices are commonly found. They are closely related to the concept of the child, which does not have a shared meaning across cultural groups. For example, while for families in the American mainstream culture children are perceived as young individuals whose development of independence is strongly supported and valued, it is not so among other cultural groups. In families of Hispanic origin, young children are believed to be totally dependent on the adults, a fact that defines the pampering and particular nurturance parents and relatives provide throughout the entire early childhood period. Contrary to families of the American culture, Hispanic parents "tend to be . . . permissive and indulgent" with their children (Zuniga 1992, p. 164). Families encourage this dependency, which gives all the family members an opportunity to create stronger bonds with the child and vice versa. Zuniga (1992) points out that rather than pushing the child to develop early skills and independence, Hispanics "placate" their children. Independence, a highly valued behavior in American mainstream culture, is not so for Hispanics. It is not uncommon to observe a Hispanic child being encouraged to keep a "babyish" behavior well beyond infancy and sometimes even until school age.

The need for a child's attainment of independence is not so relevant because traditionally, children are brought up in a network of caring relationships defined by parents, siblings, and other family members. The family places more importance in strengthening and reassuring the child's emotional ties with the family, which extends beyond the immediate family members who take care of the child. This, in turn, also affords the opportunity for the child to develop a collective orientation rather than an individualistic one. This collective orientation is also found in traditional Native American and Middle Eastern families.

Similar positions toward children are found among Asian American families. Chan (1992) reports that Asian parents consider their children until age three as "being relatively helpless," which helps explain the tolerant and permissive attitude they exhibit (p. 217). Emphasis in creating an emotionally supportive family environment supersedes attention to development of independence in the first three years of life. However, unlike the Hispanic families, as the Asian children reach the preschool stage, the Asian families prepare their children to assume responsibilities. The preschool years become a transitional stage where children are led to achieve self-discipline (Chan 1992). Life formalities are then emphasized, learned through the direct participation of children in adult activities.

Families are also expected to teach their younger members rules of social interaction. An example is learning the rules for interactions with adults and elders. The manner in which a child speaks and re-

---

IN ACTION . . .   *Childrearing*

We all have our own ideas regarding how to raise a child. These ideas are derived from what we learned through our families. However, even within families of the same culture we find differences regarding these practices. To find out if this is true, name at least five of *your own beliefs* about childrearing that are different from those of your family and friends. Then, examine each idea to see what makes them different.

sponds to adults will be different based on the family's culture. For example, American parents tend to exhibit a more permissive attitude toward children's interruptions while they are holding a conversation. A child might literally break into a conversation and yet American parents find this to be acceptable practice. This is not true of other cultures. Generally, families with Middle Eastern, Hispanic, Native American, Asian, and European roots expect their children to refrain from interrupting when adults are talking. In the same line,

they also demand from their children acceptance of their decisions, for they strongly believe that authority is not to be questioned by the young. While in a mainstream American family a child tends to talk back, this is considered unacceptable in the context of Middle Eastern, Hispanic, and Native American families (Sharifzadeh 1992; Zuniga 1992; Joe & Malach 1992).

Respect toward the elders is another concept learned through the family. Traditionally for many cultures, the elders, whether they are relatives or

---

FOCUS ON CLASSROOM PRACTICES

A CLASSROOM HOLIDAY TIME LINE

Holidays or special celebrations are a constant in every cultural group. They are also one of the things that define the diversity of ideas and experiences of children and families in our classroom. We believe that because holidays symbolize many of the values and beliefs of a group, they need to be acknowledged in the classroom. Recognition of the holidays other people celebrate is another way for children to become aware of diversity. Unfortunately, because many holidays have religious origins, this aspect of cultures is usually omitted in schools. However, there is nothing wrong with becoming aware of the names and times when other groups observe holidays.

One of the ways to acknowledge different holidays observed by families is to create a time line. This is an activity to be developed throughout the school year. We prefer a time line because unlike a calendar where holidays are lost among other events, a time line can provide a linear and clear perspective of all the celebrations observed by the children's families. Displayed conspicuously, children and families can become familiar with celebrations year-round. This activity also helps children learn about the concepts of time and space.

To create your time line, you will need to find out from families the holidays they observe. Gather your data and organize them chronologically. If you are not familiar with some of those listed, remember to ask families about them, including the time of year they are celebrated. For the time line, you can either use a roll of manila paper (size 8×11) or of plain wallpaper (the one for borders is very handy). On the time line, enter the name of the holiday and, if possible, use any of its symbols or colors. Write the names of the families that observe each holiday. As holidays approach, share them with the class. Because you are acknowledging their existence and creating awareness of the holidays, simply mention the name and any of the traditions attached to them. In this way, children will know that the family of a classmate is observing a special occasion.

not, represent a source of authority and wisdom, which in turn is acknowledged by exhibiting respect and honoring them (Chan 1992; Joe & Malach 1992). In these cultures it is common for the extended family, usually grandparents and elder family friends, to take direct part in childrearing.

❖ The Family Structure: Who Is in the Family?

A Diversity of Family Configurations

If we were to list the various family configurations represented by the children in our early childhood classroom, we would find models of single-parent families, blended families, extended families, foster families, and two-parent families among them (Figure 3.2). This proves that we can no longer identify one single model of the family as the true one. The family as portrayed in TV programs of the 50s, like "Ozzie and Harriet," is rapidly becoming the minority (Zeitlin & Williamson 1994). We need to accept that our most basic social unit has been the victim of change much like the other spheres of society (Garbarino

1992) and that today's families are structured in both traditional and nontraditional forms. It is also a fact that the nontraditional families already outnumber the traditional ones as the result of the high divorce rate in America and the rising pregnancy rate among teenage girls.

Culture Influences Family Configurations

Ask several individuals to identify members of a family and you will get a variety of answers. The reason for this is the cultural ambiance serving as a framework for the family. Although we can all agree that to have a family we need to have adults and in most cases children, we cannot so easily agree as to what specific members form the family. For some, members of a family will consist exclusively of the parents and their offsprings. For others, a family includes not only parents and children, but also blood relatives and even some very special friends not related by blood or by law.

The original concepts of family membership are lost in time. No historical proof exists regarding the origins of the family. Because there is no irrefutable evidence of family forms and their cultural origins, we can only say that they merely re-

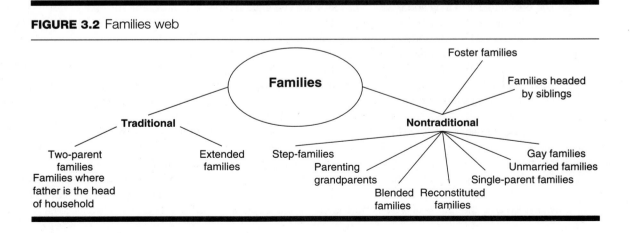

FIGURE 3.2 Families web

Families

Traditional

Nontraditional

Foster families

Families headed by siblings

Two-parent families
Families where father is the head of household

Extended families

Step-families
Parenting grandparents

Blended families

Reconstituted families

Single-parent families

Unmarried families

Gay families

flect what has become a pattern followed through time. Each of us has inherited from our families and they, in turn, from their ancestors, the ideas of family memberships.

Who Is in the Family

Comparing families across several ethnicities gives us an opportunity to appreciate the diversity of family structures. Commonly, the European American family is best described as nuclear—parents and children. Whenever asked, European Americans will commonly define their family by those immediate members in their households. Not so happens when we ask an African American or when asking Hispanics for whom family members might include even their close friends. This diversity of opinions demonstrates how culture shapes families. Being its main vehicle for the transmission of values, families will be as different as the cultural groups they represent.

Exploring who is considered "a part of the family" is an interesting way to observe the differences among cultures. For example, it is common to have Americans define their family as consisting of the mother, father, and children. Extended family members in our mainstream culture, although valued as important members, are not referred to as the "family" but as "relatives" (Hanson 1992). This view of the family, which focuses on the immediate family members, or the nuclear unit, is different from what other cultural groups acknowledge and call "my family."

According to Willis (1992), it is common to find African Americans describing their family as including more than just simply parents and children. With terms like "'my family,' 'my folks,' 'my kin,' 'my people' to identify blood relatives and to denote relationships with special friends or 'cared for' individuals who are not related" (1992, p. 131), they describe a wider concept of the family. Families of Native American roots also view the family as consisting of more than just the immediate members. Families in both these cultures are defined as including the nuclear and the extended family members (Joe & Malach 1992). A similar position is also found among Hispanics (Zuniga 1992) and Italian Americans (McGoldrick 1993) who also value and regard as family the extended members as well as those with whom there might not exist a legal relationship. For example, in both groups godparents, the Italian *comparaggio* and the Spanish *compadrazgo*, describe a way through which outside members, usually neighbors or close friends, become part of the family's network of relationships. Considered an honor, the "compadres" assume the role of parents and are expected to watch over the lives of their godchildren or "ahijados." It is not unusual to find children in care of a godparent (madrina or padrino) especially in the moments of crises.

WORKING GLOSSARY

■ **Family Structure**—"the composition and associated roles of family members" (Zeitlin & Williamson 1994, p. 43).

■ **Family Configurations**—the variety of forms depicting the combination of individuals found in a family.

■ **Traditional Family**—typically represented by being a two-parent family.

■ **Nontraditional Family**—those with configurations different from the two-parent model.

Preparing a Family Map

The diversity of family configurations in our classrooms has made knowing the members of those families a harder task. Using a family map is a valuable way of helping teachers to better grasp the internal patterns of the family. According to Zeitlin and Williamson (1994), the family map defines two important family dimensions:

1. The structure of close family support system—All those individuals holding daily or regular close interactions with the family.
2. Shared family activities—Those activities that the family participates in together including those shared among family members (p. 153).

Early childhood teachers can benefit from family maps because maps provide a close-up of the actual dynamics of its members. Directions to prepare a family map and a sample adopted from Zeitlin and Williamson appear in Figure 3.3. Maps can be developed as a part of regular meetings with families or with individuals. Careful analysis will give early childhood educators a better focused picture of the family.

Directions for Preparing a Family Map

Begin by preparing your own family map. This will provide a hands-on opportunity and improve understanding of the activity. You will need to follow these steps:

a. Take a blank copy of the map and examine it first.
b. Complete first the names of the family members currently living in the household.
c. Fill out the names of those individuals not living in the household but with whom shared activities exist on a regular basis. For example, a neighbor who baby-sits the child, or a relative (i.e., grandparents, cousins, aunts) who visits the house frequently. You may want to write their names in different color ink.
d. Describe in the space provided the kind of activities shared by the family and other outside individuals.
e. Establish the pattern of interactions by drawing lines to show who interacts with whom. If an activity is shared by all the members in the household, make sure there are lines showing this. If an activity is shared only by two members, connect only those two members with a line.

The Challenge of Working with Different Families: Implications for Teachers

Awareness of the broader concept of family membership is important for the early childhood educator. Knowing that a relative, whether an uncle or a cousin or even a close family friend, shares and cares for the child as the parents do, helps intervention and development of appropriate services. This sense of kinship that bonds many different family members as well as close individuals becomes a significant social asset for the family and for the child. It becomes their social capital, a capital that will enhance the opportunities to successfully face the demands and problems of family life (Coleman 1991). From the perspective of the child, it widens the circle of people who care and participate in his or her upbringing.

Social changes have impacted all cultural groups in our country. It is important for early childhood educators to avoid stereotyping families because of their cultural orientation. Today, because of the many social circumstances faced by people, it is impossible to assert that a family will respond according to traditional cultural patterns. Because of the effects of acculturation, some families have adapted themselves to the demands of today's social reality. Another factor responsible for the changes is the economic burdens faced by some of our families. Many otherwise traditionally nuclear families have opted for the extended family model because of economic problems. Even families of recent immigrants, which usually follow their native cultural patterns, may exhibit differences. In some cases, the strains endured by recent immigration have

FIGURE 3.3 Using a family map

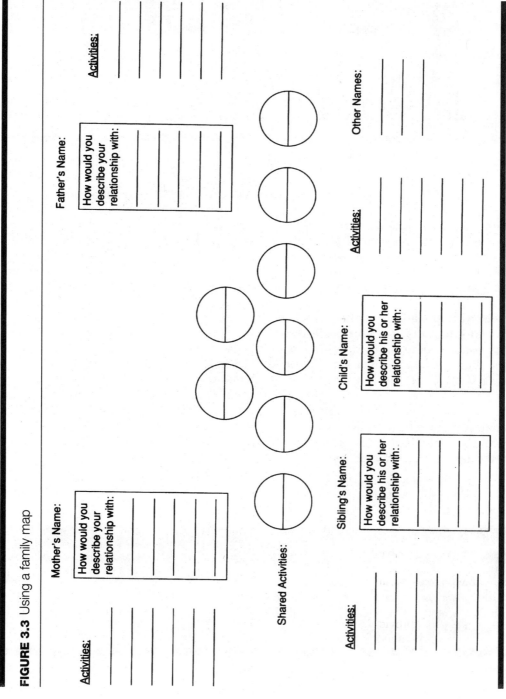

Source: Zeitlin, S., & Williamson, G. (1994). *Coping in young children: Early intervention practices to enhance adaptive behavior and resilience.* Baltimore, MD: Paul Brookes.

forced some families to adopt unique family memberships (McGoldrick 1993). Although for some immigrants these are temporary or emergency arrangements, educators need to be concerned not only with the identity of these family members, but also with how and whether they are involved in meeting needs of the child.

Family Diversity: Implications for Teachers

Early childhood educators must set aside their preconceived notions about the composition, the meaning, and the role of the family in order to become more receptive of the varieties found among their children. Accepting the fact that today's families are found both in traditional and nontraditional configurations enables the educators to objectively relate to and deal more effectively with the families of the children in their classrooms.

Who Are the Members of a Family?

The best way to determine the family configuration is by finding out who its members are. Membership implies being an active element within the family unit. It also indicates the relationship of that member to the rest of the group whereby defining the member's position within it. Today social and family researchers agree that family membership holds a wide spectrum of possibilities. No longer are these solely defined by blood or legal relationships (Garbarino 1992; Lynch & Hanson 1992). Membership in contemporary families is often defined by the particular circumstances and even crises that the family has experienced. Early childhood teachers need to be aware of these circumstances, which may help to explain the unique family structures of their students.

The fact that our classrooms are a mosaic of family configurations was proven by a group of our

Snapshot 3.2
Our Multicultural American Family: Meet the Anez-Powells

Like so many other families in this nation, the Anez-Powells are an example of the multiculturalism that characterizes today's families. Their young son, John Carver, is an example of an interesting multicultural heritage. Two cultures, two languages, and two different indigenous ethnic backgrounds describe the cultural portrait of this family. Sandra, a native of Maracaibo, Venezuela, is of Spanish and Amerindian ancestry. Her husband, Norman, is of African American and also of Native American ancestry. Proud of their rich multicultural heritage, the Anez-Powells are a good example of the cultural diversity of families in our classrooms.

graduate students who examined their respective classrooms. Using a family survey instrument (see Chapter 10), they sampled both children and parents. Simply asking the adults to name the members of their families and having children draw them, these teachers made a relevant discovery. What they found disclosed an interesting myriad of family forms. Their findings showed the following:

■ 44% were two-parent families (8% were reconstituted or blended families by remarriage)

■ 6% were two-parent unmarried families

■ 29% were single-parent (all headed by women)

■ 7% were families headed by grandparents

■ 14% were extended families.

Although it is true that the above findings cannot be used to make any generalizations, they do help us to recognize the fact that families are characterized by a diversity of configurations. Identifying the members of a family varies greatly in our society across cultures and even among our own relatives. In essence what really matters is that in spite of the unusual family structures, these units can function and fulfill the roles of a family. The strong sense of "being a family" serves to prove their validity as a social unit.

To fully understand the spectrum of dimensions of the present family, we need to examine the factors that have caused it to transform into its present state. This will help us better understand what today's family represents.

Change, a Trend for Survival

The evolution of the family has been an on-going process and is not just a phenomenon of the last decades of the twentieth century. Many who have traced its changes link them to various social and political crises like the Great Depression and the World Wars. For example, in 1934 the Hoover-Ogburn Commission, a government-appointed body, announced that since the reasons for creating a family no longer existed, it was doomed to disappear (Curran 1983). Similar voices have forecasted the same fate during the past six decades. And yet, the family remains a vital social institution. Like many other social and cultural elements, it has adapted itself to the new demands and the character of the times. You may recall that in Chapter 2 it was said that one of the ways for culture to survive is by adapting and changing itself according to the reality of the times. The family is an excellent example of that evolutionary theory.

When Did the Family Begin to Change?

The American family began its most dramatic transformation in the second half of the twentieth century as a result of political events and economic trends. Job security became a thing of the past as early as the 1930s with the unstable economy of the Depression years. The need for higher income forced both marriage partners to seek work outside the home (Coleman 1991). The participation of women in the workforce became widespread during World War II and started a decades long trend of American women as active wage earners (Piotrskowski & Hughes 1993). This pattern also established the role of working mothers, which in turn drastically altered the roles and patterns of the traditional American family. Today this practice is reflected in statistics that show

IN ACTION . . .   *Family Patterns*

■ How does your own classroom compare with these findings?

■ Is this pattern similar to that of your community? Explain.

■ Is your own family configuration reflected here?

IN ACTION . . .   *Has Your Family Also Changed?*

Early educators need to be aware of their own family characteristics. Before we continue exploring the concept of the family, let us take time to find out how and whether your families have changed. To do so, complete the questions below. They are adapted from the characteristics that traditionally depict a family (Curran 1983).

1. Who are the members that constitute your family?
2. Are they all related by blood or marriage?
3. Does your family provide for your economic survival?
4. Is your family your source of protection?
5. Has your family been the main source of social and cultural learning?
6. Is there a sense of mutual and shared responsibility among all your family members?
   ▮ What did you find out? Share your findings with a colleague.
   ▮ What are the changes, if any, that surprised you the most?
   ▮ What implications can you derive from your findings?

"56% of white married women and 72% of African American married women with children under six were employed in 1988" (Piotrskowski & Hughes 1993, p. 187). The implications for early childhood education are obvious.

The emergence of more liberal views about people's lifestyles and responsibilities in the 1960s also transformed the concept of the family. These factors directly and indirectly led the family to assume new and unique configurations. With newly developed lifestyles, the family as a social organism was forced to adapt itself (Walsh 1993). It is important to remember that the changes being experienced by American families were similarly occurring among families around the world (Figure 3.4).

A new wave of immigrants to America, particularly since the 1960s, added another element

FIGURE 3.4 Factors contributing to the transformation of the family. How many are evident in your community? In your classroom?

1. *Economic and financial situation at the national level*—the unstable economic situation forced families to become dual earners in order to preserve their survival. Women became workers outside the home, adding the role of wage-earners to that of mothers and housewives.

2. *New lifestyles*—traditional values and ideas about personal relationships changed. Along came an emphasis on individuality and a liberal view about family, sex, and interpersonal relationships.

3. *New wave of immigration*—a high percentage of new immigrants began coming into the country during the 1960s, a trend that remains true to this date. Their new perspectives added a diverse element to the social fabric of our society. With them came new ways to depict a family all based on their particular cultures.

that further diversified the traditional family. The variety of family patterns, as well as customs and traditions brought by the different ethnic groups, further altered the old family model. Your classrooms are the best examples of these fresh and varied notions of what being part of a family means.

A Pluralistic View of the American Family

The changing model of the family has contributed to the newly acquired visibility of nontraditional family forms. This has also promoted a more accepting attitude of the family as a multifaceted social unit that is the product of a pluralistic society. According to Harevan (cited by Laird 1993), the alternative family forms found in our society:

> ". . . are not necessarily new inventions. Many different forms have been in existence all along, but they have been less visible. The more recent forms of alternative lifestyles have now become a part of the official fiber of society because they are now being tolerated much more than in the past. In short, what we are witnessing is not a fragmentation of traditional family patterns but, rather, the emergence of a pluralism in family ways" (Laird 1993, p. 283).

❖ The Family, the Most Important Element in Our Lives

> "A house is just something that sits there, but a family is a group of people who love each other."
>   D. Fassler, M. Lash, and S. Ives (1988)

We are all part of a family. We are who we are because of what we received and learned from our families. The family is a basic social and cultural institution and a common characteristic of people across different cultures. The family is a basic sociocultural unit that imparts traditions and teaches shared meanings and behaviors to the individual. We only need to look at ourselves to recognize the power embedded in a family. In general, our tastes and dislikes, our beliefs, the things we prefer to eat, and even some of the phrases we use are all grounded in what we learned from our families.

Our Classroom, the Mirror of the Children's Families

Your classroom is perhaps the best place to observe how relevant and powerful families are. Every time you interact with your students, you also come in contact with their families. During the early years, families play the principal role in the lives of children. When we know the members of a child's family, even the nuances and gestures exhibited by them are understood as being characteristic of certain family members. Because families perform the role of culture interpreters for the younger generations, the ways children behave also reflect the cultures they belong to.

One of the more common ways to "see" the influence of the family is in the words and phrases children use. What the family members do, say, and wear is always noticed and modeled by children. Observing children during pretend play gives teachers excellent windows into their lives and will let them know what impacts them the most. During one of our courses, a graduate student shared the following incident she observed involving one of her pre-kindergartners:

> "I was fascinated by what Teresita did, a four-year-old whose parents came from the Dominican Republic. She was playing in the housekeeping area when I started this observation. Two other girls were with her and they were all getting dressed. She opened the handbag she was playing with and went to the mirror where she started to put on some eye make-up. As I came closer, I saw her using a black marker to draw a line around her eyes. Of course, she looked as if she had been hit by someone! When I asked her what she was doing, she remarked: 'Me estoy poniendo la raya para pasear' [I am putting on the eyeliner to go out]. I knew instantly that the idea came from her mother, a young woman who always

Snapshot 3.3
Our Multicultural American Family: Meet the Ullmeyers

These are the Ullmeyers: Peter, Angela, and little Nicole. An executive of a foreign airline, Peter, born in Germany, came to this country a little less than a decade ago where he met Angela, a German American, who still remembers how children in school used to tease her by saying "Heil, Hitler!" The Ullmeyers treasure their German ancestry. For this reason their daughter Nicole, a four-year-old, already speaks German, while learning English as well. Proud to be part of the American society, their wish is to see our country grow more tolerant toward people with cultural differences.

IN ACTION . . .   *Am I Like My Family?*

We learn so many things from our families that it is sometimes hard to realize the true realm of their influence. To find out how our families have influenced us, let's begin by finding the material things that reflect their influence. Looking around your own house, identify those things that reflect the objects, items, and patterns (although not necessarily the same) that were also found in your family's home. Consider for instance, the colors, the kind of objects and the ways they are displayed, the way your rooms are arranged, the "messes" in your kitchen, and, of course, the dishes and food you cook. How many similarities with your family did you find? If you did not find a lot of resemblances, ask yourself why you are different from your family. You will probably discover that in the similarities, as well as in the differences, the influence of your family is a common denominator. Surprised?

wears noticeable eye make-up. For Teresita, getting ready to go out implied using make-up. More importantly, this example demonstrates that even at her young age, Teresita was already modeling the accepted ways of her family."

Many of you are probably familiar with the ways young children act out the behaviors observed in their families. Take, for instance, the following example that happened in a first-grade classroom.

Anthony, a vivacious six-year-old boy of Jamaican background, was having a snack along with three other classmates, two of whom were girls. Finishing his apple, he noticed that both girls still had theirs and that the other boy at the table also had his. Extending his arm, he freely grabbed the apple from one of the girls, who loudly protested. Observing from a corner, the teacher knew that an incident was about to happen. Coming closer, she heard the following dialogue:

"Give me back my apple!" said the girl.

"Why? I'm a man," answered Anthony with emphasis.

"I want my apple now!" replied the girl.

"I told you. I'm a man and *mans* (*men*) eat more!" he said hitting the table with his fist.

Seeing that the situation was getting heated, the teacher intervened. When asked to explain his attitude, Anthony frankly said:

"My daddy gets more at home. He says *mans* need to eat more."

"But you could have asked me for another one," said the teacher.

"Daddy never asks. He takes it."

Handing him another apple, the teacher said: "Anthony, that is at your home. Here we ask when we want to have more."

❖ The Power of the Family

Entitled by society to provide the younger generations with the ideas and accepted behaviors of the group, the family serves as the prime agent for cultural learning. How strong is the power that the family exerts? We can state with certainty that its power covers every aspect of life. The younger the individual is, the more definitive and influential the power of the family is. Even before birth we begin experiencing the influence of families, and through them the culture they belong to. It is through them that we acquire the meanings and views that make us a part of our social groups.

A Child Is Born

Children are the "vessels for the passing on of culture" (Konner 1991, p. 15), representing an

---

FOCUS ON CLASSROOM PRACTICES

A CLASSROOM FAMILY COOKBOOK

One of the exciting things about cultural diversity is learning about ethnic eating habits and food patterns. Discovering what the families in our classrooms eat is not only a source for cultural awareness but also another way to emphasize likenesses and differences among families. Because all families have a favorite dish (actually, probably several favorite dishes), a good way for children and for teachers to learn about themselves is by creating a cookbook. The classroom cookbook is basically a collection of recipes of simple favorite dishes enjoyed by families. This project provides opportunities to integrate literacy, math, and science. Using a big book format, families would be assigned a page each (or two depending on the enrollment). A picture or a drawing made by the child or any family members would illustrate the pages. To collect the recipes, teachers need to send a letter to the families explaining the purpose of the activity. Ask families for very simple recipes, or those that can be made in the classroom. Possible dishes include salads, beverages, desserts, or bread-based recipes.

As recipes are collected and added to the cookbook, test them in the classroom. Give credit to the child's family whenever a recipe is prepared. On the bulletin board, announce the dish with a sign reading: "Today's special dish is _____ contributed by the _____ family." If possible, display the recipe's ingredients early so that children can examine or observe them. Plan to take pictures or videotape children while recipes are tested. These can be used for later discussions and to review specific aspects. Discuss the food value of the recipe and help children look for similarities and differences among the various dishes.

This is a project that could also increase participation of families in the classroom. It also gives teachers another opportunity to learn about the specific family cultures. For the children, learning what their classmates eat and the ingredients used will provide another window into how alike and different they are.

---

opportunity to perpetuate the ideals and values of families. Consider these comments made by future parents we interviewed:

> "She'll be an important person, maybe even a president!" "We want her to be a good wife and mother." "My baby will be proud of his color." "Whether it's a boy or a girl, I want our baby to be a good person." "He'll be a minister like his father." "We want our child to live in a country where there is freedom."

What we read in these parents' comments are not only their desires for a bright future for their children, but also the unique ideals and expectations for the new members of their culture. The thoughts parents have about their children provide glimpses of their values and ideals, knitted by the culture they belong to. For some, the arrival of a new child brings new hope for the survival of the group; for others it is a way to continue the family tradition; for others still it

means a new opportunity to accomplish some un-realized goals. Regardless of what expectations families have for their children-to-be, they represent the interplay of the cultural and personal character-istics of the group's members. Culture begins its profound influence on individuals through our families even from the moment we are conceived.

Family Rituals

For those who have younger sisters and brothers or children of their own, they know that the ar-rival of a new child entails a number of family activities. Among those activities, many repre-sent traditional rituals that people have done

Snapshot 3.4
Our American Multicultural Family: Meet the El-Kollallis

Born in Cairo, Egypt, Kamellia El-Kollalli and her husband came to the United States more than two decades ago. Like many other families, they left behind the world they knew and came "in search of a dream." Arriving in Washington, D.C., they soon began to see America through the eyes of the friends they made. The El-Kollallis raised two children and like many families with dual cultures, instilled a sense of pride in them for their Egyptian and American heritage. While believing that they and their children "are the product of the East and the West," the El-Kollallis also remember the unpleasant moments they encountered as a result of being from a different culture. Some of those most painful moments involve the discrimination their children experienced. Kamellia still remembers finding their son when he was three praying to God to make his "tan" disappear so that the other children would play with him. As the children grew older, they bore the burden of insensitive and ignorant remarks made not only by their peers but also by their teachers. At one point Kamellia's son remarked that he hoped that prejudice and ignorance would not crush his sister's self-esteem and spirit. The El-Kollallis' hope is that today's multicultural education movement can bring these damaging experiences to a halt. In spite of everything, they assert that "America is the best place to be." They also believe that the schools can help society become aware of the vast cultural treasures that people from other cultures bring to our nation.

IN ACTION . . . *Cultural Values*

Read the parents' comments again and determine the cultural values and ideals they show through their answers.

IN ACTION . . . *Family Aspirations*

All families have aspirations for their new members. To explore them, conduct a survey of your own relatives and friends with children. Begin by asking your parents what aspirations they held for you. Save their comments. As you ask others, record their answers and their backgrounds (ethnicity, social level, etc.). Compare your findings and highlight the similarities and differences. Note in particular how their aspirations for their children relate to their culture.

for centuries. They are important for they keep alive the essence of cultures. Some of these rituals are observed before the child is born while others will happen after the birth. Through time each culture has outlined a whole assortment of different practices, all intended to welcome the new member.

Many family rituals begin before birth. Selecting colors and clothes for the new baby are among the many rituals that are performed across cultures. For instance, preparing a "canastillo," a basket with all those items the baby will need, is a traditional activity among Hispanic families. A similar practice commonly found in the American culture is a "baby shower" where everyone joins in to greet the newborn with needed items. Other rituals include preserving personal items across generations. Some families keep and pass on baby clothes worn by their elders. Others use the same crib their grandparents used.

Author Margy Burns Knight (1994) has collected child welcoming practices around the world. In *Welcoming Babies,* Knight (1994) describes a series of informal and formal practices, all depicting the ways in which each society marks the arrival of its new members. Some practices involve everyone in the community while others are performed by the parents and their relatives. For example, in Nigeria some women sing after learning that the child is born (Figure 3.5), while in Afghanistan a newborn's father whispers prayers into each of the baby's ears (Knight 1994) (Figure 3.6).

WORKING GLOSSARY

▮ **Family Rituals**—practices depicting rites and ceremonies performed by families across cultures with the intent to signify and mark a particular event.

More Than Just a Name

Perhaps one of the most interesting rituals families perform concerns choosing the name for the new baby. Selecting a name for a child is a social requirement that not only gives identity but also reflects a cultural heritage and defines the individual's roots. For example, in some Asian cultures names are a way of honoring ancestors. Names are also a good way to note

FIGURE 3.5 *Welcoming Babies*

We Sing

Afam is a brand new baby. When the women near his house hear his first cry, they begin to sing, "Beautiful one, beautiful one, welcome!" When other women hear the song, they join in. Soon Afam's whole village will know that a new baby has been born.

Source: Knight 1994.

FIGURE 3.6 *Welcoming Babies*

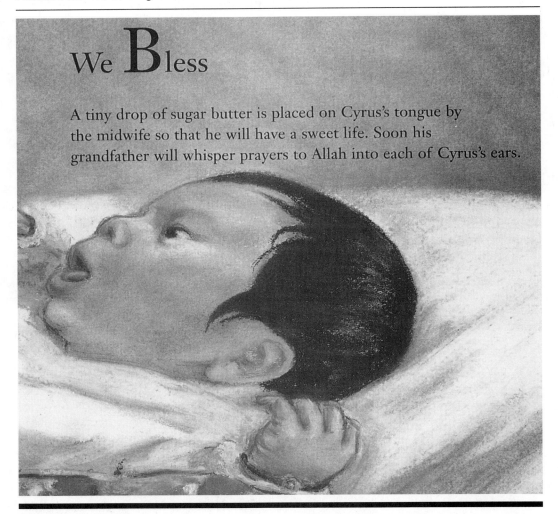

We Bless

A tiny drop of sugar butter is placed on Cyrus's tongue by the midwife so that he will have a sweet life. Soon his grandfather will whisper prayers to Allah into each of Cyrus's ears.

Source: Knight 1994.

the influence of the times. During many years that we have taught and worked in children's classrooms, we have enjoyed learning from parents the reasons behind the choices of names for their offsprings. Although there are always tendencies to choose fashionable names, we have found that there are several other motivations for selecting names, which are sometimes shared across cultural groups. Some of the main reasons are the following:

IN ACTION . . . *Welcome to the World!*

In her book titled *Welcoming Babies*, Knight (1994) presents examples of different cultural practices used to acknowledge the arrival of a new member. In our families we also have practices that we learned from our elders and that we perform when a new child is born into the family. See how many you remember or ask your relatives about things they do. Do not be surprised to find that some of these activities have been done for generations. You will see once more how powerful culture is!

1. *To honor:*
   - an ancestor—usually grandparents' names were given to a first child, especially if it is a boy.
   - a close relative, family member, or friend— names of uncles and aunts were the most common ones given along with names of recently deceased relatives. Honoring a special friend by naming a child was another common practice.
2. *To follow a tradition:*
   - naming children according to their parents' names, i.e., a boy with the father's name and a girl with the mother's name.
   - having a religious authority select the child's name (most auspicious one).
   - choosing names that are considered acceptable to the parents' religion, such as biblical names or names that honor a religious figure or a symbol.
3. *To highlight ethnic identity:*
   - selecting names that depict ethnic origin or affiliation. Names of specific ethnic groups are sometimes used to name children (i.e., Taina or Ashanti).
   - names of local and national ethnic heroes as well as events of special national significance (Bolívar, Washington).
4. *To remember a circumstance or emotion:*
   - names that depict a feeling or emotion based on the significance of the child's birth (Milagros [miracle], Joy, Aimée [the loved one]).

Learning about the significance of names has made us aware how important it is to respect and to accept a child's name, regardless of how hard it might be to write or pronounce it. Educator Samuel Perez (1994) asserts that one of the best ways to demonstrate our respect toward a family's culture is by respecting their names and avoiding their "Americanization."

Suggestions for Dealing with Names
1. Always ask the family what name they prefer their child to use. Respect their choice.
2. Ask parents why they named their child that way. This will help you not only to value the child's name, but also to find ways to enhance the child's self-concept.
3. If the name is difficult to pronounce, ask the parents to help with the correct pronunciation. Try writing it phonetically or even have the parent record it on tape.
4. If a child's name has an English translation, share it with the class. This can also become an opportunity to introduce children to a thematic unit where they can investigate origins, meanings, and other aspects of names.
5. Some children might want to adopt a nickname. Share this with parents so that they know it is the child's desire to do so.

IN ACTION . . .   *Our Names*

Do you know why you were given your name? Find out and see if it corresponds to any of the reasons we listed. What other reasons and motivations do you feel people have for naming a child? In what ways do these reflect their family and cultural values?

6. Always emphasize respect toward names. Intervene whenever a child is the target of name calling or ridicule because of his/her name. This is both damaging and humiliating for the child.

❖ **Families, the Essence of Social Life**

We hope you have realized that teaching young children presents a unique opportunity to discover their families. In every classroom in this

---

Snapshot 3.5
Names and Surnames

Family names or surnames are another relevant element that grants one both a family and a cultural identity. They are also often the focus of misunderstandings because in other cultural contexts family names follow a different practice. While in the United States a child's family name is simply that of the father with no acknowledgment of the mother's name, in other cultures, like the Hispanic, this is not the case. Although many Hispanics have adopted the practice of Americanizing their names, there are still many cases where you will find that a Hispanic child has more than one family name. The tradition in Hispanic countries dictates that children must carry the names of both parents as surnames.

Take for example the following:

| *Elena* | *Rivera* | *Cordero* |
| (child's name) | (father's name) | (mother's name) |

Although the child can be also called Elena Rivera, she still maintains "Cordero" as her other surname. This practice stemmed from the importance ascribed to legitimization of children during times when being a child born out of wedlock carried a stigma. From our own experience, we know that teachers often assume to know the child's name. To avoid misunderstanding, always ask the parents for the child's correct name.

Snapshot 3.6
Our Multicultural Family: Meet Aida Ramos-Cruz

When Aida Ramos made the decision to leave her native Puerto Rico, she had only one thought: to build a better future for her and her one-year-old child. A single parent, she came to New York almost forty years ago with only a little knowledge of the language and a firm desire to succeed. For a woman of a different culture, life in America in the 1950s and 60s was not always easy. Aida never gave up, however, in spite of the many hardships she faced. Later on, after remarrying, Aida and her husband Angel struggled to give their five children a better life in Chicago where they settled. They succeeded in keeping their cultural traditions and proudly passed them on to their children.

Today, as they enjoy their retirement in Florida, Aida and Angel look back not with nostalgia but with a well-earned sense of pride. Times were difficult but Aida agrees that there was always the knowledge that if they were willing to work, they would make it. And they did.

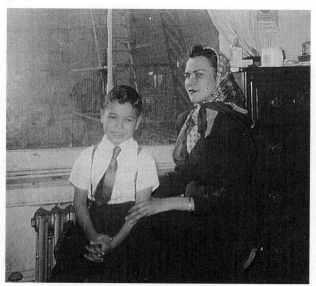

---

country we can begin not only to learn about families, but also to appreciate and value them. This is a unique opportunity to begin to understand what it means to live and be a part of this diverse American society. Because early educators are constantly trying to find more novel ways to help children, no better source and channel is found than that we have in their families. As we begin our search for ideas to reform our teaching in a responsive manner, the families in our classroom will be the first recourse to find. In the next chapter, where we will explore the needs of the child, we will see once more how relevant the family is in order to know the child we teach.

❖ Things to Do . . .

1. An excellent way to learn about families in a multicultural context is to find how they see themselves. Begin by asking a sample of your own colleagues or classmates how they define themselves as a family. You may want to ask the following questions:
   ▪ How do you define "family"?
   ▪ What makes your family *a family?*
   ▪ What would you say makes your family special or different from others?
   Once you have collected their answers, find the things in common and those where they differ. Summarize your findings and share them with your colleagues.

2. A good way to continue learning about families is to learn about their daily routines. Routines help us to "see" the culture of the family. Begin a collection of family routines. Ask your friends and colleagues and some of the parents in your class to share some of the routines they observe during breakfast, when having dinner, on Saturday and Sunday, and when having visitors at their house. After collecting your data, analyze them to find: trends in common, unusual patterns, and other peculiarities that characterize the families surveyed.

3. Because we all have an interest in learning more about different cultures, select one and do some library research about some of the family customs. Possible aspects to research

are: birth practices, child-rearing ideas, family tasks, funeral practices, and others. Write a paper about your findings and share it with your friends.

4. Using the findings from the activity listed on page 86 in this chapter where you surveyed the family configurations in your classroom, select a minimum of five children's books reflective of those configurations. Design a classroom activity to share them with your students.

❖ Children's Literature Corner

Cleary, B. (1977). *Ramona and her father.* New York: William Morrow.

Cleary, B. (1979). *Ramona and her mother.* New York: William Morrow.

Fassler, D., Lash, M., & Ives, S. (1988). *Changing families. A guide for kids and grown-ups.* Burlington, VT: Waterfront Books.

Mann, P. (1973). *My dad lives in a downtown hotel.* New York: Doubleday.

Mercer, G., & Mercer, M. (1992). *This is my family.* Racine, WI: Western Publishing.

❖ References

Bronfenbrenner, U. L. (1979). *The ecology of human development: Experiments by nature and design.* Cambridge, MA: Harvard University Press.

Chan, S. (1992). Families with Asian roots. In E. Lynch & M. Hanson (eds.). *Developing cross-cultural competence. A guide for working with young children and their families.* Baltimore, MD: Paul Brookes.

Coleman, J. (1991). *Parental involvement in education.* Washington, DC: Office of Educational Research and Improvement.

Commission on children. (1991). Beyond rhetoric. A new American agenda for children and families. Washington, DC: US Government Printing Office.

Curran, D. (1983). *Traits of a healthy family.* New York: Doubleday.

Epstein, N., Bishop, D., Ryan, C., Miller, I., & Gabor, K. (1993). The McMaster model: View of healthy family functioning. In F. Walsh (ed.). *Normal family processes* (2nd ed.). New York: The Guilford Press.

Fassler, D., Lash, M., & Ives, S. (1988). *Changing families: A guide for kids and grown-ups.* Vermont: Waterfront Books.

Garbarino, J. (1992). *Children and families in the social environment* (2nd ed.). New York: Aldine de Gruyter.

Garbarino, J., & Abramovitz, R. (1992). The ecology of human development. In J. Garbarino. *Children and families in the social environment* (2nd ed.). New York: Aldine de Gruyter.

Garbarino, J., & Abramovitz, R. (1992). The family as a social system. In J. Garbarino. *Children and families in the social environment* (2nd ed.). New York: Aldine de Gruyter.

Hanson, M. (1992). Families with Anglo-European Roots. In E. Lynch and M. Hanson (eds.). *Developing cross-cultural competence. A guide for working with young children and their families.* Baltimore, MD: Paul Brookes.

Joe, J., & Malach, R. (1992). Families with Native American roots. In E. Lynch & M. Hanson (eds.). *Developing cross-cultural competence. A guide for working with young children and their families.* Baltimore, MD: Paul Brookes.

Knight, M. (1994). *Welcoming babies.* Gardiner, ME: Tillbury Press.

Konner, M. (1991). *Childhood. A multicultural view.* Boston, MA: Little, Brown & Company.

Laird, J. (1993). Lesbian and gay families. In F. Walsh (ed.). *Normal family processes* (2nd ed.). New York: The Guilford Press.

Lynch, E., & Hanson, M. (1992). (eds.). *Developing cross-cultural competence. A guide for working with young children and their families.* Baltimore, MD: Paul Brookes.

Mayer, G., and Mayer, M. (1992). *This is my family.* New York: Golden Books.

McGoldrick, M. (1993). Ethnicity, cultural diversity, and normality. In F. Walsh (ed.). *Normal family processes* (2nd ed.). New York: The Guilford Press.

Perez, S. (1994). Responding differently to diversity. *Childhood Education* 70, 3:151–153.

Piotrskowski, C., & Hughes, D. (1993). Dual earner families in context: Managing family and work systems. In F. Walsh (ed.). *Normal family processes* (2nd ed.). New York: The Guilford Press.

Robles de Meléndez, W. (1995). *Family and school collaboration (study guide).* Fort Lauderdale, FL: Nova Southeastern University.

Sharifzadeh, V. (1992). Families with Middle Eastern roots. In E. Lynch & M. Hanson (eds.). *Developing cross-cultural competence. A guide for working with young children and their families.* Baltimore, MD: Paul Brookes.

Spradley, J., & McCurdy, D. (1972/1988). The cultural experience. Ethnography in complex society. Chicago: Waveland Press.

Walsh, F. (1993) (ed.). *Normal family processes* (2nd ed.). New York: The Guilford Press.

Willis, W. (1992). Families with African American roots. In E. Lynch & M. Hanson. *Developing cross-cultural competence. A guide for working with young children and their families.* Baltimore, MD: Paul Brookes.

Zeitlin, S., & Williamson, G. (1994). *Coping in young children. Early intervention practices to enhance adaptive behavior and resilience.* Baltimore, MD: Paul Brookes.

Zuniga, M. (1992). Families with Latino roots. In E. Lynch & M. Hanson (eds.). *Developing cross-cultural competence. A guide for working with young children and their families.* Baltimore, MD: Paul Brookes.

United Nations. (1994). *International year of the family.* New York: Department of Public Information.

"ALL children are born capable of learning."

Jean Jacques Rousseau

Who Is the Child? Developmental Characteristics of Young Children

In this chapter we will:

- define development
- describe the typical development characteristics of children
- discuss the role of the environment in the development of attitudes and behaviors of children

Key concepts:

- development
- developmental universality and individuality
- attitudes
- socialization
- prejudice
- race awareness

❖ Looking at Children: So Alike and Yet So Different

"In all children, you will find the one."
Carmen Martinez (school teacher)

We can help children understand diversity by helping them comprehend the differences and similarities of people. Helping children recognize that we share attitudes, values, and behaviors among ourselves while being distinct and separate individuals is one of the most important concepts that underlies human understanding. In this chapter we will briefly review some of the ideas of child development that define the shared characteristics of children as well as the reasoning behind the distinctive traits that give every child a unique identity. This is an essential step for educators moving into multicultural teaching.

❖ Development: The Process of Becoming

"Every time a child is born it brings with it the hope that God is not yet disappointed with man [humankind]."

Rabindranath Tagore

Whenever we enter a classroom of young children, we are faced with the wonder of life in its most vibrant form. Smiling faces, curious looks, and lively sounds all epitomize the energy of new existence that children personify. We are

"In all children, you will find the one" Carmen Martinez (school teacher).

Who Is the Child? Developmental Characteristics of Young Children

111

Many elements in the environment contribute to the positive development of the child. What elements are depicted here?

also keenly aware that each child is a separate and distinct person as well as a member of the collective of children. Preparing to offer the children the best learning environment requires a careful analysis of the characteristics that make them similar and yet individual. We particularly need to understand how children develop the beliefs, attitudes, and ideas about others that they exhibit in the classroom. This knowledge will both promote better understanding between the teacher and the students and also provide valuable information to guide the instructional practices in the classroom that will foster multiculturalism. Let us begin by briefly exploring what makes us alike: the process of development.

What Is Development?

Once life begins at the moment of conception, all human beings enter into a continuous dance of change and development. The process is completed at the end of our existence, or, as some argue, continues in other forms of life through infinity. The constancy of change that characterizes development is also what defines it. Development is an integrated and coherent process. Ludlow and Berkeley (1994) consider development as having three salient traits:

1. *It is holistic, with each organism working as a whole.* Although some of the domains may exhibit more overt changes at a specific time, in reality all the domains will be actively involved. A child's first work demonstrates the interplay of several developmental domains. For instance, the child must have the motor ability to form words, the cognitive ability to relate the sounds to an event or object, and a capacity for language that permits the sounds of the word to be perceived and reproduced.

2. *It is dynamic and intense.* Once the child is born, development begins and leads the child into an active process of change. This dynamism is best observed in the first eight years of life, when the rate of change is fastest.

Development consists of similar and diverse milestones. Awareness of developmental commonalities and differences provides guidelines for classroom teachers.

3. *It denotes a transactional process.* The individual plays an active role in the change process by altering situations as he/she is affected by changes.

A view of development as a holistic, integrated, and dynamic process is important for teachers because it explains the difference between an isolated, subject-based curriculum and a developmentally integrated one.

Because development is characteristic of all people, there are general principles that explain how children everywhere in this world develop (Berns 1994). In the same way, there are specific factors that define and give each child an individual character. Development is, then, a process of dual character: while on one hand it establishes basic and similar milestones, it also determines the way individuals acquire their unique personalities (Figure 4.1).

Universality as a Defining Character of Development

As they grow, whether in Oceania, Africa, or in this country, children of the same ages share the same physical, socioemotional, and cognitive milestones. Reaffirming the universal character of development, Konner (1991) says, " . . . infants in all cultures start out with the same biological equipment" (p. 3). This universality establishes the likenesses of children and people in general.

All children experience and share the process of development in much the same way regardless of where they live. Cross-cultural research has shown that the stages of physical growth do not vary, although the tempo may vary by race, genetic inheritance, or the physical circumstances in which a child is raised. For example, for all children, everywhere, there are shared developmental events: baby teeth erupt before the permanent ones, infants' arms exhibit more control than the legs, and fetal cartilage is replaced by bone following the same progression (Berk 1993; Konner 1991).

We also know that all children go through the same stages in learning language, no matter what their native tongue may be. From the time the linguist Noam Chomsky (1957) first defined sets of language structures common to all languages, linguists, psycholinguists, and developmental psychologists have studied how children learn these structures. They have found that language structures emerge following the same developmental progression regardless of the child's native language. For instance, babies go through stages of random vocalizations that are slowly modified as infants emulate the sounds used by parents and other caregivers. Also, children go through a stage of overgeneralizing the rules of grammar in their native language, whether it be in English or Russian. An example of this phenomenon is the child's changing of the word "foot" to "foots."

The stages of intellectual development defined and researched by the Swiss psychologist Jean Piaget and his colleagues have also been studied in children from many different countries. Among them are the children from Algeria, Senegal, Italy, Hong Kong, and Australian Aborigines. It was found that children's formal schooling and cultural

---

WORKING GLOSSARY

▌ **Development**—process of continuous change observed over time and experienced by all human beings.

▌ **Developmental Milestones**—significant events children will exhibit at different periods of life. They describe typical characteristics of a child at a certain time during childhood like the onset of talking, walking, and reading.

FIGURE 4.1 Facts about child development, ages 3–10

Age 3–4 years

Physical Development
3 years: *Average size:* 32 lbs., 38 in. tall. *Sleep:* needs 12 hrs. per day. *Perception:* still slightly farsighted—easier to see distances.
4 years: *Average size:* 37 lbs., 40 in. tall.

Motor Development
3 years: rides tricycle, can walk on tiptoe, hops with both feet, runs smoothly, walks up and down stairs one foot on each step, buttons and unbuttons, pours from a pitcher, builds tower of 9 blocks and makes bridge with 3 blocks, tries to make the basic shapes (triangles, circles, and squares), catches ball, arms straight.
3½ years: uses basic shapes, scribbles to make designs, uses circles within circles, etc.
4 years: balances on 1 foot for 5 seconds, hops on 1 foot, can walk forward heel to toe, throws ball overhand, dresses self, catches small ball, elbows in front of body, does stunts on tricycle, descends short steps, alternating feet, hand preference nearly established.

Language Development
3 years: sentences contain many words with plural endings. Uses the declarative in a raised tone to ask questions. Sometimes uses nouns or other substantives with a negative word to express negation. A greater variety of emotions is now reflected in speech. Vocabulary is about 850 words. Can understand meaning of adult speech about events that have not personally been experienced. Easily repeats songs. Begins to use subordinate sentences. Most pronunciation correct except *r, l,* and the hissing sounds.
4 years: vocabulary of about 1500 words; most grammatical endings now known; deviation from adult speech more style than grammar. Begins to use future tense; two or more ideas are regularly expressed in complex sentences. Comprehends feelings (e.g., cold, tired) and prepositions; recognizes color names.

Cognitive/Piagetian Development
3 years: *Symbolic phase of preoperational stage* still in effect. *Imagination:* ability to pretend during play develops; engages in dramatic play. *Conservation:* beginning development of the conservation of amount. *Egocentrism:* reduction in the amount of egocentrism; more able to take other people's perspectives into account. *Classification:* objects are included in a particular class for personal reasons (e.g., "this makes a house"). *Time:* talks almost as much about the past and future as about the present; often pretends to tell time and talks about time a great deal; tells how old he is, what he will do tomorrow or on his birthday.
4 years: *Intuitive phase of preoperational stage* begins to operate; the thought processes begin to involve such things as a new understanding of relationships. *Motivation:* rewards continue to need to be fairly immediate and sensual; still very sensitive to praise and attention. *Time:* past and future tenses very accurately used; refinement in the use of time words; broader concepts expressed by use of month, "next winter," "last summer"; a much clearer understanding of daily sequence of events emerges.

Social Development
Attachment: by age 4, will accept temporary absence of mother without protest and will accept substitute attachment figures (Bowlby). *Play:* at 3 years, most children involve themselves in peer play; by 4 years, most involved in cooperative play. *Social skills:* at 3 years, washes, and dries hands and face; at 4 years, dresses with or without supervision. *Phallic stage:* both sexes have sexual fantasies about their parents for which they feel guilty; stage will last until age 6 (Freud). *Sex role and identity:* knows own sex but does not realize maleness and femaleness are permanent characteristics. *Moral development:* rules of a game are sacred and unchangeable but they tend to be applied in an egocentric manner.

Self-Development
3 years: period of acute possessiveness and egocentrism. Capable of scanning and responding to inner states (e.g., identifying mood states and changes in one's own moods).
4 years: beginning to understand "mineness" and "ourness" and to see self as reflected in others. If told he is cute or devilish will include these characteristics in own self-concept. Adult responses to that image give him a positive or negative image about himself.

FIGURE 4.1 continued

Age 5–7 years

Physical Development
5 years: *Average size:* 41½ lbs., 43 in. tall. *Sleep:* needs 11 hrs. per day. *Perception:* development has advanced so that child can scan and focus reasonably well. *Body changes:* brain development at 90% full adult weight; average body temperature at normal 98.6 F; fewer stomachaches, digestive system more regular, fewer ear infections, distance from outer ear greater, respiratory infections lessened due to a longer trachea.
6 years: *Average size:* 45½ lbs., 46 in. tall. *Teeth:* at 6½ years permanent upper and lower 1st molars and lower central incisors appear.
7 years: *Average size:* 53 lbs., 47 in. tall. *Teeth:* at 7½ years permanent upper central incisors and lower lateral incisors replace baby teeth.

Motor Development
5 years: catches bounding ball with elbows at sides, balances on 1 foot for 10 seconds, skips, descends large ladder, alternating feet easily, throws well, copies designs, letters, numbers, triangles, and squares, folds paper into double triangle, tries to form pictures of animals, people, and buildings.
6 years: can walk backwards heel to toe, running speed increases, jumping forms basis of many games and improves.
7 years: balance improves, more details are added to art work.

Language Development
5 years: language increasingly resembles adult models.
6 years: average vocabulary now 2500 words.
7 years: can recall grammatical sentences rather than strings of words and can make grammatically consistent word associations.

Cognitive/Piagetian Development
5 years: *Conservation:* beginning to understand the conservation of number. *Classification:* done largely on the basis of color.
6 years: *Classification:* done largely on the basis of shape discrimination using visual perception rather than touch. *Memory:* capacity is well developed and labeling aids greatly in recalling pictures.
7 years: beginning of *concrete operational period:* capable of certain logic so long as manipulation of objects in involved. *Classification:* uses definitions for grouping centering on one dimension, but still unable to use class inclusion. *Creativity:* drawings of the human are quite well defined and designs are very representative of reality.
7½ years: *Conservation:* understanding of conservation of length, seriation, and number. *Motivation:* rewards come from correct information; begins to adopt internal standards of performance. *Humor:* ability to understand riddles.

Social Development
Period of initiative vs. guilt: the family is the main human relationship; children freely engage in many adultlike activities, and parents' patient answering of questions leads to initiative; a restriction of activities and treatment of questions as nuisance leads to guilt (Erikson). *Latency period:* not a stage but rather an interlude when sexual needs are relatively quiet and energy is put into learning skills—will continue until age 11 (Freud). *Aggression:* physical fighting often used as a means of solving problems or defending one's image. *Sex role and identity:* at 6 years, realizes that sex is a permanent characteristic. *Moral development:* rules in games are important as codes that must be respected, but they can be changed; children are more able to cooperate and share because they are less egocentric and develop a characteristic way of responding to others.

Self-Development
Understands that self is part of interrelated group of others (e.g., family, friends, kinships). Develops understanding that self is a sexual person and forms preferences for own sex. Perceives self as a moral person with goals for an ideal self. Understands self as initiator of novel and creative interactions.

FIGURE 4.1 continued

Age 9–10 years

Physical Development
9 years: *Average size:* 68 lbs., 53 in. tall. *Sleep:* needs 10 hrs. per day. *Teeth:* permanent upper lateral incisors and lower cuspids. *Perception:* well-developed ability to read fine print.
10 years: *Average size:* males, 78 lbs., 58.7 in. tall; females, 77.5 lbs., 59.2 in. tall. *Teeth:* at 10 years upper and lower 1st bicuspids and upper 2nd bicuspids appear, total now 26 teeth. *Body changes:* females begin to have rounding of hips, breasts and nipples are elevated to form bud stage, no true pubic hair yet.

Motor Development
Increased gains in vigor and balance in motor control and coordination; manual dexterity increases; greater muscular strength develops; improvement in accuracy, agility, and endurance; girls continue to run faster than boys; throwing and catching are better; jumping and climbing are done with ease and assurance; eye-hand coordination is good.

Language Development
Acquires an average of 5000 new words in this age range. Knowledge of syntax fully developed. Has the ability to understand comparatives (longer, deeper), the subjunctive (*if I were a . . .*), and metaphors (*rotten egg, dirty rat*). Language has become a tool and not just words that refer only to objects. Specialized vocabularies develop for different situations (e.g., games).

Cognitive/Piagetian Development
9 years: *Concrete operation period* still in effect: logic and objectivity increase; deductive thinking begins to appear. *Conservation:* understands conservation of area. *Causality:* has a firm grasp of cause-effect relationships. *Humor:* begins to appreciate use of certain metaphors in joking because of an understanding of the incongruous elements.
10 years: *Conservation:* understanding of the conservation of substances acquired. *Classification:* elements classified using a hierarchical construct. *Space:* able to make or interpret simple maps and distances. *Memory:* memory tasks involve use of mnemonic devices.

Social Development
Period of industry vs. inferiority: has been ongoing since age 7; the neighborhood and school are now the main source of human relationships. Children are busy learning to be competent and productive using skills and tools, exercising dexterity and intelligence to gain praise for their accomplishments leading to industry. Limitation of activities, feeling inferior, criticism, and inability to do well lead to inferiority (Erikson). *Aggression:* reduction in physical fighting to defend self-image; verbal duels now become the tool. *Sex role and identity:* at 10 years, emphasizes social roles more than physical development, believing that "men should act like men and women like ladies."

Self-Development
Develops a great variety of new skills and activities that lead to a sense of effectiveness.

Source: Berns 1994.

Who Is the Child? Developmental Characteristics of Young Children

117

IN ACTION . . . *Your Classroom Profile*

Develop a common developmental profile of the children you teach. Consider the ways in which they are alike physically, socioemotionally, and cognitively.

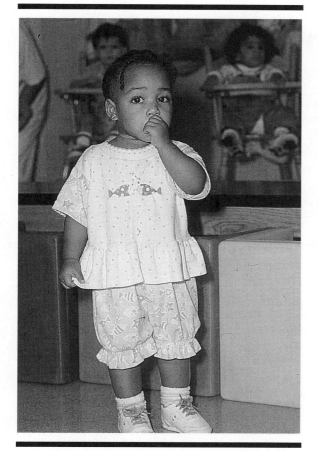

Developmentally appropriate practice (DAP) is based on the concept that all children experience common growth and development processes.

background may influence the age of mastery of specific stage-related tasks, but the progression of stages remains very consistent across cultures.

Anthropologists and psychologists have identified the common developmental tasks in social and emotional growth that children everywhere master, stage-by-stage, to become emotionally healthy adults. One of the best known of these frameworks is that of Erik Erikson. Erikson, a psychoanalyst, studied anthropological research and defined eight stages, common to all cultures, that are critical periods in social and emotional development. These stages progress from learning to trust others and accept their help, through becoming a productive member of society and helper of others (Erikson 1963).

The documented existence of these universal patterns is at the core of the concept for developmentally appropriate practices (DAP). In early childhood education, these patterns serve as guidelines for teachers who are trying to organize their teaching around the children's developmental events. For example, because of the common developmental characteristics of all four-year-olds, teachers are able to develop a program based on the general requirements of all children of that age. Developing a program based on the common characteristics of all children is also a basic principle of multicultural education.

Individuality, Also a Trait of Development

If you see a group of four-year-olds, you would probably observe that they exhibit unique

---

Snapshot 4.1
Nonverbal Communication as Another Descriptor of
Developmental Universality

One form of evidence of children's similarities across cultures comes from the work of the German ethnologist, Ireneus Eibl-Eibesfelt. For over two decades, Eibl-Eibesfelt filmed candid instances of nonverbal communication in cultures throughout the world. He captured the behaviors of people in primitive cultures such as the Yanomano of Brazil, the !Kung of Botswana, and the Tasaday of the Philippine jungles, as well as different European groups. Through his research, he was able to document similar nonverbal responses to environmental stimuli. For example, he documented similar nonverbal responses in expressing disgust at a foul odor, in hitting combined with an angry expression, and in toddlers playing with one of their mother's nipples while breastfeeding. Eibl-Eibesfelt's evidence includes observations of similar cross-cultural reactions in adults. He further documented parents showing the same facial expressions when they interacted with an infant: broad smiles, wide-open eyes, raised eyebrows, and head bobbing up and down accompanied by a high-pitched, somewhat musical vocalization.

Source: Adapted from Konner, M. (1991). *Childhood. A multicultural view* (pp. 139–140). Boston, MA: Little, Brown & Co.

---

qualities. Many factors contribute to the uniqueness of every child. The first one concerns the biological nature of each child as it relates to the parents. Because of the different genetic makeup of parents, the biological passport of each child is very unique. Stamped at the moment of conception, each child comes into this world equipped with a personalized inherited genetic code. This code determines whether he or she has light or dark skin, curly or straight hair, is tall or short, and so on. The second factor concerns the process of development. Research confirms that the development of the child is influenced by the circumstances, lifestyle, and habits of parents during the nine months before birth. Such things as the

mother's emotional readiness to accept parenthood, proper nutrition, drug abuse, and malnutrition affect the development of the unborn child. Recent evidence also demonstrates that the level of stress experienced by mothers during their pregnancy can affect the development of the fetus. A study conducted by Dunkel-Schetter, Lobel, and Scrimshaw (cited by Zigler & Stevenson 1993) proved that there was a direct relationship between the mother's level of emotional health and the baby's physical development. In their study, they "found that stress during pregnancy affects birth weight and preterm birth" (Zigler & Stevenson 1993, p. 138). Although consequences of both birth weight and preterm birth can be

Who Is the Child? Developmental Characteristics of Young Children

119

FOCUS ON CLASSROOM PRACTICES

DEVELOPMENTAL PLANNING USING UNIVERSAL MILESTONES

Developmental milestones are an important element when planning classroom activities. They provide essential information about the typical characteristics and abilities of children at different age levels. To practice how to apply these milestones to classroom planning, here is a simple exercise that will serve also as an example.

Planning for five-year-olds: Using the general description and the attributes described in the table for five-year-olds, design an activity for a group of kindergartners. Make sure that all the traits here are incorporated.

What are the children at age five typically like? Holistically viewed, they are physically active, able to make friends, more skillful in using language, and beginning to understand the qualities and attributes of objects.

Developmental Characteristics of Five-Year-Olds

Physical/Motor—able to balance on 1 foot, skip, descend a large ladder, draw well, copy designs and letters

Social—freely engage in many adult-like activities, see themselves as members of a group, like to cooperate, and begin to move away from egocentricity

Cognitive—begin to understand the conservation of numbers, learning to classify according to attributes like color; language is more adult-like

---

overcome with proper care, they do influence the development of the child.

A third factor to consider is the home environment into which each child is born. The character of the child is determined by the family experience, the cultural ideas and values of persons close to the family whether friends or relatives, and the neighborhood setting where the child grows up. For example, a five-year-old boy born in a Masai village may be given the responsibility of shepherding grazing animals. Compare this responsibility with what is expected of children of the same age in this country. We can easily see how the environment sets different behavior patterns for a child. Lastly, we must consider the

role of the culture to which the child and his or her family belong, and which establishes the way the child will learn to view the world. Berns (1994) notes that the influence of culture is such that it even controls the developmental milestones of children. For instance, in our country, "sleeping through the night" is considered an expectation for infants four to five months old. Not so in cultures where infants sleep with their mothers and nurse themselves with a "minimal disturbance of adult sleep" (Berns 1994, p. 11). Teachers of young children are discovering daily that culture is a major contributor to the identity and individuality of each child in the classroom.

Uniqueness is the most common characteristic of all children. These twins have much in common; however, they are very particular in their own ways.

IN ACTION . . . *Our Real Passport: Four Elements That Make Us What We Are*

You may have a passport that establishes when and where you were born and that declares your official identity. However, it does not say who you really are as a specimen of humankind. The self in each of us is a combination of four elements: *biological inheritance, the prenatal experience, home environment, and the culture we belong to.* Using those four elements, create your real passport. What you discover will be the real you. Try doing the same thing with your students.

Who Is the Child? Developmental Characteristics of Young Children

121

IN ACTION . . . *Developmental Factors*

■ Consider the four factors—*heredity, prenatal environment, family environment, and culture* as the major contributors to each child's identity. Are there any other elements you would add?

■ Think about yourself and describe how these four factors have affected your unique character.

Individuality Is Also the Other Parameter of DAP

Recognition of the uniqueness of each child is an important principle in developmentally appropriate practices (DAP). DAP involves adapting knowledge of the common characteristics of children in a specific age group to meet the needs, interests, and abilities of each individual child in the group (Bredekamp 1987). Developmental teaching offers children support and encouragement to be themselves, even as they learn to become part of a group. In multicultural education each child's unique cultural heritage becomes one of the individual characteristics that is supported. Children are encouraged to keep and preserve their own cultural heritage. Developmentally responsive education and multicultural education both have the goal of blending common human experiences unique to individuals and to specific cultures.

The Shaping Force of the Environment

Where we are born, and where we spend our lives growing up, molds our unique identities. The experiences we had, the friends and neighbors with whom we shared our time, all form the magic web of influences that make us who we are. As an early childhood teacher, you probably have observed how children role-play adultlike behaviors in the dramatic area. If you observe carefully, you will notice some of the social codes that the children

have already internalized. Examples include the phrases, interjections, and terms the children use in reference to bodily functions. Many times a teacher may hear children say words that are inappropriate in the teacher's frame of reference. One of the writers of this book recalls being phoned by a teacher who was so alarmed by the words used by some of the second graders that she wanted the intervention of a social worker. It was later discovered that the children were applying the terms in contexts similar to those they heard used by the adults in their neighborhoods. The only intervention needed was making the teacher aware of the influence of the immediate social environment. Provided with alternative expressions, the children eventually learned substitute words more acceptable in the school setting.

The Ecological View

Urie Bronfenbrenner's theories are of particular relevance to education for diversity. In his studies, Bronfenbrenner showed that the children in our classrooms reflect many influences of the environment. His theory looks at the environment as an ecological system where all the different forces act upon the child's development (Figure 4.2).

Bronfenbrenner interprets the influence of the environment as coming from different levels of action. Each level represents its own patterns and ways of behavior. In this sense the behaviors of

FIGURE 4.2 Bronfenbrenner's ecological model of forces acting upon the child

Ecological Level	Definition	Examples	Issues Affecting Children
Microsystem	Situations in which the child has face-to-face contact with influential others	Family, school, peer group, church	Is the child regarded positively? Is the child accepted? Is the child reinforced for competent behavior? Is the child exposed to enough diversity in roles and relationships? Is the child given an active role in reciprocal relationships?
Mesosystem	Relationships between microsystems; the connections between situations	Home-school, home-church, school-neighborhood	Do settings respect each other? Do settings present basic consistency in values?
Exosystem	Settings in which the child does not participate but in which significant decisions are made affecting the child or adults who do interact directly with the child	Parents' places of employment, school board, local government, parents' peer group	Are decisions made with the interests of parents and children in mind? How well do supports for families balance stresses for parents?
Macrosystem	"Blueprints" for defining and organizing the institutional life of the society	Ideology, social policy, shared assumptions about human nature, the "social contract"	Are some groups valued at the expense of others (e.g., sexism, racism)? Is there an individualistic or a collectivistic orientation? Is violence a norm?

Source: Garbarino 1992.

Who Is the Child? Developmental Characteristics of Young Children

123

IN ACTION . . . *Accommodating Individual Needs in Developmental Planning*

Considering the general developmental characteristics of seven-year-olds, find ways to incorporate the following individual traits into your planning.

Class profile: Your class has two children who are hearing impaired, four children who are of Native American descent, and three Hispanic children from migrant families. The rest of the children are middle class European Americans.

Consider the following: What kind of activities will you design to responsively meet the different needs of these children and at the same time meet the general developmental needs of the whole group? What developmental needs of other children will have to be addressed? What curriculum adaptations will be necessary?

Developmental Characteristics of Seven-Year-Olds

Physical—Children have improved body balance, possess better control of fine motor muscles, and are in the process of replacing baby teeth.

Cognitive—Children are in the last stages of preoperational thinking. They show cognitive shifting, are very inquisitive, and are mastering cognitive tasks. Language is almost adult-like. They are able to use grammar consistently.

Social—Children are in the period of initiative vs. guilt. They engage in many adultlike activities. They cooperate and enjoy games with rules.

Source: Berns, R. (1994). *Topical child development* (p. 28). Albany, NY: Delmar.

children in our classrooms are actually an expression of the cultural influences of their environment. The family, the relatives, the school, the peers, and the neighborhood all bestow on the child their ideas and views of life. Even within the same family, you will find that each child is different from the others. This is another example of how diversity defines humankind.

❖ Socialization: Learning to Be with Others, Learning to Be Ourselves

When children come to school, they bring with them an array of strategies to deal and get along with others. Most preschoolers in every culture exhibit the knowledge of ways to establish social relationships with others. Think about the smiles

---

WORKING GLOSSARY

▌ **Socialization**—the process through which individuals learn the accepted patterns of behavior and interactions in the context of the society to which they belong. During the process, adults pass on to the young the group's social concepts that will mold them in consonance with their patterns (Berger 1993).

Some of the forces in the environment include the geographical setting, ethnic origins, social traditions, economic status, and social patterns. Which of these forces are reflected in this illustration?

on their faces, the compliments they make about your clothing, or the way they get closer to you to catch your attention. All of these actions show that children learn ways to gain social acceptance by others. These and other behaviors are acquired through the process of socialization.

Because we live in social groups, each society has developed customs for regulating relationships

IN ACTION . . . *Acceptable Language*

Reflecting on the example of the second graders who used words accepted by their groups, think about other instances where you may have been confronted with similar situations. What did you do? Share your thoughts with the class.

Snapshot 4.2
The Environment in Action:
Culture Influences Children's Activity Levels

The child's sociocultural environment plays an important role in forming behavior. For example, Zigler and Stevenson (1993) found that the way one talks, smiles, and interacts with others is influenced by the cultural environment. Aware of the role culture plays in determining how we interact with others can help teachers understand the fact that behaviors considered normal in some cultures would not be considered normal in their own. For instance, for Hispanics, as well as for some groups with roots in the Middle East, the use of hand gestures to emphasize what is being said is considered normal. Persons from these groups tend to be very animated when talking together. In the eyes of persons with Northern European roots, a normal conversation among Hispanics can seem emotional and agitated, much like an argument.

Several studies have found that teachers tend to view behavior that may be culturally normal for Hispanics as disruptive, or as indicators of problems. Zigler and Stevenson (1993) cite the study done with Puerto Rican students. Mainstream culture teachers often misinterpreted the response styles of children of Puerto Rican origin and considered them disruptive. They also interpreted culturally acceptable interactions, such as three children talking at the same time, as signs of inattentiveness and overactivity (Bauermeister et al. 1990) Using a sample of teachers with Puerto Rican roots and of European American roots, the study showed differences between the ways in which Puerto Rican and European American teachers rated specific behaviors. Many behaviors of Puerto Rican children accepted by Puerto Rican teachers were considered distressing or in need of intervention by non-Hispanic teachers (Achenbach et al., cited by Zigler and Stevenson 1993). The different perceptions were probably due to the fact that the Puerto Rican teachers were aware of the normal behavioral responses in their culture. Although more research is needed in this area, it is important for teachers to be more aware of how children's cultural experiences shape their behavior. Perhaps a rule of thumb is to avoid making hasty judgments when children have a different social and cultural background from our own.

Source: Adapted from Zigler, E., & Stevenson, M. F. (1993). *Children in a changing world: Development and social issues.* (2nd ed.). Pacific Grove, CA: Brooks/Cole (p. 396).

Adults play a leading role in the socialization of children.

among its members. According to Elkin & Handel (1989), socialization is imperative for an individual because it is the way through which he/she learns to effectively function in a society. Children learn those formulas through the family and those around them. The older generations, be it the parents, the relatives, or the teachers, ensure that children acquire these social tools. You can imagine the extent of learning that must take place when preparing for an entire lifetime. From the simplest manners to the attitudes that one has about others, all is derived through a process that lasts as long as we are in this world. For instance, through socialization, children learn:

▐ how to interact with adults and peers

▐ how to distinguish what is good or acceptable from what is not

▐ how to behave in daily life situations

▐ how to express feelings like happiness and sadness

▐ how to perform basic activities like eating

▐ how to respond when faced with the unknown

▐ how to demonstrate affection and to whom

▐ how to show interest in something

▐ how to differentiate between what one likes and dislikes

▐ how to think about and regard others

Can you name some other things children should learn in order to become socialized?

❖ Social Learning Happens All Around Us

What are some settings where learning takes place? Contexts for learning will happen as the

Learning within the context of the family is of primary importance for a child.

child comes in contact with the family, the neighborhood, the school, the peers, and with all those in the environment. But, which ones are more important? As you probably know, the family plays the leading role in transmitting to the child the manners, views, beliefs, and ideas held and accepted by their culture (Garbarino 1992). With the rise in the number of working parents, however, day-care programs have become an influential socialization force. Many children are now getting exposed to the ideas and views of other adults and their peers earlier in life (Figure 4.3).

Along with the more traditional human socializing sources, contemporary social scientists have found that mass media has become a significant factor (King, Chipman, & Cruz-Janzen 1994). The media has provided a more accurate portrayal of the racial and ethnic demographics of American society. Two decades ago, for example, we would never have found so many news reporters, show

FIGURE 4.3 The process of socialization occurs through all the elements of our environment.

SOCIALIZATION HAPPENS THROUGH:

Family + Relatives + School/day care + Neighborhood
+ Peers + Media + Community

hosts, and artists of ethnicities other than European American. This diversity is also reflected among the individuals who are members of that industry. For today's young child, who typically spends a significant amount of time in front of the television and who "gets socialized" by it, finding out that people can succeed despite their background sends a strong positive message about diversity (Zigler & Stevenson 1993).

Learning to See the Individual in Ourselves

"I am what I am," goes a line of a song in the movie *Popeye* that reflects the self-confidence of the main character. For children to reach that same point where they can proudly affirm who they are takes a lot of effort. One of the principal goals of education for diversity is to implement practices in the classroom that contribute to the students' realization of their identities. Social identity is also something that occurs through the experience of socialization. Erik Erikson postulated that the optimal outcome of development is the achievement of identity. Miller says that "for Erikson, the essence of development is the forma-

The essential milestone of development is the building of positive self-esteem. Addressing diversity within this task is one of the primary goals of multicultural education.

tion of identity that gives coherence to one's personality" (1989, p. 191). How does this happen? How does the child come to see himself/herself? According to the social development theory, the perception of one's identity "emerges from the understanding of self as being separate from others" (Berns 1994, p. 476).

Forming Ideas About Ourselves

The quality of social interactions children have from infancy is crucial for the development of a positive self-identity. A responsive environment that supports and encourages the child and encourages a child to what Erikson called psychosocial tasks leads to a positive self-concept (Anselmo & Franz 1995). Opposite circumstances will hinder the way children see themselves. The responsibility of teachers and adults in helping children build positive self-constructive views of themselves is obvious. Children will develop a positive self-concept in an environment they trust where their ideas are encouraged and where they are seen as valuable, capable individuals.

As educators strive to create classrooms that foster and recognize the value of diversity, the implications are enormous. In every classroom it is necessary to have adults who will provide an open emotional support to all children. We cannot expect to have children "feel good" about themselves when we still find people who hold and express negative views about others based on their backgrounds. Think, for example, of the child who is constantly told that he is not capable, or whose ideas are consistently rejected for no reason. That child will find it harder to see himself/herself as a valuable individual. The way people view us during childhood remains with us for life. Here we see the implications of Bronfenbrenner's theory: that children are directly affected by the conditions of their environment. As we act to change the school environment and influence the environments in the homes, we create valuable new opportunities for children.

❖ Discovering That You Are Not Like Me

As we discussed, socialization is a process vital for human survival. As children acquire the rules of the social game, they learn to distinguish people by their attributes. However, not all that young children learn equips them with social tools valid and acceptable in a society as diverse as ours. Sometimes they acquire negative and erroneous views of those whose physical characteristics and convictions are different from their own.

While many persons still maintain that children are oblivious to racial differences (Phillips 1988), research shows that even very young children can notice differences and decode the existence of differences in their social contexts. Children begin to discriminate the existence of differences in objects and in people as early as infancy. For instance, Izard (in Berns 1994) demonstrated that infants are capable of distinguishing and reacting to different facial expressions. Perception of other differences like race, gender, social class, and physical handicaps also occurs early in life.

Developmental theory provides the best basis for arguing that early intervention is needed if children are to accept persons different from themselves. According to the theory of differentiation postulated by Eleanor Gibson (Berger 1993), the process of discriminating the details that establish the differences in objects and in people begins in infancy. Gibson saw the child as an active explorer engaged in discerning the attributes of the things encountered. She also pointed out that with experience, the child increases his/her ability to notice details (Miller 1989). Researchers

FOCUS ON CLASSROOM PRACTICES

A CLASSROOM QUILT

Quilts are a symbol of American tradition. Because they are essentially a harmonious combination of different pieces otherwise not related, they can effectively represent diversity found in our classrooms. Creating a human quilt using our young students can help them become aware of themselves. With children as the focal theme and as main artists, a class quilt can be developed early in the year. This project can be used as a culminating activity for a unit on learning about themselves.

Besides discovering how they are, this project will also help children experience working cooperatively, a valuable and needed skill for social survival.

1. Introduce the children to the tradition and meaning of quilts. Bring in a quilt for children to see and manipulate. If you do not own a quilt, parents or a colleague can lend you one. Share any of the stories about quilts like *The Patchwork Quilt* by Valerie Flournoy (1985), *Lukas's Quilt* by G. Guback (1994), and *The Keeping Quilt* by Patricia Polacco (1988). Discuss what a quilt is and the purposes of making and having one.
2. Depending on the age level of the children you teach, you may want to vary the materials used. However, we consider that using the simplest materials works best. Later on, if the interest is still there, you may move to more elaborate ones. We suggest using paper plates of different sizes and colors, which children can easily tie together with pieces of yarn.
3. Because this is a quilt about children in your classroom, each child should be represented. Give three plates to each child. On one plate they can draw a picture of themselves while on the other two plates they might describe their favorite activity and their preferred story or story character.
4. Once children have completed their plates, they can begin "quilting" the pieces. Using yarn, have children make a hole on each side of the plates. Holes can be made by punching a pencil through the plate or by using a paper hole punch. Working in small groups, children can quilt the pieces together. As each group finishes their piece of the quilt, discuss what it shows about the children "in the quilt." Begin by emphasizing the likenesses followed by the things that make them unique.
5. The completed quilt can be displayed in the classroom where it will certainly generate many interesting discussions.

Who Is the Child? Developmental Characteristics of Young Children

131

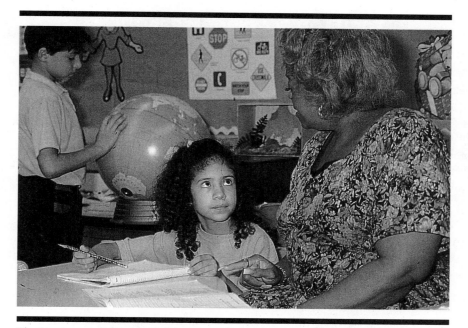

Teachers are an important influence on the positive social-emotional development of the children.

have found evidence that children perceive details like gender, age, and color.

Perception of Gender Differences

Scientists say that gender awareness occurs early and that it is shown through the verbal labels children use. Beginning at age two, according to Kohlberg (1966), children show knowledge of their own sex. Using external indicators like dress, activities, and toy preference, the child can identify the gender of self and others. Assignment of gender roles is a function of culture; therefore, children learn to differentiate gender roles through the process of socialization. Each culture determines the task and the behavioral expectations for males and females. For instance, you may have observed that male Eastern Europeans often greet each other with a double kiss or walk arm in arm with male friends. These practices are not acceptable for males in American or Hispanic cultures. Perception of what is socially established by gender is learned by participation in the culture. King et al. (1994) hold that "if young children are highly aware of the social life that goes on in their midst, then they are certainly cognizant of the sex role behavior that is appropriate in the culture" (p. 13).

Working with young children gives us a good opportunity to "see" how they are progressing in their development of gender roles. You have probably observed that although three-year-old children use terms that describe gender awareness, in reality they have not yet fully understood what "boy" or "girl" really means. Still depending on external clues (physical and societal), they have not yet developed gender consistency: the

FOCUS ON CLASSROOM PRACTICES

USING PROP BOXES TO PROMOTE AWARENESS ABOUT DIVERSITY

Helping children to become aware of diversity is one of the major goals of early childhood education. Although there are many planned activities that will promote awareness, teachers should also take advantage of the indirect or unplanned activities happening in the classroom. Particularly relevant are the experiences that occur during free play at the learning centers. Use of prop boxes (which can be located in the dramatic center) is a good way to promote awareness of diversity. Essentially, a *prop box* is a thematic collection of items suitable to foster dramatic play, role-playing activities, and open exploration. To create your prop box, you need a sturdy box with a lid. The box should be easy to handle by children and of a suitable size to facilitate storage. The next thing you need to do is identify themes for your prop boxes. Themes should stem from those same things you have observed while talking or discussing with children and from questions they have posed about any aspects of diversity. Here are some suggested themes for prop boxes and some sample props you may want to include.

1. Cooking and eating ethnic foods
   ▌ typical ethnic utensils like a wok, a *caldero* or pot, chopsticks, a cloth coffee colander or *colador,* a small barbecue grill, Indian metal serving trays, Asian and European teapots and cups, typical Amerindian serving dishes (clay, gourds), place mats, etc.
   ▌ empty boxes and cans of ethnic food; empty containers of seasonings; plastic or laminated pictures of typical ethnic vegetables and fruits.
2. Hair styling and make-up place
   ▌ empty bottles of hair products; typical ethnic hair pins and barrets; ribbons, veils, scarves, and other ethnic hair ornaments; combs, brushes, hair rollers, a hairdryer, and a curling iron (without the electric cords); ethnic dolls with different hair textures or wigs, and a wig stand; pictures of different ethnic hairstyles.
   ▌ eyeliners, kohl pencils, blush, and any other ethnic make-up items.
   ▌ earrings, necklaces, bracelets, etc.
3. Holiday decoration place
   ▌ a series of boxes for the holidays typically observed by children as well as other ethnic celebrations. Items to include:
     - typical holiday home decorations
     - songs and music
     - typical symbols
     - holiday greeting cards
     - empty boxes of typical foods
     - stories
   ▌ sample themes for holiday boxes:
     - birthdays
     - wedding items from different cultures
     - December celebrations: Kwanzaa, Christmas, Hanukkah

Focus on Classroom Practices **continued**

- January gift-giving traditions like the Three Kings (Spain and Latin America) and Befana (Italy)
- Children's Day in Korea and Japan

4. Clothes for special occasions; the sewing and dressing place:
   - fabric scraps (of different textures, colors, and prints)
   - pictures of clothing typically used by people of different ethnicities in the community and in other American communities
   - pictures of clothing worn during special occasions
   - fabric glue (to be used instead of needles)
   - a variety of sewing notions to include ribbons, yarn of different colors, buttons, sequins, etc.
   - accessories like veils, scarves, gloves, shawls, hats

5. Ethnic music and dancing
   - typical musical instruments
   - pictures of musical instruments
   - recordings of different vocal and instrumental ethnic music
   - pictures and videos of folkloric dances

---

concept that their gender will remain the same. Perhaps you have also noticed that between ages four and five, children are more likely to express and use gender stereotypes as they play (Shapiro 1994). What this reveals is that preschool children are in the process of establishing their concept of gender roles. This knowledge becomes more precise over time through increased informal social experiences. In fact, some developmental psychologists believe that clarity about one's own gender does not appear until ages seven or eight (Zigler & Stevenson 1993).

The early childhood stage is an important phase for creating awareness of gender equality. Laura Shapiro (1994) maintains that by the time children have already achieved a sense of their own gender, "the powerful stereotypes that guided them don't just disappear . . . images of the aggressive male and the nurturing female are with us for the rest of our lives" (p. 141). This statement suggests that waiting until children are more mature to address gender equality may not be as effective as dealing with it at the developmentally appropriate time.

School experiences play a leading role in helping children form their concepts of gender roles. A classroom climate characterized by equal relations and opportunities for boys and girls contributes to a sense of equality. When teachers organize their classrooms to provide experiences that invite social interactions among both boys and girls, boundaries created by gender are lessened (Thorne 1994). More attention is required to what the classroom offers and "says" to the child. Equally important are the behaviors of professionals whom children use as models. Specific attention should be given to the kinds of play occurring in the classroom. Teachers must take time to observe the gender role behaviors, labels, and activities children exhibit as they play. Derman-Sparks (1989) recommends that after an analysis of our observations, we should

---

Snapshot 4.3
Influence of Parents in Perception of Gender Roles

Research about gender awareness and roles in children has shown that parents play a leading influence. Summarizing research findings, Anselmo and Franz (1995) found that there are at least three major ways in which parents influence children's perception of gender roles.

1. Interaction with girls is characterized by being more proactive than toward boys—Research shows that mothers show a significantly higher level of protection toward girls than toward boys. Mothers tend to stay closer to girls than to boys. For example, when children fall, girls are comforted while boys are guided "to dust themselves off and get back into action" (Anselmo & Franz 1995, p. 330).
2. Parents reward boys and girls differently—There is a difference in the kind of behavior that gets rewarded by parents. For instance, boys are encouraged and rewarded when they exhibit more active exploratory behaviors. Girls are rewarded for their social responsiveness.
3. Parents tend to choose gender-related toys—Girls are encouraged to play with dolls and replicas of housekeeping items while boys are guided toward traditional male toys like cars and trucks.

Source: Anselmo, S., & Franz, W. (1995). *Early childhood development. Prenatal through age eight.* (2nd ed.). Englewood Cliffs, NJ: Merrill (p. 330).

---

reorganize the classroom learning areas to reflect a more balanced view of gender roles and to encourage "more cross-gender play choices" (p. 51). Changes should affect the entire curriculum. Literature about gender equity should be incorporated regularly into the curriculum. Titles like *Girls Can Be Anything* by Norma Klein (1973) or *William's Doll* by Charlotte Zolotow (1972) are good discussion starters with children and help them clarify stereotypes.

Counteracting Gender Stereotypes in the Classroom
1. Begin by examining your own gender stereotypes and be determined to avoid them. Remember that second to parents and family, teachers are the children's most influential models.
2. Provide opportunities for appropriate development of gender identity. Include materials that will help children form correct ideas about their anatomy and that will help them understand sex differences. Inform parents of the reasons for utilizing materials (dolls, books, puzzles) and vocabulary that are anatomically correct. Extend it to the home by providing parents with suggestions about what terms to avoid because of the confusion they create in the child.

Who Is the Child? Developmental Characteristics of Young Children

135

IN ACTION . . . *Gender roles*

The following is a conversation between two five-year-old preschoolers that took place in the classroom housekeeping area.

"Guess what? The baby is dirty," Yani said pinching his nose to indicate that the doll smelled bad. "Yani, you better change his Pamper™. You are the daddy and my daddy does that at home," Yani's playmate Sarah explained. Upset, Yani moved away from the doll. "I'm not doing that. That's girl's work and I'm a boy. I don't want to play any more," he added leaving the play area abruptly.

▮ Do you think an intervention is needed? Why or why not?

▮ What stereotypes are depicted here?

▮ What actions would you take to clarify gender stereotypes?

3. Learn about the gender roles that are assigned in the children's cultures. Be responsive to them by including opportunities for children to see that some people may hold different views.

4. Encourage participation across genders in activities traditionally assigned to either gender. For example, encourage boys to play in the housekeeping area and girls in the block area.

5. Select more children's stories about roles across gender lines and include biographies of people whose accomplishments were not restricted by gender biases.

6. Take a proactive stance and intervene whenever children express stereotypical labels. (American Association of University Women 1994; Derman-Sparks 1989; Streitmatter 1994).

Awareness of Physical Differences

One of the common areas covered in the early childhood curriculum includes the ability to recognize and discriminate details (color, form, shape). Because we live in a world of forms and colors, learning to notice these characteristics is an important way of discovering what surrounds us. This same ability enables the child to see that not all people share the same physical characteristics. Preschool children are able to discern differences like color of skin, color of eyes and hair, texture of hair, shape of the lips and nose, and other physical differences such as disabilities. Three-year-olds often reveal their awareness of these traits through their questions and comments (Katz 1982). While the timing of young children's development of awareness of specific racial and ethnic characteristics during the first three years of life is not yet clearly established, it can be argued that they derived as part of the intensive process of cognitive construction found during the first 36 months of their social life. However, research does indicate that awareness of differences as representative of race or ethnicity is developed through the influence of the family and the social environment (Banks 1992; Katz 1982; Robles de Meléndez 1992). The ideas and attitudes of the child's culture shape the notions the child will express.

Racial Awareness

"The problem of the twentieth century is the problem of the color-line."

W. E. B. DuBois (1903)

Race is a very misleading concept. So is color when we try to characterize human beings. However, since society still uses race to describe people, it is a concept children also learn through the process of socialization. Most of what the literature says about racial preferences in children comes from studies done with African American children (Kendall 1983; Derman-Sparks 1989). However limited, their findings are relevant for the early childhood educator. For instance, in her study, Phyllis Katz (1982) found that children demonstrate either a preference for their own racial group or for no special racial group. Other studies have revealed the existence of an early awareness of one's own color. In studies by Spencer and Cross (in Banks 1992), African American children showed a preference for materials (dolls, pictures) and people with Eurocentric features. One of the interesting points regarding children's awareness of color stems from the research done by Spencer, which confirmed that children were not only aware of their own race, but they also could "read" how others perceived African Americans as well as whites. Talking about Spencer's findings, Banks points out that they established that:

"Young African American children are able to distinguish their personal identity from their group, can have a high self-esteem and yet express[ing] a white bias, and that the expression of white bias results from a cognitive process that enables young children *to accurately perceive the norms and attitudes toward whites and blacks in American society*" (1992, p. 3, emphasis added).

Anselmo and Franz observe that a significant finding derived from the studies done of children's racial awareness is the fact that children of non-European background were found to be "more sensitive to racial cues and develop racial awareness earlier than other children" (1995, p. 332). Whatever the racial or ethnic makeup of the family and of the neighborhood is, it will contribute to the level of awareness children have when they come to our classrooms.

The Environment as a Source of Awareness

Anselmo and Franz (1995) contend that in cases where the family or the neighborhoods are not racially mixed, children's racial awareness will

---

IN ACTION . . .   *Are Children Aware of Color or Race?*

The following incident happened in a classroom of three-year-olds. The group was mainly Hispanic. As you read, consider the implications of what the children said. M., a fair-skinned Hispanic girl, was playing in the dolls area when two other Hispanic girls joined her. One of the girls, L., had darker skin. M. stood up and said in a commanding voice: "Vete tu eres fea!" (Go, you are ugly!) Soon a discussion began between the two children. When M. was asked why she wanted L. to leave, she answered: "Es negra, es fea." (She is dark, she's ugly.)

▌ Is the child aware of color or not?

▌ What are the implications of this incident?

▌ What would you do if you were their teacher?

Who Is the Child? Developmental Characteristics of Young Children

137

come from what the media presents. When children rely on the environment as a source of their ideas and attitudes toward racial groups, we face a potentially dangerous situation. Influenced by those they interact with, children will easily gather an array of culturally based biases and attitudes held by social groups without an understanding of the reasons behind these attitudes. This is the beginning of so many ungrounded racial prejudices still prevalent in our society. Despite the noticeable participation and presence of minorities in televised programs, television is still a powerful source of stereotypes. Laura Berk (1993) feels that television in particular is a powerful disseminator of ideas to children about racial stereotypes still common in America today.

Louise Derman-Sparks (1989), in an examination of research about biases and prejudice, found that the formation of racist views "damages White children intellectually and psychologically" (p. 4). The implications are clear: all young children are affected. Individual research of the effects of racism conducted by Bernard Kutner, Kenneth Clark, and Alice Miel (cited in Derman-Sparks 1989) demonstrated the following two main negative consequences for European American children.

1. It affected the reasoning ability of children and misled their perception of reality and thus of judgment (Kutner).
2. Children were taught to hide their own feelings toward people of other races, which encouraged the moral hypocrisy of maintaining prejudices while giving lip service to the concept of equality (Clark; Miel) (Derman-Sparks 1989, pp. 4–5).

Evidence from research and from daily life strongly confirms that contrary to what some adults still want to believe, children do see color and racial differences (Kendall 1983). Copying the behavior of those they consider their models, whether parents, relatives, or neighbors, children learn to negatively discriminate against others who are not like them. By the time they enter middle childhood, most children hold racial perceptions of others as truths. Timely action from early childhood teachers becomes the best antidote against perpetuation of misleading interpretations and concepts.

Developing a Concept of Ourselves as Social Entities

Self-perception of one's own race develops with the onset of the awareness of other races. For children with non-European American backgrounds, perception of being different from others arises early. The sources of their perceptions are many. Here we will consider three of them. The first one we need to examine is the influence of the child's parents. Many times we find that how children see themselves depends upon whether their parents' own racial identity is positive or negative. A family that feels positively about their own racial or ethnic identity will build a similar image in the child. They will also provide models for dealing with negative comments about their race or ethnic group. A positive and solid self-concept is likely to be developed by children who, nurtured by their families, see their racial or ethnic identity as equally valid as any other. When, in addition to their families, children find their classrooms supportive of their racial identities, they will grow confident and able to overcome most challenges.

The second force that shapes how we feel about our racial/ethnic identity is how others see us, and what others say about us. Children are most likely to be deeply damaged for life by racial slurs and jokes of their peers. Research has indicated that the origins of negative comments are found in the views and ideas of the children's parents and community. Instances where children replicate the words and behaviors of their parents are many. A graduate student who teaches kindergarten once told one of the authors of this book of an incident that portrays this. The student, an

---

Snapshot 4.4
Working Toward Prejudice Reduction

According to Allport (cited in Banks 1992), prejudice can be reduced when interracial situations are characterized by the following:

1. The situations are cooperative rather than competitive.
2. During the situation each individual feels of equal status to others.
3. All individuals share similar goals.
4. The contact has the approval of parents, teachers, and other authority figures.

There are obvious implications for developmental teaching in Allport's suggestions. These four characteristics of positive interracial contact situations indicate ways to plan and organize activities for young children which also respect the developmental principles. Essentially, what Allport recommends is the provision of more cooperative experiences where children will be racially intermixed and where children will find that participation has the endorsement and support of relevant adult figures. Cooperative activities should also be extended to include experiences with children and adults from diverse groups. Learning to participate and work in a group is a necessary skill children must acquire, for it serves as the basis of social life. When they form groups, teachers need to incorporate children with different characteristics: race, ethnic origin, gender, etc. However, for these suggestions to be effective, they must become standard practice.

Source: Banks, J. (November/December, 1992). Reducing prejudice in children. Guidelines from research. *Social studies and the young learner* (pp. 3–5).

African American, was teaching in a predominantly white community when one of her five-year-olds told her that she was nice but that she was "the wrong color." Feeling shocked, she asked the child why he thought she was the wrong color and the boy answered that his father had told him so. Obviously there is no such thing as the "right or wrong color." Unfortunately, episodes like this one occur in everyday life. The lesson we can learn from this is clear. Early childhood educators can counter such harmful perceptions by providing positive opportunities for children to learn about diversity issues. Although parental influences are very strong, teachers are also instrumental in reducing prejudice by providing opportunities to view and exercise equality in the classroom.

What the environment "says" is the third force that influences how we feel about ourselves. Messages in the environment play a powerful role in building a concept of one's racial characteristics. The media and the environment have often fostered negative views of certain racial groups. Cases abound of African American

FOCUS ON CLASSROOM PRACTICES

RECOGNIZING LANGUAGE DIVERSITY

Many classrooms across our country house children whose native language is different from English. For many children and parents, knowing a language other than English has not been traditionally seen as an asset, but rather as an obstacle. On many occasions, speaking a different language has resulted in discrimination. While children learn and acquire proficiency in the English language, they can also be made aware of the advantages of having or preserving the language of their own culture (Arnberg 1991). Because language is a crucial cultural element, it is important to make children aware of its value and significance. In the classroom, whether we have children who speak a different language or not, we can create awareness about the value of other languages. If you are teaching children of different language backgrounds, acknowledgment of their languages is a requirement. Here are some suggested activities:

1. If teaching children who speak a language different from English, make a commitment to use their language(s) throughout the classroom. If all the class speaks English, select a target language to be used in the classroom as activities permit.
2. As a routine, plan to label classroom items in English and in another language.
3. Learn phrases, songs, or greeting words in other languages.
4. Have classroom charts written in two languages.
5. Include books in the library corner in other languages. Include bilingual books as well. For example, good selections are Arthur Dorros' *Isla* (Dutton 1995) and Lulu Delacre's *Arroz con Leche* (Scholastic Books 1989). These titles include words and phrases in Spanish. So is *Chiemruom's Dara's Cambodian New Year* (Half Moon Books 1994), where Cambodian phrases are used throughout the text. French is used in Jonathan London's *The Sugaring-off Party* (Dutton 1995).
6. Learn the numbers in a different language.
7. Invite family members or any other persons who speak a different language to teach a simple poem or song to the class.
8. Have children who speak another language serve as tutors for the class in learning the numbers or the letters of the alphabet.
9. Bring foreign newspapers to the class. Have children browse through them at the writing center.
10. Learn to pronounce the titles of favorite story characters in another language.
11. Listen to vocal music in other languages.
12. Have someone translate the class names into another language.

Snapshot 4.5
Memories Stay With Us

What our teachers, classmates, and people in the neighborhood told us in our childhood is part of the baggage we carry with us through life. This is what Kathryn Noori (1995) found through the stories written by her college students, all prospective teachers. We chose two of them to share with you. Both stories concern African American students and reveal how negative and positive attitudes of others can influence our lives.

"I was always one of the African American students enrolled in the public school system [in New Mexico]. Not only was I aware of my 'blackness,' I was also reminded of it every time a fellow classmate or the teacher made a racist comment. I expected it from my classmates, more or less, but from my teacher—never. The remarks were often cruel and intended to make me feel like a second-class citizen (or, so I thought). For example, in 1st grade my teacher asked me to sing, 'Eenie, meenie, miny, moe, catch a nigger by the toe.' When I wanted to try out for the debate team in 5th grade, my teacher told me that people of color usually do best in athletics.

"Mrs. Gage, my 2nd grade teacher, was the person that inspired me to join the teaching profession. Mrs. Gage took a child with low self-esteem and boosted her [sic] to the sky. She was a Caucasian teacher who treated everyone equally. She didn't let your skin color determine her expectations and perceptions of you.

"Because of Mrs. Gage's kindness and caring, I have decided to become a teacher, a teacher who will encourage all students regardless of their gender, religion, race or background to be the very best they can be."

Source: Noori, K. (1995). Understanding others through stories. *Childhood Education*. 71:3 (pp. 134–136).

children asking why they are black or why they cannot have straight hair. On several occasions, one of the authors had four- and five-year-olds of Hispanic descent with Amerindian features question why their eyes were not clear like those of the dolls they play with. When asked why they preferred clear eyes, they simply said "Son mas bonitos" (They are prettier). In the same line, three-year-old African Americans told one of the authors that they wanted to have blond hair like hers instead of their own dark hair. Educators need to be particularly attentive to subtle messages that might convey a negative attitude toward a child's race or ethnic group. Formation of positive ideas about oneself is an important outcome of early childhood.

What are the physical characteristics children most frequently notice? Both the main-

Who Is the Child? Developmental Characteristics of Young Children

141

stream and culturally different child will notice the following:

1. hair texture
2. skin color
3. color and shape of eyes
4. tone of voice
5. height
6. orthopedic impairments
7. neurological impairments (particularly when they affect movement)

These physical characteristics are the same ones commonly found serving as a basis for racial slurs. However, when these are presented as unique because of one's heritage, children learn to accept them.

Children's Perceptions of Disabilities

Acceptance and integration of people with disabilities was mandated with the approval of Public Law 94-142 in 1975. Recently, the Individuals with Disabilities Act of 1990 reaffirmed the rights of the exceptional. As a result, children are more frequently exposed to people with different kinds of disabilities. This has increased the need to help children develop positive attitudes toward the disabled, a segment of the population contributing to diversity. As with racial awareness, children begin as early as age three to notice the physical disabilities of others. With the number of children with disabilities now in regular classrooms, mainstream children are very likely to be in contact with them. Since children are constant explorers, it is logical to find them asking and wondering about the physical differences they see in the disabled. These questions provide an opportunity to guide children to accept disabilities as another characteristic some people have. When trying to fight biases about the disabled, teachers need to act promptly when labeling or rejection is observed among children. This early response will stop misinter-

pretations and misled behaviors from becoming permanent.

Opportunities must be provided for children to clarify their perceptions and feelings about the disabled child or adult. An experience designed to create awareness about people with disabilities was successfully developed by Barry Friedman and Sharon Maneki (1995). They targeted blindness as the disability for their project since Maneki is a non-sighted educator. They selected a group of third graders to whom they taught the Braille alphabet. Maneki demonstrated not only how to write messages in Braille, but she also introduced the children to the special qualities of blind people. The experience helped children clarify their ideas and become more tolerant of the blind.

❖ Prosocial Skills: A Basis for Equity

One of the outcomes of the process of socioemotional development is the acquisition of prosocial behaviors and skills. Prosocial skills are defined as the ability to act in socially acceptable ways. Specifically, prosocial skills include behaviors such as respecting others and their personal property, developing empathy, exhibiting kindness, being helpful to others, defending others, and sharing with others. An important characteristic of prosocial skills is that they prepare children to do things for others without expecting rewards. Essential to children's development of prosocial behavior is their ability to see how others see a situation.

Taxonomy of Prosocial Skills

I. *Interacting with others (Beginning social skills)*
 ▪ listening
 ▪ exchanging ideas, talking in an amiable way
 ▪ following rules
 ▪ using courtesy words

■ using words to express appreciation
■ asking for help and for favors
■ showing respect for others

II. *Establishing relations with others: Making friends*
■ smiling (nonverbal behavior) to express a desire to make friends
■ greeting others
■ participating, working with others
■ sharing (expressing a desire to share; showing a willingness to share with others)
■ cooperating with others
■ being honest with others
■ using "feelings" vocabulary
■ accepting differences

III. *Showing empathy toward others*
■ showing concern for all
■ "reading" others to learn how they feel (perspective taking)
■ expressing feelings for others (going beyond the boundaries of ethnic or cultural differences)
■ taking action, directly or indirectly, to help others (advocacy)
■ demonstrating a caring, empathetic attitude
■ giving comfort to others (taking an initiative to help others)
■ dealing with differences and similarities (showing respect and tolerance toward differences, i.e., cultural dissimilarities)

(Derived from the ideas of Honig & Wittmer 1991; McGinnis & Goldstein 1991)

Being able to "walk in another person's shoes" enables the child to know what another person experiences. This perspective taking gives children the opportunity to see the problems of others and fuels the need for action on their part. The process of learning to take the perspective of another presents an optimal opportunity for multi-cultural teaching, particularly for dealing with how we think of others. Because prosocial behavior is a part of the socialization process, the classroom plays a leading role in its development. Careful planning targeted to fostering prosocial behaviors offers pertinent and developmentally appropriate ways to increase a child's awareness of diversity. Prosocial skills should be learned in meaningful contexts. When real-life situations are used, children learn to see the applicability of specific behaviors. For example, children need opportunities to examine how others feel when they use terms that are offensive or terms that reject them. Using literature is one of the ways to expose the class to issues involving the need to act prosocially. Well-selected stories offer an appropriate resource for prosocial development. Many different human circumstances are now portrayed in children's literature. Books like *My Friend Jacob* by Clifton (1980), which describes a friendship with a disabled person, and *Amelia's Road/El Camino de Amelia* by Linda Jacobs (1993), which describes the experiences of migrant families, offer excellent sources for discussion and for learning to accept others.

❖ Knowing the Child

Early educators have long known that quality services for children depend upon our knowledge of children. The same principle applies to teachers moving into multicultural teaching. Constructing a program that will effectively guide children to appreciate our social diversity begins by knowing the children we teach. This is the knowledge base for your decisions. The farther you move into multicultural education, the more you will need to know about the children in your classroom and community. Can you say that you already know them?

Who Is the Child? Developmental Characteristics of Young Children

143

❖ Things to Do . . .

1. Knowledge about what makes children uniquely individual is basic for an early childhood educator. Select three children from those you teach and begin learning about their individual characteristics. Examine their files to find data about physical traits, their families, and the elements of diversity (religion, ethnicity, language, social class, exceptionality, gender) that characterize them.

   Child's name: _____ Age: _____

Physical	Home/Family	Diversity Factors

2. The media is a powerful instrument for disseminating ideas about people. Observe any program designed for children for an hour during one week and determine what messages are presented about gender, ethnic groups, and the disabled. Include as part of your observation the commercials presented. Write a report about your findings. If you feel that changes are needed, propose them and explain your choices.
3. Considering the developmental needs of children in your class, design two experiences targeting differences that will help apply prosocial skills.

❖ Children's Literature Corner

Brenner, B. (1970). *Faces.* New York: Dutton Press.

Gabriel, V. (1982). *Ernest and Celestine.* New York: Greenwillow.

Klein, N. (1973). *Girls can be anything.* New York: Dutton Press.

Lexau, J. (1966). *The homework caper.* New York: Harper & Row.

Marzollo, J. (1980). *Amy goes fishing.* New York: Dial Books.

McGovern, A. (1969). *Black is beautiful.* New York: Four Winds.

Scott, A. (1972). *On mother's lap.* New York: McGraw-Hill.

Well, J. (1978). *Stanley and Rhoda.* New York: Dial Books.

Williams, V. (1982). *A chair for my mother.* New York: Greenwillow.

❖ References

American Association of University Women. (1994). Equitable treatment of girls and boys in the classroom. In E. Nunn & C. Boyatzis (eds.). *Child growth and development 94/95* (pp. 67–72). Guilford, CT: Dushkin.

Anselmo, S., & Franz, W. (1995). *Early childhood development. Prenatal through age eight* (2nd ed.). Englewood Cliffs, NJ: Merrill.

Arnberg, L. (1991). *Raising children bilingually: The preschool years.* Clevedon, England: Multilingual Matters.

Banks, J. (1992, November/December). Reducing prejudice in children. Guidelines from research. *Social Studies and the Young Learner* (pp. 3–5).

Bauermeister, J., Berríos, V., Acevedo, L., & Gordon, M. (1990). Some issues and instruments for the assessment of attention deficit hyperactivity in Puerto Rican children. *Journal of Clinical Psychology 19* (pp. 9–16).

Berger, K. (1993). *The developing person. Through childhood and adolescence.* New York: Worth.

Berk, L. (1993). *Infants, children and adolescents.* Boston, MA: Allyn & Bacon.

Berns, R. M. (1994) *Topical child development.* Albany, NY: Delmar.

Bredekamp, S. (ed.). (1987). *Developmentally appropriate practice in early childhood programs serving children birth through age 8.* Washington, DC: National Association for the Education of Young Children.

Chomsky, N. (1957). *Aspects of a theory of syntax.* Cambridge, MA: MIT Press.

Derman-Sparks, L., & A.B.C. Task Force. (1989). *Antibias curriculum. Tools for empowering young children.* Washington, DC: National Association for the Education of Young Children.

Elkin, F., & Handel, G. (1989). *The child and society: The process of socialization* (5th ed.). New York: Random House.

Erikson, E. (1963). *Childhood and society.* New York: Basic Books.

Friedman, B., & Maneki, S. (1995). Teaching children with sight about Braille. *Childhood Education* 71: 3 (pp. 137–139).

Garbarino, J. (1992). *Children and families in the social environment* (2nd ed.). New York: Aldine de Gruyter.

Honig, A. S., & Wittmer, D. S. (Nov. 1991). *Helping children become more prosocial: Tips for teachers.* Paper presented at the Annual Meeting of the National Association for the Education of Young Children. Denver, CO.

Jacobs, L. (1993) *El camino de Amelia.* New York: Lee & Law Books.

Katz, P. A. (1982). Development of children's racial awareness and outergroup attitudes. In L. Katz (ed.). *Current topics in early childhood education.* Vol. 4. Norwood, NJ: Ablex.

Kendall, F. (1983). *Diversity in the classroom. A multicultural approach to the education of young children.* New York: Teachers College Press.

King, E. W., Chipman, M., & Cruz-Janzen, M. (1994). *Educating young children in a diverse society.* Needham Heights, MA: Allyn & Bacon.

Klein, N. (1973). *Girls can be anything.* New York: E. P. Dutton.

Kohlberg, L. (1966). A cognitive-developmental analysis of children's sex roles, concepts and attitudes. In

E. Maccoby (ed.). *The development of sex differences.* Stanford, CA: Stanford University Press.

Konner, M. (1991). *Childhood. A multicultural view.* Boston, MA: Little, Brown & Co.

Ludlow, B., & Berkeley, T. (1994). Expanding the perceptions of developmentally appropriate practice. Changing theoretical perspectives. In B. Mallory & R. New (eds.). *Diversity and developmentally appropriate practice. Challenges for early childhood education.* New York: Teachers College Press.

McGinnis, E., & Goldstein, A. (1991). *Skillstreaming in early childhood. Teaching prosocial skills to the preschool and kindergarten child.* Champagne, IL: Research Press.

Miller, P. (1989). *Theories of developmental psychology.* New York: W. H. Freeman.

Noori, K. (1995). Understanding others through stories. *Childhood Education* 71: 3 (pp. 134–136).

Phillips, C. (1988). Nurturing diversity for today's children and tomorrow's leaders. *Young Children* 43: 2 (pp. 42–47).

Robles de Meléndez, W. (1992, July). "Creating the multicultural environment." Paper presented at the annual conference of the Florida Department of Education, Tampa.

Shapiro, L. (1994). Guns and dolls. In E. Nunn & C. Boyatzis (eds.). *Child growth and development 94/95* (pp. 140–143). Guilford, CT: Dushkin.

Streitmatter, J. (1994). *Towards class and gender equity in the classroom.* Albany, NY: State University of New York Press.

Thorne, B. (1994). Girls and boys together. . . . but mostly apart: Gender arrangements in elementary schools. In E. Nunn & C. Boyatzis (eds.). *Child growth and development 94/95.* Guilford, CT: Dushkin.

Zigler, E. F., & Stevenson, M. F. (1993) *Children in a changing world. Development and social issues* (2nd ed.). Pacific Grove, CA: Brooks/Cole.

Zolotow, C. (1972). *William's doll.* New York: Harper & Row.

"The rhetoric of equality assumes that all Americans have equal chances to succeed regardless of their actual station or circumstance in life."

Robert A. DeVillar (1994)

PART II

Exploring the Roots of Multicultural Education: Issues and Directions

From Barbara's Journal

"Now, I know that we are all products of our cultures. One of my goals is to teach my students to be proud of who they are. Until now, I've ignored the children's realities because I was too busy teaching the only way I knew how. By doing that I managed to ignore their worlds in my classroom.

"This morning when I asked one of my colleagues about teaching multiculturally, she gave me a curriculum guide from a publisher. However, it's not what I need. I want to see how other people teach about diversity, I need to have choices. I need to go back to the library. But first, I'll go to see my friends, Dennis and Belen. They said they will tell me how and why multicultural education started. Maybe this will answer some of my questions."

Barbara

"But could I be heard by this great nation, I would call to mind the sublime and glorious truths with which at its birth, it saluted a listening world. . . . Put away your race prejudice. Banish the idea that one class must rule over another. Recognize . . . that the rights of the humblest citizen are as worthy of protection as are those of the highest, and . . . your Republic will stand and flourish forever."

Frederick Douglass (1817–1895)

CHAPTER 5

Everything Started When . . . Tracing the Beginnings of Multicultural Education

In this chapter we will:

- discuss the historical evolution of multicultural education
- examine the factors that prompted the emergence of multiculturalism in education
- ponder how the civil rights movement influenced education reform
- identify the individuals who pioneered the multiculturalism of American education

Key concepts:

- civil rights movement
- equity and equality
- educational reform
- multicultural education

❖ Setting the Stage

We Believe in Children

Perhaps one of the best traits that defines early childhood educators is the fact that they are people with strong beliefs. First, they believe in children; second, they believe they can make a difference in the lives of children. They also believe in the inner beauty and potential for success every child brings to the classroom. Early childhood teachers are also dreamers. They dream all children will develop and flourish to give our society a hope for a future of continued social and national progress. Such people who dream and believe in children are committed to equality as their fundamental ideal. Early childhood teachers also realize that equality is still not fully evident in many young children's programs and services. Although considerable progress has been achieved, much still remains to be done not only in our legislatures but also in our communities and in our classrooms. Early childhood teachers believe that some of the most important victories for equal rights are won in young children's classrooms.

Understanding humankind's quest for equality will help early childhood teachers gain a better appreciation for the efforts of multicultural educators. In this chapter we will take you through time and acquaint you with some key events that have shaped the paradigm of multicultural education: equality.

Equality: A Long-term Quest

More than a thousand years ago in Greece, Protagoras, the first known professional teacher, stated that all human beings, if offered adequate learning opportunities, were capable of learning (Smith & Smith 1994). This early Greek educator

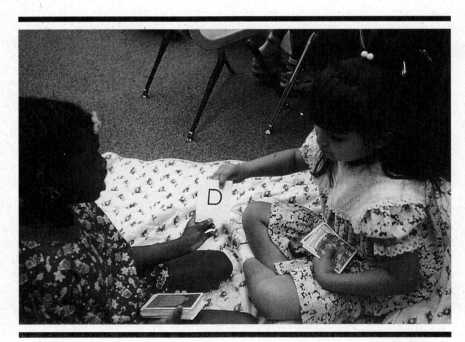

"D" is for Diversity.

also asserted that ALL individuals had the capability to "gain excellence" (Smith & Smith 1994, p. 12, emphasis added). Today, over fifteen hundred years later, those who support equality in education in our country share that same belief. Commitment to equality is also a core principle of those who advocate multicultural education. Like Protagoras, the multiculturalists believe that all children, regardless of their ethnicity, exceptionality, social class, or any other characteristic, have the right to the optimum educational environment to develop to their fullest potential.

We recognize that the future is dependent on the ability of today's children to successfully face tomorrow's challenges. Education is the tool society provides to accomplish that mission. All efforts to guarantee and support equality and equity in education are an investment in our survival as a strong advanced society. Implementing an effective multicultural education system will facilitate the successful management of the diverse environment in which we live. Quality multicultural education for all children must become one of the mandates of democracy as the United States prepares to enter the new century.

In Search of Educational Equality

"... inequality of rights has been the cause of all disturbances, insurrections, and civil wars that ever happened."

Thomas Payne

The emergence of multicultural education in the United States began with a belief in equality. Equality in the educational context implies providing opportunities to all individuals to build their own future. It also implies the availability of educational services to all individuals regardless of their social background. This ideal is one upon which American public education was built. Since the days of Horace Mann, Americans have believed that universal education is a way to "open

up the opportunities to get ahead" (Jarret 1971, p. 15). However, events have shown that this ideal has not always been attainable. Educational opportunities in the United States have been and continue to be plagued with discrimination against those who because of their social status, gender, race, or ethnicity differ from mainstream American culture. One only needs to look at some of our communities to realize that children are not being equally served. In cities and towns across our nation, hundreds of dilapidated buildings house thousands of families with children. Examples abound in the violent inner-city neighborhoods where children fear for their safety and often have to defend their lives. Lacking essential services including access to recreational areas and appropriately equipped and staffed classrooms, many of them struggle every day.

Full access to equal school opportunities has been a mandate since the 1954 landmark ruling in *Brown vs. the Board of Education* affirmed that segregated schools do not provide equal opportunity. Since then equality in education has been a zealously pursued goal. Today, it is the justification behind the efforts undertaken by those who have embraced the reform movement for multicultural education.

Looking Back Through Time

Perhaps you have wondered how long American education has focused on the elements of multiculturalism. You may have asked yourself why there are still some educators who do not adhere to its principles. The answers to these and other similar questions may lie in another important dimension of multicultural education: its chronology. As a strategy, multicultural education is a fairly recent movement, even though children of many nationalities and social characteristics have sat together in classrooms all over the country for more than two centuries. However, in the past, recognition of their characteristics, needs, and

IN ACTION . . . *Equity in Education*

Kenneth Howe, in an article on equal educational opportunity and multiculturalism, establishes three relevant issues embedded in any interpretation of equality of educational opportunities. As you read them, think about the implications they have for the education of young children.

1. Availability of desirable opportunities and the freedom to select them
2. Educational opportunities that enable the individual to succeed in life
3. Having responsible adults who will guarantee children access to equal educational opportunities

▎ Which of these three issues in your opinion is most important?

▎ In what ways are these issues related to what teachers do in the classrooms?

▎ As an early childhood professional, do you feel that children are provided with equal opportunities? Explain.

Source: Howe, K. (1992). Liberal democracy, equal educational opportunity and the challenge of multiculturalism. *American Educational Research Journal, 29* (pp. 455–470).

requirements in an effort to appropriately serve them was seldom a part of the educational agenda. The American education system was founded on the idea of equity but it was also rooted in the "melting pot" philosophy where all individuals were expected to shed their cultures of origin and become "Americans." Once the differences were melted, individuals gained the right to be part of American society. Today, we have come to realize that people can keep their individual cultures while upholding the principles of American democracy. This new vision of assimilation is much closer to the basic principles of democracy that comprise the ideological foundations of this country.

Once Upon a Time . . . Establishing the Beginning

Time exerts great influence in shaping and establishing models and patterns of movement. This is also the case with the multicultural movement. A look into American educational files reveals that prior to 1978 the *Education Index* did not contain multicultural education in its listings (Baruth &

WORKING GLOSSARY

▎ **Multicultural Education**—a process of comprehensive and basic education for all students. It challenges racism and other forms of discrimination in schools and society and accepts and affirms the pluralism (ethnic, racial, linguistic, religious, economic, gender, exceptionalities) that students, their communities, and teachers represent (Nieto 1992, p. 307).

Snapshot 5.1
Mason Street School

The Mason Street School was the first schoolhouse built in San Diego, California, in 1865. The first teacher of the school was Mary Chase Walker from Massachusetts. She described her arrival in San Diego and her early experiences at the school.

"I arrived in the bay of San Diego on the morning of July 5, 1865. It was a most desolate looking landscape. The hills were brown and barren; not a tree or green thing was to be seen. Of all the dilapidated, miserable looking places I have ever seen this was the worst. The buildings were nearly all of adobe, one story in height, with no chimneys. Some of the roofs were covered with tile and some with earth. The first night of my stay at the hotel a donkey came under my window and saluted with an unearthly bray. The fleas were plentiful and hungry. Mosquitoes were also in attendance. An Indian man did the cooking and an Irish boy waited on me at the table, and also gave me the news of the town.

"The landlord told me I could go into the kitchen and cook whatever I wanted if I didn't like the Indian's style and I availed myself of the privilege. I rented two rooms in the Robinson house for $2 a month. My school was composed mostly of Spanish and half-breed children, with a few English and several Americans. I aimed to teach what would be most meaningful to them, namely reading, spelling, arithmetic, and how to write letters. At recess the Spanish girls smoked cigaritas and the boys amused themselves by lassoing pigs, hens, etc. The Spanish children were very irregular in their attendance at school on account of so many fiestas and amusements of various kinds. For a week before a bullfight the boys were more or less absent, watching preparations, such as fencing up the streets leading to the plaza."

Source: San Diego County Historical Days Association in Wortham, S. C. (1992). *Childhood 1892–1992*. Wheaton, MD: Association for Childhood Education.

Manning 1992). A perusal of materials and titles published prior to the 1970s confirms that little or no attention was given to this topic. For instance, Frances Kendall in her important work, *Diversity in the Classroom: A Multicultural Approach to the Education of Young Children* published in 1983, terms multicultural education "a new approach to education" (p. 3). She also makes reference to all the research done in the 1970s, thus establishing the time line for the emergence of the body of investigation on the topic.

A Time Line of Multicultural Education

The struggle for educational equality through the ages has been zealously embraced by many. It has

---

FIGURE 5.1 Famous advocates of equity (fifth century B.C. to nineteenth century)

Ancient Greece	*Rome*	*Europe (16th–18th century)*	*The Americas (19th century)*
Protagoras	Quintilian	Comenius	Maestro Cordero
Plato	Cicero	Rousseau	S. Winnemucca
		Pestalozzi	M. Bethune
		Wollstonecraft	B. Washington
			F. Jackson
			J. Addams

---

also been the goal of many pacesetters in the field of early childhood education (Figure 5.1). In this section we will journey through time to find the beginnings of education for all.

❖ Early Efforts Toward Equality in Education

As you recall from Chapter 2, multicultural education is based on establishment of educational equality for all children. The concept of value of the individual and respect for human diversity has evolved slowly over the ages. Equality of educational opportunity may be a recent goal, but the notion of universal education has its roots in antiquity.

Awareness Begins in the Ancient Times

The first journey takes us to the classical times, to ancient Greece of twenty-five centuries ago. Over twenty-five centuries ago, the Greek philosopher Plato argued that education of all citizens was the one "great thing" required to assure a just and effective society. In his treatise *The Republic*, Plato outlined a society that was elitist but based on merit. Therefore, he held that each individual must receive the same initial education in the process of identifying abilities. Some would stop their training at a certain point, others would move on to leadership positions, but all would be trained as citizens. Plato asserted that women should have the same educational opportunities as men, since women had the same diversity of abilities, although at an in-

IN ACTION . . . *Checking On Our Personal Knowledge about Multicultural Education*

▋ When did you first hear about multicultural education?

▋ Do you recall any instances in which your teachers adapted the curriculum to examine perspectives other than that of the majority?

ferior level. In the context of his time the notion of educating all citizens, including women, was radical. Plato's idea had no impact on his fellow Athenians, but centuries later his work would be cited by the philosophers whose ideas influenced American democracy.

Power (1975) informs us that Plato spent little time discussing the early childhood years; however, he did advocate the use of games and toys during years 3–6. He also recognized the importance of monitoring school attendance and providing special education for the gifted. Plato demanded a state-funded, state-controlled system of education, and the use of state-approved teachers. This is the first time in history that teachers were viewed as professionals in need of professional status.

Ancient Rome also left a legacy of educational equality. In the Roman Empire most children attended public school, including girls. However, the debate over public versus private education continued for centuries after public schools were established. Two important figures of ancient Rome, Marcus Tillius Cicero (106–13 B.C.), known as Cicero, and Marcus Fabius Quintilianus (35–97 A.D.), known as Quintilian, proposed relevant changes to their education system. Both are credited with establishing the theoretical foundations of the Western education system.

Cicero, an accomplished Roman lawyer, orator, philosopher, and statesman, felt compelled to reform the Roman education system. In his landmark work *De Oratore*, published in 55 B.C., he outlined the basic principles necessary for an or-

ator's education. He believed that the purpose of education should be to create true orators "capable of thinking, speaking, and acting in a praiseworthy way" (Power 1975, p. 174). In his view, the ideal educated individual was an orator and a philosopher.

The fact that Cicero believed in the education of the elite and did not concentrate his theories on education of young children should not take away from his contributions to *how* and *when* subjects were to be taught. He proposed that the secondary schools address both eloquence and knowledge in teaching the young. A firm believer of educating through practical methods, he urged teachers to use a content with real-life applications. For the teaching of history, he also suggested using what today we call a literacy-based approach. In this way Cicero introduced pragmatism into education by replacing the teaching of history through literature. Cicero also promoted the nurturing of Greek culture and bilingualism. It was largely through his efforts that Romans initiated bilingual education and realized the importance of maintaining other people's native cultures. In the beginning of the third century, bilingual textbooks in Greek and Latin were initiated in Roman provinces (Marrou 1977). In fact, part of the Roman strategy for ruling the vast lands they conquered was to allow the inhabitants to keep their native languages and their traditions while acquiring the new customs of the empire. Needless to say, Rome became the strongest political power of ancient times (MacNeil 1989; Smith & Smith 1994).

IN ACTION . . . *Lessons from the Past*

▮ Considering Plato's ideas in the context of his times, what would you say is his contribution to the search for educational equality?

IN ACTION . . . *Roman Contributions*

▌ In what ways did Rome contribute to the search for educational equality?

▌ In today's context, what was Rome's most significant contribution?

In Quintilian we find one of the earliest pioneer educators to recognize the value of early education. Quintilian, born in Calagurris, Spain, was educated in Rome and returned to his native Spain to practice the arts and oratory. He was asked to return to Rome to be a pleader in the courts. Shortly thereafter, as laws governing education changed, Quintilian became Rome's first public school teacher. He retired from teaching and devoted himself to writing his 12-volume *Instituto Oratorio,* the most complete treatise on Roman education. Quintilian's theories of education outlined in this work set the pattern for Latin grammar schools for centuries to come. Unlike Cicero, Quintilian devoted much of his work to the education of young children. He believed in the importance of parental involvement in educating and shaping the lives of young children. This is the first time informal education was given a prominent role in early childhood. All his life he opposed corporal punishment and promoted the use of play as an important learning medium for young children. Quintilian was the first educator to emphasize the need for varied methodologies to accommodate the differences among children.

In his words, such differences were relevant to the methods used and the content of the curriculum. This part of his theory laid the foundation for humanism in education. In Quintilian's view, a good teacher had to be moral, friendly, clear, generous, and one who gave praise, characteristics that today we also seek in teachers of the young.

The Quest for Equality in Modern Times

Modern history, from the fifteenth through the eighteenth century, shows that equality had yet to be attained as of the Age of Enlightenment in the seventeenth century. Despite the efforts of many individuals, the world was still full of examples of cruel and unfair social treatment. The harsh social inequalities in Europe and the Americas continued into the eighteenth century and culminated in the French and the American revolutions, whose spirit of liberty and equality spread all over the world. The 1700s and the 1800s were also periods of unprecedented social, economic, and intellectual growth in the Western world. This period was also noted for the progressivism in educational thought that later formed the foundation

WORKING GLOSSARY

▌ **Equality**—when all individuals in a society are provided with equal access to the same opportunities and resources.

▌ **Educational Equity**—establishing the same educational resources and opportunities for all children, despite their diverse characteristics.

of the contemporary education systems in Europe and America.

To learn about the evolution of multicultural education, let us look back at a few pioneers who raised their voices in the past in support of educational equity. Believing in their cause, these leaders fought for the welfare of the children of their times, often risking their own lives and personal safety. You will see how, despite the differences in time that separate them, the advocates of multicultural education are characterized by the following:

1. awareness of inequality in educational opportunities or services;
2. recognition of unfair treatment based on gender, social class, or ethnic origin; and
3. a proactive attitude that led them to take action to resolve or modify the existing unfair conditions.

The Work of Comenius

Living in seventeenth century Europe when education was still an exclusive privilege of the wealthy, John Amos Comenius (1592–1670) was an advocate of the rights of all people to be educated. Known as the father of modern education, Comenius was born in Nivnitz, Moravia (today's Czech Republic). A Protestant scholar, Comenius is best known as an educational reformer whose greatest work is *The Great Didactic*. Although considered by historians as an educator, Comenius was primarily a clergyman and an ordained priest whose motivation in all his work was to serve God.

Education in the seventeenth century was grounded in realism. This meant putting the curriculum, methods, and students in direct contact with reality. Comenius discouraged teaching of matter that was not practical and directly related to life, reminiscent of today's effort to bring relevancy into education. He also emphasized equal education for all children, sequential learning, and the use of well-grounded lesson plans.

Comenius proposed levels of education which consisted of the Mother School, covering the period from birth to age 6; the Vernacular School from 6–12; the Latin School from 12–18, and the University School from 18–24. The Mother School curriculum was to be focused primarily on associating things with words. In the Vernacular School reading, writing, mother tongue, counting, morals, geography, topography, world history, religion, and the mechanical arts were the main subjects. Reflecting the ideas of his time, education of girls was to cease at this level. The Latin School, attended by boys, taught grammar, rhetoric, arithmetic, music, geometry, physics, astronomy, morals, history, religion, and theology. This was preparation for the University School, where the sole purpose of teaching and learning was research for discovery of new knowledge.

Much of Comenius' life was dedicated to advocating the rights of children and individuals. He defended the rights of poor children to become literate individuals and to possess basic knowledge and skills. His ideas were revolutionary for his time and it was not until the nineteenth century that his recommendations were implemented. Today, Comenius' beliefs in the responsibility of the government to provide access to education to every individual underlie fundamental educational principles in the United States.

Other Leading Figures of the 18th Century

The struggle for equality and liberty dominated the eighteenth century. Jean Jacques Rousseau (1712–1778), born of Huguenot parents in Geneva, Switzerland, became one of the most influential Frenchmen of his time. A philosopher and a political thinker, Rousseau became best known for his works *The Social Contract* and *Emile*, where he called for reforms in education and politics. His ideas about the rights of man and the responsibilities of society inspired many leaders of the French Revolution, and literally

FOCUS ON CLASSROOM PRACTICES

INTRODUCING CHILDREN TO THE CONCEPT OF INEQUALITY

An important step in teaching with a multicultural perspective is helping children develop an awareness of inequality. This is a topic that many times has been avoided in younger children's classrooms. Many consider inequality a concept that eludes the young child. However, because there are circumstances in the classroom and in the community that demonstrate inequality, children are already exposed to it. Waiting until a child enters the upper grades to bring attention to this reality is not wise. Research says that it is during the early childhood years that the basis for what is good and bad is set. This is why the curriculum needs to incorporate experiences where young children can gain a gradual awareness of their reality.

Teachers can use daily events to help children develop an awareness of inequality. Whether in the classroom or in the community, opportunities for designing such experiences abound.

Here are some tips for designing the content for teaching young children about inequality.

Suggestions for Designing a Content on Inequality

1. The first thing to do is to substitute the term "inequality" for the concept of "what is fair and unfair." This is something most young children understand early in life and can relate to.
2. Begin by identifying the areas where the child is likely to experience situations of unfairness. This will define your content. You will find examples of it in events and places familiar to the child. For example, consider the following contexts and possible scenarios:

   ▪ At home: Many chores are assigned to one family member while others do little or nothing; children leave their room disorganized and a parent has to clean it up; one family member gets to choose all the TV programs; a pet's water dish is dry because its owner does not fill it.

   ▪ In the neighborhood: A group of children make fun of an older man because of the way he walks; people refuse to say hello to the new neighbors because they are African American; people in the neighborhood want to close a shelter for the homeless; on a bus, people take the seats assigned for the elderly and disabled who then have to stand.

   ▪ In the classroom: A child refuses to let another child play with the set of Legos™; girls in the housekeeping area send boys away; some children refuse to wait their turn in the lunchroom; some children refuse to play with a child because she "speaks funny"; a child hides another child's pair of eyeglasses; children make fun of a family member because of the way she dresses; some children use racial epithets.

Focus on Classroom Practices **continued**

▮ Television programs: Consider the kind of programs children watch. Make an effort to watch them as well. This will alert you to programs whose content is likely to impact the class. If you find they are talking about a special show or program, or if the parents bring it to your attention, plan to discuss it. Discussion about a specific show or program should only take place with the whole class if the majority of children show a reaction to it.

3. Make a list of those situations that could happen more frequently. Target those first. Periodically plan weekly activities to deal with the target situations. However, it is important to remember that when a situation happens, it must be dealt with immediately. Having the children's attention and interest is essential for exploration.

4. Aside from your planned activities, make use of teachable moments. Nothing proves more effective than the magical moment when we are trying to discover the whys behind an event.

5. Select appropriate literature. Using the list of areas and topics you chose in step 2, find related literature. Today, there is a wide variety of titles for initiating discussions on practically every topic.

6. Plan concrete, child-appropriate activities. Because unfairness is an abstract concept, design experiences in ways children can relate to it literally. Remember to consider that children learn through their senses and use a variety of ways to present and foster interest in the topic.

7. Use personna dolls to introduce difficult topics particularly when they involve a child in your class (Derman-Sparks 1989). Also, use the dolls to discuss topics children may have seen on television and which require clarification.

8. Become a perceptive observer. If you have good observational skills, you will see the curriculum sprouting all around you. Observe particularly what children do and say and the gestures they make during free-choice play. Listen to what they tell you while discussing a story. These comments will let you know how children react among themselves and what levels of awareness they exhibit.

revolutionized the world and ignited the flame of liberty in Europe and in the Americas. Never before in the history of humankind had people felt the urge to be accepted and recognized as unique individuals and as equals (Baigorri 1983). Rousseau's ideas constitute the fundamental postulates of the multicultural education movement.

From the files of early childhood pioneers, we find another individual who championed the rights of all children to obtain equal educational opportunities. Johann Pestalozzi, better known for the pedagogical method that bears his name, based his ideas on the essential principle that "all people, including the poor, could and should learn" (Smith & Smith 1994, p. 190). Pestalozzi is credited with translating "Rousseau's ideas into practice, devoting his life to education of the poor" (Wortham 1992, p. 1).

An Early Defender of Women's Rights

Nearly two centuries ago, social activist Mary Wollstonecraft wrote about the unfair educational and social treatment of women in her native Great Britain. In the eighteenth century, when women were not considered as capable as men, she strongly believed women deserved equal rights. She thought women of all classes deserved better education and equal rights with men. In her passionate plea, Wollstonecraft advocated a national coeducation system where boys and girls of all social classes would receive the same kind of education (Smith & Smith 1994). An early defender of equality, her ideas opened up the debate over the rights of all individuals, regardless of their gender and social class.

People of the Americas Blaze the Trail

The names of those who fought for equality in the New World are many. Their work has become a prototype and an inspiration for all those who continue the task today. Among those to be remembered, we find men and women of both humble and noble origins. One common thread links them: their pursuit of equality and freedom for all.

What follows are a few examples of the accomplishments of some advocates of equality in education from different parts of the Americas. Among the more illustrious names are Rafael Cordero, Sarah Winnemucca, Fanny Jackson Coppin, Booker T. Washington, Jane Addams, and Miles Cary. They all honor the cause of multiculturalism and diversity in the United States.

These individuals embody the struggle of ethnic minorities in America. They are also considered pioneers of early childhood education during its early beginnings in our country.

School for the Poor

Primary education as we know it today, was a privilege of few during the nineteenth century. Illiteracy was rampant, especially among the poor, all over the world. On Luna Street of nineteenth century San Juan, Puerto Rico, Rafael Cordero, the son of free blacks and a cigar maker by trade, opened a school where he taught children of the poor and the rich (Gómez Tejera & Cruz López 1970). In his spare time, the humble "Maestro Cordero" helped the children learn to read and write, turning his tobacco workshop into a school.

When Cordero started his school, there was no official elementary education in the then Spanish ruled island of Puerto Rico.* Education was offered by private teachers who left out the children of the poor and of the blacks. Aware of their need, Cordero, whose parents were former slaves, began offering classes in 1810, 35 years before the Spanish government officially instituted elementary education (Ribes Tovar 1973). He started teaching in the town of San Germán,

---

*As a result of the Spanish-American War, Puerto Rico became part of the United States in 1898. Defeated by the United States, Spain ceded the island to the Americans. Since then, Puerto Rico has been a part of the United States. In 1917 Puerto Ricans were granted American citizenship.

later moving his school to San Juan, where he taught until his death in 1868. Hundreds of children learned to read and write with Maestro Cordero, who never charged for his lessons. Cordero's sister, also a teacher, contributed to the education of girls, directing a school in the San Juan area (Gómez Tejera & Cruz López 1970). Rafael Cordero is still remembered as the pioneer of elementary education for the humble in Puerto Rico.

Native American Champions the Rights of Her People

Sarah Winnemucca left an invaluable legacy of tenacity and faith in the education of Native American children. According to her biographer, "few people of any race have lived such a life" (Morrison 1990, p. 160). A writer and founder of the first school for Native Americans, she was described by her friend Elizabeth Peabody as the "Indian Joan of Arc" (Morrison 1990, p. 160).

Chief Sarah Winnemucca, daughter of a Paiute chief, was born in the Southwest, perhaps in 1844, and learned early in life about prejudice and discrimination. Sarah's greatest desire was to learn (Smith & Smith 1994). However, after enrolling in a convent school in California, she and her sister had to leave because of opposition by white parents. After moving back to her native Nevada, she had to work as a domestic, but she spent most of her salary on books. Sarah taught herself and became, years later, a translator and a spokesperson for the Paiutes.

Sarah later became a school assistant (Morrison 1990). In her travels in the East, she met Elizabeth Peabody, a leader in kindergarten education, and the widow of Horace Mann. Her friendship with these two influential women led her to organize a school for the Paiute children in 1886 using the proceeds of her book, *Life Among the Paiutes: Their Wrongs and Claims* (Morrison 1990). Unfortunately, her school had a brief life, closing a year later.

A New Beginning for African Americans

The education of African Americans was given a start with the abolition of slavery in the United States. Determined to become a productive part of American society and to build a future, African Americans embraced education with great eagerness. Formally, education for African Americans was undertaken by the government as part of the Reconstruction efforts after the Civil War. Under the auspices of the federal government, thousands of teachers arrived in the South, a result of the fifty-one voluntary Freedmen's Aid Societies that were formed (Smith & Smith 1994a). A distinctive attitude characterized the former slaves who attended these schools. They "emerged with a strong belief in the desirability of learning to read and write" (Anderson 1988, p. 5). This desire became the force that drove them to give their strongest support to the schooling movement. Booker T. Washington spoke of this eagerness, saying: "It was a whole race trying to go to school. Few were too young, and none too old, to make an attempt to learn" (Anderson 1988, p. 5). In the latter part of the nineteenth century, higher education would also become a reality when many schools and colleges were opened for the now-free African Americans.

The initiative of the African American community to provide education to all its members inspired many. Among the names to remember are Fanny Jackson Coppin, Mary McLeod Bethune, and Booker T. Washington.

The efforts of Fanny Jackson Coppin and Booker T. Washington, initially oriented toward vocational education, were the origin of two of today's most important institutions of higher learning: Cheney State College and Tuskegee University. In a time when American society was still coping with the realities of accepting the former slaves as equal members of the nation, Coppin and Washington proved that minorities also had a right to higher education. There are aspects of both Coppin's and Washington's lives that accent

---

Snapshot 5.2
Determination Was Her Name: Mary McLeod Bethune

Born in South Carolina in 1875, Mary was always a special person. She was the first one of fifteen children to be born out of slavery. The freedom that met her at her birth would stamp her life. Soon the little girl would show her special gifts. With the desire to learn burning strongly inside her, Mary proved to be an excellent student. Although she was eager to continue studying, she was without financial resources, and her teacher recommended her as a candidate for a scholarship. After winning the scholarship, she attended the Scotia Seminary in North Carolina and later the Moody Bible Institute in Chicago. Unable to realize her dream of becoming a missionary in Africa, Mary began a career in American education that would never end.

In 1899, she and her husband moved to Palatka, Florida, and opened a mission school, where she began to realize her true purpose.

Soon after, Mary decided to act to change the pitiful conditions of blacks in Daytona, where there was no formal school for black children. At the time, Daytona was becoming a winter resort visited by many wealthy people, particularly Northerners. Calling upon their generosity, Mary was able to open a school on October 3, 1904. The Daytona Normal and Industrial Institute for Girls opened with five students, aged eight to twelve. It started a tradition of opportunities and hope for African Americans. In the beginning students and teachers raised funds by selling ice cream and sweet potato pies. Mary's hard work and the support of many people, like John D. Rockefeller and James Gamble of Procter and Gamble, made the dream possible. Years later her school, then a college, joined the Cookman Institute, becoming the now prestigious Bethune-Cookman College.

Source: McKissack, P., & McKissack, F. (1992). *Cornerstones of freedom: Mary McLeod Bethune.* Chicago, IL: Children's Press.

---

what they believed, as well as what they accomplished. They also speak of a determination not only to better themselves, but also of their desire to make a difference in the lives of people in their communities.

From Slavery to Productive Service
Born a slave, Fanny Jackson Coppin gained her freedom when her hardworking aunt saved $125 and purchased Fanny's liberty. Years later her aunt helped her finish college, making Fanny one of the first black women to receive a degree (Smith & Smith 1994a). A college diploma opened doors to a distinguished career in education. The pinnacle of her career came while she was the principal of the Institute for Colored Youth in Philadelphia. Under her leadership, the Institute became a leading school for vocational

FOCUS ON CLASSROOM PRACTICES

LEARNING ABOUT THE MEN AND WOMEN WHO FOUGHT INEQUALITY

Children can increase their awareness of inequality when they learn what it actually does to real people in the context of daily life. Because literature has a special appeal for children, the use of biographical literature and historical fiction is particularly effective. One of the benefits of biographies is that they help children build a sense of the different kinds of inequalities real people have experienced. When concretely presented (using artifacts, role-playing), historical fiction is a "true voyage into time." A list of suggested titles is included here. Ask the school librarian and check your local library for additional and recent titles.

Suggested Titles

*Ashabranner, B. (1986). *Children of the Mayas: A Guatemalan Indian Odyssey.* New York: Dodd.

Bains, R. (1982). *Harriet Tubman: The road to freedom.* New York: Troll.

Carrick, C. (1985). *Stay away from Simon!* New York: Clarion.

*Davis, L. (1982). *Behind barbed wires: The imprisonment of Japanese Americans during World War II.* New York: Harper & Row.

DeKay, J. (1969). *Meet Martin Luther King Jr.* New York: Random House.

Delacorte-Taylor, M. (1987). *The gold Cadillac.* New York: Dial Books.

Franchere, R. (1970). *Cesar Chavez.* New York: Crowell.

Greenfield, E. (1973). *Rosa Parks.* New York: Crowell.

Howard, E. (1987) *Edith herself.* New York: Atheneum.

Monjo, F. (1970). *The drinking gourd.* New York: Harper & Row.

Neimark, A. (1983). *A deaf child listened: Thomas Gallaudet, pioneer in American education.* New York: Morrow.

Patterson, L. (1965). *Little Frederick Douglass.* New York: Garrard.

Stanley, D., and Vennema, P. (1988). *Shaka: King of the Zulus.* New York: Morrow.

Wolf, B. (1978). *In this proud land: The story of a Mexican-American family.* New York: Lippincott.

*Titles are appropriate for elementary-age children; however, teachers can retell these stories.

studies. In the 1950s the Institute became Cheney State College.

Booker T. Washington learned he was a free person when "a Union officer appeared on his owner's porch and read the Emancipation Proclamation" (Smith & Smith 1994, p. 335). This marked the beginning of a courageous and historic life for young Booker T. In 1872, Washington started his formal education at the Hampton Normal and Agricultural Institute. Smith and Smith (1994) write that "his entrance exam was very unique: the principal asked him to clean a room" (p. 336). Dedicated to his goal, Booker dusted and cleaned and passed the "exam." Despite hard work and disappointments, he never lost hope and became a brilliant teacher. Today, Booker T. Washington is remembered as the founder of the prestigious Tuskegee University in Alabama.

Hull House: The Work of Jane Addams

The founder of Hull House, Jane Addams, was born in Cedarville, Illinois, in 1860. Born to a well-off family, Jane attended college and traveled throughout Europe. It was during her travels that she became aware of the needs of the poor and witnessed the efforts of some dedicated individuals to alleviate their problems. After visiting the People's Palace, built in one of the poorest neighborhoods in London, where services for the poor were offered, Jane returned home determined to do something for the underprivileged (McPherson 1993). In 1889 she moved into a rented house on Halsted Street, located in one of Chicago's poorest areas. At the time, Chicago was called "a city of a million strangers" (McPherson 1993, p. 28) due to the recent influx of many immigrants. It was not long before the Hull House became a haven for many newcomers in the Chicago area. Among Jane's first projects was a kindergarten that in less than a month had twenty-four children in attendance with seventy

---

Snapshot 5.3
The Atlanta Compromise

The Atlanta Compromise is a significant event not only in Booker T. Washington's life but for social relations at the time. With a captive crowd, Washington seized the moment to deliver the message that would color race relations for the next two decades. Although in his message we find that segregation was accepted by Washington, we also see him opening up the opportunities for the progress of African Americans. Concerned with the future and cognizant of the impending need to improve the social conditions of his people, he seized the opportunity to make a call for what would benefit African Americans.

Bennett (1994) writes: "With a strong and convincing voice, he said: 'In all things purely social we can be as separate as the fingers, yet [he balled the fingers into a fist] one as the hand in all things essential to mutual progress.'" These words, which exposed the truth about a powerful society, became known as the Atlanta Compromise, a compromise to work together for the sake of the country.

Source: Adapted from Lenore Bennett (1994). 10 most dramatic events in African American history. In J. Kromkowski (ed.). *Race and ethnic relations 94/95.* Guilford, CT: Dushkin (pp. 134–137).

more on the waiting list (McPherson 1993, p. 33). Addams dedicated her entire life to social justice, struggling to open opportunities to families and children of the poor. Her philanthropic work was extended to serve people and children throughout the world. Jane Addams was awarded the Nobel Peace Prize in 1931. Today, the Hull-House Association still serves needy children and adults in the Chicago area.

Japanese American Relocation Camps

During the 1940s another educator made a difference in the lives of others. Miles A. Cary organized educational services for thousands of Japanese American children in relocation camps. The magnitude of his accomplishment must be measured in the context of one of the most shameful periods of American history.

To many American citizens the mere term "relocation camp" is not something they recognize in the context of our country's history. For a great majority, it was not something they read about in their history books. Relocation camps represent an injustice committed during World War II against one of our country's ethnic minorities, the Japanese Americans.

On December 7, 1941, the Japanese delivered a surprise attack to the American base in Pearl Harbor, Hawaii. This marked the entrance of the United States into the Second World War. At the time, the United States had a significant Japanese American minority population already settled in the United States. Many of the members of this group had been born in America and had ancestors who had been citizens of this country for generations. Despite this fact, it was not long before the government, fearing another attack and trying to prevent what they thought could be anti-American activities from the Japanese immigrants, decided to confine this group to mass detention camps. Thus emerged the concept of camps where these "potential enemies" could be "relocated" while the nation was at war (Okihiro 1993).

Camps were established to house nearly six million Japanese Americans, including more than 33,000 children. This experience forever marked the lives of those children who came to live behind barbed wire. For them, life changed drastically. George Takei, Mr. Sulu on TV's "Star Trek" series, whose family spent time at Camp Rohwer, Arkansas, when he was a child, remembers in his 1994 book how this isolation deprived him and other children of the precious privilege of fantasy. He records vivid memories of a certain Christmas when he and the other Japanese American children in the camp wondered if Santa Claus was going to come. He describes his feelings when he discovered that the long-awaited Santa in the "wrinkled red suit" had a Japanese face:

> This Santa was a fake. I knew what Santa looked like. Mama had taken me to visit him the previous Christmas at May Company Department Store in downtown Los Angeles. I met him. I sat on his lap. I talked to him. And he wasn't Japanese . . . I guessed the real Santa probably couldn't get past the barbed wire fence (Takei 1994, p. 39).

In the midst of these unfortunate circumstances the work of educator Miles A. Cary stands out. An innovator by nature, Cary was also a voice that spoke against the unfair relocation of Japanese Americans. Cary, who believed relocation was an immoral act, accepted responsibility for organizing educational services in the Poston Relocation Center (Smith & Smith 1994). This dusty area in the Arizona desert housed more than 4,000 JapaneseAmericans. Poston, the school designed by Cary, became a spiritual oasis for hundreds of students who lived there. Cary hired Japanese teachers and opened special programs that even included a student newspaper (Smith & Smith 1994). Today, many of these people remember that going to school at Poston

---

Snapshot 5.4
Impressions

George Takei was four years old when he learned that his family could no longer live as free people. The following are his impressions of the moment when he and his family were forced to leave for the camp.

"Then a terrible war had broken out, and my father's whole world was blown away. All people of Japanese ancestry in America were to be immediately removed to internment camps, leaving everything behind. So much was irretrievably lost. The business—abandoned. The rented house on Garnett Street—hurriedly vacated. The car sold for the best offer, five dollars—better to get something than leave it behind. But the new refrigerator got no offer. It nearly killed Mama to have to abandon it to the vultures. Everything other than what we were allowed to carry—all abandoned. All memories now. All fleeting as the sand blowing past the window. All gone."

Source: Takei, G. (1994). *To the stars. The autobiography of George Takei.* NY: Pocket Books (p. 16).

---

was the best part of the years they spent behind the fences.

A Legacy of the Past
It is said that the past holds undeniable truths. It also allows us to better focus the lens through which we look at life. Before continuing our search for the genesis of multicultural education, it is important to assess what we have learned from the past.

1. Awareness of inequality has existed since ancient times. Education for the poor and gender equity have been two areas of early awareness.
2. Despite the awareness, actions by society to correct inequality have been delayed, or never taken.
3. Both men and women played active roles in exposing and disclosing the existing inequities.
4. Realization of unfairness in various aspects of life established the beginnings of the concept of *diversity* (gender, social class).

5. Of the many cries for equality, only a few resulted in concrete deeds. Often, only a few benefited from the change. However, the changes served to strengthen the desire for fair service for all.

❖ The Road to Multicultural Education

Considering the impact education has on the life of a young child, teachers know that to provide a developmentally appropriate environment, the nature and needs of the child must be reflected in the program. Today, diversity is a major element to be considered when designing programs for the young, according to research on best practices. However, this was not always so. According to multiculturalist James Banks (1992), multicultural education is a phenomenon of the 1960s. As pointed out earlier, little or no effort was made until then to accommodate the needs and particularities of children with diverse backgrounds. Various factors are responsible for this delayed awareness.

1. Slavery was abolished in 1865 after Abraham Lincoln issued the Emancipation Proclamation, but history shows that acceptance and entry into society of the free African Americans was a slow and painful process. Numerous accounts tell of unjust and unfair acts committed against former slaves through the following decades.
2. During the late nineteenth and early twentieth centuries, while the United States was coping with the new societal role of African Americans, waves of immigrants were pouring into this country. The demographic changes caused by this population presented new challenges. The fact that many new immigrants belonged to ethnic and racial groups different from those of the first settlers set in motion a new period of discrimination.
3. Court rulings lent legal validity to segregation and affirmed differences among people based on race. Among these rulings were the Supreme Court's 1883 declaration that the Civil Rights Act of 1875 was unconstitutional and the Court's approval of "separate but equal" facilities in *Plessy vs. Fergusson* (1896).
4. Policies that accented the differences between specific ethnic groups and the majority were still enforced. Examples include the policy that led to the incarceration of Japanese

---

Snapshot 5.5
Plessy vs. Fergusson (1896)

Justice Harlan expressed his disagreement with a decision that sanctioned the practice of assigning separate seats in public places based on race, in an eloquent letter. According to the court ruling, the separate assignment did not imply that blacks or any other ethnic minorities were to be seen as not equal to whites.

". . . In respect of civil rights, common to all citizens, the Constitution of the United States does not, I think, permit any public authority to know the race of those entitled to be protected in the enjoyment of such rights. . . . In the view of the Constitution, in the eye of the law, there is in this country no superior, dominant, ruling class of citizens. There is no caste here. Our Constitution is color-blind, it neither knows nor tolerates classes among citizens. In respect of civil rights, all citizens are equal before the law.

"In my opinion, the judgment rendered this day will, in time, prove to be quite as pernicious as the decision made in the Dred Scott Case."

Source: *Plessy vs. Fergusson* (1896). In J. Kromkowski (1994) (ed.). *Race and ethnic relations 94/95*. Guilford, CT: Dushkin (pp. 10–16).

Americans at the start of World War II, and the reaction against Mexican immigrants, which led to "Operation Wetback" in the 1950s (U.S. Commission on Civil Rights in Kromkowski 1994).

African Americans found the legal and social obstacles present in our country unbearable. Their frustrated hopes and the feeling of powerlessness nurtured the spirit that ignited and sustained the civil rights movement of the 1960s. Two events in the 1950s fueled the beginning of this struggle for equality. The first was the landmark Supreme Court decision of *Brown vs. the Board of Education of Topeka, Kansas,* in 1954, which ruled that segre-

gated schools did not provide equal opportunities. The Brown decision reversed the view the Court had taken in *Plessy vs. Fergusson;* separate but equal facilities were now considered unconstitutional. This decision marked the end of the legal segregation in American schools and initiated equalization of education services. It can also be said that it established the beginning of multiculturalization of our schools. The desegregation of schools that followed the 1954 Brown decision was enforced throughout the 1960s largely as a result of the work and the determination of the leaders of the civil rights movement.

The second event was the Rosa Parks incident, which took place on December 1, 1955, in Mont-

---

Snapshot 5.6
What Started Brown vs. the Board of Education?

To many, the events that led to the landmark decision of 1954 have faded. Briefly, let us recall the incident that initiated this historic lawsuit.

During the 1940s, the unfair and unequal conditions of schools for African Americans had become obvious. During this time, the National Association for the Advancement of Colored People (NAACP) had brought the issue to local and national attention. It was 1947 when Esther Brown, "a thirty-one-year-old white woman" (Tushnet 1987, p. 139), became concerned about the state of schools for African Americans in South Park, outside of Kansas City. Initially, Brown tried to persuade the school board to improve the grade schools but failed. She then consulted about the situation with an attorney from Topeka, Elisha Scott, finding that there were legal grounds in the issue. According to Kansas law, segregation was permitted "only in school districts larger than South Park" (Tushnet 1987, p. 139).

Determined to fight for what was right and equal for black children, Brown, along with the parents and children of South Park, boycotted the schools. The rest is history. With the support of the black community, Brown moved the case forward, achieving one of the major victories in the struggle for social justice.

Source: Tushnet, M. (1987). *The NAACP's legal strategy against segregated education, 1925–1950.* Chapel Hill, NC: The University of North Carolina Press.

gomery, Alabama. The tired Ms. Parks refused to move from the seat designated for "white" people, even though a white man was left standing (Asante & Mattson 1991). She was arrested, jailed, and tried for breaking the law. The entire black community rose to her defense. The result was the famous Montgomery bus boycott. The entire black community refused to ride the public transportation system. After many months, the city capitulated, and blacks were free to sit anywhere they wished on buses. The incident sparked the unification of African Americans across the South and marked the official beginning of the civil rights movement. The Rosa Parks incident brought prominence to a young attorney, Martin Luther King, Jr., who joined her in the noble cause (Asante & Mattson 1991, p. 72).

The inability of many mainstream Americans to accept the decision to desegregate, and their efforts to set the fight for equality back, served to unite the African Americans in the greatest struggle for freedom and equality known to this country. Civil rights became a major issue in national elections. Civil rights issues were also vigorously pursued by many black-led activist organizations. Among the most prominent were the National Association for the Advancement of Colored People (NAACP), formed in 1909 by W. E. B. DuBois and a small group of African Americans and white supporters, and the Congress on Racial Equality founded in 1942. The strides made during the civil rights movement in the 1960s were numerous and costly. Unfortunately, many setbacks were suffered in the 1980s and 1990s, causing the fight for equality to continue. Ensuring that the constitutional rights of all are protected and guaranteed to people regardless of their origin, race, or religious affiliation is still at the forefront of the agenda of various groups, especially that of the African Americans.

A major social force of the 1960s, the civil rights movement survived tragedies, humiliations, and injustices to win many major battles fought for the dignity of the individual. Among these were battles

IN ACTION . . . *The Impact of a Court Ruling*

Here is James Farmer's description of the impact that the *Brown vs. the Board of Education* had upon the civil rights movement. While you read it, imagine how civil rights activists felt at the time. Think how it relates to multicultural education.

"The Brown decision set in motion boundless energies, spawned by the promise of Jeffersonian egalitarianism but penned up by the delay of fulfilling that promise. From Little Rock to Oxford, Mississippi, and throughout the South, children and youth of irrepressible and heroic dimensions rose and the barriers came down. There were other foci in the equality drive of the 1950s and 1960s. There were boycotts and freedom rides; sit-ins at lunch counters; voter registration drives; lynchings and killings; and admission of black students to all white universities. Dr. Martin Luther King, who with his charismatic appeal succeeded in mobilizing as much as one-fourth of the entire black population, as well as millions of whites, led marches for across-the-board desegregation and for universal dignity of man. One of the most successful civil rights demonstrations was the march on Washington in 1963, which was conducted in support of the decision that segregation of educational facilities by race was unconstitutional."

Source: Wortham 1992 (p.47).

FIGURE 5.2 Recent history of equality in education

1954 Supreme Court decision in *Brown vs. the Board of Education* declares segregation unconstitutional.

1964 The Civil Rights Act is passed by Congress, outlawing discrimination in accommodations and employment. Economic Opportunity Act initiates Head Start, Job Corps, Neighborhood Youth Corps, Upward Bound, Aid to Dependent Children, and Food Stamps.

1965 The Voting Rights Act abolishes literacy tests. Passage of the Elementary and Secondary School Education Act fuels antipoverty programs.

1965 Project Head Start begins. Other programs like Project Follow Through, Home Start, and the Migrant Program are developed to serve children at risk.

1966 The Coleman Report discovers that segregation of educational services is still rampant. Equity in educational services has not yet been achieved.

1974 Passage of the Bilingual Education Act as a result of the decision in *Lau vs. Nichols* (1974).

1975 The Education of All Handicapped Children Act (P.L. 94-142) is approved, recognizing the rights of children to be educated.

1986 P.L. 99-457 amends the Education of the Handicapped Act (EHA) and establishes early intervention services for infants, toddlers, and their families.

1990 Americans with Disabilities Act (P.L. 101-336). A landmark act, it establishes civil rights protection against discrimination for all American citizens with disabilities. Protection covers employment in the private sector, access to public services, public accommodations, transportation, and telecommunications.

1990 Education of the Handicapped Act Amendments of 1990 (P.L. 101-476). Renames the EHA as the Individuals with Disabilities Education Act (IDEA). It also adds two new categories of disabilities, autism and traumatic brain injury; requires all IEP's to incorporate a statement of required transition services beginning no later than age 16; and expands the concept of related services to include rehabilitation counseling as well as social work services.

---

for registration of black voters, desegregation of public facilities and private businesses, and desegregation in schools. The progress made in the area of equality in recent years can be traced to victories won by the supporters of the civil rights movement who continue their work today (Figure 5.2).

❖ The Birth of Multicultural Education

"The multicultural approach to education reconstructs the entire education process to promote equality and cultural pluralism."

Christine Sleeter (1993)

Educators attribute the contemporary beginnings of multicultural education to the events and the social climate of the 1960s. According to Gollnick and Chinn (1990) interest in ethnic studies was brought to attention in the 1960s and early 1970s. Major socio-political events like the assassinations of John F. Kennedy, Martin Luther King Jr., and Robert Kennedy; the "hippie movement"; the anti-Vietnam War movement; the sexual revolution; and the new drug culture created a climate of unprecedented change in American society. It was in this atmosphere of uncertainty and flux that multicultural education got its start.

The issue of inequality, central to many social and political movements of the 1960s, gave way to initiatives like the War on Poverty of 1964. During this time, people realized that children of minorities were at a disadvantage with respect to the children of United States mainstream culture. Although this view of minorities led to misconceptions about the "culturally deprived," it acknowledged the existence of different cultural backgrounds. Concerted efforts made to bring people out of their "disadvantages" gave way to a number of important social and educational programs. It is through these efforts that the government affirmed its interest in children. As a way to equalize opportunities for all, educators like Jerome Brunner and Edward Zigler advocated the development of programs to serve the children of the poor and those of culturally different backgrounds.

One of the best known of these programs was Head Start, begun in 1965 as part of President Lyndon B. Johnson's War on Poverty. Still in existence today, it is the federal government's longest-lasting and most effective program for the very young. Initially, Head Start was designed as an eight-week summer intervention to give disadvantaged children a "head start" before they entered kindergarten. The program was designed to foster development of learning patterns, emotions, skills, and attitudes that "would protect the children against the pattern of poverty" (Wortham 1992, p. 51). As a result of its overwhelming immediate success, Head Start soon expanded into a year-round program that provided not only learning experiences but also health care, parent education, and meals. Soon a network of community agencies to assist parents was added.

The concern for the future success of Head Start students resulted in the founding of Follow Through, a program designed to facilitate the transition of children into the primary grades. Begun in 1967, the program served the needs of children of low-income families enrolled in kindergarten through third grade.

Efforts to address diversity and equity were also seen in the modest efforts of universities to include in their curricula views about other cultural groups and issues on discrimination. Because of the interest in specific ethnicities, early programs were basically designed as single group studies (Sleeter & Grant 1993). Banks (1993) points out that "the first responses of schools and educators to the ethnic movement were hurried [and] . . . without the thought and careful planning needed to make them educationally sound or to institutionalize them within the educational system" (p. 5). The efforts to include other cultures into the curriculum largely took part on campuses of socially progressive universities and colleges across America. Audiences for these courses were usually composed of minority students representing the same groups targeted in the courses (Banks 1993; Gollnick & Chinn 1990). Banks, who established five evolutionary phases for the development of multicultural education (Figure 5.3), labels this initial stage as "monoethnic studies" (1988).

The focus on various minorities in the form of "multiethnic studies" also emerged in the 1970s. Interest was mainly on the comparative examination of the experiences of different cultural groups. This led to a "multiethnic education approach," focused on racial and ethnic minorities, where a more general audience participated.

There were notable efforts made on the part of some early childhood educators. Among these efforts were the "Bank Street readers," a basal series developed by the Bank Street College of Education. These readers portrayed children of different races and ethnic groups and social settings. Social studies curricula have long included themes about diversity. During this period, it began to reflect the characteristics of the already pluralistic American society. Bolstered by the development in 1976 of the *Curriculum Guidelines for Multiethnic Education*, social studies curricula began to incorporate more aspects about different cultural groups (National Council for Social Studies 1992). Early childhood curricula were

FIGURE 5.3 James Banks' (1988) phases of multicultural education evolution

Phase I—*Monoethnic studies courses:* African American educators demand revision and rewriting of textbooks.

Phase II—*Multiethnic studies courses:* Schools begin to offer courses focused on different minority groups. Curriculum begins to include comparative views of cultures.

Phase III—*Multiethnic education:* Educators initiate a curricular reform to incorporate and integrate elements of other ethnic groups across disciplines.

Phase IV—*Multicultural education:* Curriculum includes perspectives of the nature of American pluralism. A wider focus is used to address the perspectives of other cultural groups.

Phase V—*Multiethnic-multicultural education:* Awareness about cultural diversity is slowly occurring. Educators are taking steps to establish education about cultural diversity as a general educational goal.

developed around topics like families here and in other countries, what children do in the United States and in Japan, and what children do in schools in other countries. Specific curricular guides were designed to provide children with opportunities to discover their similarities with children in other cultures. One example of this movement was the social studies program developed for kindergartners in Puerto Rico (Robles de Meléndez 1985). Among the program's goals was the idea of offering five-year-olds opportunities to explore their similarities with children in India. Continuing with this multiethnic focus, first graders studied the family in a cross-cultural context, with units about families in Japan and the Navajo culture.

Efforts Toward Equal Services for Children

"By the safeguard of health and the protection of childhood we further contribute to that equality of opportunity which is the unique basis of American civilization."

President Herbert Hoover (1929)
Excerpt from the Announcement of the
White House Conference on Children

The rapid industrial growth during the early 1920s and, later, the need for workers during World War II, forced many women of poor and middle class families to get jobs and leave their children at home. According to Hymes (1977), during World War II "America needed woman-

IN ACTION . . . *Early Experiences with Other Cultures*

▮ Can you recall the topics about other cultures you studied during kindergarten/primary school?

▮ What was their focus?

power to win the war. [So] the government set up and supported child-care centers for the young children of war-working mothers" (p. 6). This established early childhood services for children of the working class. In accordance with the earlier traditions regarding American society's commitment to children of the working poor, services expanded steadily through the 1950s. They received their major endorsement through the compensatory education movement of the 1960s.

The spirit of the 1960s was the perfect breeding medium for social reform. Thousands of people across the country, representing all the ethnic and cultural minorities, joined hands with African Americans to bring inequality to a stop. The constancy of their efforts for achieving equality was the force that rang the bell for action for children. With the understanding that children of the poor (who at the same time represented the ethnic minorities) would do better if offered additional educational services, the greatest revolution for young children began to unfold. It was because of the belief that *early intervention* was a way to ameliorate differences in social experiences that the public and the government took a decisive interest in young children (Peterson 1987). Growing out of the War on Poverty and the civil rights movement, the government decided to improve services for children living in poverty. At the time "some 35 million citizens were estimated to be living in poverty in the midst of what seemed to be an affluent American society" (Peterson 1987, p. 125). Recognizing that children from socially and economically disadvantaged environments were entering school less equipped for success, many initiatives were undertaken to serve the culturally diverse child. Targeting those from low socio-economic communities across the nation, the government began focusing its efforts on children from the various ethnic minorities. Although many programs were designed during

the 1960s to meet their needs, two in particular stand out: Head Start and Follow Through.

A Head Start for American Children

It is the summer of 1965 and the beginning of Project Head Start. Approximately 2,500 Child Development Centers have been established to serve more than 550,000 children across the nation (Osborn 1996). The program was designed to provide learning experiences to children entering first grade in the fall of 1965 and who had not experienced kindergarten or preschool. Centers opened their doors to children in urban areas, on Indian reservations, and in places as far as Guam, Puerto Rico, and the Virgin Islands.

Head Start also proved that, to serve children, educators needed to involve the community and parents as partners. The experiences during the days and weeks of that memorable summer session in 1965 marked the first substantial efforts to reduce inequality. The program was a first effort to directly empower citizens by involving them in the educational decision-making process. James Hymes (1977) recalls that Head Start programs opened and blossomed thanks to responsive communities everywhere. Knowing that this was an opportunity for their children to have a better education, people gave their full support to the project.

The need for parents and teachers to work as partners was realized through the concept of the *child development center*. Different from the classroom, the child development center affirmed the roles of parents and the community in a child's education. According to Osborn "in concept it [the child development center] represents drawing together all the resources—family, community, and professionals—which can contribute to the child's total development" (1996, p. 298).

Designed as a comprehensive program for preschool children, Head Start was founded on

A rich environment plays an important role in the learning process of young children attending Head Start in this classroom in Florida.

the belief that a child's success was not to be defined only by intellectual growth but rather by a holistic perspective of the individual child. Consideration of the integral development of young children has since been the driving force behind Head Start services. Following this holistic view, interventions were planned to include a variety of direct and preventive services. Today, interventions take place through the following:

▌ Individualized developmental education services.

▌ Health services. Comprehensive medical, dental, and mental health services are offered. Preventive health is among its objectives.

▌ Nutrition services. Since its beginning, Head Start has emphasized the need for children to be well fed. Balanced meals (breakfast, snack, and lunch) are served family style, in what has become another trademark of this program. A strong nutrition program complements the meal services.

▌ Family services. A full range of social services is offered. Their purpose is to promote the best conditions for an improved quality of family life. A well-planned parenting skills empowerment program is also part of the services. Here parents/families refine and acquire knowledge to enhance their child-parent relationships and interactions.

Since 1972, Head Start has served children with special needs. Today, at least 10 percent of its enrollment must be allocated to children with disabilities (Peterson 1987). Constant training and in-service activities prepare the staffs of Head Start programs to offer quality services to children with disabilities. A full range of support services is offered to meet the needs of the disabled child.

Serving primarily ages 4–5, Head Start recently extended its services to infants and toddlers. Through the Comprehensive Child Development Program (CCDP), children of low-income families receive full services. This initiative is intended to prove that intervention begins at birth, something that most early educators have advocated for years.

Currently, Head Start serves more than 700,000 children (infants to preschoolers) representing almost 40 percent of those eligible (U.S. Department of Health and Human Services 1993). Sixty-seven percent of its enrollment are ethnic minorities, with African Americans and Hispanics as the largest groups.

Today, Head Start continues to be the optimum "head start" for thousands of children. Celebrating its 30th anniversary in 1995, Head Start is the longest-lasting program stemming from the 1964 War on Poverty.

Project Follow Through
Established in 1967, Project Follow Through, a federally funded program, was also a part of the

Head Start is characterized by a wide variety of personal and individual services for children.

IN ACTION . . . *Learning More About the Head Start Program*

To appreciate the relevancy of the Head Start program, try the following:

▌ Interview someone who experienced Head Start during its beginning years. Ask about the kinds of activities and materials used and, especially, about the nature of the children enrolled.

▌ Visit your local Head Start office and find out about its services. Identify the populations being served.

▌ Visit a Head Start classroom. Compare its program with other early childhood services.

▌ Read about the origins of the program. Look for: Zigler, E., and S. Muenchow (1992). *Head Start: The inside story of America's most successful educational experiment.* New York: Basic Books.

initiatives of the War on Poverty. The Follow Through project originated in an effort to extend and continue the benefits of Head Start into the K–3 level (Goffin 1994). Full intervention services were offered to children and their parents. Using the same parameters as Head Start, the project provided its services to low-income children and families. This once again offered an opportunity for cultural minorities to benefit from a well-designed educational strategy. Like Head Start, Follow Through was an opportunity to test and develop a wide variety of early childhood curricular models. Essentially, efforts were made with the purpose of finding what approaches would work best for children (Goffin 1994). Stacie Goffin points out that the project "was implemented using 13 different curriculum models at 80 different school sites across the country" (p. 23). Follow Through classrooms were established in every state and in other parts of the nation. For example, in Puerto Rico Follow Through characterized itself by the use of the open classroom strategy. Under the sponsorship of the Puerto Rico Department of Education, teachers K–3 received periodical training and support. Follow Through proved that continuity of services at the early childhood level was a key to the child's success (Wortham 1992). Unfortunately, the program was phased out in the 1980s.

The Road Is Finally Laid

As public interest in diversity issues increased during the 1970s and 1980s, educators began to realize that efforts alone were not sufficient to effect true educational reform. Baruth and Manning (1992) note that the negative attitudes of teachers also influenced the effectiveness of the multiethnic education approach. In time, the scope of multicultural education gave way to a broader view of cultures and encompassed the total school and classroom environments. This inclusive perspective was reinforced by the passing of Public Law (P.L.) 94-142, the Education for All Handicapped Act in 1975, which recognized the rights to equal education for the handicapped. The Individuals with Disabilities Act (IDEA) of 1990 reaffirmed the commitment to serve the exceptional.

As we move through the 1990s, awareness and acknowledgment of the rights of all individuals has increased. Current efforts, termed by Banks (1988) as "multiethnic-multicultural education," focus on awareness of and consideration for the needs of the child as an individual with diverse cultural characteristics. This approach also includes developmental appropriateness as a necessary component for implementation of effective programs for culturally different children.

Today, as early childhood educators prepare themselves to enter a new millennium, their realization of the responsibilities toward children is heightened. A desire to reach all the children we teach has become clear to many more educators. Although we feel optimistic about the future, we also realize there is still much to be done. We count on those of you who believe in unity and equality to bring equitable and fair education to all children who will help us build a strong and prosperous nation.

Moving Ahead

The history of efforts toward the multiculturalism of American education and, particularly, of early childhood education, is still young. Although much has been accomplished, many areas still require reform as our society grows more diverse. Many chapters remain to be written. Which one will you begin?

❖ Things to Do . . .

1. What are the main components of the multicultural education movement? Select three that you think are the most relevant.
2. Choose your favorite advocate of equality from the individuals mentioned in this chapter. Do some library research to find at least two other characteristics that highlight his or her contributions.

3. Equality is a very difficult concept to define. To gain some insight as to how people see it, ask ten people to define it. But first, write down your own definition. Begin your interviews and make sure to jot down their responses. Examine their responses to find the similarities and differences. Then, redefine equality to reflect what you learned. Share your findings with a classmate or colleague.
4. Equality is the catalyst for development of multicultural education. Do you think your school provides equal opportunities to all children? What areas do you think still require improvement? Explain.
5. Baruth and Manning (1992) have written that some teachers' attitudes toward multiethnic education are negative. Do you agree or disagree with their statement? If you agree, why is multicultural education a problem for some? How can this problem be overcome? Explain.

❖ Children's Literature Corner

Adler, D. (1989) *Picture book of Martin Luther King, Jr.* New York: Holiday.

Davidson, M. (1986). *I have a dream. The story of Martin Luther King, Jr.* New York: Scholastic Books.

Freeman, D. (1968). *Corduroy.* New York: Puffin.

*Hamilton, V. (1985). *The people could fly: American black folktales.* New York: Knopf.

*Hansen, J. (1986). *Which way freedom.* New York: Walker.

*Haskins, J. (1993). *The march on Washington.* New York: HarperCollins.

---

*These titles are recommended for retelling or for teacher's information. Their content is at the 4–6 grade level; however, teachers can adapt the stories for the children they teach.

*Levine, E. (1993). *Freedom's children. Young civil rights activists tell their own stories.* New York: Putnam.

Little, L. J. (1988). *Children of long ago.* New York: Philomel.

Williams, S. A. (1992). *Working cotton.* Orlando, FL: Harcourt Brace Jovanovich.

Yashima, T. (1955). *The crow boy.* New York: Viking.

❖ References

Anderson, J. D. (1988). *The education of the blacks in the South 1860–1935.* Chapel Hill, NC: The University of North Carolina Press.

Asante M. K., & Mattson, M. T. (1991). *Historical and cultural atlas of African Americans.* New York: Macmillan.

Baigorri, P. (1983). *Historia de la filosofía* [History of philosophy]. Madrid, Spain: Santillana.

Banks, J. (1988). *Multiethnic education* (2nd ed.). Boston MA: Allyn & Bacon.

Banks, J. (1992). Introduction. In Task force on ethnic studies. Curricular guidelines for multicultural education. *Social Education* 56: 5 (pp. 274–294).

Banks, J. (1993). Multicultural education: Characteristics and goals. In J. Banks & C. Banks (eds.). Multicultural education: Issues and perspectives (2nd ed.). Boston, MA: Allyn & Bacon.

Banks, J., & Banks, C. (eds.). (1993). *Multicultural education: Issues and perspectives* (2nd ed.). Boston, MA: Allyn & Bacon.

Baruth, L., & Manning, M. L. (1992). *Multicultural education of children and adolescents.* Boston, MA: Allyn & Bacon.

Bennett, L. (1994). In J. Kromkowski (ed.). *Race and ethnic relations 94/95.* Guilford, CT: Dushkin.

Derman-Sparks, L., & A.B.C. Task Force. (1989). *Antibias curriculum: Tools for empowering young children.* Washington, DC: National Association for the Education of Young Children.

Goffin, S. (1994). *Curriculum models and early childhood education: Appraising the relationship.* New York: Merrill.

Gollnick, D., and Chinn, P. (1990). *Multicultural education in a pluralistic society* (3rd ed.). Columbus, OH: Merrill.

Gómez Tejera, C., & Cruz López, D. (1970). *La escuela Puertorriqueña* [The Puerto Rican school]. Sharon, CT: Troutman.

Howe, K. (1992). *Liberal democracy, equal educational opportunity and the challenge of multiculturalism.* American Educational Research Journal 29 (pp. 455–470).

Hymes, J., Jr. (1977). *Early childhood education. An introduction to the profession* (2nd ed.). Washington, DC: National Association for the Education of Young Children.

Jarret, J. L. (1971). *The meanings of equality.* In S. M. McMurin (ed.). *The conditions for educational equality.* New York: Committee for Economic Development.

Kendall, F. (1983). *Diversity in the classroom. A multicultural approach to the education of young children.* New York: Teachers College Press.

Kromkowski, J., (ed.) (1994). *Race and ethnic relations 94/95.* Guilford, CT: Dushkin.

MacNeil, E. (1989). *Historia de occidente: Manual de historia.* Río Piedras, PR: Editorial Universitaria.

Marrou, H. (1977). *A history of education in antiquity.* London: Sheed & Wavel.

McKissack, P., & McKissack, F. (1992). *Cornerstones of freedom: Mary McLeod Bethune.* Chicago, IL: Children's Press.

McPherson, S. S. (1993). *Peace and bread. The story of Jane Addams.* Minneapolis, MN: Carolhorda Books.

Morrison, N. (1990). *Chief Sarah.* Portland, OR: Oregon Historical Society.

National Council for the Social Studies. (1992). Guidelines for multicultural teaching. *Social Education* 1: 56, No. 3 (pp. 274–294).

Nieto, S. (1992). *Affirming diversity.* New York: Longman.

Okihiro, G. (1993). The victimization of Asians in America. In J. Kromkowsky (ed.). *Race and ethnic relations 94/95,* pp. 114–122. Guilford, CT: Dushkin.

Osborn, K. (1996). *Project Head Start: An assessment.* In K. Paciorek and J. Munro (eds.). *Sources. Notable selections in early childhood education.* Guilford, CT: Dushkin.

Peterson, N. (1987). *Early intervention for handicapped and at-risk children: An introduction to early childhood-special education.* Denver, CO: Love Publishing.

Power, E. J. (1975). *Main currents in the history of education* (2nd ed.). New York: McGraw-Hill.

Ribes Tovar, F. (1973). *100 biografías de Puertoriqueños ilustres* [100 Biographies of Illustrious Puerto Ricans]. New York: Plus Ultra Educational.

Robles de Meléndez, W. (1985). *Guía para la enseñanza de los estudios sociales en el kindergarten* [Guide for the teaching of social studies in kindergarten]. San Juan, PR: Editorial del Departamento de Instrucción Pública.

Sleeter, C., & Grant, C. (1994). *Making choices for multicultural education* (2nd ed.). New York: Merrill.

Smith, L. G., & Smith, J. (1994). *Lives in education: A narrative of people and ideas* (2nd ed.). New York: St. Martin's Press.

Smith, L. G., & Smith, J. (1994a). *Education today: The foundation of a profession.* New York: St. Martin's Press.

Takei, G. (1994). *To the stars. Autobiography of George Takei.* New York: Pocket Books.

Tushnet, M. (1987). *The NAACP's legal strategy against segregated education, 1925–1950.* Chapel Hill, NC: The University of North Carolina Press.

U.S. Commission on Civil Rights. In J. Kromkowski (ed.) (1994). *Race and ethnic relations 94/95.* Guilford, CT: Dushkin.

U.S. Department of Health and Human Services. (1993). *Creating a 21st century Head Start: Final report of the Advisory Committee on Head Start Quality and Expansion.* Washington, DC.

Wortham, C. S. (1992). *Childhood 1892–1992.* Wheaton, MD: Association for Childhood Education International.

Zigler, E. F., & Stevenson, M. F. (1993). *Children in a changing world: Development and social issues* (2nd ed.). Pacific Grove, CA: Brooks/Cole.

"Multicultural education is not tasting ethnic food and learning ethnic dances . . . It is much more complex and pervasive than setting aside an hour, a unit or a month. It should influence the whole curriculum."

Gollnick and Chinn (1990)

CHAPTER 6

Approaches to Multicultural Education: Ways and Designs for Classroom Implementation

In this chapter we will:

- ▮ define keys concepts: curriculum, approach, model, design
- ▮ examine models for multicultural education
- ▮ establish the applicability of multicultural approaches in the early childhood context

Key concepts:

- ▮ approach
- ▮ model
- ▮ design
- ▮ curriculum
- ▮ anti-bias

❖ Time for Decisions

We begin this chapter with the assumption that you have made a decision to bring multicultural education into your classroom. Congratulations! Now, it is time for decisions.

Having looked at some of the ideas that describe the origins of multicultural education, it is time to search for ways to translate the ideas into practice. Hopefully, by now you have accomplished two things: you have realized the importance of multiculturalism and you are determined to make multicultural education benefit your young students. These resolutions are a part of the first phase, "exploring and thinking," experienced by teachers when moving toward acceptance of multicultural education. The next two phases, "making choices" and "activating ideas," are related to implementation and practices (Figure 6.1).

Why Engage in Educational Reform?

What you are about to begin can best be defined as educational reform in action. Teachers throughout the United States already know or have heard that multicultural education is one of today's educational priorities. Many of them experience diversity daily in their own classrooms as a result of cultural diversification in communities across this country. Consequently, conscientious teachers of the young have come to recognize the challenges of teaching culturally diverse children. They are aware that providing developmentally appropriate responsive educational programs now requires a different method of delivery. This constitutes educational reform.

Getting to Work

It seems that the transition from believing in multicultural education to putting it into practice should be a simple process. However, many early childhood educators find themselves facing barriers. In recent years, whenever teachers were asked about major obstacles to translating multicultural education into practice, the answers have been the same: "How is it done?" and "How can I do it?" Reflected in these questions are two major issues. The first question reveals the problem of finding a design or pattern to follow as a practical model. The second presents a dual issue: (1) the functional quality and feasibility of the model, and (2) the appropriateness of that model to the teacher's own classroom. The need for guidelines to adapt any chosen model is always

---

FIGURE 6.1 Phases of multicultural education

Moving into Multicultural Teaching

Phase I: *Exploring and Thinking*
Inquiring about the need and the supporting rationale. Reflecting upon our findings. Formulating a personal conviction. Establishing why multicultural education is considered important [both for the child and personally].

Phase II: *Making Choices*
Selecting and deciding on the ways to design the program. Exploring the available models, approaches, practices, and materials. Reconfirming the decision to teach multiculturally.

Phase III: *Activating Ideas*
Implementing the program. Constant revision to redirect the efforts.

a concern when dealing with innovation. The absence of both model and guidelines has often accounted for the inertia found among teachers. Lack of adequate knowledge is also a reason given by teachers when they are asked why multicultural education has not yet become a part of their school's curricula.

We believe that when teachers are empowered, the desire to affect change is heightened and their willingness to engage in change increases. This book is intended to empower you to transform those desires and aspirations into reality by:

1. assisting you in making a decision to teach in a multicultural way;
2. providing the relevant knowledge that will help you implement a multicultural program.

In this effort, we adhere to the principles drawn from Paulo Freire's ideas. Central to his concept of *critical pedagogy* lies the importance of knowledge and the power it offers to those who possess it (Freire 1970). Well-informed teachers, within the context of Freire's thesis, can become effective participants and serve as leaders in the movement of multicultural education.

In this chapter we will examine some of the existing models and approaches of leading multiculturalists. Part III of this book is designed to answer the question "How can I teach multiculturally?"

❖ Exploring Models and Approaches

The terms *approach* and *model* are often used interchangeably in education. Essentially, they indicate what a teacher does to orient, organize, and deliver the curriculum.

Establishing Definitions

An **approach** is a set of guidelines that defines an overall method used to attain a specific purpose. An approach dictates ways to present, develop, and select topics for classroom instruction. In the context of multicultural education, an approach describes techniques and practices for dealing with diversity issues. Whole language and collaborative learning are two examples of instructional approaches.

A **model** is a conceptual framework of sequential stages and processes designed to meet a specific purpose or to complete a process. Models can be structured or fluid. A structured model is one where procedures and ways to implement them are specified and required to be followed. On the other hand, fluid models allow for modification as required by the target population. They are often named after or attributed to leading authorities in a special field or discipline. Bank Street and High Scope are examples of models as is Meisel's model for early childhood assessment.

Theory-based → CURRICULUM MODEL ← *Provides direction*
↑　　　　　　　↑
Suggests teaching practices Defines teaching philosophy

Gordon and Browne (1989) state that curriculum "can become, literally, everything that happens in the course of a school day" (p. 310). Williams (1987) notes that the term curriculum can have many different meanings. For some educators curriculum will be what is established by their school districts, while others will consider it to be what they construct based on their experience and knowledge about children. However, Williams adds that most early childhood educators will see the curriculum as centered and emerging from the whole child. This idea is in agreement with the essential parameters of developmental appropriateness and is relevant for teachers examining ways to bring multiculturalism into the early childhood classroom. For the authors of this book, the multicultural curriculum is what emerges after a careful analysis of the needs and interests of the child, and also of the societal needs particular to the community. In this process, we see teachers as being instrumental in creating a culturally responsive curriculum.

Like templates, curriculum models also provide directions for implementing educational programs. A curriculum will also provide ways to organize the educational environment. Evans (Goffin 1994) explains that a curriculum model also "refers to a conceptual framework for decision making about educational priorities, administrative policies, instructional methods, and evaluation criteria" (p. 15).

A variety of models and implementation plans have been proposed since the beginnings of multicultural education in the 1960s. The central tenet in all of them is that awareness and knowledge about the many cultures in our society promotes the understanding necessary for optimizing personal interactions. What model to select is the option of the teacher. As you examine the approaches and models presented in this chapter, take notes on their characteristics and ways in which they align with the curriculum. More important, start pondering how they would respond to the needs of the children you teach. Remember that it will be possible to provide a quality program only when you consider the cultural reality of the children you teach as well as their needs. To help you reaffirm your decision to begin teaching multiculturally, bear in mind the following goals York (1991) identifies for multicultural education of the young child.

York's Goals for Multicultural Education
1. Recognize the beauty, value, and contribution of each child.
2. Foster high self-esteem and a positive self-concept in children.
3. Teach children about their own culture.
4. Introduce children to other cultures.
5. Provide children with a positive experience exploring similarities and differences.
6. Encourage children to respect other cultures.
7. Increase children's ability to talk and play with people who are different from them.
8. Help children to be group members.
9. Talk about racism and current events regularly with children.
10. Help children live happily and cooperatively in a diverse world.
11. Help children notice and do something about unfair behavior and events. (York 1991, pp. 24–25)

Guidelines for Examining Models

Selecting what we like is not always an easy task. As you read through this section, you will begin to make choices about the models you prefer. It is best to acquaint yourself with all of them before making your choice. Remember that engaging in successful educational reform requires much reflection. The list of guidelines in Figure 6.2 will assist you in examining the different multicultural models.

❖ Models of Multicultural Education

Models of multicultural education are of two types: those developed through an analysis of existing practices and those that are based on specific approaches or theories. James Banks (1993) and Christine Sleeter (1994) developed their implementation models through the analysis of existing practices. These models provide frameworks and recommendations for practice. Among the theory-based models are those of Louise Derman-Sparks (1989) and Frances Kendall (1983).

Proposed models for the implementation of multicultural education all have in common the fact that they evolved out of the efforts begun in the 1960s. They also share the belief that persistence in the use of a mainstream-centric curriculum does not facilitate the attainment of the *e pluribus unum* (out of the many, one) which ac-

---

FIGURE 6.2 Guidelines for the evaluation of teaching models

Name of Model: _____

Age/Grade Level I teach: _____

A. Main Tenets of the Model
   1. What are the basic assumptions and theories about the nature of multicultural education on which the model is based?
   2. What are the emphases?
   3. Check for Developmentally Appropriate Practices (DAP)
      a. Are the tenets consistent with the DAP criteria?
      b. Are the beliefs consistent with research and theory regarding:
         (1) children's social and emotional development?
         (2) children's intellectual development?
B. Goals of the Model
   1. What are the expected outcomes?
   2. What kind of materials, if any, are needed?
   3. DAP check
      a. Are activities adequate for the age level of the children I teach?
      b. Are the activities consistent with child development principles?
C. Personal Opinion
   1. Do I agree with the model's tenets?

   Yes, I agree because _____
   _____
   _____
   _____

   No, I do not agree because _____
   _____
   _____
   _____

   2. As an early childhood educator, do I agree with the goals and practices of the model?
   3. Do I believe I can implement the model in my classroom? (If the answer is no, why not?)

---

cording to Banks (1994), is the ultimate goal of American education. James Banks (1993) says that insistence on following current mainstream-centric curricula is detrimental not only to children of diverse backgrounds but also to mainstream children. In his opinion, mainstream-centric curriculum is negative for mainstream students because it provides

"... a misleading conception of their relationship with other racial and ethnic groups, and denies them the opportunity to benefit from the knowledge, perspectives, and frames of reference that can be gained from studying and experiencing other cultures and groups. A mainstream-centric curriculum also denies ... the opportunity to view their culture from the perspectives of other cultures and groups" (p. 195).

Recognizing that infusion of multiculturalism in education is essential for all children, educators like James Banks, Christine Sleeter, Carl Grant,

Frances Kendall, and Louise Derman-Sparks have designed different educational implementation models. Each of these educators has analyzed existing practices, giving us an account of the process. They also propose models most consistent with their beliefs.

Although none of these educators, with the exception of Kendall and Derman-Sparks, focus their ideas specifically on early childhood education, their observations provide the practitioner with relevant information to add to the knowledge base. We understand that other frameworks have been proposed by educators and social researchers who are exploring for more answers. For the purposes of this chapter, we will limit our inquiry to the models of authors already mentioned. Our decision is made based on the fact that these models provide more opportunities for teaching young children. These models are also basic and open frameworks allowing teachers to add their own elements or build their own frameworks. If at any point you feel that the curricular ideas proposed in a model do not fit into your philosophy of early childhood education, we urge you to review its main tenets for suggestions and ideas for designing your own multicultural curriculum. Our experience indicates that one way for teachers to teach responsively is by designing their own teaching model. We hope this discussion will assist educators in building models based on the realities of the children in their classrooms.

Banks' Levels of Integration of Multicultural Content

James Banks, one of the leaders in multicultural education in the United States, has studied the evolution of multiculturalism since its beginnings. For Banks (1993), multicultural education is an idea, an educational reform, and a process based on the premise that all students, despite their backgrounds, should have equal educational opportunities. That premise sustains the need for venturing into educational reform for diversity.

A witness to the ways multiculturalism in schools has evolved through time, Banks comments on and describes the various approaches that have been used during the last three decades. The common link in all these approaches is curricular change. Change, in Banks' view, happens as ethnic and multicultural content is integrated into the existing curriculum, with integration taking place at varying levels. Banks has defined four levels of multicultural curricular integration. These levels are of ascending value, relating to both degree of complexity and degree of commitment to multicultural education (Figure 6.3).

Level 1—The Contributions Approach

Level 1 in Banks' typology is described as the "Contributions Approach." At this level, teachers continue using their regular curriculum to which they add "ethnic heroes and discrete cultural artifacts" (1993, p. 198). Occasionally, ethnic contributions are also presented through a selection of holidays. These insertions play no role in changing the already existing curricular goals and objectives. Inclusion of these ethnic names and objects have basically the effect of "filling in" rather than affecting change (Figure 6.4).

Comments about Level 1

Using level 1 requires very little knowledge by teachers about the multicultural material added to the curriculum. Because these topics are presented as brief snapshots, relevant aspects of specific cultures are not really focused. Actually, if teachers are not careful in their selection and presentation of the topics, it is possible to find concepts displayed in stereotypical ways. Although well intentioned, this practice communicates misleading information to the child. An example of commonly shown stereotypes is the sole use of "gauchos" to depict Argentinians, or to portray

FIGURE 6.3 Banks' levels of integration

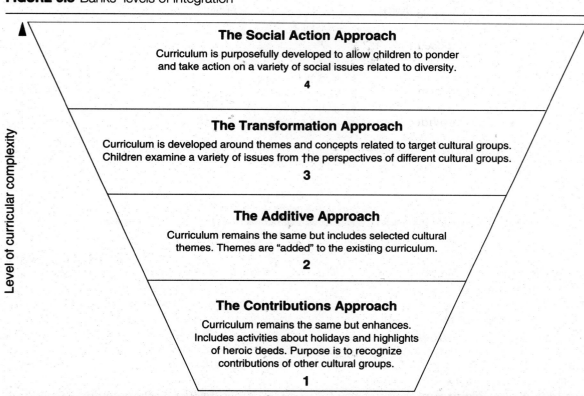

Level of curricular complexity

The Social Action Approach

Curriculum is purposefully developed to allow children to ponder and take action on a variety of social issues related to diversity.

4

The Transformation Approach

Curriculum is developed around themes and concepts related to target cultural groups. Children examine a variety of issues from the perspectives of different cultural groups.

3

The Additive Approach

Curriculum remains the same but includes selected cultural themes. Themes are "added" to the existing curriculum.

2

The Contributions Approach

Curriculum remains the same but enhances. Includes activities about holidays and highlights of heroic deeds. Purpose is to recognize contributions of other cultural groups.

1

Source: Adapted from J. Banks, (1993). Approaches to multicultural curriculum reform. In J. Banks & C. Banks (eds). *Multicultural education: issues and perspectives* (p. 199). Needham Heights: Allyn & Bacon.

Calypso dancers as representative of all the people in the Caribbean. One of our students told us that her second grade class doubted her Japanese heritage because she did not wear a kimono!

We have a responsibility to remember the power that teachers exert over children. We must remember that information presented in class often remains with our students through a lifetime. If cultural contributions are not carefully selected, students are likely to derive little from these experiences, since the topics presented are usually not examined in detail and are presented out of context (Banks 1993).

An important point regarding the level 1 approach is that it serves as a beginning step for many educators who decide to infuse perspectives of diversity into their curriculum. Such efforts deserve to be acknowledged and commended because the teachers are demonstrating an initial level of awareness. Providing teachers with support and opportunities for learning more about how to integrate ethnic topics into the

FIGURE 6.4 Examples of ethnic content in level 1

Topics teachers include when using the contributions
approach may be:

Heroes
- Eugenio M. de Hostos
- Benito Juárez
- Martin Luther King, Jr.
- Pocahontas

Artifacts
- food (eating tamales)
- dances (dancing a Venezuelan "joropo")
- crafts (making an "ojo de Dios")
- musical instruments (playing a ukulele)

Holidays
- October: Hispanic heritage month
- January: Chinese New Year
- February: Black history month
- May: Cinco de Mayo

curriculum is crucial at this point. This can help teachers continue the process of curricular change.

Level 2—The Additive Approach

The additive approach, or level 2, is based on the addition "of content, concepts, themes, and perspectives to the curriculum without changing its basic structures, purposes, and characteristics" (Banks 1993, p. 201). In this approach teachers select an ethnic topic and plan activities around it. In Banks' opinion, this second level implies a first step toward the transformation of the curriculum. Success of this approach depends on how the teacher organizes the presentation of the chosen concepts in accordance with the developmental levels of the children. Examples of how this level could be practiced in the early childhood classroom appear in Figure 6.5.

Level 3—The Transformation Approach

The third level, the transformation approach, represents a phase of substantial changes. At this level, teachers reconstruct the curriculum on the assumption that the content should address the

targeted problems with consideration for the views of other groups. Content based on the transformation approach is designed to enable students to examine the issues from a variety of perspectives. Because the students look at the problem from a variety of angles, they gain an enhanced concept of the reality or of the time being studied. For example, in studying the discovery of the Americas, the teacher would lead children to ponder the meaning of this event, not only from the point of view of the discoverer but also from that of the indigenous people of the continent. Another example is presented in Figure 6.6.

Comments on the Transformation Approach

Banks (1993) recommends that teachers applying the transformation approach remember that the key lies in the presentation of logically infused "perspectives, frames of reference, and content from various groups" (p. 203). He warns against adding topics to the already existing curriculum and recommends fusing the new with concepts already familiar to children. For the early childhood teacher, this also means selecting materials

DEFINING A CONTRIBUTION

Perhaps you have already decided to follow the contribution approach. However, selecting what to include is sometimes difficult. Because you want to develop a good curriculum, it is important to begin defining what constitutes a cultural contribution. This will help you select appropriate themes.

Cultural contributions are those cultural details currently defining a culture and the events or actions that either made lasting changes or that dramatically affected the culture. The following example will help you identify and select key elements for your curriculum.

When identifying cultural contributions look for the following:

▮ *Events of lasting effect:*

- Independence of a country

- Abolition of slavery (In our country and in other parts of the world. For instance, in Puerto Rico the abolition of slavery is officially observed on March 22)

- Discoveries and inventions

    - geographical discoveries, like the discovery of the Americas or of the Pacific Ocean by the Europeans

    - scientific discoveries, such as the botanical work of George Washington Carver

    - inventions like the helicopter by Russian scientist Igor Sikorsky

▮ *Foundations of leading organizations:* (for example, the Red Cross, the United Nations)

▮ *People who have distinguished themselves because of a heroic deed or for their contribution to our society*

- Heroes or distinguished people. For example: Mahatma Gandhi, leader of the nonviolent movement that led to the independence of India; Harriet Tubman, an African American woman who risked her life for the cause of freedom; Simón Bolívar, leader of the Latin American independence movement; African American poet Maya Angelou.

▮ *The Arts*

- music

- dances

- drama

- literature and poetry

- crafts and decorative arts

▮ *Beliefs and Traditions*

- festivals

- folklore

- myths

FIGURE 6.5 Working with the additive approach

Applying the Additive Approach in the Classroom (4–5-year-olds)

Main Theme: Things we like to eat at home and at school

Concept: Food

Integration: Social Studies, Science, Math, Literacy

Topics to explore:
1. Foods we like
2. Food we eat for breakfast
3. Food we eat at school
4. Food children eat in Japan and Mexico*

Literacy (books):

Objectives: Learning new words; learning food words; learning words in other languages; comparing and contrasting; sequencing; retelling.

Books to share and discuss with children:
1. Carle, E. (1970). *Pancakes, pancakes.*
2. Brown, M. (1947). *Stone soup.*
3. Brandenburg, A. (1976). *Corn is maize: The gift of the Indians.**
4. Hitte, K. (1970). *Mexicali soup.**
5. Morris, A. (1989). *Bread, bread, bread.**
6. Baer, E. (1995). *This is the way we eat our lunch: A book about children around the world.**

Social Studies Activities

Objectives: Identifying eating patterns; investigating the eating schedule in other countries; discussing how fruits and vegetables get to the grocery store; locating places where our food comes from; mapping.
1. Preparing charts describing what children prefer for breakfast, dinner.
2. Making a graph to show what the class favorite fruits, vegetables, etc. are.
3. *Taking a field trip to an ethnic grocery store to identify what they have.
4. Preparing a cooperative map to show the places/countries where our preferred food items come from.
5. *Learning the names of favorite dishes in another language.
6. *Discussing the eating schedules in other countries.

Science/Cooking Experiences

Objectives: Observing changes in food (when mashed, ground, cooked); tasting; comparing flavors; identifying vegetables and fruits with similar colors.
1. Making apple sauce
2. *Making Mexican quesadillas (cheese-filled tortillas)
3. *Making an Asian vegetable salad
4. Tasting different types of cheeses
5. *Comparing different types of breads (flat or unleavened, sweet, salty, crusty, etc.)
6. *Preparing a cooperative vegetable soup with vegetables from different countries, for instance, root vegetables, pumpkin, white sweet potatoes, plantains

Art Experiences

Objectives: Using art to represent one's ideas; using common house items to create art; working cooperatively.
1. Preparing a picture menu
2. Making "food mobiles"
3. *Preparing a cooperative mural about food children eat in the U.S.A., Japan, and Mexico

---

* Indicates insertion of ethnic content.

FIGURE 6.6 Transformation Approach: Let's talk about ornaments

---

A kindergarten teacher who uses the level 3 approach would make the following changes in the curriculum:

Theme: Things we wear and use

Topic: We all use personal ornaments

Concepts:
1. People are alike and different in many ways
2. People wear different objects
3. Personal ornaments have special meanings for people

Skills:
1. Looking for details
2. Observing and classifying
3. Identifying things that are alike and different

Goals:
1. To understand that most people use and wear personal ornaments (watches, bracelets, hair pins, scarves, necklaces, etc.)
2. To become aware of the different ornaments (earrings, Hindu dots (vindi), rings, African kefte, etc.) that people in our community use
3. To realize that people with different cultural roots prefer different ornaments
4. To understand that ornaments have special meanings for people
5. To comment on the different occasions people use ornaments (weddings, birthdays, holidays, etc.)

Learning Centers:
1. Housekeeping area: A variety of clothing reflective of what people in the community wear; an assortment of clothing and accessories used by the target cultural groups
2. Art/Manipulatives: A variety of materials to create ornaments and crafts. Materials will include beads, coconut shells, dry leaves and flowers, etc. Have materials used for women's makeup (for example, kohl pencils, blush, etc.). Do the makeup on paper plate faces for different occasions.
3. Math/Science: Estimate how many pieces of coconut are needed to make a necklace. Taste raw coconut and coconut flakes to compare their taste.
4. Movement: Listen to music typically used during special occasions (weddings, birthdays, etc.). Respond to the music by creating steps. Learn a typical dance.

---

that will not only respond to the developmental levels and interests of children but will also be pertinent to the child. In this type of approach, considering the surrounding reality of the child is crucial to making the curriculum valid and culturally responsive. We say responsive because children are not only discovering their cultural identities, but are also provided with opportunities to discover other cultural entities. Teachers working with level 3 know that it requires constant planning and a great deal of flexibility to ac-

commodate necessary changes. The flexibility gives teachers an opportunity to offer a pool of socially significant experiences for the young children in their classrooms.

Level 4—The Social Action Approach
The social action approach is the highest level in Banks' typology and "includes all the elements of the transformation approach but adds components that require students to make decisions and take actions related to the concept, issue, or

FIGURE 6.6 continued

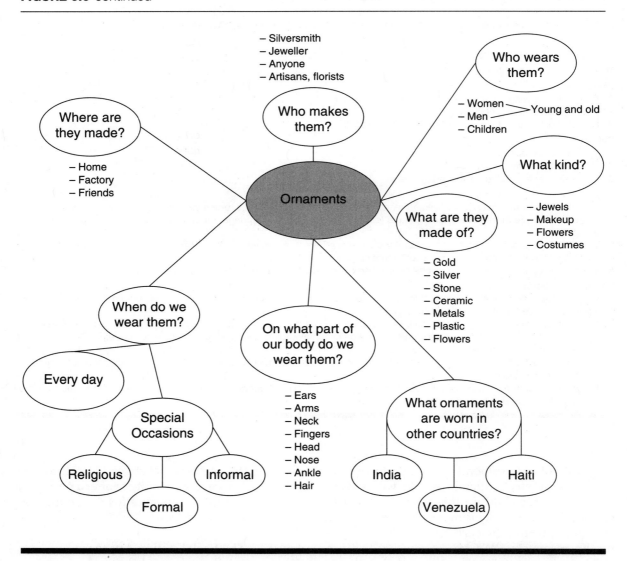

USING THEMATIC TEACHING TO CREATE THE LEVEL 3 CURRICULUM

We know that translating ideas into action is sometimes a hard thing to do. When some of our students began exploring how to apply the transformation approach, they felt overwhelmed by the task. As we talked with them we discovered that they were trying to transform their entire program at once. We suggested that they start small by changing one small portion of the curriculum first. With that advice in mind, one of our students who teaches first grade chose to focus on the movement curriculum. Using thematic teaching as her strategy, she decided to target her activities on learning games from different cultures. She began by first selecting games played by people in the children's community (mainly European American) and then added games representing Asian and Hispanic cultures. Group games and musical games and dances were selected, providing opportunities for children to employ a wide variety of skills within the framework of play.

Using references like *The Multicultural Game Book* by Louise Orlando (Scholastic 1993) and Jane Caballero's *Children Around the World* (Humanics 1990), our student began to compile ideas for her curriculum. The result was an appealing curriculum where children were introduced to diversity through one of the best cultural artifacts: games. As she told us later, this initial trial with the transformation approach was the bridge she used to move into other areas of multiculturalism. In her words, once she "tasted" teaching in a different way, she just could not go back to her old curriculum.

Theme: It Is Playtime!

▮ Favorite games of our families
  ▮ Games from the African American tradition (*hot butter beans; skelly; Rolly Polly; tin can alley; hand soccer; four squares; jack rocks*)
  ▮ Traditional games of European American families (*hide and seek, hopscotch, tops, etc.*)
  ▮ Games from the Hispanic tradition (*arroz con leche; Doña Ana, etc.**)
  ▮ Games and dances from other countries
      1. Ghana- The clapping game**
      2. Zaire - Catching stars***
      3. Taiwan - Clapstick blind man's buff**
      4. China - 1,2,3 dragon ***
      5. Haiti - Manee Gogo **
      6. Jamaica - Sally Water **
      7. Puerto Rico - Ambos a dos; Candela, candela
      8. Chile - Guessing game (¿Quién es?**)
      9. Mexico- La raspa
      10. Brazil - Bossa Nova

*Delacre, L. (1992). *Arroz con leche.* New York: Scholastic Books.
**Nelson, W., and Glass, B. (1992). *International playtime: Classroom games and dances from around the world.* IL: Fearon Teachers' Aids.
***Orlando, L. (1993). *The multicultural game book: More than 70 traditional games from 30 countries.* New York: Scholastic Books.

problem studied in the unit" (1993, p. 205). Teachers using level 4 have two major goals, both consistent with early childhood aspirations and practices (Bredekamp 1987). These goals are

1. To prepare children for social criticism (ability to examine and analyze social situations and to originate and participate in the social change process); and
2. To prepare children to become decision-makers (learning decision-making skills).

Classroom instruction based on level 4 is characterized by intense activity rather than the passive examination of issues and events from both the past and the present. Children operating in level 4 are asked to analyze facts and practices closely. For example, a social analysis of a topic may be presented for the purpose of examining the issue of fairness. A goal of level 4 is to confront children with situations describing unfair events, for the purpose of leading them to take action. Expected behaviors include proposals of alternative views and suggestions of corrective measures for a situation. Teaching such a topic in a multicultural environment becomes a true social learning experience for children who will learn that they can become agents for social change.

Developing a curriculum based on level 4 requires a careful selection of issues characterized by both relevancy and developmental pertinence. Lesson plans following the social action approach have the four major components shown in Figure 6.7.

Teaching with the social action approach lends itself to introducing children to topics that are not often studied in the classroom. Some of these topics, such as prejudice and racism, might be considered controversial by school colleagues and parents. Therefore, teachers who decide to teach about such issues will need to carefully select materials and topics and spend more time preparing to teach. Communication with families must be incorporated into the process if this approach is to

be successful. A simple letter stating the topic and the purposes for studying it will not only help clarify doubts but it will also allow families to see the need for the activities.

Creating a socially responsive curriculum in level 4 is a challenging and exciting experience. This is a level that teachers can reach after they have gained experience and confidence dealing with the multicultural content. It is advisable to try the other levels before venturing into this highest one. Remember, moving toward reform takes time!

The Sleeter and Grant Typology for Multicultural Education

The model developed by Christine Sleeter and Carl Grant is a product of their extensive and continuous research in multicultural education. As they explain, the five approaches were constructed from their varied experiences as educators and social scientists and their extensive analyses of multicultural curricula in grades K–12 (Sleeter & Grant 1994). The approaches are structured around the social diversity issues of race, class, disability, and gender. The typology also serves as a way to observe how multicultural education has evolved since its inception. Stacey York (1991), in reviewing the typology, comments that although the research did not focus on primary education levels, Sleeter and Grant's ideas are still relevant to early childhood education. We agree with her opinion because the typology offers an array of possibilities from which early childhood professionals can choose and adapt the one that best fits their needs. In Sleeter and Grant's typology, multicultural education is offered through the following approaches:

1. Teaching the exceptional and the culturally different
2. Human relations
3. Single-group studies

FIGURE 6.7 Teaching components of the social action approach

1. *A decision problem or a question* (An issue or situation that requires attention)
   Example: Children are posed with the problem of a child who is being rejected by others because he speaks with an accent. Because of what is happening, the child does not want to come to school. Is there anything we can do? Is it right for others to make fun of him because of his accent?

2. *An inquiry that will provide children with data related to the problem* (Questioning to discover the real cause of the problem; who is affected and how are they affected; and examples of the problem)
   Example: Lead children in the analysis of the situation with questions such as:
   ▌ What do we know about the boy/girl who has a problem?
   ▌ Is it wrong or bad to be different? Why?
   ▌ What happened to make the boy/girl feel bad?
   ▌ Is he the only one who is different in our classroom/school?
   ▌ If he/she is rejected, who else might feel rejected, too?

3. *A value inquiry and moral analysis* (Discussions, role-playing, presentation of different cases with the same issue)
   Example: Children will read and discuss selected readings to further illustrate that what happened was wrong and that it hurts people. For instance, they could discuss stories like *All Kinds: Who Cares about Race and Colour?* (Child's Play International 1989) and *Crow Boy* (Yashima 1955).

4. *A decision and a list of social actions to be taken* (A final determination of the case and a list of needed actions to correct the issue)
   Examples:
   ▌ Working in small groups, children can prepare an action plan to avoid similar situations. Children can also create a slogan to help them reinforce their commitment to what they have decided to do. For example, declaring the classroom as a place where "Everyone is welcome because we are all the same."
   ▌ Children can be prompted to take actions using questions such as:
   – What will this class do from now on?
   – If you find that someone is making a bad comment about another child, what should you do?
   – Can we help others understand what our beliefs are? How?

Source: Adapted from Banks, J. (1993). Approaches to multicultural curriculum reform. In J. Banks & C. Banks (eds.). *Multicultural education: Issues and perspectives* (pp. 205–207). Needham Heights, MA: Allyn & Bacon.

4. Multicultural education
5. Education that is multicultural and social reconstructionist

Approach I: Teaching the Exceptional and the Culturally Different

The first approach is a description of the programs many educators find in their districts. However, in terms of specific directions to design classroom practices or to organize activities, it bears little value for the early childhood teacher. The essence of teaching the exceptional and the culturally different is based on the factors that make some students different from the mainstream. These factors include having a particular disability, being a part of a lower social class or minority group, having a different language, or being a low-achieving female (Sleeter & Grant 1994). These factors are also seen as areas that create problems requiring corrective actions. Actions are taken with the purpose of facilitating the child's entrance into the existing social structure of our country. The belief here is that if children are taught according to their needs, they will be able to perform effectively.

Teachers following this approach adapt instruction to the students' skill levels and particular

FOCUS ON CLASSROOM PRACTICES

SELECTING EARLY CHILDHOOD CONTENT FOR THE LEVEL 4 CURRICULUM

Working with Banks' level 4 requires careful preparation. It particularly requires effective selection of the issues children will explore. One of the ways to find sound and child-valid topics is to create a list of possible areas requiring social action both at the community level and at the national/international levels. In doing this you will need good observation and analytic skills. As you exercise them, you will find that there are plenty of areas to study. We have listed some suggestions to help you select themes for your classroom. When considering what topics or social issues to include, look for:

▪ **Issues arising from the classroom/school interaction patterns:** For example, an incident of name calling, cases of lack of acceptance of some children and adults because of their religious ideas, reluctance to interact with adults based on their appearance.

▪ **Issues from the community:** For instance, cases of violent acts, situations of unfair practices against elderly people, loss of a recreational area, presence of homeless people.

▪ **Issues at the national/international level:** Possible topics are poverty; cases of unfairness because of people's status; loss of housing because of commercial expansion or construction; cases of violence against families; situations forcing people to leave their countries (immigrants and refugees); effects of epidemic diseases; needs of communities after a natural disaster.

▪ **Issues from the past:** Examples include examining the life of African Americans during the years of slavery, emotions of Africans as they were taken away from their homeland, reactions of Native Americans as they were forced to abandon their land and lifestyles, heroic accomplishments for the cause of justice, children and the Holocaust, the life of immigrants.

learning styles. Curricular practices are targeted to help the student "fill in the gaps in basic skills and knowledge" (Sleeter & Grant 1994, p. 42). These practices are based upon three important elements or bridges.

1. **Bridge I:** relating the curriculum to experiences and interests of children.

2. **Bride II:** using the children's native languages.
3. **Bridge III:** using a variety of strategies to attack and fill in the academic gaps.

School programs following this approach are structured in four different ways. Sleeter and Grant state that one form is when schools keep the exceptional or culturally different child in the

---

IN ACTION . . .   *Thinking About Banks*

After learning about the levels or approaches that educator James Banks proposes, take time to reflect and ask yourself the following questions:

▌ Which one(s) attract me the most? Why?

▌ Which one(s) have I already used? What was my experience?

▌ Which one(s) can I use with my children?

▌ Which one(s) seem to be most developmentally appropriate? Why?

---

regular program to which adaptations are made. A second approach is to keep the child in the same school program while offering help and enrichment "at the preschool level and before and after school" (Sleeter & Grant 1994, p. 68). Pull-out programs, the third way, are those in which the child spends some time away from the regular classroom receiving additional support. The fourth structure is assignment of children to an entirely different program where they remain until they have overcome their deficiencies and can be integrated into the regular school program. (This practice is being reconsidered as a result of the movement toward inclusion.) Examples of this approach can be found in:

1. ESOL programs
2. Chapter I programs
3. Bilingual kindergarten programs
4. Self-contained special education programs
5. Programs for children at-risk
6. Head-Start; Even-Start programs

Commenting about the first approach, Sleeter and Grant say that it reflects the ideas of those who perceive our society "as the land of opportunity and as a good, technological society that is constantly improving itself" (1994, p. 79). For this reason the exceptional and culturally dif-

ferent child needs help to enter the American mainstream.

Approach II: The Human Relations Approach
Contrary to the first approach, Sleeter and Grant's second approach offers teachers specific ways to create and organize a multicultural curriculum. Grounded on the idea of prosocial behaviors, the concept of human relations evokes many ideas but essentially brings to mind the desire for positive interaction among people. Central to this approach is promoting positive feelings in children that lead them to a sense of unity, tolerance, and acceptance of social diversity within the existing framework of American society. With such expectations all children become the target. The goals of this approach are

1. To help students communicate with, accept, and get along with people who are different from themselves
2. To reduce or eliminate stereotypes that students have [or might have] about people
3. To help students feel good about themselves as individuals and as members of the group they belong to
4. To prevent situations where children offend others by putting them down because of their

affiliations or characteristics (Sleeter & Grant 1994, pp. 86–87).

Teachers need to observe four basic principles when the human relations approach is used. First, this is a comprehensive approach, requiring infusion of its tenets throughout the entire curriculum. Sleeter and Grant recommend that this kind of program become schoolwide to avoid sending mixed messages to students. As a second principle, they recommend using a variety of teaching strategies where children are actively engaged. Use of real life and child-relevant experiences are recommended in following the third principle. Lastly, activities should be built around success for all children. Teachers should avoid competition and in its place should emphasize participation and involvement as end goals for classroom experiences. Themes could include:

1. *We are friends*
2. *We care for people*
3. *Sharing with our friends*
4. *I am important*
5. *My family and yours*
6. *We all have feelings*
7. *Friends everywhere*
8. *We can all play together*
9. *We all live and work together in a community*
10. *We are alike and we are different*

The goals and principles of human relations are consistent with the ideas of many early childhood professionals. However, concerns about this approach have been expressed by some educators. To effectively organize a human relations curriculum, teachers need to keep in mind that the emphasis is on the development of prosocial behaviors as the vehicle to promote positive interactions among all. Because the risk of falling into the trap of stereotypical and condescending material is always present, this approach requires an in-depth examination of the ideas and topics to be included. Topics and activities must be age-

appropriate and culturally sound. Teachers need to check materials constantly to verify that opportunities to develop a sense of fairness and equality are appropriately presented. In fact, use of this approach can provide relevant enabling experiences for teachers, preparing them to engage in more complex approaches to multicultural education.

Approach III: Single-Group Studies

The single-group studies approach represents one of the three more complex ways to multicultural education. The term, coined by Sleeter and Grant, defines those programs in which a particular cultural group or element of diversity becomes the focus of study. Promotion of social equality for a special group, as well as the recognition of that group, is the essence of the single-group studies approach. Advocates of this approach believe that exposing students to the realities of a specific group will result in the reduction of social stratification. Targets commonly chosen include women, ethnic groups such as Asian Americans, people with disabilities, gay people, or the working class (Sleeter & Grant 1994). An important goal of this approach is to provide students with relevant knowledge that will encourage their willingness "to work toward social change that would benefit the identified group" (Sleeter & Grant 1994, p. 124).

When using this approach, early childhood teachers need to consider that effective teaching requires integration of subject areas. If topics are taught in isolation, they will contribute little to the development of ideas. Because children learn when concepts are presented in a holistic way, presentation of target topics must permeate all classroom activities. As we design curricular activities, it is important to remember that learning occurs as a result of the child's exposure to a continuum of logically related experiences. Effective planning of the single-group approach resembles thematic teaching, where children are immersed in the

FOCUS ON CLASSROOM PRACTICES

PLANNING ACTIVITIES FOR THE HUMAN RELATIONS APPROACH

Structuring an effective human relations curriculum means that we are going to select goals and objectives that are child-appropriate. It also means that we will use child-appropriate strategies as well. We begin by establishing target goals similar to those proposed by Sleeter and Grant. Using them as guides, we then select a number of basic concepts. Finally, in choosing a teaching strategy we opt for literature-based thematic teaching. The result, shown below, is a teaching framework easily adaptable to any age level. As you read it, think about ways to adapt it for your own classroom.

Sample Framework Using the Human Relations Approach

Goal I: To get along with people who are different from ourselves

Theme 1: We all have things that makes us special

Concepts:

▮ Discovering ourselves: Finding that we all are special in some way

▮ Accepting differences in ourselves and others

▮ Becoming friends with all the children in our class

Goal II: To eliminate and fight against stereotypes about people

Theme 2: We are all alike and diverse

Concepts:

▮ Welcoming people as they are

▮ Clarifying our ideas about ourselves and others

▮ We listen and think: Learning to stop words that hurt

Goal III: To feel proud about one's identity

Theme 3: We are happy being what we are

Concepts:

▮ Valuing ourselves and our families

▮ Feeling proud of our identities: Learning who we are (ethnicity, religion, language, etc.)

▮ Accepting others

Goal IV: To become aware of unfairness and to take action

Theme 4: You and I can help make a better society!

Concepts:

▮ Working with everyone: Learning to be a good member of my classroom and school

▮ We can do it: Helping stop unfairness

▮ We can help make everyone feel accepted

topic throughout the entire program. Opportunities for application are crucial in this approach, both for assessment purposes and as ways to provide the child with instances showing the actual need and importance of the concepts explored.

Topics for single-group studies can be organized around investigative questions (Figure 6.8).

Classroom teaching structured around single-group studies requires careful preparation and knowledge about the chosen group. Sleeter and Grant recommend using authentic materials produced by and focused on members of the targeted group. This step is relevant if teachers want to demonstrate how people in that group perceive and feel about given events or facts. An accurate portrayal of the group's opinions and feelings will help students determine if equality exists. These studies would also help the children learn how each group interprets and views social reality. For example, children can examine the importance of knowing how to address an Hispanic adult (by

either his/her title rather than by the first name, if you are not a close friend). This will help them learn how social relationships are interpreted by that group.

Because of its empowering character, this approach is particularly valuable in helping children learn about themselves and their own culture (York 1991). Effectively used, this approach is also valuable in helping the child develop a proactive awareness about social and cultural issues.

Serious attention should be given to the selection of topics chosen in single-group studies. York (1991) notes that this approach has been misinterpreted by many educators who turned "the model into another form of classroom entertainment" (p. 26) by focusing on less relevant aspects like food, dances, and folktales. As with any other approach, caution should be placed not only in the selection of topics but also in their treatment and presentation. There are many times that, in spite of the best teaching intentions, topics are presented in a trivial and stereotypical form. Good planning and reflection are the best way to infuse quality into our teaching experiences.

Approach IV: Multicultural Education

The multicultural education approach is based on the importance and value of cultural pluralism in American society. A main tenet of this approach is that the United States is like a "tossed salad or a patchwork quilt" made up of distinct parts to create a wonderful new whole (Sleeter & Grant 1994, p. 170). Rather than focusing on a specific curriculum topic, multicultural education is viewed as a comprehensive curriculum reform process affecting all aspects of schooling. Important to the organization of the curriculum are the social contextual realities and experiences pertinent to the classroom audience. This approach shares similar characteristics with Banks' level 3. Basic to the multicultural approach are the ways in which students are led to analyze social issues involving bias, prejudice, and racism.

FIGURE 6.8 Topics for single-group studies at the primary level

---

▪ Life of homeless children
  (Who are the homeless? Who can become a homeless person? How does it feel when you do not have a home? Who helps the homeless? How can we help the homeless?)

▪ Learning about people with disabilities
  (What does it mean to have a disability? How do people with disabilities feel? How can we help?)

▪ Learning about refugees
  (Why do people leave their countries? How can we help?)

▪ Valuing our elders
  (Who are our elders? Why are they important to us? What can we learn from them? How can we show respect and appreciation toward our elders?)

▪ Learning about children in other neighborhoods
  (Where do they live? What activities do they do? What are their schools like? What games do they play? What do we have in common? In what ways are they unique?)

FIGURE 6.9 Parameters of the multicultural education approach

1. To promote cultural values.
2. To promote human rights and respect for those who are different from oneself.
3. To promote alternative life choices for people.
4. To promote social justice and equality for all people.
5. To promote equity in the distribution of power and income among groups.

Source: Gollnick & Chinn 1990 (p. 31).

Gollnick and Chinn (1990) have developed goals for the multicultural education approach (Figure 6.9).

Nieto (1992) claims that effective multicultural education programs require modifications to the entire school "culture." Such changes encompass not only the materials but also the content, which should be drawn out of the cultural baggage or background of the students. Practices like ability grouping, the behaviors and attitudes of teachers and staff, and the ways parents are involved in the school should be reviewed and changed. These changes reflect what several authors have agreed on: multicultural education is a process of total education reform (Banks 1993; Gollnick & Chinn 1990; Kendall 1983; Nieto 1992).

Although ideally this is an approach for implementation at the school level, it also provides direction for the early childhood teacher. When implemented, this approach requires the following steps:

1. *Knowledge of the Classroom Cultural Composition:* Essential to any successful activity is knowing what the cultural identity of both the class and the community are. This step requires a clear concept of the cultural setting where our teaching takes place. No responsive planning can be done without a realistic assessment of our classrooms. It is important to remember that elements of diversity such as religion and gender are also considered cultures. Questions to answer are:
   - What are the cultures/diversity found in my classroom?
   - What are the cultures/diversity found in this community?

2. *An Appraisal of the Existing Curriculum:* Before you begin changing your curriculum, take time to analyze what you have. In other words, do not discard everything yet! In the process of determining the "fit," you will undoubtedly discard some topics and keep others. To expedite this analysis, we suggest you review your curriculum framework or the list of topics planned for the year and check off those that correspond to the cultural diversity of your class and the community. The example below illustrates the process of deciding the "cultural fit."

What I currently teach	Children's cultures found in my classroom	Is there a cultural match? (A "NO" means I need to add or change)

3. *Establishing Goals and Selecting Topics:* This step leads the teacher toward making specific curriculum decisions and creating the curriculum framework. Using the information gathered in step 1, begin to outline your main targets or goals. Teachers following a mandated curriculum find it necessary to do some revisions in order to identify topics that match their targets. Once your goals are established, begin to select your content, that is, the themes and topics you want to explore with the class. Instead of choosing the content

for an entire year, begin by simply listing those you could develop in a month's time. Designing activities for only a month at a time will also prove easier. Remember that your activities should be age-appropriate. Finally, implement the curriculum.

4. *Periodical Review/Assessment Plan:* Taking time to review what actually happened is an important step. Having a simple assessment plan will help you identify the effective parts of the curriculum and alert you to the areas that need improvement. An assessment plan could actually consist of three simple questions:

  ▮ How did children react to the activities/materials?
  ▮ Am I satisfied with the outcomes of the activities? Why?
  ▮ Were my goals/objectives met? How?

Approach V: Education That Is Multicultural and Social Reconstructionist

This approach is the most complex one in the Sleeter and Grant typology. It is also the one they prefer. The name itself—education that is multicultural and social reconstructionist—indicates a higher level of sophistication. The goal of this approach is to foster a belief and a sense of social equality and cultural pluralism so that students will want to become actively engaged in achieving equality. A major expectation and a result of this approach is to have students become active participants in the elimination of social oppression. In general, teachers will find that this approach has many ideas in common with Banks' level 4.

Implementation of the multicultural and social reconstructionist approach presents two important challenges: 1) a need to redesign the total educational program to reflect the needs of diverse cultural groups; and 2) an openness to have children's questions, ideas, and proposals for dealing with current social issues. Sleeter and Grant present three advantages that support their selection of the multicultural and social reconstructionist approach. These same points become teaching guidelines when developing the classroom curriculum.

1. It targets issues and problems that have a current impact on some of the students.
   Classroom application: Developing a curriculum that deals with existent issues or problems at the classroom level or in the community. Activities and materials would directly reflect issues currently faced by children.

2. It allows students "to take an active stance," offering opportunities to present alternatives to the existing situations.
   Classroom application: Curricular topics would tackle problems about unfairness. Activities would be based on a participatory philosophy where children would take the role of active decision makers. Children would have a leading voice in establishing course of action to resolve situations of unfairness and discrimination.

3. It helps students participate and work as a group "to speak out, be heard, and effect change" (p. 247).
   Classroom application: Teaching activities will be designed around the concept of the project approach and the group investigations strategy (Joyce & Weil 1992). Here children would work as a group in cooperative activities for the purpose of finding ways to resolve or to confront events and situations requiring action. Activities would engage children in discussions helping them work out ideas together.

The multicultural and social reconstructionist approach represents a more direct way of dealing with social issues than the other models do. Given its complexity, educators are advised to carefully reflect on the requirements for its implementation (Sleeter & Grant 1994).

FOCUS ON CLASSROOM PRACTICES

THE GROUP INVESTIGATION MODEL

Aimed at offering children opportunities to develop skills needed to interact in a group and to become effective group members, the group investigation model (GIM) encourages the development of a sense of social life (Joyce and Weil 1992). Using the classroom as a model of the community/larger society, children are led through active participation to learn how to be group members and interact with others. Using cooperative inquiry, children are guided to problem-solve or investigate specific situations. Properly used, the GIM could be considered an effective and practical way for teaching children not only academic concepts but also providing experiences to participate in the social process. Joyce and Weil further emphasize that, besides its instructional effects, it also has relevant nurturant outcomes. They specifically identify the following significant nurturant effects, all relevant to multicultural teaching:

1. To encourage a sense of respect for the dignity of all and a commitment to pluralism
2. To instill a commitment to social inquiry
3. To foster a sense of independence as learners

Sharing elements with the project approach and cooperative learning, activities designed according to the GIM consist of the following phases:

Phase I: Children encounter a puzzling situation. The teacher, acting as a facilitator, describes and presents the problem to the class.

Phase II: Children are led to freely discuss and comment on the problem or situation. The teacher monitors the discussion, posing questions to help [clarify any angles].

Phase III: With the help of the teacher, study areas are identified and groups are formed. Members of each group are democratically assigned tasks and roles.

Phase IV: Working in their groups, children look for resources and collect information.

Phase V: Each group takes time to examine what they have collected. Decisions are made as to what else needs to be investigated. The teacher acts as a facilitator during their meeting.

Phase VI: Children in each group present their findings. New areas of study are identified.

Using the Sleeter and Grant Typology in Early Education

The five approaches suggested by Sleeter and Grant are a collection of options early educators can also consider. Like those proposed by Banks, these approaches also vary in complexity. We believe that the following approaches are adequate ways to teach multiculturally in an early childhood context: *human relations, multicultural education, and education that is multicultural and social reconstructionist.* Approach number one, teaching the exceptional and culturally different, we consider to be a mandate in terms of educational services required by this population. We also recognize that it needs to be infused with true perspectives about diversity issues. The single-studies approach, despite its positive characteristics, does not represent a way to infuse the entire curriculum, which is what multicultural educators view as effective practice. Because of its "add-on" character as Sleeter & Grant point out (p. 162), this approach can easily lead to bringing into the classroom irrelevant issues that will contribute little or nothing to the overall goals of multicultural programs. If this is the approach of your choice, remember that a conscientious and careful selection of topics is required for its successful implementation.

Concerns About the Human Relations Approach

Despite the advantages of the human relations approach, there are also some concerns. Some educators caution that the issue of the quality of the classroom experience is something to be carefully considered. Unfortunately, there have been times when the classroom curriculum has been characterized by trivial and stereotypical activities. Generally, this has happened when children are presented only with situations where no inquiry into social realities takes place. It can also occur as a result of poorly selected materials that are not reflective of the characteristics of local and national diversity. An effective human relations curriculum not only needs to emphasize social harmony, equality, and justice, but it also needs to confront children with an accurate portrayal of our society.

Reflecting on Approaches 4 and 5

Sleeter and Grant's last two approaches, multicultural and social reconstructivist, are more complex. They offer a more direct way to bring diversity issues into the young children's classroom, and employ strategies similar in nature to those found in the anti-bias curriculum. We believe that approaches 4 and 5 present good choices for teachers after they have gained experience in teaching multiculturally.

Which Approach Should Teachers Select?

Which approach to select depends on teachers and on their classroom circumstances. Because not all teachers are at the same level of professional development, it is important to select an approach that will compliment the teacher's strengths. How confident we feel as we deliver our program is basic to the success of any intended reforms. We support Sleeter and Grant's recommendation that teachers begin teaching about diversity by using the human relations approach. As a first step, an appropriately designed human relations curriculum offers the teacher ample opportunity to *begin* gaining experience in teaching about diversity. Selecting and organizing activities, leading the child to see how alike people are, and establishing the importance of the shared equality are all a part of an initial level that teachers can gradually surpass as they become more experienced in dealing with multicultural issues. Accomplishments on this level provide teachers with the necessary knowledge and skills to introduce the child to the more serious issues that are targeted by approaches 3 through 5.

IN ACTION . . . *Thinking About Sleeter and Grant*

Having examined Sleeter and Grant's five approaches to multicultural education, let us reflect on what we found. Try to answer the following questions:

▮ Have you used any of these approaches before?

▮ What other choices can you use to implement multicultural education?

▮ Which of these five approaches do you prefer? Why?

▮ Which approach is most appropriate for your classroom?

The Anti-Bias Approach

Developed by Louise Derman-Sparks, an early childhood educator, the anti-bias approach to curriculum centers on changing existing social inequalities. This approach proposes to eliminate the sources of stereotypes that lead individuals to form prejudices and cultural biases. The anti-bias approach is founded on the "practice of freedom" as defined by Paulo Freire. According to Freire (1970), people need to be able to face their social reality critically and propose ways to transform inequalities. Derman-Sparks asserts that this conceptual stance is "fundamental to anti-bias education" (Derman-Sparks 1989, p. ix). It has the potential to equip children to take action to stop injustice against themselves or others.

The anti-bias approach to multicultural education was developed especially for early childhood education. It is based on a belief that young children can be guided to develop positive attitudes toward social diversity. The anti-bias approach is grounded in cognitive theory and research on concept formation. Derman-Sparks contends that children will develop positive attitudes toward diversity and adopt a proactive stance against unfairness if the classroom offers experiences where they can see people responding against unfair situations and accepting differences, and where

the children themselves are encouraged to act in the same fashion.

Four central goals define the philosophy of the anti-bias approach. They also indicate the developmental appropriateness of the approach (Figure 6.10).

Teachers following this approach find themselves eliminating the color-blind or color-denial position which "assumes that differences are insignificant" (Derman-Sparks 1989, p. 6). They find themselves dealing directly with prejudice, racism, and stereotypes as they arise. As teachers deal with unfair situations, children join them, learning how to take action to correct a given

FIGURE 6.10 Curriculum goals of the anti-bias approach

Every child will be able to:

▮ construct a knowledgeable, confident self-identity

▮ develop comfortable, empathetic, and just interaction with diversity

▮ develop critical thinking skills

▮ develop the skills for standing up for oneself and others in the face of injustice

Source: Derman-Sparks & A.B.C. Task Force 1989 (p. ix).

circumstance. The model is intended to assist children in acquiring attitudes and behaviors modeled in the context of direct confrontations.

The Derman-Sparks anti-bias model differs from the multicultural model in the way it presents and addresses the content. Basically, it refrains from assuming the tourist-like curriculum where the child "visits" a culture and usually learns about its more exotic details. Such curricula only offer glimpses of cultures, contributing little to development of awareness and knowledge about the daily life and problems people face in other cultures. Derman-Sparks provides specific guidelines for avoiding a tourist approach to curriculum (Figure 6.11).

Two other important differences in the anti-bias approach are the inclusion of other components of diversity and the use of a developmental framework. Perhaps the best way to characterize

---

FIGURE 6.11 Guidelines for avoiding a tourist approach to the curriculum

1. Connect cultural activities to individual children and their families.
2. Remember that, while cultural patterns are real and affect all members of an ethnic group, families live their culture in their own individual ways.
3. Connect cultural activities to concrete, daily life.
4. Explore cultural diversity within the principle that everyone has a culture.
5. Have cultural diversity permeate the daily life of the classroom through frequent, concrete, hands-on experiences related to young children's interests.
6. Avoid the editorial "we" when talking to children ("we" implies homogeneity).
7. Explore the similarities among people through their differences.
8. Begin with the cultural diversity among the children and staff in your classroom, then focus on the diversity of others.

Source: Derman-Sparks & A.B.C. Task Force 1989 (pp. 57–58).

---

the anti-bias approach is to state that it is targeted at preventing the formation of misconceptions about the individual and group. The approach offers a way to help children deal with the diversity embedded in our society through activities that are based on principles of child development. For that reason, it is an excellent strategy for the early childhood classroom.

Another Model for Early Childhood Education

Frances Kendall, an early childhood educator, sketched a model based on the framework of the developmental-interaction philosophy, the same model used by Bank Street, and late Hilda Taba (Kendall 1983). Kendall believes that existing racism can be overcome through education, and she aspires to help the child learn to affirm his/her cultural differences and to respect those of other people. In her model, she bases the success and the attainment of these goals on the teacher, as the pivotal element in the process of multicultural education. She believes that "teachers are models for children; therefore, they should show respect and concern for all people" (Kendall 1983, p. 1). In Kendall's view, the focus of any multicultural program begins with enabling teachers: first, to recognize their own beliefs and, second, to learn how to implement the program. These insightful ideas are extremely relevant not only to the early childhood teacher but also for those aiming to initiate school-wide programs (Figure 6.12).

❖ Reflecting on the Approaches for Multicultural Education

The challenge of multicultural education has such dimensions that the best approach is still to be designed. In the interim, there are several choices available to the early childhood educator. The ones

---

FIGURE 6.12 Kendall's goals for multicultural education

---

1. To teach children to respect others' cultures and values as well as their own
2. To help all children learn to function successfully in a multicultural, multiracial society
3. To develop a positive self-concept in those children who are most affected by racism—children of color*
4. To help all children experience both their differences as culturally diverse people and their similarities as human beings in positive ways
5. To encourage children to experience people of diverse cultures working together as unique parts of a whole community

---

*The term "children or people of color" refers to children of origins other than European American. In this book, we have excluded this term because it emphasizes not only a misleading human element but also one that has been responsible for many painful incidents. Kendall 1983 (p. 3).

presented in this chapter are only a few considered more relevant by the authors. Other models have also been proposed by concerned educators.

As you prepare yourself to become a multicultural educator of the young, it is important that you take time to reflect on the kind of classroom environment you want to create. Ask yourself:

1. Why do I want to teach in a multicultural way?
2. What are my expectations of multicultural education?
3. What do my students need?
4. What are the cultural challenges present in my community?
5. Would my teaching be more developmentally appropriate if I infused the multicultural perspective?

The more time you take to reflect on your convictions regarding multiculturalism, the more certain you will become of the direction you wish to take. This will help guide you in planning the multicultural program you want to establish. Of all the decisions to make in multicultural education, the hardest one is resolving to change our teaching strategies. If you have resolved to do that (and we hope you have!), other decisions regarding teaching multiculturally will come more easily.

❖ Things to Do . . .

1. Define the following key concepts: approach, model, and curriculum. Reflecting on your own school, find examples of an approach, of a model, and of a curriculum.
2. Examining the typology of James Banks, think about examples to describe each of his four levels.
3. It is always important to know how other teachers feel about the curriculum. For that purpose, share Banks' typology with at least three teachers. Be sure to jot down their comments. Do an analysis of your findings and determine the approaches of their preference.
4. Banks and Sleeter and Grant's typologies have common points. Examine both carefully and find the common elements.
5. Define the anti-bias approach. Does this model have any points in common with the other approaches? Explain.
6. After exploring the different approaches to multicultural education, which one would you select? Why?
7. Some people have argued that many of the approaches to multicultural education are not suitable for the early childhood classroom. What is your opinion? Why?
8. Thinking about the multicultural approach you chose for question number 6, prepare a draft of the changes you would need to make

in your classroom to implement it. After completing your draft, go back to it and find:
a. the five major changes
b. the three hardest changes
c. the five easiest things to change
d. three initial changes.

❖ Children's Literature Corner

Coerr, E. (1993). *Sadako*. New York: Putnam's Sons.

Daly, N. C. (1986). *Not so fast Songololo*. New York: Atheneum.

Griego, M., Gilbert, B., and Kimball, S. (1981). *Tortillitas para mama and other nursery rhymes*. New York: Holt, Rinehart, & Winston. (Spanish and English)

Jacobson, P., and Kristensen, P. (1986). *A family in China*. New York: Bookright Press.

Levine, E. (1989). *I hate English!* New York: Scholastic Books.

Morrow, M. (1990). *Sarah Winnemucca: Native American stories*. Austin, TX: Steck-Vaughn.

O'Kelley, M. (1991). *Moving to town*. Boston, MA: Little, Brown & Co.

Williams, V. (1982). *A chair for my mother*. New York: Greenwillow.

Wolf, B. (1974). *Don't feel sorry for Paul*. New York: Harper & Row.

❖ References

Banks, J. (1993). In J. Banks & C. Banks (eds.). *Multicultural education: Issues and perspectives* (2nd ed.). Needham Heights, MA: Allyn & Bacon.

Banks J. (1994, May). Transforming the mainstream curriculum. *Educational Leadership* 5: 8 (pp. 4–8).

Banks, J. & Banks, C. (1993). *Multicultural education: Issues and perspectives* (2nd ed.). Needham Heights, MA: Allyn & Bacon.

Bredekamp, S. (ed.) (1987). *Developmentally appropriate practice in early childhood programs serving children birth through age 8*. Washington, DC: National Association for the Education of Young Children.

Derman-Sparks, L., & A.B.C. Task Force. (1989). *Antibias curriculum tools for empowering young children*. Washington, DC: National Association for the Education of Young Children.

Doll, R.C. (1992). *Curriculum improvement decision making and process* (8th ed.). Boston, MA: Allyn & Bacon.

Freire, D. (1970). *Pedagogia del oprimido* [Pedagogy of the oppressed]. Madrid, Spain: Siglo Veintiuno Editores.

Goffin, S. (1994). *Curriculum models and early childhood education: Appraising the relationship*. New York: Merrill.

Gollnick, D.M., & Chinn, P.C. (1990). *Multicultural education in a pluralistic society* (3rd ed.). New York: Merrill.

Gordon, A., & Browne, K. (1989). *Beginnings and beyond*. New York: Delmar.

Joyce, B., and Weil, M. (1992). *Models of teaching*. Englewood Cliffs, NJ: Prentice Hall.

Kendall, F. (1983). *Diversity in the classroom: A multicultural approach to the education of young children*. New York: Teachers College Press.

Nieto, S. (1992). *Affirming diversity: The sociopolitical context of multicultural education*. New York: Longman.

Sleeter, C.E., & Grant, C. (1994). *Making choices for multicultural education* (2nd ed.). New York: Merrill.

Williams, L. (1987). *Determining the curriculum*. In C. Seefeldt (ed.). *The early childhood curriculum* (pp. 1–12). New York: Teachers College Press.

York, S. (1991). *Roots and wings: Affirming culture in early childhood programs*. St. Paul, MN: Redleaf Press.

"Guideline #7: Curriculum respects and supports individual, cultural and linguistic diversity. Curriculum supports and encourages positive relationships with children's families."

National Association for the Education of Young Children
and National Association of Early Childhood Specialists
in State Departments of Education (1992)

PART III

Into Action: Implementing a Pluricultural Program for Children

From Barbara's Journal

"It's hard to believe that we have had such inequity in education in a country where liberty and freedom are so valued. This whole idea of multicultural education finally makes sense to me. Now, I understand why my friend Belén tried to teach her class that we are all one and that they need to help others underhand that. Gee, it was funny to see how she told her first-graders that they can best help our country by preventing unfairness. I remember how they admonished a fifth-grader who was calling another boy names because the boy wore very thick glasses. It worked! The fifth grader was so embarrassed!

"I want to start my new year on a different note. I don't know how I will do it yet. I do know that I want the children to learn to accept and respect others. More than that, my classroom will be the place where children will learn to enjoy this diverse world they live in. It will be a challenge. So, let's see what happens."

Barbara

"Multicultural education, reflecting the diversity of American society, can become a part of the classroom in all programs for young children."

Jeanne Morris (1983)

CHAPTER 7

The Classroom, Where Words Become Action

In this chapter we will:

■ define components of curriculum design

■ discuss and suggest a process for assessing the curriculum

■ describe the role of teacher as curriculum designer

■ depict the impact of developmentally appropriate practices in the curriculum

■ define the characteristics of an early childhood multicultural educator

Key concepts:

■ curriculum

■ process and content

■ curriculum reform

■ needs assessment

❖ Reaffirming the Decision to Teach Multiculturally

Every day in classrooms across America children and teachers join in the magical journey of schooling. Through this experience children begin to understand at an early age what it is to be an American. This discovery process takes place primarily in the classroom. Therefore, it is imperative that the instructional practices in the early years reflect the true nature, values, and needs of our society. To accomplish this in a meaningful way, we must look for effective inclusion of multiculturalism into the curriculum.

Making the transition to a multicultural educational program requires not only time and careful preparation, but also an examination of our curricular practices. Such analysis must cover all aspects of teaching: the beliefs, the content, the activities, the materials, and the classroom environment. In this chapter, we will explore the ways teachers moving into multiculturalism need to transform their teaching.

When you make the decision to infuse the multicultural perspective into your teaching, you make a commitment to invigorating your instructional practices and providing children with learning experiences that are valid in the context of today's world. Teachers who become multicultural educators are also responsive to the particular developmental demands that children bring to the classroom. For example, we know that young children at a certain stage of their development are very curious. They may frequently raise issues about other people's characteristics, like the European American child who asks, "Why is she so dark?" when referring to an East Indian classmate. The Asian American child may find his classmates giggling at him because of the shape of his eyes. Incidents like these are used by some professional educators as knowledge-building experiences. However, not all early childhood educators perceive these as opportunities to prepare children for increasingly complex social interactions in our multicultural world.

Let us keep in mind the assumptions outlined by Hernández (1989).

1. It is increasingly important for political, social, educational, and economic reasons to recognize that the United States is a culturally diverse society.
2. Multicultural education is for ALL students.
3. Multicultural education is synonymous with effective teaching.
4. Teaching is a cross-cultural encounter.
5. The educational system has not served students equally well.
6. Multicultural education is synonymous with educational innovation and reform.
7. Next to parents, TEACHERS are the single most important factor in the lives of children.
8. Classroom interaction between teachers and students constitutes the major part of the educational process for most students (emphasis added, pp. 9–11).

Our determination should be reaffirmed by the realization that teaching multiculturally means teaching all children. In the next sections, we will examine some of the relevant steps we must take to reach that goal.

❖ Where Do We Start?

There are many steps to be taken as you move onto teaching with a multicultural perspective. The first step is to look at yourself. You must recognize how important you are as a teacher and even more as a professional early childhood educator. As a professional educator you are the best champion children have. Their hopes for a responsive education are placed on you.

Let us examine those qualities and characteristics that make you the key to a successful multicultural program.

Teachers: the Key to the Success of Multicultural Education

Teaching transforms lives, according to the old adage. Good teaching, as defined by leading educators and professional organizations, happens when teachers care and look for ways to reconcile the child's own needs with the aspirations of education. Some of these aspirations are grounded in the principles of developmentally appropriate practices (DAP). Teachers of young children need to incorporate both the perspectives of diversity and DAP into their instruction in order to respond to the whole child. The authors of this book recognize this as the essence of a multicultural teacher.

Good multicultural programs for children exist because some teachers have a special commitment to children. This special sense of responsibility is what helps these professionals look for ways to organize their classroom environment in developmentally and culturally responsive ways. Teachers who achieve this balance are the professionals every child deserves and needs. They also model ideal ethical traits that should distinguish all early childhood educators.

Let us begin by examining the characteristics that define good multicultural teachers. This will help us identify the qualities we seek in an early childhood multicultural educator. Banks (1988) lists the following as essential traits of an effective multicultural teacher.

1. **knowledge:** about the social sciences and about pedagogical principles.
2. **clarified cultural identification:** possesses "a reflective and clarified understanding of his or her cultural heritage and experience of how it relates to and interacts with the experiences of other ethnic and cultural groups."

3. **positive intergroup and racial attitudes:** exhibits and practices a positive attitude toward others regardless of their ethnic or cultural differences.
4. **pedagogical skills:** has effective and valid instructional knowledge (Banks 1988, p. 169).

Another set of teacher characteristics is offered by Nieto (1992). In her opinion, "becoming a multicultural teacher . . . means becoming a multicultural person" (p. 275). She further states that to become multicultural one must be reeducated in three specific ways. This triad also describes the traits of the multicultural educator.

1. **knowledge:** learning more about pluralism and how it is reflected in people and in our interactions.
2. **honest assessment of our own biases:** accepting that we all hold biases, sometimes very well hidden inside ourselves.
3. **ability to view reality through a myriad of perspectives:** learning to approach reality from more than one way.

According to Lillian Katz (1984), the early childhood professional is characterized by the ability exhibited in handling situations in the classroom. In her view, a professional "considers the most reliable knowledge about how children learn plus the goals of the parents, the school, and the community at large" (p. 3). Katz indicates that the professional knowledge teachers possess should come from the sound interdisciplinary background, with child development principles serving as the core.

Drawing upon the ideas of leading educators and the ideal traits defined by professional organizations like the National Association for Education of Young Children (NAEYC) and the Association for Children Education International (ACEI), we can now draw a profile of an early childhood multicultural teacher.

An early childhood multicultural teacher . . .

1. has a sound knowledge about child development that he/she uses and applies in classroom teaching;
2. believes that multiculturalism is an integral part of our society and that schools need to incorporate multiculturalism into their programs;
3. is committed to helping the child face and understand our social diversity;
4. is aware of his/her own ideas about diversity, biases, beliefs, and works to clarify them, and recognizes and accepts his/her own diversity and that of children;
5. holds high expectations equally for all children and helps all children to develop to their fullest;
6. works and interacts in a respectful way with all parents as partners and collaborators for the benefit of the child;
7. is willing to try out new methods and materials to accommodate the needs of children;
8. is constantly assessing his/her own teaching to guarantee its responsiveness to the children's needs;
9. is constantly searching for new approaches, and/or methods to improve her/his multicultural teaching;
10. has a classroom environment where tolerance, respect, and openness to learn and understand others are its essential characteristics;
11. keeps a positive, willing, and open attitude toward self and others as professionals; and
12. recognizes that reality is a composite of many different perspectives.

These characteristics describe a classroom leader, the teacher, who will use her/his skills and knowledge on behalf of children. This list of at-

FIGURE 7.1 Multicultural early childhood teachers are leaders

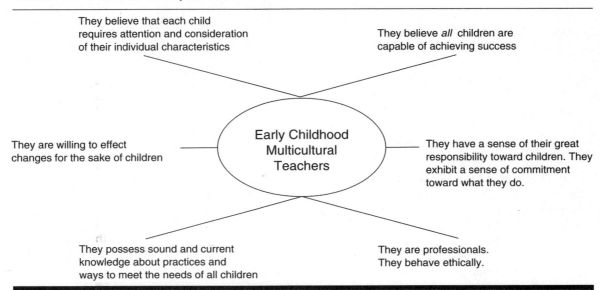

They believe that each child requires attention and consideration of their individual characteristics

They believe *all* children are capable of achieving success

They are willing to effect changes for the sake of children

Early Childhood Multicultural Teachers

They have a sense of their great responsibility toward children. They exhibit a sense of commitment toward what they do.

They possess sound and current knowledge about practices and ways to meet the needs of all children

They are professionals. They behave ethically.

IN ACTION . . . *Reflecting Upon the Profile of the Early Childhood Educator*

▮ Which of the characteristics of an early childhood multicultural educator mentioned here describe you?

▮ Which do you think are the most important ones?

▮ Which ones would you say are the hardest to achieve? Why?

▮ What other descriptors would you add to the list?

tributes also reflects a composite of knowledge and values, both personal and professional, that depicts an educator who is personally and professionally willing to take action and to set direction (Figure 7.1).

Becoming a Good Multicultural Early Educator

You probably realize that many of the essential characteristics of multicultural educators are attributes that you already possess and that there are others that you still need to achieve. Because all professionals are constantly growing and improving themselves, it is to be expected that there will be areas where you will need further development. Learning about our own teaching strengths and weaknesses is an important step for a teacher who is moving into multicultural education. This knowledge determines the directions and the intensity of changes you need to make.

Educators who make a commitment to undertake multicultural teaching often discover that they possess many more good teaching qualities than they had thought. This knowledge reassures them and acts as a catalyst for change. The change process is described in Figure 7.2. The first two steps will be the focus of this chapter.

❖ Exploring Our Teaching Environment

Good and effective multicultural education requires sound and objective knowledge of the place and program where we teach. In the next section, attention is placed on learning more about our classrooms, our curricula, and, in general, our programs.

WORKING GLOSSARY

▮ **Multicultural Early Childhood Educator**—a teacher with a professional commitment to offer children ages 0-8 specially designed developmental experiences where both the child's immediate multicultural realities and those of our nation are considered and valued. This educator tailors the curriculum to the developmental and cultural needs of children for the purpose of helping them learn to interact and succeed in the American multicultural society.

FIGURE 7.2 Steps toward multicultural teaching

I. **Knowing ourselves as teachers:** Who am I as a teacher? Self-assessment, where teachers examine their own teaching and beliefs.

II. **Assessing our present practices:** Where do I stand now? What kind of program do I offer my students? Analysis of current curriculum to determine the content and processes used. What is the school context like? What should my teaching be like? What do my students need?

III. **Designing the program:** Which goals and objectives will I have? What approach will I use? What materials and resources do I have and need?

IV. **Implementing:** When will actions take place? How can I find out about their effects?

Where Do We Start?

We first need to know where we are before any changes can effectively take place. Imagine you have been invited to a party and you want to buy something new to wear. Without any further information or details about the event, it would be impossible to buy clothes to suit the occasion. You might like to wear elegant evening attire, but if the activity turns out to be an outdoor picnic, you probably will find yourself totally out of place. You might be an excellent guest, but if you do not prepare yourself for an event, you will probably have a difficult time trying to fit in. The same concepts apply to curriculum change. When planning for school and classroom change, it is important to have a clear understanding of the setting where the change will take place. A thorough knowledge of the classroom environment and the pupils helps the teacher set realistic expectations. Doll (1992) reminds us that effective planning happens only when those involved in the planning are a part of the environment where the plan will be implemented. Good planning aimed at producing long-lasting transformations is based on sound knowledge of the children we teach. This is not only common sense, but something that has been advocated by many distinguished educators. John Dewey, who advocated an active and child-based curriculum, argued that good curriculum was determined by its relationship to society. Educational directions, according to Dewey, should emerge from the people and the societal context. Consideration of the social context, he felt, provides the appropriate and essential bases to plan and design school activities. Dewey believed that changes cannot take place without consideration for their applicability. This important point regarding applicability reaffirms the need to know our settings. To know the settings where we work, means to do a "reality check," to ascertain the characteristics of that setting.

Applying Dewey's ideas of an effective curriculum for young children means considering three essential ingredients: the *reality of the community,* the *nature of the family,* and the *children's developmental needs.* Incorporating all three elements into the curriculum will result in a culturally sensitive and developmentally appropriate curriculum we aspire to realize in every early childhood classroom in our country.

Why Planning Is So Important

Literature abounds in examples of well-intended innovations that never met with success. Upon close examination, it becomes evident that many failures were due to inadequate investigation of facts in the planning phase. Deciding to teach multiculturally already places us close to the finish line. But to cross it and remain winners requires having clear objectives and expectations. Taking time now to carefully plan and assess your setting will prove beneficial for determining present and future directions. Let us try to avoid failure and take some time to do that important "reality check."

IN ACTION . . . *Looking at Your School*

- How well do you think you know your school?
- What details about your classroom do you feel you do not know will enough?
- What are the major tenets of your program?
- What should be the essential characteristics of your multicultural program?

Knowing Your Program

Being early childhood educators has provided us with first-hand experiences about how children learn. One very important lesson we have mastered is that learning does not happen in isolated bits and pieces. The same is true of teaching. It is an important part of the growth process, complemented by familial and societal experiences. To make teaching a truly integrated intellectual and social experience, materials and the school environment must mirror the community of children and parents served (Bredekamp & Rosegrant 1992). It is, therefore, essential to examine the nature of the settings where teaching takes place. The knowledge gained from this experience often prevents disappointment. By determining the particular attributes that depict a community, the early childhood educator comes to know the needs of the stakeholders, which in turn will determine the direction of required change. The assessment of the setting needs to be undertaken by other school professionals as well as by the individual classroom teacher. Ornstein and Levine (cited by Ornstein & Hunkins 1993) suggest that to generate success, changes must be school-focused and adapted to reality.

The Needs Assessment: How to Gain a True Perspective on Our Practices

A well-known principle in early childhood education is to never assume that we know what the child needs or knows. In fact, this is why we are constantly observing and checking what children do and say in our classrooms. In the multicultural early childhood environment, verifying and checking what children bring into the classroom is crucial. Time spent in assessment is as important as selecting materials and designing activities. Actually, this is what guarantees that we are taking the right developmental direction.

Teachers of young children in today's diverse classrooms need to confirm that their teaching strategies meet the needs of their students. The process requires that the teacher identify the specific areas of concern from which the educator will later develop instructional goals and expectations. This process is better described as a *needs assessment.*

"A needs assessment permits determination of needs either in broad, general terms, with reference to several goals, or in specific terms, with reference to pinpointed goals," (Doll 1992, p. 339). Identification of needs can take place through both formal and informal processes. The outcomes of both reveal "where we are" (Doll 1992, p. 339). Needs identification should provide the teacher with a three-dimensional sense of the setting. It should provide information regarding: a) the community where the school is located or serves (in case children are bused in); b) the school itself as an entity formed by faculty and staff; and c) the children and their families. Getting a feel for the setting as seen from these

---

Snapshot 7.1
Never Assume You Know Everything About Your School

One of the authors of this book gave her graduate students in an early childhood education course an assignment to prepare a profile of their school and community. Students were expected to determine the ten essential elements that define the school and the community that teachers need to consider in their planning of the multicultural curriculum. Many of the students, being practitioners, commented that they could write the ten elements without doing a survey.

When the time came to report the findings, the majority of students (almost 90 percent) reported that there were more details about their school than they realized. Answers such as: "I can't imagine that I knew so little!" "Now I know what my class needs!" or "I have gained a totally new perspective of my class," were common reactions. The fact is that these professionals, some of whom have worked in their settings for a number of years, never grasped the essence of their school environment. So even if you think you know your classroom and school, take time to find out how much you *really* know.

---

perspectives can be very time-consuming. However, there are informal ways for teachers to obtain valid, relevant information. Doll (1992) suggests several ways for determining needs that may be helpful to the classroom teacher:

- interviews
- open-ended inventories
- reports of critical incidents
- records of discussions
- test results and scores
- notes taken during meetings
- interviews with parents or children, and
- personal observations

To those suggested by Doll, we add:

- written communications from parents
- students' portfolios

- children's drawings
- comments made by children or parents
- children's reactions: during story time; to materials; to situations.

The classroom teacher may use all of the data sources described above to provide insights needed to structure the desired changes.

When doing a needs assessment at the classroom level, it is probably easier if the teacher follows a basic outline covering the relevant areas. Such outlines can serve as "factual maps" once the assessment has been completed. Two examples of multicultural profiling, one using questions and another based on webbing, are described. Both address the same four basic areas and differ only in one being more formal, a questionnaire (see also Figure 7.3), than the other, a web (Figure 7.4). Regardless of the method followed, it is important at this stage to

---

FIGURE 7.3 Needs Assessment for an Educational Setting

(Sample Questionnaire)

A. The Community
1. What is the cultural and ethnic makeup of the community?
2. What languages are spoken?
3. What are the immediate priorities of the community?
4. What are the main community issues?
5. How do the community members feel toward the school, toward my classroom?

B. The School
1. What is the cultural and ethnic makeup of the school?
2. What is the diversity profile of the school?
3. What attitudes do teachers and staff have toward diversity?
4. Is anyone engaged in a multicultural program? What approaches are they following?
5. Are multicultural programs among the school's priorities?
6. Would the faculty, administrators, and staff support my efforts?

C. Children and Families
1. What are the families like? Socioeconomically, how are they defined?
2. What elements of diversity are reflected in these families?
3. What are some of the essential needs of families?
4. What are their religious affiliations?
5. Can I address those needs in my classroom?
6. What are the traits that, ethnically and culturally, characterize children in my classroom?
7. What diversity issues are unclear to my students? (For example, language differences, equality, interracial relations)
8. How do children see me?

D. The Classroom
1. What are the ethnic and cultural origins of the children in this classroom?
2. What opportunities do they have for dealing with diversity at the school?
3. Generally, how do children interact in this classroom?
4. Have there been any incidents because of racial or cultural differences?
5. Are there children who tend to use racial slurs or pejorative terms against others?
6. How do they respond when a person with given cultural characteristics comes into the classroom?

FIGURE 7.4 Using an "assessment web" (Barbara's findings)

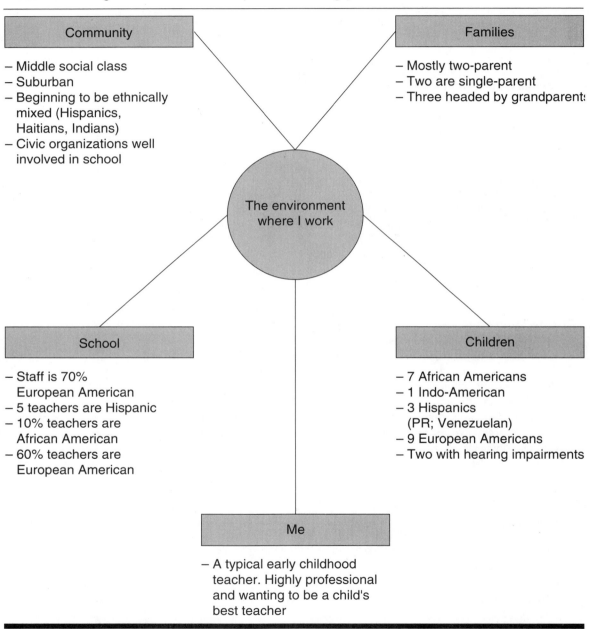

ascertain and clarify the conditions of the environment. Remember that the information collected here will become your planning blueprint.

Because many educators enjoy brainstorming or webbing ideas, an assessment web could be the one they prefer. More informal in nature, it is also open to including any other areas teachers might deem necessary. The example in Figure 7.4 is only a sample of an assessment web. Early childhood educators might want to add to or modify it to suit their own settings.

Assessing the School-Parent Environment

A thoughtful analysis of the data collected during the community and school assessment is critical to the reform process entailed in multicultural education. The data will form the framework for future actions and assist in bringing reality into the classroom. It will help determine and explain future decisions and actions. More specifically, this information will help establish the instructional content and processes for children taking part in the multicultural program. For instance, in this chapter we will see why our kindergarten teacher, Barbara, chose to address disabilities in her curriculum.

❖ Assessing Curriculum Programs

Once knowledge about the setting has been gained, it is important to look at the curriculum. Fundamental to any classroom change is the clear knowledge one has about the way the program is organized. Teachers need to understand their programs in terms of content and instruction. A knowledgeable assessment of the curriculum will help the teacher determine, conceptually, where she/he stands. Outcomes of this analysis will help determine the curriculum areas in need of change and prioritize those in need of urgent attention.

What to Assess in the Curriculum?

According to Ferguson (1987), the purpose of the multicultural classroom is to assist children in learning about themselves. We find this to be most appropriate in the context of the early childhood classroom. Essentially, it is congruous with the principles of developmentally appropriate teaching. To begin trying to answer the question: *What to assess in the curriculum?*, we need to first realize that children come to school to learn to be valuable individuals as well as to learn the specifics of

IN ACTION . . . *In this section we discussed two assessment formats: the factual map and the assessment web. Considering them:*

❙ Which of these two formats would you prefer?

❙ If you were to construct your own assessment, what other areas would you include? Why?

❙ What data sources would you add?

academics. This is possible if the teacher offers learning in a context where recognition of each child's unique background and characteristics permeates all experiences. Children growing up in school environments that show and lead them to respect differences are personally enriched. Ferguson (1987) states that in such classrooms students learn to derive ideas and knowledge from others and come to recognize that there are many more ways of looking at things than just those of their own cultural groups. Any classroom that adheres to the principles of developmental appropriateness mirrors Ferguson's ideas. Establishing that kind of learning environment is largely the function of the curriculum *process* and *content*.

Let us briefly review some definitions about curriculum. According to Piaget and Dewey, early childhood curriculum includes all the experiences the child encounters in the classroom and in the school. More recently, McCracken (1993) has stated that it is *all* that children find happening in a classroom. Curriculum, in this sense, becomes all the opportunities that teachers present to children with the purpose of introducing new concepts and ideas. Using a constructivist focus, Forman and Kuschner (1983) define curriculum as a series of "learning encounters" that begin when teachers have a clear vision of the purposes and objectives to be pursued by children. This is followed by the teacher's selection, preparation, and organization of the learning environment that presents the children with purposeful challenges. These "encounters" happen in all learning areas, including those occasions when the child is confronted with his/her own differences or those of other children and adults.

In early childhood education the curriculum becomes those learning encounters teachers prepare for children to foster knowledge building. The knowledge to be built in multicultural teaching includes concepts about oneself and others in the context of a diverse society.

What Is Curriculum Content?

All classroom teaching presupposes a content. Content, according to general curriculum theory, is the "what" selected for learning (Oliva 1988). Many teachers call it the "stuff" they teach. The context is considered appropriate when the concerns and the needs of the students and of society are addressed in ways that will provide opportunities for students to grow cognitively, psychologically, and socially (Bredekamp 1987; Ornstein & Hunkins 1993).

Selecting the Early Childhood Content
A curricular content is typified by seven major characteristics: self-sufficiency, significance, validity, interest, utility, learnability, and feasibility or practicality. These seven points, which appear in Figure 7.5, also serve as criteria for teachers who are in the process of establishing and selecting the classroom content.

Using Child Development Concepts
When selecting content for young children, important instruments to guide our decisions are the developmental milestones children experience at given ages. To design an appropriate content, our curricular decisions need to be supported by those universal milestones that define children's development. Developmental milestones serve as a blueprint from which our classroom-specific planning will emerge. A summary of developmental milestones is included in Chapter 4.

Using a Child-Centered Curriculum
Good teaching practice tells us that in child-centered programs, the content emanates from the child. The "curriculum is based on both age-appropriate and individually appropriate information," (Bredekamp 1987, p. 3). Because children are the *raison d'etre*, or the reason for what we do, in early education, everything we

---

FIGURE 7.5 Seven-point criteria for content selection: A synthesis perspective

---

1. **Self-sufficiency:** As the leading criterion, early childhood teachers should select suitable content, where children will be offered the opportunity to develop their potential and form their own identities. Educational equality and its enabling effect on the child is an important aspect of self-sufficiency in multicultural programs.

2. **Significance:** What is learned will be relevant if it relates meaningfully to the child's experiences. Content needs to be chosen not only on the basis of its academic (skills, concepts) relevancy, but also because of its social and affective (attitudes, social skills behaviors) pertinence. A multicultural curriculum is primarily different from others because of its cultural significance.

3. **Validity:** Content must be authentic and accurate in order to be valid. Teachers need to constantly verify their sources to meet this criterion. When dealing with issues about diversity, this requirement becomes particularly relevant. Almost daily, social scientists are gaining new knowledge that expands the content of curriculum.

4. **Interest:** Curriculum content must arouse curiosity and a desire for further knowledge. Classroom experiences that are interesting to the child should be based on a sound knowledge of age-appropriateness and the preferences of children. In a multicultural approach, the interests of the children tell teachers what topics to address and to what degree of intensity.

5. **Utility:** Curriculum content must also be useful. Content is useful if the child derives meaningful knowledge, attitudes, skills, or perspectives. For multicultural teaching this implies the type and quality of enabling views and ideas that the child is to gain.

6. **Learnability:** Any curriculum that is well organized presents the content in ways that facilitate a child's learning. A logical curricular structure establishes a sequence based on the abilities and needs of the learner. When selecting multicultural content, teachers must be sure that the topics selected are at a level of complexity that the child can understand and that they reflect a logical progression in the treatment of themes (depth and breadth).

7. **Feasibility:** Time, availability of resources, knowledge, and expertise are constraints that, if not properly considered, will affect and determine the success of the content. Any multicultural curriculum needs to consider these and other issues.

Source: Adapted from Ornstein, A., & Hunkins, F. (1993). *Curriculum: Foundations, principles, and theory* (pp. 281–282) Boston, MA: Allyn & Bacon.

plan and do revolves around the child's needs (Jones & Nimmo 1994). Planning in child-centered environments begins with teachers carefully observing to determine the things children like and feel curious about. The child-centered curriculum essentially emerges through our interactions with children.

Two kinds of child-centered curricula are usually observed in early education. One is the developmental curriculum the teacher builds, based on the needs children demonstrate through a developmental assessment. If you were to follow a developmental curriculum, you would begin by examining the results of the needs assessment and using the data to guide you in selecting age-appropriate themes your children will explore. The result of this approach is typically a master list of flexible topics offered throughout the year. The list is flexible because as other needs or interests arise, teachers add them to the master plan. Another form is the *emergent curriculum,* commonly utilized at the preschool level. This curriculum is based on the demonstrated interests and needs of the children. Instead of selecting topics from a list of yearly suggested themes, teachers construct experiences for children based on daily observation of their interests and concerns. The emergent curriculum may be based on areas that present difficulties for the children, topics that arouse

FOCUS ON CLASSROOM PRACTICES

USING A CONCEPTUAL SCHEME TO CREATE THE MULTICULTURAL CONTENT

Trying to choose the essential concepts for our multicultural curriculum is not a simple task. It means addressing how culture influences the myriad of human behaviors and interactions (Banks 1994). Banks recommends choosing high-level key concepts that are interdisciplinary in nature and organized around five main areas. Considering the developmental characteristics of young children, we adapted Banks' list, selecting those most appropriate. We also added some that seemed pertinent in a young child's classroom. The result is a master list of concepts teachers can use as a tool for content selection.

Key Multicultural Concepts

I. Main Concept: *Culture, ethnicity, identity*

- culture
- cultural beliefs
- cultural symbols
- cultural celebrations
- ethnic groups in U.S.A./in my community
- cultural diversity
- cultural groups

II. Main Concept: *Socialization and interaction*

- child-rearing patterns
- family patterns
- values
- self-concept
- social interaction patterns
- racism
- prejudice
- discrimination

III. Main Concept: *Intercultural communication and perception*

- languages
- communication patterns
- nonverbal communication
- symbols
- world/life view (how they see and interpret events)
- oral traditions
- literature and folklore (literary and musical)

Focus on Classroom Practices **continued**

IV. **Main Concept:** *Power and status*

  ▮ social classes

  ▮ locus of influence

  ▮ status of women, men, elders, and children

V. **Main Concept:** *The movement of ethnic groups*

  ▮ migration

  ▮ immigration

  ▮ purposes of migration and immigration

  ▮ immigrants in the community

Source: Adapted from Banks, J. (1991). *Teaching strategies for ethnic studies,* 5th ed. (p. 61). Boston, MA: Allyn & Bacon.

---

their curiosity, or themes that help them gain broader social understanding.

Defining the Curriculum Process

The curriculum process includes the methodology and procedures teachers follow to deliver their content (Ornstein & Hunkins 1993). The process entails the strategies, techniques, and overall methods used in the classroom to convey specific content and skills. What processes the teacher selects will influence the child as a learner. As we mentioned before, in the early childhood classroom, proper selection of the process must consider the child's developmental level and specific individual needs.

Some of the most helpful and specific guidelines for selecting teaching procedures are offered in Bredekamp's (1987) book *Developmentally Appropriate Practices for Programs Serving Children from Birth to Age 8.* Based on child development principles and best teaching practices, Bredekamp advocates the integrated curriculum approach as the most developmentally appropriate method for teaching young children. She states that since young children learn in a holistic

---

WORKING GLOSSARY

▮ **Early Childhood Curriculum**—the formal and informal experiences through which young children are empowered to continue the process of knowledge acquisition and development.

▮ **Content**—the topics, concepts, and themes selected for children to experience in the classroom.

▮ **Process**—ways and procedures used by teachers to deliver the curriculum content.

FOCUS ON CLASSROOM PRACTICES

ADDING THE APPROPRIATE PERSPECTIVE ABOUT ETHNICITY TO THE CURRICULUM

In his book *Teaching Strategies for Ethnic Studies* (1991), James Banks shares some concerns about what the multicultural curriculum often presents. His remarks are particularly important when teachers strive to create a responsive curriculum. According to Banks (1991), when planning multiethnic experiences, some educators assume that an ethnic group is monolithic and homogeneous or characterized by a single set of traits.

Nothing is further from reality than to presume that all people from a cultural group possess identical qualities and views. Just as children from the same family have different characteristics, so do cultural groups.

Banks adds that another problem is that educators tend to believe that self-esteem and the academic achievement of youth from other cultures will be enhanced by teaching mostly about heroic characters and achievements of individuals of their cultural background, while demonstrating how their ethnic group has been victimized by the mainstream culture (Banks 1991). The implications are clear. When the curriculum is built solely on the cultural past and a one-way description of a culture, despite the positive intentions of teachers, it will lack responsiveness and appropriateness.

Both of Banks' observations have relevance for the classroom teacher. If we are to design curriculum presuming that all members of a group have similar needs and reactions, the result would be a curriculum where we risk finding not only stereotypical information about these groups, but presentation of their daily existence. To avoid falling into this kind of curricular trap, we recommend answering these questions:

▮ Have I used more than one source to get information about the target cultural groups?

▮ Have I also considered and examined materials written by members of the culture I am targeting?

▮ Have I included materials and activities based on assumptions or on what I believe about other cultures?

▮ Does the content offer a balanced view of the past and present realities of the target culture?

fashion, experiencing the totality of a moment rather than in bits and pieces, they benefit more when learning is structured in similar ways.

When teaching the young child it is important to realize that the traditional division of curriculum into academic subject areas like social studies, literacy, science, math, and others carries no logical meaning. Integration is especially well facilitated when themes or topics are used. The project approach is an example of such an integrated teaching strategy (Katz & Chard 1989). Integrated teaching is easily combined with other strategies such as cooperative learning and group investigation. Working in small groups, children explore and build knowledge as their projects are developed.

Thematic teaching, a practice commonly used in whole language or literacy-based instruction, is also a developmentally appropriate approach for early childhood programs. In thematic teaching, all curriculum areas are integrated into the study of a particular theme. As a teaching strategy, thematic teaching, as proposed by John Dewey and by William Kilpatrick in the early decades of the century, provides an opportune instructional strategy for multicultural teaching. We will see its applicability in Chapter 8.

The project approach is not the only way of teaching about diversity. Additional suggestions for processes as well as content related to multicultural teaching can be found through several sources. Among these are the *Curriculum Guidelines for Multicultural Education* from the National Council for the Social Studies (NCSS 1992) and the key document *Expectations of Excellence: Curriculum Standards for Social Studies* (NCSS 1994). The *Curriculum Guidelines for Multicultural Education* (NCSS 1992) offer teachers specific suggestions on what and how to approach the teaching of culture at the primary level. An insightful source of ideas for curricular methodology is Louise Derman-Sparks' (1989) *The Anti-Bias Curriculum: Tools for Empowering Young Children.*

Snapshot 7.2
The Project Method, Origin of the Integrated Curriculum

The integrated curriculum, a commonly used method of instruction with young children, was developed by William Kilpatrick, a progressive educator. Kilpatrick, a colleague of John Dewey, was one of the supporters of the child-centered approach that gained popularity during the 1930s. By merging the then-current behavioristic ideas represented by Watson and Thorndike with the progressive philosophy of Dewey, Kilpatrick formulated the "project method," or purposeful activity. The basic concept centered on engaging children in activities ranging from classroom to community projects. These projects, which were to be child-selected, would offer a means to logically explore various subjects at the same time. Kilpatrick felt that it was the child who needed to explore and search for answers while the teacher served as a facilitator and guide. Today, his ideas have been brought back to the classroom through the reformulation by Lillian Katz and Sylvia Chard in what they have called the "project approach."

Sources: Katz, L., & Chard, S. (1989). *Engaging children's minds: The project approach.* Norwood, NJ: Ablex; Ornstein, A., & Hunkins, F. (1993). *Curriculum foundations, principles, and theory.* Boston, MA: Allyn & Bacon.

FOCUS ON CLASSROOM PRACTICES

USING THE NCSS PERFORMANCE EXPECTATIONS TO TEACH ABOUT
CULTURE AT THE EARLY CHILDHOOD LEVEL

The teaching of culture and cultural diversity at the early childhood level is an important step in developing a sense of pride and awareness about one's culture. It is also the first step toward the individual's realization about the existence of diversity. The performance expectations outlined by NCSS become a required tool as the early childhood teacher builds classroom experiences around the concept of culture. According to NCSS (1994), teaching about culture and cultural diversity at the early childhood level should lead children to:

a. explore and describe similarities and differences in the ways groups, societies, and cultures address similar human needs and concerns;

b. give examples of how experiences may be interpreted differently by people from diverse cultural perspectives and frames of reference;

c. describe ways in which language, stories, folktales, music, and artistic creations serve as expressions of culture and influence the behavior of people living in a particular culture;

d. compare ways in which people from different cultures think about and deal with their physical environment and social conditions;

e. give examples and describe the importance of cultural unity and diversity within and across groups.

Source: National Council for the Social Studies. (1994). *Expectations of excellence: Curriculum standards for social studies* (p. 33). Washington, DC.

❖ Discovering the Reality of Our Programs

Now that we have reviewed some of the main curriculum concepts, let us begin investigating our programs. Basically, we need to determine what activities and/or practices we currently use. Once we know where we stand, the next step is to design a plan where we want to be.

This is Where We Are; This Is Where We Want to Be

According to a statement presented jointly by the National Association for the Education of Young Children (NAEYC) and the National Association of Early Childhood Specialists in State Departments of Education (NAECS/SDE) (1991), multiculturalism should be embedded in every program for young children. The statement on the ideal curriculum reads:

> The curriculum embraces the reality of multiculturalism in American society by providing a balance between learning the common core of dominant culture knowledge (for example, English language, democratic values) and knowledge of minority cultures. Curriculum accommodates children who have limited English proficiency. All cultures and primary languages of children are respectfully reflected in the curriculum.
>
> (NAEYC & NAECS/SDE 1991, p. 30)

It is clear that if schools remain mainstream-oriented and unresponsive to our pluralistic context, education will be doing a disservice to our children and to our country. Carol Phillips (1988), a remarkable early childhood educator, urges teachers to break away from school practices that perpetuate inequities. She asks her early childhood education colleagues to use their own power to build nurturing classrooms where children will come to appreciate and value social diversity.

Mirroring Our Classrooms: An Example

Many things are clearer and easier to understand when we observe others in action. We want you to come into the classroom of our kindergarten teacher Barbara who has decided to "turn around" her teaching. As you may recall Barbara, who teaches in a suburban school somewhere in this country, was introduced earlier in this text. Well grounded in her belief that teaching can help eliminate prejudice and racism, Barbara has decided to take action and incorporate diversity into her teaching. Before you catch up with her through her journal entries, examine your personal convictions about multiculturalism! You can be like Barbara and write down your beliefs and the reasons you think establish the need for a different program. Save your ideas in a journal or on index cards and revisit them later. You may want to see if your views remain the same.

There is an important purpose in our writing this book: We want you to become a successful multicultural educator for two important reasons. First, to ensure that your children get the education they deserve, and second, we need to keep you as part of the force of new multicultural teachers who are setting the pace for others.

Focusing Our Lenses: Ways to Go

We hope you will join us as Barbara continues her journey. She is now ready to begin the most serious part: moving from ideas to action. Let us follow her as she takes steps to transform her teaching.

The first thing Barbara did was to answer three very general questions about her curriculum in order to get an overview of her own practices. The questions she asked herself were

1. Does my current program reflect the diversity of my students' community?
2. Do I teach in ways that reflect the lives of my students, and does my teaching help them affirm their identities?
3. Am I providing each child with skills to deal and interact with people who are different from him/herself?

Questions such as the ones listed here, which are based on the ideal curriculum defined by NAEYC and NAECS/SDE (1991), help establish the overall nature of our practices. It was by answering these questions that Barbara identified her need to change to a program focused on diversity. Some of her findings were as follows.

Question 1: "I teach basically about the mainstream culture, and what white people do. I haven't included anything in my curriculum either about the farmers or the migrant workers that abound in this area, or about the people from other countries that have started to move into this community. I do include holidays like Cinco de Mayo and Dr. King's birthday but nothing else."

Question 2: "Very few things are included about the things and customs of Velia, Etienne, and Lavania's cultures. I've taught mostly what the teacher's guide says, where little acknowledgment is made about diversity."

Question 3: "I'm sure that I have guided them to be respectful towards others but I guess they forgot that when they called the custodian names because he limps or when they refused to play with Etienne because he was the 'wrong color.' I realized now that I

IN ACTION . . .   *What About Your Teaching?*

You read Barbara's answers to three very important questions. Now, we would like to ask you to answer those same three questions. Use the questions below and reflect on your own answers.

▌ Were any answers similar to/different from Barbara's? Why?

▌ What have you discovered about your teaching?

▌ What did you learn?

should have used those times to help them learn that words hurt as much as when they hit you."

Barbara's Findings

What Barbara found supported her idea that her classroom teaching needed a change. She recognized herself as failing to serve those children who were ethnically different, but also failing to help children accept and encounter people with physical disabilities and racial differences. The most relevant thing is that, as a professional, Barbara had already made the determination to add "multiculturalness" to her classroom teaching. Multiculturalness, according to Davidman and Davidman (1994), is the perspective and posture the teacher assumes and imparts through her/his classroom practices, even when teaching an all European American class. Simply said, multiculturalness is a quality that must define classroom teaching. This is a point that we find necessary to emphasize, because there are still many who believe that these efforts are important only when culturally diverse children are concerned. On many occasions the authors of this book have heard students say that they have no need for a multicultural program because they do not have any multicultural children. When asked what they meant, they have responded that their class "is all white." In another instance, one of the authors recalls that, while presenting at one of the national early childhood conferences, someone commented that she had no need for multicultural programs because all of her students were from minority groups, so "what else could I teach them since they already know everything about themselves?" We believe that we need to offer multicultural programs to all children so each child can develop positive perspectives toward people in our country that can be used throughout life. We also hope for multiculturalness to soon become the character that permeates the teaching and learning processes in our country.

Finding Instruments to Examine the Curriculum

We already know that Barbara concluded that something had to change. However, wanting more specific directions, she decided to identify with precision the areas where help was required most. This is an optional step. Perhaps for some teachers the realization that a change is needed is enough to move ahead. If teachers feel confident with the information gathered in this way, they should move on. However, others may want to follow Barbara's example and consider more information.

Barbara Sets Up Her Plan

Getting ready to begin a more in-depth analysis, Barbara made another comment in her journal: "Will I be able to go ahead?" The reader might have a similar question. This is, after all, an expected reaction, for this is the very step where people often tend to shy away from the task that lies ahead. York (1991) says that, before beginning a multicultural program, one should expect "to be awed and amazed, scared and overwhelmed, and finally excited and full of anticipation" (p. 32).

Having made a decision to go on, Barbara's next concern was what instrument to use to evaluate her program. She knew there were several options:

∎ *reviewing professional literature to find an existing assessment instrument*

∎ *using an instrument already available at her school or school district*

∎ *designing her own assessment*

Assessment Instruments Recommended in the Professional Literature

Various examples of instruments for initial assessment are found in the professional literature. They present several advantages. One, they are readily available. Second, they constitute good sources of information for educators planning to create their own instruments. Third, they provide helpful indicators of the areas we must address when moving into multicultural teaching. We will look at only a sample of those we consider relevant and useful for the early childhood educator.

Hernández's Teacher Survey

Hilda Hernández (1989) recommends a basic teacher survey for assessing existing practices. The instrument she describes is adapted from the one used by the Long Beach Unified School District in California. In that survey, four areas are examined: content, instructional approaches and strategies, school climate, and parent/community involvement. Hernández places special emphasis on the content, where she assesses five aspects. Questions are formulated to elicit how the content addresses areas and issues such as human dignity and worth, ethnic studies, intercultural studies, differences and similarities, and human and intergroup relations. Some sample questions include: "To what degree do pupils exhibit pride and acceptance of self and abilities?" "To what extent do pupils recognize and accept differences as positive?" "To what degree do pupils feel pride in their ethnic heritage?" (Hernandez 1989, p. 174).

Baruth and Manning's Criteria

Baruth and Manning (1992) suggest a criterion that provides both the categories/areas of intended change and the standards required for these changes. They offer as an example a seven-point questionnaire, which we have adapted for the early childhood setting.

1. **Evidence of multicultural perspectives:** Are multicultural perspectives already incorporated throughout the entire school, my classroom curriculum, and my classroom environment?
2. **Attitudes toward diversity:** Do my attitudes and those of the rest of the teachers, administrators, and staff members indicate a willingness to accept and respect cultural diversity?
3. **Instructional materials/resources:** Do classroom materials—manipulatives, books—recognize the value of cultural diversity, gender, and social class differences?
4. **Teaching strategies/activities:** Do curricular activities and methods provide children with opportunities to work and play together in a cooperative fashion?
5. **School-wide activities:** Do general school activities reflect cultural diversity?

6. **Parent/community views:** Do my curricular planning efforts reflect the reality (views and opinions) of families and the community?

7. **Language diversity:** Do my curricular efforts include bilingual perspectives or provide assistance for students with limited English-speaking skills (when teaching children who are bilingual or who are learning English as a second language)? (Baruth & Manning 1992, p. 180)

Checklists and Questionnaires

Checklists are another effective source of information teachers can easily use. Because of its closed-answer format, a checklist is easier to tabulate and summarize. Kendall (1983, 1996) proposes a checklist to assess each aspect of the classroom environment. Through her checklist, the teacher takes time to examine each detail of the young children's classroom through which information and knowledge-building opportunities are offered. Kendall says that in assessing each area, teachers will identify the curriculum areas that need improvement (1983, p. 102). An interesting feature of her checklist is its proactive character, which asks the teacher to think about alternative ways that would correct what is done or what is missing.

The Southern Early Childhood Association (SECA) has a checklist specifically designed for teachers to appraise the level of diversity in their classrooms. Developed by Peck and Shores (1994)

and simple to administer and tabulate, it provides the teacher with an easy way to mirror their classroom practices. The SECA checklist is included in the appendix.

A more formal checklist is the one prepared by the Task Force on Ethnic Studies from NCSS. *The Curriculum Guidelines for Multicultural Education of the National Council for the Social Studies* (NCSS 1992) is a thorough and detailed instrument useful for both pre-assessment and evaluation of school/classroom practices. The checklist is based on the twenty-three guidelines identified by the Task Force as essential to an appropriately implemented multicultural program at the preschool–12 levels. Extensive and broad in scope, it is a helpful tool for the early childhood educator who is trying to initiate a program on diversity. The detailed list helps reemphasize the belief that for a program of this nature to happen, it must include the entire environment.

A questionnaire based on the five dimensions needed for the implementation of multicultural education identified by James Banks (1994) is recommended by Robles de Meléndez (1994). The five dimensions include: (a) content integration; (b) knowledge construction; (c) prejudice reduction; (d) equitable pedagogy; and (e) an empowering classroom culture and structure. There are questions addressing each dimension, which provides teachers with a detailed a profile of their practices (Figure 7.6).

WORKING GLOSSARY

▪ **Checklist**—an assessment instrument, usually consisting of "go" or "no go" choices used in an educational setting to collect factual data about student behaviors, physical arrangements, use of materials and activities, and student achievement, among others, that are objectively observed in the classroom.

▪ **Survey**—an oral or written assessment instrument designed to get specific answers from a designated constituency. Similar to a questionnaire, a survey usually consists of a list of open- or closed-ended statements designed to elicit information about targeted points or issues.

FIGURE 7.6 Profile of multiculturalism in the classroom (based on Bank's five dimensions)

A. Content Integration:
1. What is my curricular content? What topics do I explore with children?
2. Is diversity reflected in my classroom topics? How?
3. Are there opportunities for children to ponder similarities/differences?
4. Are materials and resources reflective of the children's/nation's diversity?
5. Are topics on diversity consistently included? How often?

B. Knowledge Construction:
1. Are experiences offered for children to examine and discover likenesses/differences?
2. Are experiences at the cognitive developmental level of the child?
3. Is the classroom arrangement/materials exposing children to diversity?
4. Are questions used to guide the child as he/she ponders reality rather than providing the answers?

C. Prejudice Reduction:
1. Is the classroom (materials, books) free of cultural stereotypes?
2. When they occur, are misconceptions examined and clarified?
3. Is the teacher proactive and not "color-blind" when situations arise?
4. Are positive attitudes toward diversity modeled and encouraged?
5. Does the classroom atmosphere inspire respect and tolerance?

D. Equitable Pedagogy:
1. Are all children treated equally?
2. Are all children offered a sense of success?
3. Do I show to every child that I believe in what he/she can do?
4. Do I adapt/change the curriculum for the child?
5. Do I show children that I respect and value their cultural identities?

E. An Empowering Classroom/School Culture:
1. Are my children screened/assessed in a developmental fashion?
2. Is the child's cultural identity acknowledged when planning/teaching?
3. Is my teaching mindful of the community's identity?
4. Is the classroom constantly acknowledging the children's identities?

Source: Robles de Meléndez (1994). *Theory and practice in early childhood education. Study guide.* Fort Lauderdale, FL: Nova Southeastern University.

Assessment Tools Used in Schools or School Districts

Attention given by schools and districts to education for diversity has dramatically increased in the past five years. This heightened awareness is a result of advocacy efforts made by the leading professional organizations and increasing diversity within our communities. Data about the ethnic and social nature of the student body is regularly collected. Information is routinely gathered about student exceptionalities, and about the number of children speaking native languages other than English. What use is made of these statistics depends upon the priorities and commitments of the various schools and school districts. The data are not always used to readdress the curriculum to students' needs.

Many schools have made attempts to change their practices because of student diversity. These efforts might represent interests coming from the district personnel, from a group of teachers, or from administrators. It might also happen that the change to multiculturalism is generated by one educator who decides to reform her/his teaching. Regardless of where the initiative comes from, schools have started to use and design data-gathering instruments. Most schools use checklists and surveys designed at the district level or by teachers and multicultural specialists (Figure 7.7). If your school has such a list and you have never used it, ask other teachers about their experiences with the instrument. Their comments may provide valuable insights. In some cases, multicultural instruments are generated by national organizations like the National Association for the Education of Young Children (NAEYC), Association of Children Education International (ACEI), or the Southern Early Childhood Association (SECA).

Multicultural assessment instruments should always be closely examined to determine whether they are congruous with developmental practices. Teachers are urged to change inappropriate items to reflect appropriate practices for their level of teaching. Using or even adapting existing instruments saves the time needed to design new ones.

What Barbara Chose as an Assessment Tool

As you recall, Barbara, the kindergarten teacher moving into multicultural teaching, was trying to get a good instrument to assess the nature of her instruction. She found the existing multicultural tools in her school helpful but not appropriate for an early childhood setting. So she decided to design her own. This is what she wrote in her journal.

> What I want to find out is just what I am really doing. I guess I can get that if I just look at what I plan, do and use with my class. Yes, that's what I'll do. I am going to create my own assessment instrument. I'm sure that I'll find surprises but . . . that's OK. After all I just want to be a good teacher. So, here I go!

❖ Designing Multicultural Assessment Tools

The decision to construct a multicultural instrument of your own may result from the uniqueness of your setting and the makeup of your students. Regardless of the reason, preparation and good planning are in order. Before designing a multicultural assessment tool, it is necessary to search the literature and learn not only what the content of such instruments should be, but also how to apply good principles of instrument design.

Educator Howard D. Hill believes that teachers of minority students should become effective facilitators of learning and achievement. For that to happen, he urges teachers to ask themselves four key questions that detect the skills and attitudes one needs when working with diversity. Hill's questions remind educators not only to consider the students but also themselves as implementors of the process.

- *What is it that helps students learn?*
- *What is it that teachers can do to aid their students in learning?*
- *What teacher qualities, personal and professional, do I possess that help or hinder student learning?*
- *What skills must teachers possess if they are to facilitate learning and achievement for minority students?* (Hill 1989, p. 11)

What Needs To Be Assessed: Key Points in Young Children's Programs

The first thing our kindergarten teacher, Barbara, did was to analyze the nature of her existing program. We can follow her discovery process by

FIGURE 7.7 Assessing children's awareness about diversity (Clark County, Las Vegas, NV)

PROJECT MCE
CLARK COUNTY SCHOOL DISTRICT
COMPENSATORY EDUCATION DIVISION

STUDENT ATTITUDE ASSESSMENT

Directions: Place an X in front of each item you agree with:

_____ 1. I know someone who can speak another language besides English.

_____ 2. I know some words in another language besides English.

_____ 3. I like to try foods from other countries.

_____ 4. I know at least two other countries in which they speak Spanish.

_____ 5. I know at least two other countries in which they speak French.

_____ 6. I know at least two other countries in which they speak _____.
fill in language

_____ 7. I would like to learn about how people in other countries live.

_____ 8. I can sing a song in another language.

_____ 9. I can find Nigeria on a map.

_____ 10. I can find Puerto Rico on a map.

_____ 11. I can find _____ on a map.
        country

_____ 12. I have talked to someone from another country about where they came from.

_____ 13. I know (or have read) at least one Native American story.

_____ 14. I know (or have read) at least one story from a far-away country.

_____ 15. I know (or have read) at least one _____ story.
        specific culture

_____ 16. I know where to find books about different cultures in the school library.

Curriculum & Instruction Center, 601 N. 9th St., Room 30, Las Vegas, NV 89101

examining her journal. Let us find out what she learned about her classroom.

1. *Checking for developmentally appropriate practices (DAP)*

The first thing to keep in mind is that multicultural teaching and DAP are equal partners in education for diversity. Barbara, as a kindergarten teacher, is committed to teaching in a developmentally appropriate way. For Barbara, following the DAP guidelines begins with her review of the "green and white book," Bredekamp's (1987) *Developmentally Appropriate Practices for Programs Serving Children from Birth to Age 8*. Parts 4 through 7 offer clear portrayals of children's behaviors and characteristics for ages birth through 8. Although an experienced teacher, Barbara needed to reinforce her knowledge of the guidelines. Reviewing professional sources is an important step because it gives teachers a chance to validate their own knowledge and practices.

If you begin your discovery process in the same way as Barbara, be very honest with yourself in determining whether your teaching truly responds to developmental principles. If you find that in some areas you are not applying DAP, do not despair. Simply write the problem areas down as things to work on (Figure 7.8). It is very common to find that many early childhood educators do not follow appropriate practices in all aspects of their teaching. You will find that those points requiring attention will be adjusted as you move toward multicultural education. Because multicultural education is a part of DAP, you will see that, as you learn more, your entire teaching and learning will become immersed in it.

2. *Identifying "things-that-happen" in the classroom*

Analyzing the program in our classroom is easier when we think of it as "what happens" (McCracken 1993, p. 4). The topics and themes the children explore and the materials they use rep-

FIGURE 7.8 Barbara's findings

DAP areas Barbara needs to work on:

▮ More age-appropriate literacy materials
▮ Increase opportunities for thinking, pondering (use more questions)
▮ Work on the learning stations (more areas for working independently)

resent the real curriculum. How these topics are presented and developed depends on the particular instructional strategies and processes employed by the individual teacher. To further analyze this, ask yourself, *"What do I teach and how do I teach it?"*

a. What are the themes/topics that children work with in this classroom? (Content)
b. How do they learn about those themes? What things do they do? (Process)
c. What do we use when we work with a topic? (Resources/Materials)

An honest answer to each of these questions will help identify the classroom reality. These questions also identify the same three elements needed to create the real curriculum: the content, the process, and the resources.

a. **The Content:** When answering the first question regarding the topics and themes, it is advisable to check your lesson plans for the past month. Retrospection will tell you where your emphases have been. A way to keep track of this analysis is to use 3×5 cards or even sticky notes and jot down what diversity topics you targeted. Also, write the dates on which they occurred to determine whether these instructional events only happened when observing holidays.

b. **The Process:** For the second question that addresses the process, it is helpful to write some of the activities that were used in the classroom. Try to remember how all the children responded to the experiences. Determine whether at the end of each experience all the children came away knowing that they were successful in their own way (Gollnick & Chinn 1990).

c. **Resources and Materials:** Identifying the classroom materials and resources is a way of judging whether children are provided with things that either reflect their own background or that of others, or if the materials are inappropriate or missing from the classroom. Use of ethnic items helps children clarify their perceptions about the cultures of others. When listing your resources, recall how many times you have invited people of various cultures from the community to visit your class. Ask yourself if those times included only holidays, or if they happened during the "multicultural month." Derman-Sparks (1989) notes that for teachers to establish a bias-free environment, children need to have their parents and other community members regularly involved in the classroom, not just on special occasions.

3. *Find what my classroom has: What the child sees*

The classroom environment is another area to examine. Learning is not limited to what the teacher presents or asks the children to do. It also includes messages sent by the classroom environment. Therefore, it is necessary to detect the kinds of messages sent to the children through such media as pictures, manipulatives, and literature. Derman-Sparks (1989) believes that the environment is a powerful knowledge-building instrument. She recommends that teachers carefully analyze the environment as a first step toward change. She

states: "What is in the environment also alerts children to what the teacher considers important or not important. Children are as vulnerable to omissions as they are to inaccuracies and stereotypes: What isn't [seen] can be as powerful a contributor to attitudes as what is seen" (p. 11).

Your analysis should begin with what you have on the walls. After all, whatever you have hanging on the walls is what sets the atmosphere in your classroom. Using 3×5 cards, list the kinds of pictures and decorations in your classroom that reflect diversity. This means finding out, for example, whether the pictures reflect a balance of ethnic backgrounds and include the cultures of your children. Determine whether pictures show activities commonly engaged in by your children's parents. You also need to see whether the manipulatives and other play materials, like dolls, reflect diversity. Check the literacy area to see whether the books address a variety of multicultural themes. A detailed listing of environmental elements to check appears in Figure 7.9.

Putting Things Together

Verifying developmentally appropriate practices, analyzing the curriculum, and taking an inventory of the classroom environment are the three tasks that must be performed by every early childhood educator who has made a commitment to teach in a multicultural way. This information can be collected in a variety of formats. Since the findings will be for your own use, you should use the methods of collecting information you find most convenient and appropriate. What is important is to assess the program honestly and thoroughly so that the results of the inquiry present an accurate picture.

Here is how our friend Barbara went about this assessment process. Being experienced in thematic teaching, she was very familiar with webbing, a way to graphically brainstorm and conceptualize a problem, topic, or issue. Barbara

FIGURE 7.9 Checking the classroom environment for diversity

ELEMENTS OF DIVERSITY

	Ethnicity	Gender	Social class	Disability	Age
Pictures/Posters					
Books					
Housekeeping items					
Manipulatives					
Art materials					
Dramatic area					
Music					

Comments:

• Things I need to change:

• Things I need to add:

Enter a check mark (√) whenever you find something in the classroom that complies with these elements of diversity

FIGURE 7.10 Action map

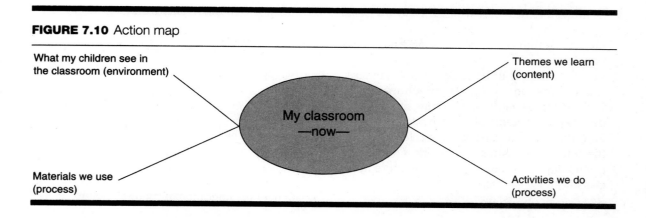

decided to use a web for her assessment. At the center of a large piece of cardboard, she drew a circle and labeled it "My classroom now." Inside the circle she wrote the diversity characteristics of her classroom. Branching out from the center were the following areas:

1. Themes we learn about (Content)
2. Activities we do (Process)
3. Materials we use (Process)
4. What children find/see in the classroom (Environment).

Using 3×5 cards, she jotted down her findings. Then she pasted them to their respective locations. As a working action map (Figure 7.10) the web became a practical way to portray her classroom and her teaching.

Setting Directions
Like Barbara, go ahead and choose a special way to assess your practices and your classroom. You probably have your own way of gathering information about your practices or you may want to modify what Barbara did. Regardless of which avenue you decide to follow, we want to encourage you to get a feel for what you actually do. This is an important step, for it will make you more aware of the need for a multicultural cur-riculum. We will examine Barbara's findings in the next chapter.

❖ Things to Do . . .

1. Identify five early childhood teachers working in multicultural education. Have them examine the list of characteristics of the early childhood multicultural teacher defined in this chapter. Have them point out those characteristics they find most relevant and ask them to explain their choices. Find out what other traits they believe should be listed.
2. Examine your curriculum to determine whether it reflects integration of diversity topics. See if the topics are integrated throughout the content, or if they appear only when a holiday is observed.
3. A tourist approach looks at multiculturalism as a visitor does when traveling to another country—by focusing on the folklore, the exotic, and the historical aspects. Examine your curriculum and determine whether you are following a tourist-like approach. If you are, propose two alternative ways to modify your present curriculum.

4. Changes begin when we clearly know what needs to be transformed. Use the assessment web that Barbara followed and assess your classroom.
5. Visit five early childhood settings and assess the environment, using the guidelines presented in this chapter. Determine the areas that most frequently appear in need of change.
6. Find the ethnic and social characteristics of the community where you work. Then, determine what materials you could include in the classroom to represent them.

❖ Children's Literature Corner

Ata, T. (1992). *Baby rattlesnake.* San Francisco, CA: Children's Book Company.

Atkinson, M. (1979). *María Teresa.* Carrboro, NC: Lollipop Power.

García, M. (1987). *The adventures of Connie and Diego: Las aventuras de Connie y Diego.* San Francisco, CA: Children's Book Press.

Lee, J. (1987). *Ba-Nam.* New York: Henry Holt & Company.

Mckissack, P. (1992). *A million fish. . . . more or less.* New York: Alfred A. Knopf.

Medearis, A. (1991). *Dancing with the Indians.* New York: Holiday House.

Sakai, K. (1990). *Sachiko means happiness.* San Francisco, CA: Children's Book Company.

Stock, C. (1984). *Emma's dragon hunt.* New York: Lothrop Lee & Shepard Books.

❖ References

Banks, J. (1988). *Multicultural education,* (2nd ed.). Newton, MA: Allyn & Bacon.

Banks, J. (1991). *Teaching strategies for ethnic studies,* (5th ed.). Boston, MA: Allyn & Bacon.

Banks, J. (1994). Transforming the mainstream curriculum. *Educational Leadership* 8 (pp. 4–8).

Baruth, L. G., & Manning, M. L. (1992). *Multicultural education of children and adolescents.* Needham Heights, MA: Allyn & Bacon.

Bredekamp, S. (ed.). (1987). *Developmentally appropriate practice in early childhood programs servicing children from birth through age 8.* Washington, DC: National Association for the Education of Young Children.

Bredekamp, S., & Rosegrant, T. (eds.). (1992). *Reaching potentials: Appropriate curriculum and assessment for young children,* vol. I. Washington, DC: National Association for the Education of Young Children.

Davidman L., & Davidman, P. T. (1994). *Teaching with a multicultural perspective.* New York: Longman.

Derman-Sparks, L., & A.B.C. Task Force. (1989). *Antibias curriculum tools for empowering young children.* Washington, DC: National Association for the Education of Young Children.

Doll, R. (1992). *Curriculum: Decision making and process* (8th ed.). Boston, MA: Allyn & Bacon.

Ferguson, H. (1987). *Manual for multicultural education* (2nd ed.). Yarmouth, ME: Intercultural Press, Inc.

Forman, G., & Kuschner, D. (1983). *The child's construction of knowledge: Piaget for teaching children.* Washington, DC: National Association for the Education of Young Children.

Gollnick, D. M., & Chin, P. C. (1990). *Multicultural education in a pluralistic society* (3rd ed.). New York: Merrill.

Hernandez, H. (1989). *Multicultural education: A teacher's guide to content and process.* New York: Merrill.

Hill, H. D. (1989). *Effective strategies for teaching minority students.* Bloomington, IN: National Educational Service.

Jones, E., & Nimmo, J. (1994). *Emergent curriculum.* Washington, DC: National Association for the Education of Young Children.

Katz, L. (1984). The professional early childhood teacher. *Young Children* 39, 5 (pp. 3–10).

Katz, L., & Chard, S. (1989). *Engaging children's minds: The project approach.* Norwood, NJ: Ablex.

Kendall, F. (1983). *Diversity in the classroom: A multicultural approach to the education of young children.* New York: Teachers College Press.

Kendall, F. (1988, November–December). Creating a multicultural environment. *Pre-K Today* (pp. 34–39).

Kendall, F. (1996). *Diversity in the classroom. New approaches to the education of young children* (2nd ed.). New York: Teachers College Press.

McCracken, J. (1993). *Valuing diversity: The primary years.* Washington, DC: National Association for the Education of Young Children.

Morris, J. (1983). *Classroom methods and materials.* In O. Saracho & B. Spodek (eds.). *Understanding the multicultural experience in early childhood education.* Washington, DC: National Association for the Education of Young Children.

National Association for the Education of Young Children & National Association of Early Childhood Specialists in State Departments of Education (NAECS/SDE). (1991). Guidelines for Appropriate Curriculum and Assessment in programs serving children ages 3 through 8. *Young Children* 46, 3 (pp. 21–38).

National Council for the Social Studies. Task force on ethnic studies. (1992). Curriculum guidelines for multicultural education. *Social Education* (pp. 274–294).

National Council for the Social Studies. (1994). *Expectations of excellence: Curriculum standards for social studies.* Washington, DC: NCSS.

Nieto, S. (1992). *Affirming diversity: The sociopolitical context of multicultural education.* New York, NY: Longman.

Oliva, P. (1988). *Developing the curriculum* (3rd. ed.). Glenview, IL: Scott Foresman.

Ornstein, A., & Hunkins, F., (1993). *Curriculum: Foundations, principles, and theory.* Boston, MA: Allyn & Bacon.

Peck, N., & Shores, E. (1994). *Checklist for diversity in early childhood education and care.* Little Rock, AR: Southern Early Childhood Association.

Phillips, C. (1988). Nurturing diversity for today's children and tomorrow's leaders. *Young Children* 43, 2 (pp. 42–47).

Robles de Meléndez, W. (1994). *Theory and practice in early childhood education: Study guide.* Ft. Lauderdale, FL: Nova Southeastern University.

Robles de Meléndez, W. (1995). *Family and school collaboration: Study guide.* Ft. Lauderdale, FL: Nova Southeastern University.

York, S. (1991). *Roots and wings: Affirming culture in early childhood programs.* St. Paul, MN: Redleaf Press.

"To fully participate in our democratic society . . . all students need the skills a multicultural educationcan give them to understand and to thrive in a rapidly changing, diverse world."

James Banks (1992)

CHAPTER 8

Preparing to Bring Ideas into Action

In this chapter we will:

▌ discuss ways to bring multicultural education into practice

▌ select multicultural approaches for the young children's classroom

▌ give examples for establishing goals and objectives in multicultural programs

▌ organize the early childhood multicultural curriculum following developmentally appropriate practices (DAP)

Key concepts:

▌ goals and objectives
▌ curriculum
▌ curricular approaches
▌ content
▌ planning

❖ A Time for Ideas: Planning for Multicultural Teaching

The time has come to begin one of the most exciting parts of multicultural education: the planning phase. This is when you take the most concrete and definitive steps. More than anything, this will be a challenging time. We will begin by reviewing some basic concepts of curriculum planning. Then, we will move to examine the planning process in the early childhood classroom context.

Building Our Teaching Blueprint

Like architects and engineers, early childhood teachers have blueprints to guide their work. We call it the curriculum and refer to it as a blueprint because it lays out the routes of knowledge we will take during the learning journey with our students. Curricular blueprints vary as much as a blueprint of a high-rise differs from one of a single-family house. However, curricular blueprints share many elements in common. For example, instructional content is organized by combining knowledge, the needs of learners, societal goals, and personal ideals into a coherent instructional plan. Designing new instructional blueprints is a complex process that requires the use of many talents and resources such as originality, knowledge, creativity, and funds.

Curriculum development has traditionally been delegated to school curriculum specialists and commercial experts associated with publishing firms. You probably have seen many or used some of these curricula. In the area of multicultural education, however, we find that teachers have played a major role in the curriculum development of programs focused on diversity. This can be attributed to such factors as the relatively recent emergence of multicultural education as a curriculum component; the evolving nature of multiculturalism; lack of commitment and resources on the part of the schools to develop special curricula; and the interests and initiatives of teachers who wish to align their practices with reality. Whatever the reason, classroom teachers have played an important role in developing multicultural curricula. Curriculum development provides a special opportunity for teachers to implement the wealth of their ideas and explore new ways of transforming classroom teaching. Like everything new, the task is a challenging one that requires good planning, hard work, and patience. Because of the versatile nature of multicultural programs, educators who took part in the process report that they found it necessary to spend more time planning the experiences for their students than they did when developing more traditional curricula.

Making Dreams into Reality

Inclusion of multiculturalism at all levels of education is slowly becoming a reality. The process has been facilitated by the rapid transformation of America's pluralistic society. The social and cultural changes have been the major catalysts in convincing educators that appropriate preparation of students must include new ways of dealing with the present and the future society.

Many early childhood educators are committed to multicultural education. Designing effective curricula centered on the individual needs of children and their social environment is one way of fulfilling that commitment. However, the implementation of multicultural programs has been difficult for many teachers, not because it requires skills, creativity, and knowledge, but because it often lacks the other essential element: support. We believe that if teachers had the necessary encouragement and support, there would be many more quality programs about diversity.

The authors of this book believe it is important to eliminate the myth about the impossibility of implementing a multicultural curriculum, especially at the young children's level. Thousands of

IN ACTION . . .   *"I think I can, I think I can"*

Remember *The Little Engine That Could?* Well, like it, we want you to become very optimistic and positive about what you are able to do as a multicultural educator. We want you to be able to affirm, "I know I can." Complete the following two sentences:

▮ I know I can become a multicultural educator because . . .

▮ I know I can build a good curriculum because . . .

As we continue this chapter, keep these two statements in mind. They well serve to remind you that you can do it!

teachers throughout this country have already embraced this approach and experienced success. They recognize the crucial role multiculturalism plays in the educational process and life, in general. This book is designed to offer support to early childhood practitioners who need and want to reform their teaching. This chapter contains practical ideas to help you launch your program. Before you proceed, let us go back and see how Barbara, our kindergarten teacher who embraced multicultural education, is doing.

From Barbara's journal

Last time we encountered Barbara in Chapter 7, she was in the process of assessing her program with an informal assessment instrument. Barbara's principal also helped her locate the faculty responses to a multicultural assessment done the previous year. Having analyzed the results, Barbara is ready to begin the implementation. There are many decisions she needs to make. Barbara's journal entry shows her concerns.

> "I know where I want to go: I want to teach responsively. How to do that is what I need to work on. Honestly, I feel some apprehension. Will I make the right decisions? Will my teaching be what my students need? I guess I will know that only after I start making the changes. All I know is I have to do it!"

❖ Planning and Organizing: The Critical Steps

Having to structure "what will happen in the classroom" is a threatening experience for many educators. However, teachers need to be assured that because of their immersion in the classroom, they have the practical experience and the knowledge necessary for designing effective curricula. Additional enabling forces are the teachers' dedication to their profession and their belief in equality for all children. Stephen Corey, cited by Glickman (1990), said "Learning that changes behavior substantially is most likely to result when a person himself [sic] tries to improve a situation that makes a difference to him [sic]" (p. 393). In other words, the conviction educators possess determines the success in any educational effort.

Multicultural reform has caused many educators to assume the role of curriculum innovators. According to Tanner and Tanner, cited by Glickman (1990), teachers engaged in curriculum improvement can be described as being at the creative-generative level. This level involves finding answers to already identified problems. Teachers engaged in the process of changing to multicultural teaching are doing that with exceptional creativity. It can even be said that their creativity is nurtured by their commitment to multiculturalism and their devotion to young students.

Doll (1992) states that teachers are particularly well-equipped for the role of curriculum improvers. He describes three main factors that qualify teachers to be effective curriculum developers: (1) constant interaction with children; (2) knowledge of teaching practices; and (3) constant exposure to ideas and suggestions coming from their colleagues (pp. 390–391). As an early childhood educator or a prospective one, you probably would agree that Doll is right: We certainly have the qualities to create the best kind of curriculum!

Early Childhood Teaching Prepares You For Curricular Change

The vary nature of the field of early childhood education prepares teachers to engage in curriculum planning. A review of developmentally appropriate practices (DAP) reminds us that the real curriculum is constantly being redesigned as the young students in the classroom reveal their needs and interests. Good professionals recognize that developmentally effective teaching can only happen if they are able to alter instructional plans to respond to the needs of young learners.

Curriculum development tasks for traditional and multicultural instruction include writing and readjusting the content of lesson plans, trying to find manipulatives for the classroom, and searching for appropriate literature. An additional task for teachers to remember when planning to teach multiculturally is to become more aware and be perceptive of the students social interactions in the classroom. A careful assessment and a perceptive analysis of how children deal with each other and how they face social issues will be a source of data revealing how your activities impact children, as well as a guide for finding new directions for your curriculum. In the next sections we will explore the specific steps for making your multicultural curriculum a reality.

❖ What Is Planning? Do We Need to Plan?

Planning is an essential part of any change process whose primary purpose is to set directions to achieve specific goals in organized and logical ways. Good planning is a critical phase of the curriculum development process. Consequences of efforts undertaken without a solid plan are obvious. Confusion, inappropriate use of resources, vagueness, and unclear goals are among the characteristics of an unplanned curriculum. In the classroom these results are often observed in the students' apathy and lack of interest in what is studied.

IN ACTION . . .   *Ask the Experts in the Field*

No other person can provide you with more expert information about planning than an early childhood teacher. That is why we want you to informally interview at least three early childhood teachers. Simply ask them to share what kind of curriculum they use, how they plan their activities, whether they often change them to suit the children's needs, and how they make such changes. Share your findings with class.

To facilitate curriculum planning, teachers can select from a number of models. Some are more technical in nature than others. For example, a commonly used one is Tyler's Model, also known as the "Eight Year Study" because it was based on a longitudinal study conducted between 1933 and 1941. Tyler's classic paradigm is structured around four basic principles: *purposes, selection of experiences, organization of experiences,* and *evaluation* (Ornstein & Hunkins 1993). This is the first time that the focus of curriculum shifted from the individual student to the whole program and connected the educational goals and objectives with methodologies and outcomes. Tyler's Model had a major impact on education and still continues to be widely used today.

Another important model was originally designed by Hilda Taba for a social studies curriculum. Taba's model is based on the belief that teachers are the ones to design the curriculum. The model incorporates and expands Tyler's steps by adding the assessment of needs to the process (Ornstein & Hunkins 1993). We are certain that as you read its description, you will find many elements in common with what we do in the early childhood classroom.

The Transformative Curriculum

More recently, the model of transformative curriculum has been proposed by several curricularists. This model contends that curriculum is made anew as teachers and learners find new

---

FOCUS ON CLASSROOM PRACTICES

APPLYING TYLER'S CURRICULAR MODEL

Ralph Tyler's model for curricular design is still useful. Many early childhood teachers are probably using it without even realizing that they are doing so. Tyler's four basic principles offer teachers a simple way to create an effective multicultural curriculum. Here we provide a sample idea to transfer this early paradigm onto your daily planning.

Topic/Theme: _____

Objectives (purposes)	Activities (selection of experiences)	Scheduling of activities/learning centers (organization of experiences)	Assessment (evaluation)
		Monday: Tuesday: Wednesday: Thursday: Friday:	

FOCUS ON CLASSROOM PRACTICES

MODEL OF CONCEPT DEVELOPMENT

A noted curricularist, Hilda Taba, is also remembered for her model of concept development. In her curriculum model, she places the responsibility on the teachers, whom she considers to have the best practical knowledge necessary to design classroom experiences. Her model consists of seven major steps and is described as a grass-roots approach.

Step #1: **Diagnosis of needs**—identification of the needs of the audience, the students.

Step #2: **Objectives**—based on the identified needs, objectives are formulated.

Step #3: **Content selection**—content is selected in consonance with the objectives.

Step #4: **Organization of content**—content is arranged in a logical sequence considering what is age-appropriate.

Step #5: **Selection of learning experiences**—teachers select the instructional methods.

Step #6: **Organization of activities**—following the sequence and organization of the curriculum, activities are then chosen.

Step #7: **Evaluation**—the means to assess and determine the outcomes are established by the teacher.

Source: Adapted from Ornstein, A. C. & Hunkins, F. (1993). *Curriculum. Foundations, principles, and theory.* (2nd ed.). Boston, MA: Allyn & Bacon (pp. 268–269).

---

meanings to what is experienced, an idea in consonance with many of the views about constructivism. The model, proposed by James Henderson and Richard Hawthorne (1995), is formulated around the vision of curriculum that will make sense to both the teacher and the child.

This model is founded on a premise that teaching is for understanding and not for the sole transmission of bits and pieces of knowledge. Here, the learner is to be an active participant and not just a receiver of what is planned. The teacher is not just delivering the content, but

---

WORKING GLOSSARY

▌ **Planning**—process through which actions are taken and decisions are made to accomplish a chosen goal and the directions and procedures for implementation are selected and organized.

▌ **Eclectic**—a combination of two or more ideas or approaches to produce a new vision, solve a problem, achieve a goal, or define a position.

FOCUS ON CLASSROOM PRACTICES

USING TABA'S MODEL

Early childhood teachers can easily apply Taba's model to what they design. Her ideas are especially helpful whenever we are beginning to develop a new thematic unit. We will suppose that you already have a theme in mind. Let us incorporate the questions described here into your development of a unit based on this theme.

Taba's question-based process for building an instructional unit:
   I. What interests/questions have the children shown, expressed? What concepts and skills do they need to acquire/explore? What ideas do they have about this theme? (*Needs assessment*)
  II. What do I want children to learn through this unit? What will the children derive from the unit? (*Objectives*)
 III. What topics would be interesting/important for them to explore? What ideas should they explore? (*Content selection*)
  IV. What is the age-appropriate way to present the topics? (*Content organization*)
   V. What teaching strategies will I use? What materials do I need? (*Teaching methods.* For example: use of learning centers, small group work, etc.)
  VI. What activities should I include? What areas will I integrate? (*Organization of activities*)
 VII. What should I use to assess the children's reactions? (*Evaluation, assessment*)

---

rather building the content from what is jointly experienced with the child. Reflective of the child's interests and of what teachers sense is relevant to present, this model is emergent in nature. It has three important requirements that appeal to early childhood teachers.

1. Educators need to be constantly observing and assessing what the children do and express in the classroom.
2. Teachers must be aware of "what happens" in the school environment and in the community.
3. Teachers must possess good skills to transform the information gathered from the child and the environment into a meaningful set of curricular experiences.

Using an Eclectic Model

The authors of this book believe in an eclectic model for curriculum development that includes elements from several models. The model is based on Taba's ideas (Ornstein & Hunkins 1993), as well as on the concepts of the transformative curriculum (Henderson & Hawthorne 1995). It also includes the principles of child development as interpreted by the developmentally appropriate practices (DAP), to ensure the curriculum remains responsive to the child. The model consists of four steps presented in Chapter 7: (1) assessment of the setting, (2) assessment of practices, (3) design, and (4) implementation. Like Taba's model, our model encourages teachers to be the proponents of curriculum reform (Figure 8.1).

To be effective, a curriculum needs to have personal relevance, an idea espoused by Dewey many decades ago. Dewey believed that children show involvement in things in which they find a purpose commensurate to their interest. A child uses interests as a catalyst to guide the process of knowledge construction. The dynamic interaction between the child and the challenges found in the environment, in this case the classroom, establishes the active construction of new ideas (DeVries & Kohlberg 1987). Dewey's ideas correlate with the Piagetian principles of knowledge construction that form the basis of the child-centered curricula. These principles also underlie an effective classroom curriculum intended to develop multicultural perspectives.

Teachers should aspire to build meaningful hands-on curricula for students (Bredekamp & Rosegrant 1992). A curriculum formulated on the realities of the child's world offers purposeful and challenging experiences. A relevant curriculum consists of experiences that keep the child constructively engaged. For that reason, our model places special emphasis on the careful appraisal of the settings where the child interacts: the family, the neighborhood, the community, and the school.

What Do We Do Next?

Assessing the environment and appraising classroom practices were the first two steps of the curriculum model proposed by the authors of this book. In Chapter 7, together with Barbara, you assessed the physical environment in your classroom and you made an appraisal of your classroom practices. After reviewing the findings, both you and Barbara are ready to begin the curriculum design and implementation.

FIGURE 8.1 Curriculum design for multicultural education

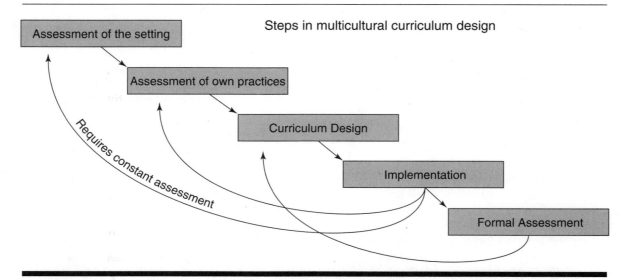

Steps in multicultural curriculum design

Assessment of the setting

Assessment of own practices

Curriculum Design

Implementation

Formal Assessment

Requires constant assessment

❖ Setting Directions: A Curriculum Design of Our Choice

A careful analysis of findings collected during the assessment stage leads to the next step of *how* to reorganize the curriculum, or the *design.* When selecting a design for multicultural education, it is important to decide which approach to use (Figure 8.2). As explained in Chapter 6, there are a variety of ways in which education for diversity can be delivered. At this point, it is important to take time to choose the approach that really appeals to you. Remember that this new pattern for organizing your teaching does not have to be your final choice. If you find it to be unsuitable for your students' needs or for your setting, feel free to try another model. Once an approach has been selected, the design of your curriculum can begin.

Choosing a Successful Approach

Teachers searching for an appropriate curriculum approach will encounter several suitable options. Practitioners who believe that their teaching will be enhanced by using ideas from various models are encouraged to combine them in the most effective ways. Combining ideas from different approaches results in an eclectic approach. For example, Banks's additive approach can be used

---

FIGURE 8.2 Synopsis of sample approaches for multicultural education

---

Curriculum Approaches

▮ Banks's four levels to integration of multicultural content (additive, contributions, transformational, and the social action approach)

▮ Sleeter and Grant's typology of practices

▮ Derman-Sparks's anti-bias approach

▮ Frances Kendall's model for early childhood multicultural education

---

in conjunction with the anti-bias approach proposed by Derman-Sparks. This was Barbara's choice because she believed that the combination of the two will best serve her students' needs and because she felt she could manage it well. In her journal, she wrote:

> "I like the approaches of James Banks. Level four (social action approach) is particularly appealing; however, I don't think I'm ready to try it yet. I also like the anti-bias model of Derman-Sparks. What should I select? My teaching is mainly thematic. Perhaps I can use themes where I could blend the anti-bias approach with the contributions level. That's what I'll do. We'll see what happens!"

Like Barbara, you may want to select an approach compatible with your professional expertise. It is always advisable to choose a less difficult model in the beginning, and then, as you gain confidence, progress to the more complex one.

❖ Making Decisions: What Barbara Did

All educators experience difficulties associated with decisions regarding best practices. Many of us have also experienced the disappointment associated with something that did not work as planned. Learning how to design effective programs through good planning will maximize success in the classroom. Effective planning will allow teachers to:

▮ identify the students' needs (review assessment data)

▮ prioritize the needs

▮ set realistic expectations (goals and objectives)

▮ gain confidence in their teaching strategies

One thing is true: No teacher is exempt from planning regardless of how experienced or how

IN ACTION . . . *Choose Your Own Approach*

▪ What curriculum development approaches have you been using in your instruction?

▪ How much do you know about the approaches discussed in this chapter?

▪ What approaches seem to be most compatible with each other?

▪ Which one is the approach of your choice? Why?

new to the teaching profession. This includes Barbara, who decided to begin planning by reviewing the findings of her assessments. You may remember that she recorded her data on a web. Webbing provides a holistic view of data and facilitates visual analysis. The conceptual format of the web also makes it easy for Barbara to locate the teaching areas she will target for action (see Figure

Figure 8.3 Holistic panorama of a classroom

THE SETTING

Community:	Families	Children:
▪ ethnicities	▪ configurations	▪ ethnicities
▪ services	▪ cultures	▪ languages
▪ social class	▪ ethnicities	▪ cultures
▪ agencies	▪ languages	▪ interests
▪ languages	▪ customs	▪ other variables
▪ other variables	▪ religions	
	▪ needs and issues: (disabilities, employment)	

THE CLASSROOM

School	Me as a teacher
▪ faculty ethnic makeup	▪ my ethnicity
▪ programs for the exceptional	▪ my cultural beliefs
	▪ my customs
▪ school services	▪ my share of other aspects of diversity

8.3). If you used a web for your assessment and analyzed the information, you can select the key areas you wish to target simply by highlighting them with a marker.

Choosing Priorities

Early in this book, we examined some of the goals of multiculturalism. Reviewing them again is particularly helpful when trying to define priorities in multicultural education. For example, the goals defined by Francis Kendall (1983) over a decade ago reflect the same purposes advocated today by many educators and early childhood organizations. Kendall's goals incorporate the current directions and concerns for multiculturalism in the early childhood classroom. They can serve as an appropriate guide in establishing priorities. Additional definitions of goals can be found in York (1991) and the guidelines published by the National Council for the Social Studies (NCSS 1992).

Kendall's Primary Goals for Multicultural Education
1. To teach children to respect others' cultures and values as well as their own.
2. To help all children learn to function successfully in a multicultural, multiracial society.
3. To develop a positive self-concept in those children who are most affected by racism—children of color.

4. To help all children experience in positive ways both their differences as culturally diverse people and their similarities as human beings.

5. To encourage children to experience people of diverse cultures working together as unique parts of a whole community.

The next step after selecting the appropriate goals is to prioritize them. Some teachers may find this difficult because of their desire to attend to the needs of all children. However, it is important to initially focus on only a few goals that will target the needs of the majority of the students in your class.

Priorities Show Us the Way

A thorough examination of the characteristics discovered in the assessment phase will help you realize how diversity is reflected in your setting. In Barbara's case, she discovered the following:

▮ a variety of ethnicities (European American, Indian, Hispanic, Caribbean)

▮ several different multilingual backgrounds (three different native languages still spoken at home)

▮ two main racial groups (dark and light skin)

▮ various programs for exceptional children in which her students participate either directly or indirectly

▮ increasing ethnic diversity in the community.

The five diversity features Barbara identified will serve as the foundation of her program. Here are the priorities she listed for her kindergartners.

1. Helping children to deal positively with their own cultural identities; providing opportunities for children to become aware of other kinds of cultural identities.

2. Learning to live with diversity that surrounds them.

3. Helping children reject unfairness.

What If My Classroom Is "Monocultural"?

You probably noticed that priority #1 had a dual objective. In the second part Barbara refers to children "becoming aware of other kinds of cultural identities." This is a very important objective because it will not limit the scope of Barbara's multicultural activities to only those cultural groups already found in the community. In fact, she is determined to offer her students a much wider view of diversity. She began her planning by observing one of the basic rules of multicultural education: considering first the ethnicities present in her class (Derman-Sparks 1989). Then, she thought about other groups children should learn about. We want to emphasize this point because this is where most multicultural planning fails. Effective multicultural curricular planning requires teachers to consider not only the groups the children represent, but *also others not present in the classroom and in the community*. There are reasons to support this decision. First, with the high population mobility in our country, children have the potential of being exposed to many forms of cultural diversity. Second, the media (TV, movies, etc), a powerful source of cultural interaction for children, presents diversity on a very broad scale. It is, therefore, logical that these experiences also should be brought into the classroom. We recommend that early childhood educators include information about one additional cultural group not present in the children's community, as a minimum.

Some teachers comment that they only focus on a few concepts of diversity because their classrooms are "monocultural." To them we want to say that educators have a responsibility to offer children opportunities for getting a realistic view of the social environment in which they live. In order to do that, we need to offer them opportunities to expand their scope of understanding about others. We also believe that true "monocultural" classrooms are very unlikely to exist in our present society when we consider the comprehensiveness of diversity. Remember that diversity includes not only ethnic differences, but a wide range of other factors like religion and physical disabilities that influence and determine people's behaviors and views about life. So, if your classroom happens to be characterized mostly by a single diversity element, make sure to incorporate those the children would most likely interact with. The number of other cultural groups you would incorporate into the curriculum depends on the developmental level of your students as well as on the interests and the needs of the school and the community.

Now, try to identify your own priorities that will constitute the basis of your multicultural program. Write them down and use them as guides throughout your planning phase.

❖ Focus on the Environment

The first tangible changes toward multiculturalization should take place in the classroom physical environment. Because in early education the classroom environment is another teaching and learning tool, we need to focus our attention on it first. Berry and Mindes (1993) recommend making changes in the physical arrangement before moving to the curriculum content. Change is more visible when dealing with the concrete rather than the abstract. Seeing visible changes will give the teacher a more immediate sense of accomplishment that will motivate future efforts.

Taking Action: Changing the Physical Scenario

In Barbara's journal:

> "I just finished taking the inventory of my classroom and I can't believe what I found! I thought this was going to be the easiest part of my planning because I was sure I had plenty of materials my children could relate to. But, gosh, I'm shocked! No ethnic dolls at all. Actually, they all look alike. At least I do have nice posters with children of different ethnicities. But, books . . . two or three books about African Americans and nothing on any other groups. Well, I'm afraid I have a lot of work to do."

What gives you the first impression of any classroom? Without any doubts what you *see* sends the initial messages we use to form a frame of reference for that particular setting. This is also how children form impressions and interpret the environment. Early childhood educators (Derman-Sparks 1989; York 1991; Bredekamp & Rosegrant 1992; Berry & Mindes 1993; Jones & Nimmo 1994) agree that the classroom environment is an important teaching-learning component of the educational process. Unlike in other grades, the total classroom environment plays a crucial role in the development of young children. It is considered an essential medium for learning because every aspect of the classroom serves as a stimulus for challenging the child during the intensive knowledge construction phase that occurs during the early school years. This is why many early childhood educators spend much ef-

---

IN ACTION . . .   *Identifying Priorities*

▮ What are your priorities?

▮ How did you identify them?

▮ Do you agree with Barbara's choices? Why?

Figure 8.4 A classroom menu for the most discriminating tastes

Housekeeping area: kitchen area (cooking and eating utensils, make-believe food items); living room (furnished! and including a phone, decorations); bedroom (including a baby area, a closet or trunk with clothes, shoes, bags, accessories)

Art area: easels for free painting; a variety of painting materials (finger paint, sponge painting, vegetable painting, straws for blow painting, leaf printing, modeling clay, and others)

Block area: blocks of different sizes, props to play with the blocks like cars, trucks, people, animals

Drama area: different props, costumes, hats, puppets, paper to draw and/or to make a scene

Literacy and writing areas: books, newspapers, catalogs, magazines, pictures, phone book, taped books

For writing: paper, templates, pencils, pens, crayons, and other writing materials

Water and sand tables: containers, pails, floating objects

Manipulatives: puzzles, games, beads

Music area: a variety of musical instruments like drums, tambourines, maracas, cymbals, and others

---

fort in constructing classroom environments that offer something for every child.

The physical arrangement of an early childhood classroom is very complex. There is much to include and so much to choose from! Typically, early childhood classrooms offer a wide range of possibilities. Just look at the wealth of activities learning centers can provide the child (Figure 8.4).

All objects in the classroom have the potential of influencing the child. Teachers must constantly examine the contents of the environment because children have "fewer strategies for coping or responding to any negative impact from the space around them" (Watkins & Durant 1992, p. 69). Watkins and Durant (1992) recommend taking time to observe the layout of the classroom. This will allow teachers to determine the learning and the emotional atmosphere conveyed to the child. They further say that if children find a sense of ownership in the classroom, they will react more responsively to it.

In Chapter 7, we shared several ideas on how to assess the classroom. For instance, observe the interest areas first, then move to the literacy resources, and, then examine everything that hangs on the walls. Your appraisal can be facilitated by using an observation instrument. The *Checklist for diversity in early childhood education and care* (Peck & Shores 1994), published by the Southern Early Childhood Association (SECA) is an excellent example. This instrument is designed around three important areas: the overall image of the classroom, the materials in the interest areas, and the diversity of languages.

WORKING GLOSSARY

▪ **Classroom Environment**—the overall result of the arrangement and disposition of materials and equipment within a given learning setting. It is designed to promote the physical, cognitive, and social–emotional development of young learners.

Using the NAEYC Accreditation Criteria as a Tool for Action

In Chapter 7 we learned that Barbara discovered many elements in her classroom incompatible with a program emphasizing diversity. She decided to review the guidelines of the National Association for the Education of Young Children (NAEYC) and to look for information regarding the inclusion of diversity.

The NAEYC accreditation criteria include two items that specifically address diversity in the classroom. The first item, B-5a, deals with the physical environment, while the second, B-7h, addresses the instructional processes. Criterion B-5a serves as a guide for initiating the classroom transformation.

> B-5a. Multiracial, nonsexist, nonstereotypic pictures, dolls, books, and materials are available. (NAEYC 1991, p. 146)

Anatomy of Criterion B-5a: Expanding the Meaning

There is a consensus among early childhood educators about the importance of inclusion of diversity in early childhood experiences. However, data collected by NAEYC validators who visit early childhood facilities for accreditation purposes indicate that inclusion of diversity cannot be easily validated. Some educators argue that the reason is unclear requirements, while others believe that they are too stringent to be fully met. NAEYC validators report that B-5a, the easier of the two standards, often puzzles teachers and directors who frequently ask the team members for advice about how to comply. An analysis of the criterion may help us understand its intent better.

All materials (for example, dolls, manipulatives, music, pictures, posters, books, puppets) in the classroom reflect the following characteristics:

▪ **Multiracial:** the classroom portrays those cultures reflected by the children, those found in the community, and those children find in the media (the national level).

▪ **Nonsexist:** classroom reflects a balanced view about gender roles as depicted through activities and materials. Children are aware that the classroom interest centers and materials are not gender specific.

▪ **Nonstereotypic:** materials (like artifacts, manipulatives), pictures, and literature are free of biased or misleading representations. For example, ethnic groups are appropriately portrayed.

Many educators are inexperienced in analyzing classroom materials for multicultural, sexist, and stereotypical traits. This makes it difficult for them to create environments without biases. We believe that as awareness about diversity increases, professionals will become more conscious of diversity issues and will develop the expertise that will help them eliminate biases and prejudice in the classroom.

We Need To Be Practical!

Transforming the physical environment of a classroom requires time and a budget, both of which may sometimes be unavailable. Teachers are advised to proceed slowly in transforming their classrooms. Begin by generating a list of all things needed to achieve a cultural balance in the classroom. Concentrate on removing all images that either distort or misrepresent cultures and people. Notice what is missing. Derman-Sparks (1989) asserts that what is omitted in the classroom can be as negative as what is inaccurate and sterotypical.

Selecting one learning area to change at a time rather than trying to change them all at once is a good idea. More details about materials and guidelines on how to select activities and resources will be described in Chapter 9.

FOCUS ON CLASSROOM PRACTICES

DRESSING UP THE VISUAL ENVIRONMENT

Pictures play an important role in diversity. What the child finds in the classroom visuals sends powerful messages about multiculturalism. It particularly shows the child what the teacher values as exemplary ideals of people and actions. There are many ways to get good visual multicultural materials for our classrooms. We are sure you probably know about some sources already. So, we want to suggest some additional sources.

Sources for Visual Materials

1. Journals, magazines, and even newspapers are sources of pictures about different ethnic and cultural groups. If using newspapers, the Sunday edition is the one that offers the best array of choices. Remember to look for those pictures where people are presented in nonstereotyped ways.
2. Commercial sources: Among the many available sources, you may want to check the following:

   ▪ **National Women's History Projects** (7738 Bell Road, Windsor, CA 95492): A nonprofit educational organization, they carry a variety of posters about women representing a variety of diversity characteristics. Among their products are: "Notable Women Photo Displays" (set I and II) with examples of distinguished women in American history; poster sets (for example, *Women of Hope: Latinas Abriendo Camino; Women of Hope: African-Americans Who Made A Difference; Celebrate Women's History-a Coloring Poster,* etc.)

   ▪ **Poster Education** (Box 8774, Asheville, NC 28814 Tel. 800-858-0969): Emphasizing geography, they have very good sets of colorful posters about Native Americans that include lesson planning ideas. Also a good selection of posters about different geographical regions of the U.S. as well as posters about places around the world.

   ▪ **Camera-Mundi, Inc.** (Amatista #8 Villa Blanca, Caguas, PR 00625): Excellent photo and picture sets depictive of Hispanic family traditions, occupations, food, children's games, etc. Good source for early childhood bilingual teaching and training materials.

   ▪ **NAEYC** (1509 16th St. NW, Washington, DC 20036): Good source for reasonably priced classroom posters.

Teachers should focus attention on the nature of materials used and displayed in the classroom. They need to determine if classrooms are free of stereotyping and biased representations. A good way to do that is to pretend that you are a child and record the messages you receive from the classroom setting. Appraising the environment should be a slow and deliberate process. In the end, you will be surprised to "see" the messages being sent directly and indirectly to some students on a daily basis.

IN ACTION . . .   *Classroom Messages*

Consider what messages your classroom environment conveys. With the eyes of a child, look and find ideas conveyed through your classroom environment. After your survey is over, write down what things made you feel "bad" and what made you "happy," the way a child might.

Changes Will Yield New Insights

Changes in the environment will result in a variety of responses from the students. Perceptive teachers will use these responses to generate additional ideas that will assist them in moving into the more complex part of multicultural education change process: the content.

Establishing the Content

The traditional curriculum has given way to the new multicultural one as a result of the growing diversity of our society, which is mirrored in our schools. The acceptance of the multicultural curriculum is the result of not only the societal trends,

FOCUS ON CLASSROOM PRACTICES

GETTING OTHERS TO HELP US ASSESS OUR CLASSROOM ENVIRONMENT

While it is true that sometimes we fail to detect the stereotypes used and present in our classrooms, it is equally true that we can find help. Where? Here are some suggestions:

1. Begin by asking yourself: Does everything I have in this classroom reflect my own cultural style? Are there any objects that show my acceptance of the children's cultures? If I were in a different culture, what things would make me feel accepted?
   Being honest in your answers helps you discover what your classroom fails to reflect.
2. Colleagues: If there are some teachers already teaching multiculturally, visit their classrooms. Talk to them and observe what they have and how they arrange the environment. Ask them to share some tips. Invite them to "see" your classroom and ask them to suggest ways to improve it.
3. ESOL teachers and exceptional education teachers: These professionals can also provide good ideas about how to meet diversity. They are especially capable of identifying stereotypical or culturally biased objects and materials.
4. Parents and community members: If you have parents from a variety of cultures, have some of them share their impressions of your classroom. Ask them what things about their cultures they would like to see in the classroom. They can probably become the sources of additional materials and cultural activities.

but also of the new assumptions about teachers, students, and learning. Today's educators realize that culture as a framework for the curriculum blurs the boundaries between the lives of children, the schools, and society at large. It aids in unifying knowledge and skills with the cognitive, emotional, and psychomotor development of the whole child. Choosing the content that will meet the mission of the multicultural curriculum presents a real challenge.

Setting Expectations: Goals and Objectives

Every curriculum contains a plan based on expectations and suggested ways to meet those expectations. Expectations are the reasons and the purposes of the learning the students are supposed to accomplish. In education, the reasons and purposes are also known as goals and objectives.

Multicultural Education Encompasses the Whole Child

The purposes of a multicultural program will depend on the established priorities. The teacher needs to keep in mind a whole-child approach when selecting curriculum priorities. A whole-child program considers the intricate interactions between the environment and the child. For that reason, the targeted instructional areas must reflect what is pertinent and relevant to the children. Pertinence is achieved when the curriculum addresses points that convey meaning to the child. This is where teachers need to reconcile the developmental characteristics of the children they teach

with the expected aims of the program. More specifically, this means paying special attention to the principles of child development in the physical, cognitive, and social-emotional domains.

Knowing what happens to students during various life stages helps to establish meaningful goals for any program and particularly for a multicultural one. For example, knowledge of the social-emotional and cognitive characteristics of five-year-olds will permit selection of literature materials at the correct level. Similarly, knowledge of young children's physical needs and capabilities will offer a solid basis for choosing and structuring experiences for motor skill development.

Multicultural Education Is Grounded in General Educational Goals

The goals and expectations of multicultural programs are not isolated from the goals of general education. The National Standards, also known as *America 2000*, establish the educational aspirations for all American students.

The first standard addresses the national concern for appropriate early education. Goal 1, in Snapshot 8.1, states that every child will begin school ready to learn. It also specifies what schools must provide and do for children. Embedded in this goal is more than just providing the child with developmental readiness for learning. "Ready to learn" also implies that children have a positive concept about themselves as individuals. This means that young children are ready to learn only after they have established

---

WORKING GLOSSARY

▮ **Goal**—a statement that defines the intent and aspirations of a program or of an activity.

▮ **Objective**—a statement that establishes the specific purposes for an activity or exercise. It describes the nature and the level of knowledge the student will derive from the experience.

PLANNING FOR THE WHOLE CHILD

Developmental teaching has a basic rule: Consideration of what the child needs is essential for creating an effective curriculum. The same rule applies to multicultural education. Planning for the whole child means considering how the child's developmental needs are met through the selected curriculum content. An example of this is presented here. Derived from one of Barbara's priorities, see how she began to identify ways to fulfill the children's developmental needs while using a multicultural content.

Barbara's priority #1— Helping children to deal positively with their own cultural identities; providing opportunities to discover other kinds of cultural identities.

1. Topic: Discovering what makes us alike and different
2. Target areas and sample activities:
   a. Language/Literacy
      - Write their names in the air. Use sandpaper letters to form their names. See who has the longest/shortest name.
      - Name soup (identifying the names of our classmates). Find out how many of the classmates' names have the same first initial.
      - Show and tell about "What I can do best."
      - Read and discuss the book, *This is the way we got to school,* by Edith Baer (1994, Scholastic).
   b. Cognitive Skills
      - Discuss the things we like to eat, play with, do, etc. Do a Venn diagram to find out what things we have in common as a group or with a class member.
      - Discuss breakfast preferences. On paper plates children will draw and share what they usually have for breakfast. Prepare a graph to see how many children prefer the same items for breakfast.
      - Measurement. Find out how many have the same height/weight. Discuss findings.
   c. Social Skills
      - Use manner words. Learn to say greetings in different languages.
      - Work cooperatively to create a class mural about "How alike we are."
      - Prepare a "This is Me" book.
      - Learn the song "We are alike" (following the tune "Are you sleeping?" or "Frere Jacques" in French:

         We're alike, we're alike.
         Yes, we are. Yes, we are.
         (Name of child) can dance and jump (substitute with those things the class found in common)
         And so do I.
         We're so much alike.
         Oh, that's nice!
   d. Art/Fine motor skills
      - Explore with different art forms. Use paper plates and cut-outs from magazines to create "Me mobiles" (things children like to do).
      - Create tactile self-portraits. Use skin-color paints, fabrics, buttons, yarn (for hair), etc.
      - Prepare brown-bag puppets about our favorite pets and improvise a skit.

FIGURE 8.5 Wheel of developmental areas

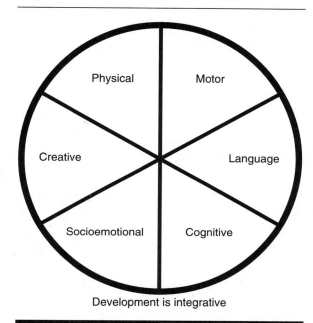

Development is integrative

forts made in schools. They define in broad, long-range terms what children are to gain from the teaching-learning process. In early education, goals need to respond to the developmental characteristics of children. When trying to establish the goals for a program built around diversity, teachers must consider the developmental aspects along with the concepts to be taught. This establishes realistic and achievable purposes for the program (Figures 8.5 and 8.6).

Be Realistic When Setting Expectations

Goals and objectives should be established based on realistic expectations of what the child can accomplish. This involves considerations of special elements that must underlie the teacher's approach to the children's learning process. The following are the elements to consider:

▮ What is *developmentally sound* for the group
Consider the age level and developmental needs of the learners. Select objectives you know they need and can meet. Your best guide comes from your own observations of children and from reviewing the outcomes of assessment activities. For instance, most of your four-year-olds require experiences to strengthen oral expression and build social skills. These areas should become priorities as well as guides in your planning.

▮ What is *meaningful* to the group
Consider the interests and things familiar to the class. Weigh how much interest children would have if presented with experiences to

identities and self-concepts that allow them to feel good about themselves. Early in life a child's personal identity is constructed through familial relationships, interaction with peers, and relationships formed with other members of the community. This entire process is influenced by the child's culture. The process of forming a sense of identity is more complex when children enter school and encounter others whose ways are different. The new conflict that this creates can be resolved positively if children have a strong self-concept based on positive feelings about their own cultural identities.

In Writing: My Goals and Objectives Are . . .

A program is established when the goals and objectives are defined. Goals are the purposes of ef-

FIGURE 8.6 Goals define objectives

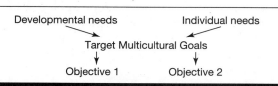

Snapshot 8.1
Goal 1: Readiness for School

By the year 2000, all children in America will start school ready to learn.

Objectives:

▊ All disadvantaged and disabled children will have access to high quality and developmentally appropriate preschool programs that help prepare children for school.

▊ Every parent in America will be a child's first teacher and devote time each day helping his or her preschool child learn: parents will have access to the training and support they need.

▊ Children will receive the nutrition and health care needed to arrive at school with healthy minds and bodies, and the number of low weight babies at birth will be significantly reduced through enhanced prenatal health system (p. D-1).

---

further explore those topics. Observe children, talk to them, and listen to them while working at the learning centers, and you will learn what they value as important. Do webbing experiences around some topics to detect what they know and how much interest they have in those themes. Use the children's interests, not yours, as a guide for planning.

▊ What is *relevant knowledge* versus what is trivial
Consider what will provide valuable experiences and knowledge children can use to build upon. Stay away from what seems "nice" but where significant ideas are not gained. It is important to consider if the content will provide opportunities for learning accurate and valid information about their own diversity and that of others. Consider also if what is presented is just mere frills that usually carry little value and sometimes lead to stereotypes.

▊ What are the children's *prior knowledge*
Always consider the children's experiences. Awareness of the children's family backgrounds and personal life experiences will let us know what "baggage" they bring to our classroom. Always value what they bring, and use it to plan activities to either foster exploration of new concepts or to expand and refine what they already know.

▊ What is *culturally relevant* to children
Consider the immediate cultural world of the children. Be aware of the elements of diversity they represent. Knowing the children's families and the neighborhood environments also provides clues as to what is significant to the child. For example, if a child holds religion and a physical exceptionality as his/her distinctive diversity traits, find out how they are viewed by the child, the family, and his/her culture. Use this knowledge to select materials and content congruous with the re-

alities they represent. Consider presenting the special qualities of this child to the rest of the class to help them learn about and become aware of differences.

One of the most important aspects of an appropriate curriculum in the early grades is the logical way in which it blends learning and developmental principles with the construction of knowledge (NAEYC & NAECS/SDE 1991). In multicultural programs, the type of knowledge to be learned is determined by the established educational priorities in a given setting. An example of locally relevant educational priorities are those that Barbara determined after analyzing the findings from her assessment. Appropriate multicultural curriculum is also based on aspects and interests legitimately related to the children's lives. The combination of the children's needs, the aspirations of the program, and the identified priorities constitute a pedagogically sound program. Target outcomes should reflect a logical balance between what the school determines as relevant educational aspirations, what the child is capable of doing, and what is relevant to the child. These principles must be applied in designing all effective early childhood education programs including those focused on diversity.

Formula for Appropriate Early Childhood Education Programs

developmental needs + individual interests + educational priorities = appropriate goals

Selecting Relevant and Developmentally Appropriate Goals and Objectives

Teachers preparing to establish expectations for multicultural programs need guidelines. We recommend three specific sources. Two of them address early childhood practices while one is a document addressing multicultural programs. The two early childhood sources are the *Guide-*

lines for appropriate curriculum content and assessment in programs serving children ages 3 through 8 (NAEYC & NAECS/SDE 1991), and *Developmentally appropriate practice in early childhood programs serving children from birth through age 8* (Bredekamp 1987). The third is the *Curriculum guidelines for multicultural education* (NCSS 1992).

Details about practices and content selection ideas for early childhood education are contained in the documents prepared by NAEYC and NAECS/SDE (1991) and in Bredekamp (1987). Clarification and description of what is a developmentally appropriate program practice is addressed by both sources. In the guidelines provided by NAEYC and NAECS/SDE (1991), detailed information for preparation and selection of curricula is provided. Bredekamp, on the other hand, presents descriptions of practices. Both sources serve as the knowledge base for early childhood professionals who wish to make competent decisions. The guidelines from the National Council for the Social Studies (NCSS 1992) provide the framework and the rationale for multicultural programs. They also serve to establish directions and purposes for a multicultural program in early childhood education.

Using Professional Guidelines

Guidelines for Appropriate Curriculum Content and Assessment in Programs Serving Children Ages 3 Through 8 (NAEYC and NAECS/SDE 1991): contains twenty specific guidelines required for child-appropriate programs. "To judge curriculum appropriate and acceptable, positive evidence should exist that *all* guidelines are met" (NAEYC & NAECS/SDE 1991, p. 31).

Although all of the guidelines stated by NAEYC and NAECS/SDE (1991) apply to early childhood education, some have a more direct relationship to multicultural curricula. Guideline #7 specifically addresses the need for diversity in the curriculum. Guideline #7 states: "Curriculum respects and supports individual, cultural, and linguistic diversity. Curriculum supports and encourages positive relationships with children's families" (NAEYC & NAECS/SDE 1991, p. 32). Description of those considered most relevant, in addition to guideline #7, and their implications for design of multicultural programs follows.

Key curriculum guidelines for multicultural programs found in the NAEYC and NAECS/SDE (1991) document

■ **Guideline #3:** *Curriculum addresses the development of knowledge and understanding, processes and skills, dispositions and attitudes.*
Implications: Multicultural programs are designed to help the child gain relevant cultural knowledge as well as skills and attitudes required to live in a socially diverse community.

■ **Guideline #6:** *Curriculum content reflects and is generated by the needs and interests of individual children within the group. Curriculum incorporates a wide variety of learning experiences, materials and equipment, and instructional strategies to accommodate a broad range of children's individual differences in prior experience, maturation rates, styles of learning, needs, and interests.*
Implications: Content of multicultural programs addresses topics relevant to children. Activities and strategies respect children's learning needs.

■ **Guideline #8:** *Curriculum builds upon what children already know and are able to do (activating prior knowledge) to consolidate their learning and to foster their acquisition of new concepts and skills.*
Implications: The content of a multicultural program considers the cultural baggage the children bring to the classroom. Teachers use children's cultural knowledge as a foundation on which to structure the program.

■ **Guideline #9:** *The curriculum provides conceptual frameworks for children so that their mental constructions based on prior knowledge and experience become more complex over time.*

Implications: A multicultural curriculum has conceptual pertinence. Children experience cultural concepts that facilitate and engage children in the development of a relevant cultural knowledge base.

■ **Guideline #12:** *The content of the curriculum is worth knowing; curriculum respects children's intelligence and does not waste their time.*
Implications: A multicultural curriculum engages the child in cognitively sound activities. The content is free of triviality or "touristlike" approaches. It respects and recognizes the child as a serious learner.

■ **Guideline #16:** *Curriculum emphasizes the value of social interaction to learning in all domains and provides opportunities to learn from peers.*
Implications: Multicultural activities encourage social interactions as a means of promoting understanding of relevant societal principles and prosocial behaviors (i.e., empathy, cooperation, fairness, tolerance).

■ **Guideline #20:** *The curriculum is flexible so that teachers can adapt to individual children or groups (NAEYC & NAECS/SDE 1991, pp. 31–34).*
Implications: Multicultural programs should not follow a fixed or closed structure. They are characterized by their capacity to alter and adapt accordingly to the needs of children.

Bredekamp's developmentally appropriate practices.

Equally important for a multicultural curriculum design are the principles of developmentally appropriate practices described in Bredekamp (1987). Bredekamp's guidelines do not address multicultural education in detail, but they establish recognition of diversity as an essential element of appropriate practice. A review of what constitutes acceptable in early childhood education provides teachers with a practical reference for program design. Teachers should use Bredekamp's text to verify what represents valid procedures for the age level they teach.

Guidelines for multicultural programs

The National Council for the Social Studies has been a leader in supporting curriculum reform addressing ethnic and cultural diversity. The first set of NCSS curriculum guidelines for multicultural education were developed in 1976. The original was reviewed and revised in 1992 by the Task Force on Ethnic Studies, led by James Banks. These guidelines provide a rationale for multicultural education, 23 guidelines for curriculum design, and an evaluation instrument. The guidelines provide a framework for action in grades preschool through 12. The principles of ethnic and cultural diversity provided by the guidelines serve as a rationale for program restructuring. Of particular importance to the early childhood educator are the following:

1. Ethnic and cultural diversity should be recognized and respected at the individual, group, and societal levels.
2. Ethnic and cultural diversity provides a basis for societal enrichment, cohesiveness, and survival.
3. Equality of opportunity must be afforded to all members of ethnic and cultural groups.
4. Ethnic identification for individuals should be optional in a democracy (NCSS 1992, pp. 277–278).

According to the Task Force, the goal of schools "should be to help attain a delicate balance of diversity and unity—one nation that respects the cultural rights and freedoms of its many people" (NCSS 1992, p. 278). The direct implication for early childhood educators is: The development of an effective sense of respect and tolerance begins in childhood. For that reason, programs for the young need to embrace this premise as one of their goals. This goal also emphasizes the importance of an antibias curriculum whose purpose is to provide experiences that help young children develop positive social attitudes.

❖ Putting Everything Together

We have discussed several essential elements that will help create a child-responsive multicultural program. Let us review what we learned.

Things I can use in planning my program:

▌ results from classroom assessment (children, community, environment, my current curriculum)

▌ list of priorities identified from the assessment data

▌ professional guidelines

It's Your Turn, It's Your Decision!

The next step is to begin drafting your goals and objectives. This phase requires independent decision making. Now, you must assume a leadership role and define the specific goals for your program. The writers of this book have purposely avoided prescription of a specific approach, or even of a specific set of objectives and goals in order to empower teachers to design their own educational improvements. It is our opinion that teachers have been prevented far too long from making curriculum decisions for which they are qualified and to which they are entitled. It has almost become a tradition that teachers are to follow curricula written by individuals completely unfamiliar with their classroom experiences. This practice has started what Gay (1992) calls a cycle of dependency where others tell teachers what to do. In our experience, when teachers are entrusted with the task of educational reform, the results are highly positive for both the child and the teacher. That is why we believe that with the knowledge you have acquired, you can choose the most appropriate targets for your program. Only when

Snapshot 8.2
Using the NCSS Guidelines to Design the Curriculum

During a course in early childhood education, a group of students examined how the guidelines for multicultural education from the NCSS apply to the design of classroom objectives. Working in small groups, the class determined that the document was a helpful resource for the classroom teacher. The class, where 60 percent of the students were early childhood practitioners, used the document to draft learning objectives they would follow in their own schools. A sample of what one of the groups developed is included. The NCSS guidelines addressed by each objective appear in parentheses.

Learning Objectives (Group III):

1. To provide children with enhanced opportunities for practicing cooperative learning (NCSS 11.0).
2. To generate from students a sense of shared "communality," of "being alike" through realizing that the diversity of cultures also shows patterns of similarity (NCSS 10.0; 2.0).
3. To increase the level of self-confidence in one's own cultural identity (NCSS 6.0).

Guidelines considered most relevant for the classroom teacher are the following.

Relevant NCSS Guidelines for Early Childhood Education Planning

1.0 Ethnic and cultural diversity should permeate the total school environment.

5.0 The multicultural curriculum should reflect the cultural learning styles and characteristics of the students within the community.

6.0 The multicultural curriculum should provide students with continuous opportunities to develop a better sense of self.

10.0 The multicultural curriculum should promote values, attitudes, and behaviors that support ethnic pluralism and cultural diversity as well as build and support the nation-state and the nation's shared national culture. *E. pluribus unum* should be the goal of the schools and the nation.

11.0 The multicultural curriculum should help students develop their decision-making abilities, social participation skills, and sense of political efficacy as necessary for effective citizenship in a pluralistic democratic nation.

12.0 The multicultural curriculum should help students develop the skills necessary for effective interpersonal, interethnic, and intercultural group interactions.

14.0 The multicultural curriculum should include the continuous study of the cultures, historical experiences, social realities, and existential conditions of ethnic and cultural groups, including a variety of racial compositions.

15.0 Interdisciplinary and multidisciplinary approaches should be used in designing and implementing the multicultural curriculum.

16.0 The multicultural curriculum should use comparative approaches in the study of ethnic and cultural groups.

17.0 The multicultural curriculum should help students to view and interpret events, situations, and conflict from diverse ethnic and cultural perspectives and points of view.

19.0 School should provide opportunities for students to participate in the aesthetic experiences of various ethnic and cultural groups.

21.0 The multicultural curriculum should make maximum use of experiential learning, especially local community resources (NCSS 1992, pp. 280–288).

teachers themselves select and establish the program goals can we say that children will reap the benefits of a culturally responsive and pedagogically sound program. Examples and models presented in this book are only intended to illustrate the process, but they do not pretend to be "the way" to construct a multicultural program. With that point clarified, let us see what Barbara, our kindergarten teacher, decided to do.

Barbara Sets Directions for Her Teaching

"It's not easy," Barbara wrote in her journal as she was planning her course of action. Gathering the data and the guidelines, including the "green and white book," she began to identify her goals. Simultaneously, she highlighted the guidelines she believed would help her meet her program priorities.

To facilitate the process, Barbara decided to use a planning matrix as a "teaching blueprint." Using a large piece of paper (like those from a flip chart pad), she outlined the essential elements of her program. Next, she wrote down the program

expectations as she envisioned them. Visualization is an important planning strategy used in many different endeavors by creative individuals. Creating a new multicultural program also requires the teacher's ingenuity and vision as well. This is the time to start dreaming, so feel free to go ahead!

Barbara's next steps were to choose the most relevant professional guidelines to form a framework for action. For example, she chose two guidelines from the NCSS (1992) document (6.0 and 12.0), and three from the NAEYC and NAECS/SDE (1991) statement (6, 8, 12).

Barbara decided to target all of her priorities even though she was focusing on the multicultural perspective. If you remember, her priorities were (1) to help children develop a positive understanding of their identities, (2) to help them interact positively with the diversity surrounding them, and (3) to have children become proactive in rejecting unfairness. Barbara's decision to target all three areas is based on her belief that they are interrelated. Children need to develop a positive understanding of their own identities before they can interact positively with those around them. Learning about diversity will result in proactively rejecting unfairness. Barbara also believes that accomplishing these three priorities will build the foundation for the rest of her program.

You need not follow Barbara's ambitious path. Remember that all of us have a need to feel successful, and setting more modest targets may help you achieve that. Working with one program priority at a time can be just as effective. The important thing to remember is that you are continuing to transform your teaching! Figure 8.7 contains suggestions to help you get organized and get started by asking yourself a few questions.

Barbara recognized that teaching multiculturally involves an acceptance of a philosophy based on principles of equality. Adopting a whole new theoretical perspective is a complex process that cannot be rushed. Barbara decided to give herself time by setting aside the program priorities and looking at the content.

❖ Selecting the Content for Multicultural Teaching

Content, in curricular terms, is the *what* included for the purposes of learning (Ornstein & Hunkins 1993). There are many divergent opinions regarding what constitutes content in the context of early childhood education. This is partly due to the many instructional modalities associated with the field. Each early childhood instructional model has its own particular way of constructing or selecting the contents of instructional experiences (Roopnarine & Johnson 1993). However, one thing on which most early childhood educators agree is that there is a given and basic set of ideas regarding the content children should learn. It is an accepted notion that early childhood teachers will use a variety of ways to teach that basic content.

Scholars of multiculturalism believe that instructional content is the major conduit for infusion of diversity into educational program. The *what* the child discovers in the classroom has a decisive impact on the child's development of ideas and acquisition of knowledge. For that reason, the content needs to be worthy of learning. Earlier in this chapter, we defined the characteristics of classroom content. Among the characteristics mentioned were the need for *validity, usefulness, interest, and significance.* We believe that those four traits should serve as guiding principles in selecting and establishing the content of a curriculum for diversity in the early childhood classrooms.

Infusion of Diversity as a Key Strategy

One of the questions most commonly asked by teachers is: "How can I change what I teach?" Or, "How can I prepare a new content?" Behind their

IN ACTION . . . *Choosing Professional Guidelines*

▌ Why do you think Barbara chose those specific guidelines?

▌ Do the guidelines have relevance to her classroom characteristics?

▌ Which guidelines would you choose for your program? Why?

▌ How do you envision your multicultural program?

FIGURE 8.7 Teaching blueprint (planning matrix)

I. What kind of multicultural program do I want? Your answer will include aspects of your personal philosophy.

II. What guidelines will I follow? We suggest you review some of the ones presented earlier in this chapter.

III. What are the priorities I will target? In determining the answer to this question, you will have to define priorities similar to the following ones.

Priority #1 To deal positively with the children's cultural identities.

Priority #2 To live with the diversity in the school and the community.

Priority #3 To learn to reject unfairness.

IV. How can I meet my priorities? Remember that priorities become goals. (Use the charts to plot your answers to the rest of the questions.)

Goal:	Goal:

V. What are my objectives for meeting the goals? These are the specific targets from which you will later generate activities.

Objective #1	Objective #2	Objective #3

VI. Comments/changes? Remember to conduct periodical self-assessments during the planning process.

August:	October:	January:	May:

questions one can sometimes detect a reluctance and a realization that the task may be difficult. The teachers using prescribed or mandated curricula are often even more hesitant about the transition to multicultural teaching. The writers of this book understand that preparing and organizing a new curriculum content is not only a difficult activity, but one requiring time and experience. We, therefore, recommend content infusion as a method to facilitate that process.

The multicultural content infusion is a strategy used to incorporate the perspective of a pluralistic society into the existing curriculum. It allows the teachers to continue using the existing curricula and, at the same time, incorporate new material. This also gives the teachers more confidence in the transformation process. In the approach recommended by James Banks (1992), the first two levels for content integration, the contributions and the additive levels, represent examples of content infusion. Banks recommends demonstrating the ways of achieving infusion.

The teachers can infuse the curriculum by introducing appropriate views and ideas about diversity into the context of the curriculum. To accomplish that successfully, teachers must have a thorough knowledge of various diversity concepts (Figure 8.8).

Teachers of young children need to begin the infusion process by examining the topics and the units taught through a prescribed curriculum. A careful analysis will reveal *how* the topics can accommodate the inclusion of diversity perspectives. The process will also show *where* and *what* type of multicultural views and ideas need to be included. To begin, simply take your current

FIGURE 8.8 Content infusion happens when the perspectives of diversity are incorporated into the content

views of diversity → **CONTENT** ← views of diversity

planning book or the curriculum guide and perform the following steps.

Steps for multicultural content infusion

1. If you use an emerging curriculum (built around the interests of the child), or if you follow a teacher-made curriculum, go through your lesson plans and find the topics, or themes, you teach. List them. If you use a prescribed curriculum, check your guide and list all the topics/themes/units that you teach.
2. Review the profile of your students and look for the traits that are descriptive of cultural diversity (ethnicities, religion, languages, social class, exceptionality).
3. From the list of topics/themes/units, circle or highlight those that you find lend themselves best to infusion of diversity. Begin first by considering to incorporate those characteristics that are found in your classroom, then consider those of others.
4. Next, brainstorm how you could incorporate diversity into the selected topics. Begin by asking yourself: What other views could help children expand their understanding of this topic? Write down all the ideas you think are plausible.

WORKING GLOSSARY

▪ **Multicultural Content**—the "what" children experience, which is defined by its significance, validity, interest, and usefulness.

5. Gather all the ideas and rewrite your list of themes or units including the additional diverse perspectives. The only way to know if your approach will work is to try it with your students. So, the next step is implement your ideas!

6. Keep notes during the lessons on the children's reactions. This will help you assess the success of your venture and offer constructive information for revisions.

Avoiding Infusion of Trivial and Stereotypical Content

Too many times we find children involved in experiences that are purely fun and that do little to expand their level of knowledge about human diversity. This commonly occurs when content without relevance is infused into the curriculum. The result is called trivializing.

The rule for avoiding trivializing is to first identify how a selected topic is consistent with the curriculum. Second, it is necessary to determine whether what is incorporated bears any valuable learning, particularly whether it will contribute to the understanding of life in our diverse society. To prevent choosing unimportant topics for infusion, we should ask ourselves:

▪ Is the topic presenting, elaborating, and/or expanding concepts on diversity that are commonly and currently found among the target groups?

▪ Does the topic fit logically into the child's learning/experiencing? Does it give a sense of real learning versus the unimportant?

▪ Can the topic be made to include the perspectives of how the people with diverse cultural views would behave or react to it?

▪ Is the topic reflective of issues that commonly happen to children in this classroom or to people in our community?

▪ Does the topic offer opportunities to present other positions that expose the children to divergent views or allow the children to respond to it?

▪ Can the topic serve as a link to discuss emotions and feelings as perceived through the eyes of the children?

▪ Can the topic facilitate clarification of stereotypes and biases? How?

Barbara's Experience

Barbara reviewed her curriculum and selected the areas for infusion of diversity. She found that this enhanced her content and made it more realistic and interesting. She also noticed that her teaching became more child-oriented because she was including the points that pertained to the immediate reality and life of her students. In other words, her curriculum became pertinent and relevant. Let's look at one of the topics she enhanced with diversity:

Theme: All about me

My purpose: To engage children in an analysis of the things that make them special individuals. To actively establish why we feel proud about our cultural identity.

Things (topics) to work on: (see Figure 8.9)

Stories to share:

▪ *Clothes from Many Lands* (M. Jackson)

▪ *All the Colors of the Skin* (K. Kissinger)

▪ *Bread, Bread, Bread* (A. Morris)

▪ *How My Parents Learned to Eat* (I. Friedman)

▪ *A Boy Named Jafta* (H. Lewin)

▪ *How Emily Blair Got Her Hair* (S. Garrison)

▪ *This Is the Way We Eat Our Lunch* (E. Baer)

▪ *Mel's Diner* (M. Moss)

▪ *Birthdays! Celebrating Life Around the World* (E. Felman)

IN ACTION . . .   *Your Own Theme*

▌ If you were to teach the theme, "All about me," what would you include?

▌ How would you reflect the diversity in your classroom?

▌ What literature, manipulatives, and class objects would you use?

▌ What are some of the key questions you would ask the students?

▌ Create your own web to organize your plans.

FIGURE 8.9 Infusing the perspective on diversity

	All about me	
Topics	**Possible Activities**	**Perspective on Diversity**

Topics
- I am like you but I'm different, too
- Things I can do
- Stories I like
- Stories my friends like
- Where do I come from? (community, state, country)
- Things my friends and I enjoy doing
- Things I do at home
- Things I do in the classroom
- My favorite game
- Clothes I like to wear
- My favorite words
- Things I like to eat
- My favorite song

Possible Activities
- Visit local grocery store to pick favorite fruits, vegetables
- Learn games from other countries
- Invite parents to tell us about their favorite games and songs
- Read stories from other countries, Learn about the authors
- Prepare a graph about the physical characteristics of children in the class
- Learn words in other languages (greetings, names of food)
- Look at the pictures of children from Haiti/India to see how they dress. Compare with how we dress in U.S.

Perspective on Diversity
- Learning about what children in other states and countries do (i.e., India, Haiti)*
- Learning about the communities of other countries
- Stories children like in other countries
- Games from other countries
- Activities children do in other countries
- Clothes children use in, for example, Haiti and Venezuela
- Learning basic words in other languages
- Typical snacks and food in other places
- Music children sing in other countries

*Emphasis on what is current in those countries or cultures.

❖ What Is the Next Step?

"There is still much to be done. My next steps are to focus on the classroom materials, and on the actual experiences. I know there are many things I need to consider before I am done," Barbara wrote in her journal. That will also be our task as our journey takes us to Chapter 9.

❖ Things to Do . . .

1. Thinking about your classroom (or future classroom), describe the approach you would choose to implement your program for diversity. Give two reasons for your selection.
2. Considering all the steps involved in good classroom planning, which one would you say is the most important and why?
3. Some teachers believe they can initiate a program transformation "overnight." Do you agree or disagree? Give specific reasons for your position.
4. Using the blueprint that Barbara followed to plan her program transformation, determine if it would facilitate the beginning of multicultural teaching in your classroom. Explain your answer.
5. Define multicultural infusion. Look back and see how Barbara implemented the process. Then select a theme for your curriculum and try to do the same.
6. There are many teachers who are already teaching multiculturally. A few of them may be at your school. Interview them to find out what planning strategies they use.

❖ Children's Literature Corner

Crew, D. (1991). *Big mama's.* New York: Greenwillow.

Hoffman, M. (1991). *Amazing Grace.* New York: Dial.

Kroll, V. (1992). *Masai and I.* New York: Four Winds.

Mendez, P. (1990). *The black snowman.* New York: Scholastic Books.

Ringgold, F. (1993). *Aunt Harriet's underground railroad.* New York: Crown Books.

Small-Hector, I. (1992). *Jonathan and his mommy.* New York: Little, Brown & Company.

Williams, K. (1991). *When Africa was home.* New York: Orchard Press.

❖ References

Baer, E. (1994). *This is the way we go to school.* New York: Scholastic Books.

Banks, J. (1992 November/December). Reducing prejudice in children. Guidelines from research. *Social Education* (pp. 3–5).

Berry, C. F., & Mindes, G. (1993). *Theme based curriculum goals, activities and planning guides for 4's and 5's.* Glenview, IL: Goodyear.

Bredekamp, S. (ed.). (1987). *Developmentally appropriate practice in early childhood programs serving children birth through age 8.* Washington, DC: National Association for the Education of Young Children.

Bredekamp, S., & Rosegrant, T. (ed.). (1992). *Reaching potentials: Appropriate curriculum and assessment for young children.* Vol. I. Washington, DC: National Association for the Education of Young Children.

Derman-Sparks, L., & A.B.C. Task Force. (1989). *Anti-bias curriculum. Tools for empowering young children.* Washington, DC: National Association for the Education of Young Children.

DeVries, R., & Kohlberg, L. (1987). *Constructivist early education: Overview and comparison with other programs.* Washington, DC: National Association for the Education of Young Children.

Doll, R. (1992). *Curriculum improvement: Decision making and process* (8th ed.). Boston, MA: Allyn & Bacon.

Gay, G. (1992). Effective teaching practices for multicultural classrooms. In C. Díaz (ed.). *Multicultural education for the 21st century.* Washington, DC: National Education Association.

Glickman, C. D. (1990). *Supervision of instruction* (2nd ed). Boston, MA: Allyn & Bacon.

Henderson, J. G., & Hawthorne, R. D. (1995). *Transformative curriculum leadership.* New York: Merrill.

Jones, J., & Nimmo, J. (1994). *The emerging curriculum.* Washington, DC: National Association for the Education of Young Children.

Kendall, F. (1983). *Diversity in the classroom. A multicultural approach to the education of young children.* New York: Teachers College Press.

National Association for the Education of Young Children and the National Association of Early Childhood Specialists in State Departments of Education. (1991). Guidelines for appropriate curriculum content and assessment in programs serving children ages 3 through 8. *Young Children,* 43, 3 (pp. 42–47).

National Council for the Social Studies Task Force on Ethnic Studies. (1992). Curriculum guidelines

for multicultural education. *Social Education* 56, 5 (pp. 274–294).

Ornstein, A. C., & Hunkins, F. (1993). *Curriculum. Foundations, principles, and theory* (2nd ed.). Boston, MA: Allyn & Bacon.

Peck, N., & Shores, E. (1994). *Checklist for diversity in early childhood education and care.* Little Rock, AR: Southern Early Childhood Association.

Roopnarine, J. L., & Johnson, J. E. (1993). *Approaches to childhood education* (2nd ed.). New York: Merrill.

Sleeter, C., & Grant, C. (1994). *Making choices for multicultural education. Approaches to race, class, and gender* (2nd ed.). New York: Merrill.

Watkins, K., & Durant Jr., L. (1992). *Complete early childhood behavior management guide.* West Nyack, NY: The Center for Applied Research in Education.

York, S. (1991). *Developing roots and wings. A trainer's guide to affirming culture in early childhood programs.* St. Paul, MN: Redleaf Press.

"An environment that is rich in possibilities for exploring gender, race/ethnicity, and different-ableness sets the scene for practicing anti-bias [and multicultural] curriculum."

Louise Derman-Sparks (1989)

CHAPTER 9

Activities and Resources for Multicultural Teaching: A World of Possibilities!

In this chapter we will:

- discuss the characteristics of a child-appropriate environment
- establish guidelines to select developmentally appropriate multicultural materials
- give examples of appropriate activities for multicultural teaching

Key concepts:

- instructional materials
- instructional experiences
- learning encounters
- antibias, multicultural resources

❖ Building a Classroom for Our Multicultural Society

We learned in the previous chapters that the classroom is a very important place of learning for young students. This is where the microcosm of reality is encountered in forms of new ideas, concepts, and social interactions the student experiences. The classroom environment is, therefore, a vital component of the multicultural education transformation process. In this chapter, we will discuss how to design appropriate activities, materials, and resources that will help the students learn about diversity. You will see how the ideas discussed throughout the book become classroom practices.

Remembering Classrooms

We know from many years we spent in schools as students that not all classrooms are alike. Some we remember by the hard seats, others by the funny windows. We remember the pictures on the walls that gave us our first glimpses of the far away world, and the phrase on top of the chalkboard that seemed to admonish us every day. Perhaps the maps and replicas of houses and ships in the social studies classroom come to mind when you try to remember one of your old classrooms. Rosales (1992), who came to the United States from another country, recalls her impressions of the first American classroom she encountered. "My eyes were fixed on the door. It was closed and it remained closed *all the time!* I couldn't help

IN ACTION . . . *Your Classroom Memories*

▐ What do you remember about the classrooms of the schools you attended?

▐ If you are currently teaching, what does your classroom say to those who enter?

but miss the classrooms in my island where the doors were always open, where I could always see the sky and hear the world outside. And, we had windows from which we could see the mountains and hear the noises of the airplanes ready to land. This room has those high windows that don't let you see anything. Here, well, it's different. One feels like being trapped inside the room." (n.p.)

The classroom environment is an important teaching vehicle at the early childhood level. It is not only a place where the teacher and the students meet, but a part of the teaching process because it is a communication medium. We need to look closely at the impressions and messages conveyed to the children through the classroom environment. What makes classrooms so powerful?

The Many Environments of a Classroom

The organized and informal activities that take place in the classroom consist of complex intellectual and social actions that are a microcosm of the real world. Individuals, young and old, who find themselves in classroom settings create ideas, make discoveries, exchange views, and rehearse ways to interact in a larger social context. Changes in visions, positions, and attitudes are

Figure 9.1 Classroom environments

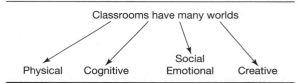

often among the outcomes derived from classroom activities.

Classroom activities and events can be classified into four major worlds or environments: the physical, the cognitive, the social-emotional, and the creative (Figure 9.1). The four environments are relevant to teaching because they comprise an appropriate educational setting.

The Physical Environment

The physical environment is considered the most overt of the four classroom worlds. It is defined by all the objects found within an identified space. The space itself is something over which the teacher usually has little or no control because it is assigned by someone else (Brewer 1992). Adequate classroom space is frequently a problem in

WORKING GLOSSARY

▐ **Classroom Environment**—the sum of all the parts that comprises a teaching/learning setting. It includes the space, the social and emotional atmosphere, the cognitive, and the creative opportunities.

the early childhood programs. According to the accreditation criteria from the National Association for the Education of Young Children (NAEYC), space should be allocated according to the number of children enrolled. A minimum of "35 square feet of usable playroom floor space indoors per child" is required as acceptable physical space (NAEYC 1991, p. 43). NAEYC standard indicates that the physical environment must be of high quality because it affects the behavior and development of people.

The physical environment also encompasses the equipment, the furniture, and the teaching materials located in the classroom. The adequate and developmentally based combination of all of these elements is what makes a good classroom for children.

Classrooms for children need to be attractive, colorful, and stimulating. Anne Taylor and George Vlastos (1983) indicate that the physical environment "does make a difference in, and directly contributes to, a child's behavior and learning" (p. 25). This has implications for multicultural teaching in terms of the development of appropriate behaviors and attitudes, a major goal in multiculturalism.

The efforts of many early childhood educators have been hindered by the disregard for the physical setting as a determining element for success of children. John Holt (cited by Ornstein & Hunkins 1993) once pointed out the value of the physical setting as being an effective motivator of students. He also stated that if the role of the learning setting was more seriously considered in the teaching-learning process, teachers would achieve more success. In Holt's opinion, "We would have to worry less about 'motivating' students, about finding ways to make good things happen, if we would just provide more spaces in which good things *could* happen [space induces children] to generate places and moods" (Ornstein & Hunkins 1993, p. 284).

The Cognitive Environment

A classroom is a place of continuous intellectual activity. Intellectual or cognitive activity is described as the process of forming and acquiring ideas and concepts. Cognition thrives in young children when they are given opportunities to experience and discover realities on their own. One of the major ways for children to grow and develop cognitively is through play. A good cognitive environment is one that facilitates experiences that challenge and allow the children to discover and construct their reality. They are expected to make errors during the process. For Piaget, this stage of error-making is as important as that of discovering the truth (DeVries & Kohlberg 1987). Teachers act as facilitators and companions for the children as they work around the challenges. Questions rather than answers abound, for the intention is to lead the children into self-discovery. Learning about diversity issues depends on cognitive processes where children are led to ponder experiences and examine consequences rather than be told the "accepted truths." An accepted truth for a child is what he/she has gathered by him/herself, what the child owns. An appropriate cognitive environment for children allows for this sense of ownership to develop.

The Social-Emotional Environment

The social-emotional environment can be perceived by the "feeling" one gets from being in the classroom. Social interactions in the classroom between the teacher and the students, as well as among the students themselves, can clearly convey a sense of welcome and respect, or of something quite the opposite like fear and rejection. Because the early childhood level deals and focuses on children between birth and age 8, attention to the social and emotional development is fundamental. Much of the children's time is dedicated to further development of this area. The relative limited social experience of the child points to the need to make social-emotional development a major focus of the teacher's efforts. The classroom, thus, literally becomes a social-emotional laboratory where behaviors and attitudes are experienced, modeled, and explored.

Behaviors are actions exhibited by individuals in response to certain situations or stimuli. Attitudes are the dispositions people have toward others and/or to a circumstance that guide their overt and covert behavior. The behaviors and attitudes of adults and of other children convey messages to a child that a child can use to con-struct his/her own responses and ideas. Class-rooms are the ideal milieu for the development of some of the positive attitudes and behaviors related to basic elements of multicultural education like tolerance, understanding, and acceptance of the cultural differences present in our society (Figure 9.2).

The Creative Environment

Creativity can be defined as the special ability to see things in unusual or unconventional ways (Cropley 1992). A classroom where nontraditional ideas and views are fostered among young children is an ideal setting for promoting creativity. An environment that is open and flexible serves as a vehicle for growth and development especially if the children are encouraged to find alternative ways to approach realities. For example, children are encouraged to find solutions to situations presenting unfair treatment to others. Creativity is an important resource in multicultural education and an essential element of the classrooms where teaching about diversity is taking place.

Making the Best Use of Teaching Environments

For years, educators have focused attention on the intellectual content taught in schools. Little attention, however, has been paid to the setting, or the physical space, where instruction takes place. Comments about procedures, goals, and objectives abound in curriculum materials, but directions how to organize the stage, the classroom, are much more difficult to locate. In teaching for diversity, the role of the physical context is as important as what is discussed and shared. A teacher of young children knows that imagination and ability to conceptualize are sparked when the children are surrounded by an environment that is visually and emotionally inviting. To

---

Figure 9.2 Words can reveal the emotional atmosphere of a classroom

What are the messages conveyed? Which ones are culturally and developmentally appropriate?

"You can do it. Try it again!"

OR

"You never seem to do anything right. Do it again."

"Perhaps you want to ask Jeannie if you can use her tempera."

OR

"That's Jeannie's. You can't use it."

"You did work a lot today. Maybe tomorrow we can work some more on that."

OR

"Why are you so slow?"

Comments can send strong messages to a child. Think about the impressions that these comments make:

1. ". . . he can't do it. He doesn't know English."
2. ". . . they can't understand the story. In their country they do not have things like that."
3. ". . . oh well, she is LD, you know."
4. "It doesn't look like food to me." (referring to an ethnic snack)
5. "I learned to read already. If you don't learn, that's up to you."
6. "Here we use utensils, not our hands!"

maximize the power of the classrooms, let us examine how they can be made into powerful instruments of education about diversity.

❖ A Classroom for Teaching About Diversity

The multicultural classroom is a place where the teacher attempts to guide the young students through the process of learning to live with diversity. This process of social transformation requires a special setting conducive to the children's dreaming and fantasizing, and for skill building and socialization. Such classrooms already exist in many schools across the United States. But, many more need to be transformed into the learning settings that children deserve and need. Difficult to accomplish? Yes, but not impossible. Let us find out what we need to do to make our classrooms become the exciting environments where learning about diversity can take place.

In Search of the Multicultural Classroom Setting

You remember how Barbara, the kindergarten teacher we have been following, started making changes in her teaching. Now, as she plans to begin the selection of the classroom activities, she realizes that she first has to consider her setting. This is what Barbara wrote in her journal:

> "Nothing will ever succeed if I don't start making changes in the classroom. I realize that what I currently have in the work and play areas sends contradictory messages to the children. I want everything to be consistent with what I am trying to do. My next move: find out how I can make the classroom more culturally responsive."

Barbara has learned that young children absorb the information transmitted by the classroom environment both directly and indirectly. These transmissions occur largely through the

senses, the major learning avenues for young children. She now recognizes that the setting plays an important role in the teaching-learning process. Barbara also realizes that children have specific predispositions toward learning what Howard Gardner calls "intelligences" (cited by Armstrong 1994, pp. 2–3). Gardner contends that multiple intelligences are the capacities and abilities of humans to master skills and concepts through one of the seven intelligences: language, logical-mathematical, spatial, bodily-kinesthetic, musical, interpersonal, and intrapersonal. This theory requires congruency between the classroom environment and children's learning styles. In multicultural teaching, congruency needs to be achieved among the children's learning styles, the environment, and the curriculum goals.

What Do We Find in the Classroom?

Before we begin thinking about what to change, let us consider the physical components of the classroom. Essentially, three elements make up the classroom: the space and the arrangements of objects, the interest areas, and the instructional resources. Awareness about these elements will help target our change efforts (Figure 9.3).

A Flexible Space Where Objects are Carefully Arranged

All classrooms consist of space designated for teachers and students of a particular age level. The organization of that space is what "personifies" early childhood education classrooms.

Equipment and furniture in young children's classrooms are child-size and multifunctional. This gives each classroom its own character. For example, tables and chairs are not just for children to sit on and work, but also to utilize for other purposes. A table turned on its side can become a puppet theater or it can serve as a work place for arts and crafts. Because of its flexible utilization, teach-

Figure 9.3 Multicultural ECE classroom arrangement

Space	Interest areas	Arrangement	Instructional Resources
– Flexible; well ventilated and lighted.	– Includes the following: housekeeping; art; dramatic play; blocks; literacy; language; discovery; manipulatives.	– Equipment is flexibly arranged and periodically modified.	– A variety of non-biased, nonsexist, multicultural materials exists.
– Meets DAP criteria for physical space.		– Children use arrangement freely.	– Resources reflect the characteristics of children, their families, and the community.
– Includes access to a DAP playground.	– Includes rotating areas. Area can be converted to accommodate new interests or topics.	– Display of objects and materials are child-oriented and reflect a learning target.	– Labeling in more than one language is observed.
	– Interest areas are periodically rotated or modified to replicate organization in other cultural groups (i.e., the dramatic area, the house-keeping area).	– Needs of exceptional children are reflected in the arrangement.	– Pictures, posters, and other visual aids reflect diversity.
			– Emphasis on what is actual practice or typically current is depicted in the resources.
			– A balance between what is current and what is traditional is found in the materials.

ers need to ensure that the arrangements correspond not only to the age level of the group, but also to their needs. For instance, children with exceptionalities may require specific furniture or particular arrangements in a classroom.

The Interest Areas

The space in early childhood classrooms is distributed into learning or interest areas (NAEYC 1991). Terms like learning area, center, or station refer to those spaces "where certain activities can take place and certain materials are stored" (Brewer 1992, p. 99). A major portion of what the child learns occurs in these learning centers .

Learning areas are used to offer a variety of instructional experiences. Each learning center is usually organized around specific developmental area or topic, intended to further the develop-

ment of young students. Having an adequate quantity of materials allocated to each learning center is very important. Quality, the type of material, and its presentation influence the children's responses and their learning. That is why special attention should be given to the messages that learning centers "give" to the child. What to include for diversity will be described later during this chapter.

Instructional Materials

Didactic or instructional materials are the common denominator of all classrooms. Instructional materials include a broad category of objects ranging from the sophisticated commercially produced resources, to the classroom posters, the objects hanging from the ceiling, and the costumes in the play chest.

All objects that comprise the classroom environment have the potential of influencing the children. Consider, for instance, the impact of a poster of community helpers where all the pictures depicting professionals like the physician, the lawyer, and the engineer are portrayed as European Americans, while the custodian and the sanitation employee are depicted as minorities. The message sent is obviously a subtle but an influential one for the children who are just beginning to form ideas about the world.

❖ Guidelines for a Multicultural Classroom Environment

There are several resources that can help the teacher answer the question: *"What characteristics of the classroom make it suitable for teaching about diversity?"* In Chapter 7, you learned about several tools used for multicultural assessment purposes. Each instrument gave a description of what the multicultural classroom should include. Let us summarize the ideal aspects as defined by a few well-known multicultural educators.

There are many sources of valuable ideas for creating the ideal classroom environment for teaching about diversity. We examined the ideas of several multicultural authors and of some professional organizations regarding their visions of the ideal classroom (Banks 1988; Derman-Sparks 1989; Hernandez 1989; Neugebauer 1992; Mc-Cracken 1993; Matsumoto-Grah 1992; Nieto 1992; York 1991; Peck & Shores 1994; Davidman & Davidman 1994). Although some of these authors were not talking specifically about the early childhood classroom, their insights provide important information (i.e., Banks 1988; Davidman & Davidman 1994; Hernandez 1989; Nieto 1992). Through our analysis we found that they emphasized the importance of seven specific areas.

We have chosen to examine these elements in a slightly different configuration.

▌ learning materials—including all manipulatives, books, toys, props, classroom decorations, and everything written

▌ art

▌ literature

▌ music and movement

▌ games and play activities

▌ attitudes and behaviors

▌ activities

We will focus our attention on the first five. The remaining two, attitudes and behaviors and ac-

---

IN ACTION . . . *Powerful Images*

Try to remember the images that made an impression on you as a child and still have an impact on you today. They could have been a part of your classroom, a store display window, a neighbor's house, or a television program.

▌ How did you react to a powerful image when you first noticed it?

▌ Was anyone with you at the time, and how did that person react?

▌ Does that image still have the same power for you today? Why?

▌ Does that image have the identical impact today? Explain.

IN ACTION . . . *What's Your Opinion?*

In regard to the classroom aspects that were suggested as important to consider, what is your opinion?

▌ Do you agree with these categories? Why?

▌ Would you add any others? Which ones?

tivities, will be discussed in another section of this chapter.

In order to better understand the multicultural classroom environment, there are several questions we need to ask ourselves about the five elements we will analyze. For example:

▌ What does each of these categories represent?

▌ How do they contribute to a successful multicultural education program?

▌ What should each one be like in a multicultural classroom?

▌ What does each one consist of?

These are the questions that we plan to answer as we "walk through" the early childhood classroom.

Learning Materials

Children use didactic materials to experience, ponder, produce, and process ideas. Instructional materials are necessary resources that help children acquire and shape knowledge. Forman and Kuschner (1983) state that materials are an important resource to provoke cognitive construction in the child. Because of this, teachers need to become aware of what happens when children use the entire classroom environment as a learning resource. A first question to ask ourselves about what materials to choose is: *Are these resources developmentally appropriate?* Guidelines to help teachers answer this question are presented in Snapshot 9.1, where we summarized Forman and Kuschner's recommendations for selection of the developmentally appropriate classroom materials. Their suggestions offer teachers ways to choose resources based on the constructivist, or the building block, view of children's cognitive development. These suggestions are pertinent because multicultural education for young children includes the principles of child development.

Good multicultural classroom materials need to be free of biases, stereotypes, and misrepresentations regarding diverse cultures. Teachers need to be especially careful when selecting multicultural materials because of the tendency to seek

WORKING GLOSSARY

▌ **Bias**—"any attitude, belief, or feeling that results in and helps to justify unfair treatment of an individual because of his or her identity" (Derman-Sparks 1989, p. 3).

▌ **Stereotype**—"an oversimplified generalization about a particular group, race, or sex, which usually carries derogatory implication" (Derman-Sparks 1989, p. 3).

Snapshot 9.1
Selecting Quality Developmental Instructional Materials

Teachers should exercise caution when choosing materials for young children. Here are some helpful tips for selecting items for the early childhood multicultural classroom.

1. Do not rely on the titles of commercial materials. Sometimes they are deceiving! Take time to carefully read the instructions and examine the materials.
2. Choose materials with various ranges of difficulty that present challenges. Avoid materials that only serve one purpose or one skill level. They will be interesting for children when seen for the first time, but they will not hold their interest for long.
3. Select materials that will make the child think. Try to stay away from resources that are too simple, or easy for a child to figure out.
4. Choose materials that can be transformed. It is preferable to have items that can be used in different ways.
5. Have materials that allow children freedom to work with them. For instance, avoid items that do little to encourage the child to try several possible answers.

Source: Adapted from Forman, G., & Kuschner, D. (1983). *The child's construction of knowledge. Piaget for teaching children.* Washington, DC: National Association for the Education of Young Children (pp. 189–191).

what is "beyond the usual" (Thompson 1993, p. 29). Jeanne Morris (1983) warns that teachers cannot rely on the content of a resource, but rather they need to verify the nature of didactic materials by asking: Do these materials present an accurate, bias-free and stereotype-free picture of diversity?

Karen Matsumoto-Grah (1992) establishes seven guidelines for selecting materials that include all the aspects of diversity. She recommends observing to determine if materials:

1. present the contributions of groups other than European Americans; reflect a cross-cultural perspective of what women have contributed.

2. portray people, including women, across socioeconomic classes and religions who are free of stereotypes (for instance, European Americans portrayed as upper-class and minorities as poor).
3. depict religious issues appropriately "when religion is integral to the context of the subject."
4. give socially balanced views of "famous people," that is, include the outstanding people from both the privileged and the working classes.
5. reflect the cultures and ethnicities of the classroom children and of their community.
6. exhibit and include the native languages present in the class (for example, if the class

has children who speak Spanish and French-Creole, materials in those languages should be available).

7. are at the developmental level of the children and offer challenges with opportunities to experience success (p. 105).

Both Kendall (1983) and Derman-Sparks (1989) call attention to the need for teachers to ensure that the classroom resources are totally bias-free. In their opinion, during the formative years it is of utmost importance to make the classroom a place where the child will experience and encounter human and social differences as something typical of all people. The emphasis should be placed first on targeting unbiased representations in materials. This means paying attention to what and how material is presented in a resource (see Figure 9.4).

Avoiding "Token Diversity"

Many times we find classrooms that exhibit what is called "token diversity" (Derman-Sparks 1989). Tokenism happens, for instance, when there is just one doll or an artifact of a given ethnic group. It is a way of minimizing the existence of certain cultures and groups like women and the elderly. Token representation reduces the importance and significance of the contributions and roles of a group (King, Chipman & Cruz-Janzen 1994). More importantly, a minimal inclusion of the elements of diversity will not transform your classroom into the culturally responsive setting.

Two main reasons for tokenism are the lack of awareness among teachers about the importance and the need to establish appropriate settings for diversity, and the lack of time to transform the classroom environment. In examining the first one, we find that many new and experienced teachers throughout this country still refuse to acknowledge the importance of teaching multiculturally. Some of them still argue that in the past, children learned fine without any special materials "about the others." Others still cling to the traditional phrase: "Children don't see colors. They only see children." Research does not support either one of these positions (King 1990). Teachers must allocate time for choosing good,

---

Figure 9.4 Ways to appropriately depict a cultural group

What is presented shows
— A variety of gender roles, racial and cultural backgrounds
— A variety of occupations
— A variety of ages
— A variety of abilities (includes special-needs individuals from different backgrounds)
— A variety in time (past and present) and place (local, national, international)

How it is presented portrays
— An assortment of social contexts
— Contrasting lifestyles and configurations
— A variety of languages (those of the children must be acknowledged first, and then others as chosen by the teacher)
— An assortment of representations or symbols to depict a given event or fact
— Different social and racial groups
— An accurate portrayal of racial characteristics (pictures do not use the Caucasian facial traits to depict different races/ethnic groups)

child-appropriate materials and for adapting the classroom environment because of the significance multiculturalism has on the future of our children.

The best way for teachers to avoid tokenism is to not display the single item, like a doll, from a specific culture and to save it until other items are acquired. Another solution, as observed in some classrooms, is to use pictures along with the dolls or real objects. Teachers in a preschool visited by one of the writers, for example, selected magazine and catalog pictures of ethnic dolls, pasted them on pieces of cardboard, and laminated them. The pictures were placed among the real dolls. The children used the paper dolls in much the same way as they used the real ones because of the magic of "pretend play."

When to Keep and When to Remove Materials
You may find that some of your multicultural materials do not meet the criteria for appropriate classroom resources. Decisions to remove a given item should be based only on the character of the stereotypic or misleading information that it contains. Even materials depicting stereotypes can serve as a teaching resource (Derman-Sparks 1989). Used only by the teacher, and not available to the class, they can be kept as part of the materials.

There are two things that can be done before making the determination to remove any inappropriate resources from the classroom. One, incorporate the cultural elements into the existing material; and two, consider the possibility of altering or transforming the materials. You need to start by checking to see how the resource could be altered or modified in any way possible (Derman-Sparks 1989). For example, a set of manipulatives depicting people can be altered by adding some figures with different ethnic characteristics. The dramatic area can be enhanced by adding masks representing different ethnicities. Artifacts com-

---

Snapshot 9.2
"I'm not that doll!"

A student visiting a mostly European American kindergarten classroom overheard a discussion among three girls. Two of the girls were European Americans and one was an African American. The girls were working in the dramatic area. One of the girls was holding a black doll. Everything had been going well until one of the girls called the black doll "Elissa," the name of the African American child. "That's not me. I told you. Give her another name!" said the child, clearly upset. Judging by Elissa's reaction, this was not the first time this happened. The two girls continued calling the doll by the same name. "Oh, yes, see, it has her face. It is Elissa," said the younger one, while her friend gave an affirmative nod. This time, Elissa snatched the doll away and threw it into the trash can. At that point the teacher intervened and took the opportunity to "talk about" what happened. While talking with the children, she realized that the African American doll was the only ethnic doll in the classroom. The teacher realized what negative affect "tokenism" can have on children.

IN ACTION . . . *Inexpensive Multicultural Resources*

Teachers frequently ask where to find good pictures as well as other ethnic materials. We have found that there are three good sources. Two of them provide excellent pictures and learning resources. They are the United Nations International Children's Emergency Fund (UNICEF) and the National Geographic Journal. A third source is any local ethnic store that actually carries not just exotic things, but the things people actually use. There are many others.

▮ Which additional sources can you recommend?

mon to specific cultures and a balance of gender objects can also be included. In the case of pictures and posters, you can prepare collages using pictures portraying other cultures. You can also paste pictures over those in posters or even in books (Derman-Sparks 1989). This will visually change and broaden the resources. For the manipulatives area, puzzles reflecting different elements of diversity can be easily made by teachers or volunteers. Thompson (1993) suggests preparing puzzles with laminated pictures. Pictures of the class can also be utilized and added as part of your resources.

In one instance, in a classroom with two-year-olds, teachers enhanced their resources by simply using the pictures of the children, of the children in other classrooms, and of the members of the staff. Taped to a table and to one of the walls, the photographs offered the children a display of racial diversity associated with familiar faces. In another case, first-grade teachers began changing their classrooms by adding labels and signs in languages other than English. With the help of other teachers, they also wrote the names of the class in two languages, Spanish and Arabic. The classroom soon became an interesting place to visit, where children began to look for their names and the names of their peers. This helped them to expand their awareness of the representations in other languages. It was also a thrill for

the students to understand they could establish their identities in other cultures by writing and recognizing their names.

Art as a Source for Awareness About Diversity

The art center is another important place in the classroom. Art serves the purpose of offering children the opportunities to explore the ways to use the materials to represent what they perceive through their senses. Art is a powerful source for learning that can also facilitate learning about diversity.

The colors of the paints are the first art objects that should be changed. Adding more browns, tans, and black induces the child to notice other color tones. Creative ways of developing these tones include using chocolate or coffee, which can be diluted to create various shades of brown. Having children work with such color tones is an appropriate way to facilitate understanding the role of melanin as the agent responsible for the different skin tones of people. A third-grade teacher devised the activity described in Snapshot 9.3 to clarify that no one is truly white.

Art can help young children dispel the most damaging of myths: that people are divided by the color of their skins (Allport 1958). Tempera paints, crayons, and markers can be selected to

Snapshot 9.3
Discovering the Colors of People

The first-grade class was working on a project, "Friends Across the Border," when the teacher discovered that most of the children thought the people in the countries neighboring the United States were "not white." This incited an argument among some fair-skin Hispanics who refused to be described as "not white," arguing that their skin was as light as that of others in the class. Everything reached a climax when several members of the class agreed that: "They can't be white because they speak Spanish." The teacher understood that the children were not only using race, but also language to define others. She decided to do something immediately to correct the misconceptions.

The teacher proceeded to divide the class into teams of five. Then, using white play dough as well as different shades of play dough that resembled the various colors of the skin, she asked the children to match the play dough to the colors of the skin of their group members.

The results were recorded on a graph. Upon completing the survey, the teacher entered the names of the colors the children chose during the discussion. The colors ranged from peachy, rose, dark peach, to tan, burnt brown, and "kind of creamy vanilla." All names were accepted and entered. Then, the groups began to share their findings. At the end, the column that read "white" was empty, while the rest of the entries appeared in all of the other categories. "What do we see in this graph?" "Where do we have most of the names? Where do we have the least names, or no names?" Without hesitation, the answers began to show the truth. Entries of colors with a variety of fancy names were entered in the graph. At the end, no entries were made for the category depicting "white." "No one is really white," said a child of very fair skin, who described himself as being "golden vanilla." "Why do they say that people are white or black? They lied to us," said one girl.

The teacher, by using self-discovery, helped the children to clarify the ways of looking at others, and ensured the continuous harmony in the class.

include more colors reflecting the range of skin tones. There are effective multicultural art materials such as the multicultural crayons that contain many varieties of skin shades. Another very useful item is the multicultural modeling clay. Play dough can also be shaded by teachers to produce various skin shades using powdered tempera and even cocoa powder (Thompson 1993). Whether teacher-made or commercially produced, multicultural art supplies should be available in the classroom at all times.

Activities and Resources for Multicultural Teaching: A World of Possibilities!

287

Easy to make multiracial play dough

You will need the following ingredients:
   4 cups corn starch
   1 cup salt
   1 1/2 cups water
   powdered tempera (brown, red) or cocoa
   2 1/2 cups water

Mix all the ingredients. The amount of tempera or cocoa to add will depend on the skin colors you want to make. Place on medium heat for 5 minutes, until it thickens. Remove from heat. Cover the pot with a wet paper towel. When cool, knead for about 5 minutes, working on a surface covered with waxed paper. When making objects, allow them to dry before painting.

Felt and construction paper in shades of brown and black are other important materials to include in the art center. Art paper should also be changed and varied (Thompson 1993). Traditionally, only white paper has been utilized. However, when children are drawing pictures of themselves, family, and friends, they should find paper in shades that more accurately reflect their reality. The shades of tan and natural are more appropriate than the plain white paper. An inexpensive source is the packing paper that comes in a natural shade. Also useful are the brown grocery bags. Manila folders and a roll of manila paper are additional sources of art materials.

Educator Aurelia Gómez (1992) states that crafts are one of the universal elements that define people across cultures. Crafts have the power to captivate the interest and the imagination through artistic expression. Crafts are an excellent source of learning about ourselves and about other people. Because arts and crafts represent how individuals have learned to make art with what is present in their environments, they become a source for valuing and appreciating people's resourcefulness and creativity.

Arts and crafts activities contribute to the holistic development of the child by providing opportunities for "actively solving problems, thinking critically, becoming visually literate, making aesthetic decisions, weighing and measuring, expressing themselves, using their imaginations, communicating with peers, and developing motor skills" (Gómez 1992, p. 7). Children need to have access to the materials used in handicrafts in order to explore and experiment. Part of the classroom art area should include selected art forms and handicrafts from the children's own cultural groups, as well as from other groups they will learn about. A sample of the materials listed below can enhance the child's perspective of other people. In parentheses, we have indicated the cultural groups that more frequently use these art materials. You may add some others.

Common art materials used by different cultures

▮ dry gourds, dry coconut shells, beans, seeds, leaves (Caribbeans, Africans, Native American groups)

▮ feathers, clay, colored beads, strings (Latin Americans, Native American groups)

▮ yarn, scraps of fabric, sequins, glitter, watercolors (Asians, Europeans, Latin Americans)

▮ straw, sticks, twigs, raffia (Latin Americans, Native American groups, Africans, Asians)

▮ sea shells, dry fish scales, coral rocks (Caribbeans, Asians)

A preschool teacher once shared another interesting source for materials described in Snapshot 9.4.

The colors white and black have been ascribed with the symbolism of good and evil in the Western society. Unfortunately, this concept has been extended into the racial context that children encounter very early in life. Classroom activities can be designed to disperse and correct these unfounded views. Teachers can set aside specific days when the only art items to be used are those of less frequently used colors, like blacks and

---

Snapshot 9.4
Teachers Are Always Resourceful!

The first-grade teacher ran out of art paper one day. She found some brown boxes that had been discarded and had an idea. She cut the boxes into pieces of various sizes, she placed them on the art table, and waited for the reactions. When children asked what they were, she said they were "special art canvases for pictures they could easily hang after they finished them." The result was a lot of "artistic canvases" the children displayed around the classroom. The experience was so successful that the teacher decided to make corrugated cardboard a permanent part of the art supplies.

---

browns. This is a way of helping children overcome their socially based fear of these colors. For instance, a preschool or kindergarten class can take a field trip around their neighborhood to see all the things that are the various shades of brown or black. We can already anticipate a long list of items! The realization that these colors are a part of our daily life is a start for children to see that there is nothing mysterious or malicious about them.

The Literacy Area

Literature is one of the most powerful sources of ideas, personal values, and wisdom. Donna Norton (1995) says that literature plays an important role in helping people learn and appreciate their very own cultural heritages. She further maintains its critical relevance in a multicultural society like ours.

Carefully selected literature can illustrate the contributions and values of the many cultures. It is especially critical to foster an appreciation of the heritage of the minorities in American society. A positive self-concept is not possible unless we respect others as well as ourselves; literature *can contribute considerably* [emphasis added] toward our understanding and thus our respect (1995, p. 4).

Some of the impressions, fantasies, and words many of us still cherish are from the stories, the rhymes, and the poems we heard or read when we were children. Our favorite books made us dream of unknown places and people. The benefits of literature go beyond the pleasure and enchantment they give us. Literature is a complementary developmental element for the young child. Joan Glazer (cited by Norton 1995) has listed four ways that literature promotes good emotional development. According to Glazer, a good selection of books in the classroom can (1) help children see

---

WORKING GLOSSARY

▮ **Multicultural Literature**—the collection of literature depicting ethnic groups and other elements of diversity.

that other people also share emotions and feelings just like they do; (2) facilitate the exploration of feelings and emotions from a variety of perspectives; (3) show different ways to deal with emotions and feelings; and (4) demonstrate that at times what we might feel might be in conflict with our own emotions (Norton 1995, p. 25).

Literature is one of those common denominators found across cultures. We can learn about the ideas, the beliefs, the values, and the struggles of daily life in any country around the world through literature. Because of its powerful character for cultural transmission, literature is an ideal resource for multicultural education. In the opinion of Tway (cited by Norton 1995), "In a country of multicultural heritage, children require books that reflect and illuminate that varied heritage" (p. 224).

The emphasis on whole-language teaching has opened the door to more quality literature for children. With it, a profusion of ethnic literature has also emerged because of the recognition given to the absence and misrepresentation of cultural groups. Today, most classrooms have a good supply of multicultural books. Discovering what kinds of books are in the classroom is important because of the power literature has for young children. Bonnie Neugebauer (1992) recommends assessing the classroom library corner to determine: (1) how the books portray the characters; (2) the type of situations they present; (3) the value, accuracy, and appropriateness of the illustrations; (4) the nature of the messages conveyed in the stories; (5) the credibility of the author and illustrator to tell the story and portray the characters; and (6) whether the stories depict the ethnic groups and the diversity of the class and community (Figures 9.5a and 9.5b).

Sources of good multicultural literature have significantly increased. Many book publishers

Figure 9.5a Multicultural literature evaluation criteria

Evaluation Criteria

Multicultural Literature

1. Are the characters portrayed as individuals instead of as representatives of a group?
2. Does the book transcend stereotypes?
3. Does the book portray physical diversity?
4. Will children be able to recognize the characters in the text and illustrations?
5. Is the culture accurately portrayed?
6. Are social issues and problems depicted frankly, accurately, and without oversimplification?
7. Do nonwhite characters solve their problems without intervention of whites?
8. Are nonwhite characters shown as equals of white characters?
9. Does the author avoid glamorizing or glorifying nonwhite characters?
10. Is the setting authentic?
11. Are the factual and historical details accurate?
12. Does the author accurately describe contemporary settings?
13. Does the book rectify historical distortions or omissions?
14. Does dialect have a legitimate purpose and does it ring true?
15. Does the author avoid offensive or degrading vocabulary?
16. Are the illustrations authentic and nonstereotypical?
17. Does the book reflect an awareness of the changing status of females?

Source: Norton 1995.

have begun to include titles covering all aspects of diversity. For example, a series of *Big multicultural tales* has recently been published by Scholastic Books, Inc. The series includes stories from Russia (*Little Masha and Misha the bear*), Haiti (*Horse and toad*), Kenya (*The crocodile and the ostrich*), and a story about the Pueblo Indians (*Coyote and the butterflies*), among others. Several book publishers and distributors like Savanna Books, Just Us Books, Children's Book Press, Children's Press, and Jacaranda also specialize in the distribution of ethnic literature. Most local libraries also include multicultural books in their children's sections.

Using Journals, Magazines, and Newspapers

Journals, newspapers, and magazines are considered a part of literature that can be used to en-

hance the children's learning process. They are excellent sources of pictures children can view while learning about their world and the worlds of others who inhabit our society. Periodicals and newspapers in different languages should be included in the classroom literature areas. They provide unique opportunities for the children to explore the linguistic symbols of other languages. Analyses of the various sections, such as the advertising section, found in the foreign papers can turn into interesting activities for the children. Teachers can obtain foreign papers and journals from local bookstores, at the airport newspaper stands, and, in some cases, from the local ethnic stores. Other sources are the donations made by the children's parents or by the staff members who buy ethnic publications. Teachers are advised to examine the donated literature materials

Activities and Resources for Multicultural Teaching: A World of Possibilities!

291

Figure 9.5b Using literature to develop multicultural awareness. Sample planning web.

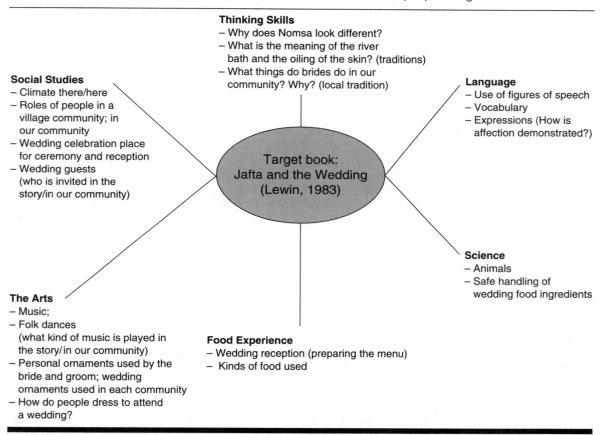

Thinking Skills
– Why does Nomsa look different?
– What is the meaning of the river
  bath and the oiling of the skin? (traditions)
– What things do brides do in our
  community? Why? (local tradition)

Social Studies
– Climate there/here
– Roles of people in a
  village community; in
  our community
– Wedding celebration place
  for ceremony and reception
– Wedding guests
  (who is invited in the
  story/in our community)

Language
– Use of figures of speech
– Vocabulary
– Expressions (How is
  affection demonstrated?)

Target book:
Jafta and the Wedding
(Lewin, 1983)

Science
– Animals
– Safe handling of
  wedding food ingredients

The Arts
– Music;
– Folk dances
  (what kind of music is played in
  the story/in our community)
– Personal ornaments used by the
  bride and groom; wedding
  ornaments used in each community
– How do people dress to attend
  a wedding?

Food Experience
– Wedding reception (preparing the menu)
– Kinds of food used

Source: Robles de Meléndez & Henry 1994.

carefully to verify the appropriateness and the quality of the content.

There are many journals that can be added to the book center. For example, *National Geographic* and *World* (both from the National Geographic Society); *Faces: The Magazine about People* (Cobblestone Publishing); and the *Smithsonian* (from the Smithsonian Institution) make good additions to the classroom literature corner. They can be found in most public and school libraries.

Newspapers are an inexpensive source of rich cultural materials. They offer glimpses into the realities of other individuals and groups. A newspaper also reports on current views, attitudes, conflicts, and values of different ethnicities. Newspapers can help the child to discern a variety of human characteristics through the racial and physical portrayals of people living in our communities.

We know a second-grade teacher who developed a project about people solely from newspapers. During an entire year, her students saved those pictures they thought best portrayed different people. Over 800 pictures pasted on tagboard became a permanent picture file that captivated the children's imagination throughout the year.

Pictures are another important element of any literature corner. Journals, newspapers, and magazines are good sources of provocative illustrations. We have found that postcards are an inexpensive source of good pictures, as well. Most people who travel are tempted to bring home cards that end up not being used. They can become an excellent resource in the classroom. Robles de Meléndez (1992) recommends professionals to use their "teacher's eye" in selecting postcards when traveling. The good "eye" alerts us to the images the children enjoy and savor in their imagination. Postcards can easily be used to make picture books that will expand the literacy resources. A map, or a world globe, should always be close to the literature area for easy consultation. The notion of "here and there" gives appropriate opportunities to compare and contrast for the purpose of finding out what makes us so alike!

Postcards have been successfully used by Bucher and Fravel, Jr. (1991) to teach about communities and local history. The postcards were organized into thematic areas (architecture and historical scenes; major industry scenes, agriculture, transportation; environment and tourist sites) that provided a wealth of perspectives for children. Teachers can also organize their postcards by major themes, and either file them by those topics or make picture books with them. A list of possible themes commonly found in postcards is given in Figure 9.6.

Ways to Enhance the Literature Area

An optimal literature area can be built by using some of the resources common to all schools: the stories of children and families. Grandparents and senior volunteers are invaluable sources of information and anecdotes of other people's ways. Teachers can have the elderly as guest "tellers" and record their stories to form an additional "story bank" for later enjoyment. This is also a way to save the wisdom of the past for future generations and to develop an appreciation for the elderly, a diversity group frequently overlooked.

Patricia Raymond, a kindergarten teacher from Ocala, Florida, did an oral history project with the elders in her community. Her goal was "to build a bridge of memories past and present by joining kindergarten students with 'grandparents'" (1992, p. 224-L). With the support of an Elizabeth Breathwaite Mini-Grant from the Association for Childhood Education International (ACEI), she began taping the stories of grandparents to enhance her classroom listening center.

Figure 9.6 Ways to organize pictures and postcards

Sample theme topics in postcards
- How we dress (clothing)
- Things to eat
- Flowers and trees
- Faces
- Places to visit
- People's hats
- Musical instruments
- Celebrations/festivals
- Houses and buildings
- People everywhere
- Colors and decorations
- Natural landscapes
- Fun places

Our classroom listening center became a time machine as students listened to older members of the community read familiar stories on tape and record reacted situations and instances from their lives. The readers readily shared personal glimpses of their childhood that delighted the children.... Even on tape the warm, soothing voices of older friends bring smiles to children's faces (Raymond 1992, 224-L to 224-P).

Persona Dolls, Another Useful Literacy Resource

All of us have enjoyed the stories told by puppets at one time in our lives largely because we believed they were real. That is precisely why the persona doll is another child-appropriate resource (Figure 9.7). A persona doll is a vehicle for telling stories about the lives of children and their families developed by Kay Taus (cited in Derman-Sparks 1989). According to Taus, persona dolls also bring into the classroom the lives of people who have "differences that do not exist within one classroom" (p. 16). Each doll acquires a "persona" from a character it represents in a story. A script accompanies the doll, which periodically visits the classroom and becomes a part of it. Intended to serve as a teacher resource, persona dolls should be kept in the teacher's area. However, they are available to children whenever they ask for them. Stories with persona dolls are created from four main sources.

1. issues emerging from the children's lives and experiences
2. current world and community events
3. relevant information that the children should learn
4. significant historical events (Derman-Sparks 1989, p. 18)

Music and Movement Experiences

Another of the universal traits that characterizes human cultures is music and its counterpart, movement. They are considered important because they provide avenues to become culturally literate (Lemlech 1994). Children seem to have a natural inclination toward anything involving rhythm and body movement. They are constantly exposed to a variety of experiences in the classroom such as listening to music, singing, performing, and movement that contribute to their holistic development. Singing and dancing is incorporated into many daily activities like story time, circle time, outdoor play, and so on. Because of the appeal these activities have for the child, they also serve as an avenue of learning about themselves and about others.

Folk songs and ethnic music need to be incorporated into the regular curriculum so as to initiate an appreciation for these art forms. They should not be limited to whenever a given holiday approaches. Reserving ethnic music and dancing for specific dates only serves to reinforce

Figure 9.7 Sample persona doll story

USING PERSONA DOLLS

One of the ways to establish a diversity responsive classroom environment is by incorporating characters that reflect the cultural nature of your group and of the community. Teachers know that puppets, dolls, and masks are good developmental resources that spur the child's imagination. They also serve to stimulate the child to talk, revealing feelings and emotions otherwise known only to the inner self. When addressing issues of diversity, a persona doll (Derman-Sparks 1989) helps teachers to focus on a variety of situations suitable for discussion.

But, what is a *persona* doll? Basically, it is any resource used to personify a given character. What makes it different is the fact that in this case the doll is given a specific personality that will reflect any of the variables that define the concept of diversity (i.e., ethnicity, religion, social class, gender, handicappism, race). The object receives personal attributes that establish a very distinguishable identity; that is, it becomes a "person."

The goal behind each doll is to provide teachers with a resource they can use to help children face situations that are typical for people of diversity. Using the principles of storytelling, the doll is then used as the key character in teacher-made stories that are shared with the children. They can become permanent "members" of the classroom, helping children to learn how "they view" different circumstances as they arise. Placed in the housekeeping area or in the "guest visitor" corner, children can reflect and reenact their problems.

Designs of *persona* dolls will be as varied as classrooms are. The basic rule is to frame them according to the diversity parameters characteristic of the community and those of children. In this way they become a device to help teachers address issues before or as they arise. Also, they will serve to expose children to aspects of diversity that are not part of their environment. For example, in a school with a predominantly upper-middle class student population, a teacher might use the *persona* dolls to expose children to issues like homelessness. Another use would be to have children share specific problems faced by handicapped persons. Issues of race and ethnicity are equally feasible to be displayed through the "personas."

If you are planning to use the dolls, here are three key suggestions to remember.

1. Have a clear purpose for each "personality" that will enter into your classroom. Ask yourself: "*Why is _____ in our classroom? What will the children derive, learn through _____?*"
2. Create a believable story about the character. Dolls must present daily life situations faced by people of those same characteristics. Remember, children are to construct ideas through their stories, thus, stories must be faithful to the diversity circumstance that is being personified. Avoid unreal, hard to believe personalities. Select situations you are familiar with, that will also be at the child's level. Ask yourself: "*Is the character an example of a real person? What makes the character authentic?*"

Activities and Resources for Multicultural Teaching: A World of Possibilities!

295

Figure 9.7 continued

3. Use appropriate artifacts or materials to design and prepare the persona dolls. Avoid objects that would misrepresent the character. Remember, you are dealing with very sensitive issues! Ask yourself: *"Is the characteristic an accurate portrayal? Is it realistic?"*

STORIES TO ENHANCE THE CHILD'S PERCEPTION OF SOCIAL DIFFERENCES

Topic:
  Learning about the contribution and role of farm workers in our society.
Goal:
  To enhance the social value of migrant workers.
  To learn about family life in a migrant worker community.
Concepts:
  —Work as a valuable activity
  —Interdependence
  —Migrant/farm worker
  —Pride in one's social world
Focus on Diversity:
  Social class; ethnicity
Materials:
  —Map of Florida; world map
  —Persona dolls
  —Pictures of flowers, live flowers and ferns

Procedure:

Using a persona doll, the teacher will introduce "Guillermo," a child whose parents are migrant farm workers.

Guillermo came to Crescent City, Florida, two months ago. His father works in a fern farm. He likes this town because it is less warm than Homestead where they lived before. Guillermo also enjoys the new apartment where he lives with his family. Now, after losing everything they owned during the "huracán Andrés," he finally has new clothes and, in particular, a new pair of tennis shoes that shine at night!"

His father works all day long. With his little sister, he goes to school while his mother stays at home taking care of Lalito, his baby brother. In the afternoon, when he comes back home, he likes the "pupusas" that his mom prepares.

Today he feels very proud. He just learned that the ferns that his father helps to grow are highly valued in countries far away from Florida. Yesterday, when he went to the packing house, he saw how they prepared the ferns for their long trips. He saw the farm owner and a man from an airline making all the shipping arrangements. With a lot of care, every fern was carefully wrapped and placed in special boxes.

Figure 9.7 continued

Guillermo was going to ask where they were being sent when he heard the "capataz," his father's boss, saying: "those ferns are going to Amsterdam." "There they are used to make all the finest bouquets," said the person from the airline. He talked about the huge flower market in Amsterdam where ferns are sold and distributed all over.

Guillermo felt proud to hear that those plants that his father grows are so important. This morning, during circle time, he told his kindergarten teacher about the ferns. And he also said that there is something else he wants to learn, where is Amsterdam?

To think and do . . .

1. If you were Guillermo's teacher, what would you do with his question?
2. What activities would you design to involve the rest of the children?
3. In what ways could you use this opportunity to enhance the child's self esteem?
4. Think about other circumstances or stories that define the daily lives of children with
   diverse cultural backgrounds. Select one and describe how you can address their
   situations to make the rest of the class aware of the things that they all have in common.

a sense of cultural remoteness of a particular group. Typical ethnic musical instruments need to be included in the music and listening center. When integrated into the regular plan of experiences, children learn to hear and sing the music of other countries as logical expressive representations of human beings.

Music is also known for being able to convey emotional feelings, which children seem to emulate easily (Haines & Gerber 1992). This affective characteristic of music offers an opportunity for learning about the similarity of feelings people express through music. An effective strategy is to organize your musical selections as well as dances according to the many emotions that originate from life events and which are shared by all people. Children can listen to the tone and rhythm used to describe the different feelings and emotions and form body movements to accompany their interpretations. Introducing some of the typical dances can also occur as part of their learning about things people share. For example, dances commonly performed during weddings or other festivities provide an understanding of the existing multiple views.

Possible themes to select and incorporate ethnic music into the curriculum

Life events

▌ happiness (marriage, births, successes, holidays)

▌ sadness (death, losses)

▌ solemnity (graduations, patriotic events, some cultural celebrations)

Daily life

▌ home and family

▌ nature

▌ motherhood/fatherhood

▌ children

▌ games

Which other ones can you name?

Music of different cultural groups is easily obtainable through most local public libraries. Many libraries even include typical musical instruments from the various cultural groups. Performers like Ella Jenkins, Raffi, and Hap Palmer have recorded multicultural music appropriate for young children. Most music stores now have an ethnic music section where teachers can also find adequate instrumental and vocal pieces. When making selections, remember to look first for the musical representations of those cultural groups present in your classroom, and then look for others.

Suggested ethnic musical instruments for the classroom

▌ Native American: drums, horns, conch shells

▌ Caribbean; African: guitars, maracas, *güiros* (gourds), percussion instruments

▌ Latin American: guitars, tambourines, wind instruments (for example, the Andean quena), xylophones (to represent the *marimba*), maracas

▌ Asian: string instruments, percussion instruments

Games and Play, the Medium of All Cultures

Jean Piaget defines play as a natural and inherent characteristic of individuals found across cultures. He established that children respond spontaneously to any game-like activity. This inclination of children to respond simultaneously to any

---

IN ACTION . . . *Stories for Persona Dolls*

▌ Using what Taus recommends as possible sources for persona doll stories, identify two topics for each of those four sources. State why they would be meaningful to your students.

▌ What additional categories could be added to Taus's list of topics?

game-like activity is what facilitates the acquisition of knowledge across cultures. Piaget's theory stresses the role of play as a common learning strategy and a central channel for knowledge formation about the world. Aside from their recreational aspects, play and games are found to keep their power throughout our lives.

Educator Frances Kendall (1983) believes play "enables children to grow out of their egocentric and ethnocentric picture of the world" (p. 18). Play and the games children learn offer an excellent foundation for developing and increasing the awareness about human diversity. Mary Renck Jalongo (1992) says that children, despite their differences, share the culture of childhood through play, another universal characteristic. She contends that the attributes of play make it a vital resource for teaching about diversity. Jalongo suggests that culture influences play in the following ways. Play is

1. voluntary and intrinsically motivated: It is initiated by things that present challenges and where children find an interest.
2. symbolic and meaningful: Children will assign meanings to their play items as they serve to bridge realities.
3. active and pleasurable: The child's social context will determine the kind and type of activities.

4. rule-governed: Rules established by children reflect the cultural values they know. Encountering different views is a way to learn about the ideas of others.
5. episodic: Experiences shape the roles and purposes of play (Jalongo 1992, pp. 54–55).

Observing what the child does when playing in the learning centers offers a window into the cultural ideas and values the child is acquiring. Some classroom areas are especially conducive to revealing the role culture plays in the child's interactions. For example, the block and dramatic centers serve as stages for children to practice and apply their social and cultural ideas. Attention to what takes place there helps the teachers follow the dynamic life of their students.

Games from the students' cultures should be the first ones to consider when teaching about diversity. Information about traditional game activities can be located in libraries and through the physical education specialists in the schools. A good way to begin is by inviting parents to share some of their favorite childhood games with the children. Learning games enjoyed by significant adults helps children to value their experiences. Fingerplay, rhymes, and songs usually accompany many of the ethnic and folk games, which makes them a source of integrated learning. *Arroz con leche: Popular songs and rhymes from Latin Amer-*

IN ACTION . . . *Play in the Classroom*

▌ Consider the types of play taking place in your classroom. Think about ways to enhance them for the purpose of multiculturalism.

▌ To encourage learning about others, what items would you add to the block area or to the dramatic area? Why?

ica by Lulu Delacre (1989), a collection of the best traditional children's folklore, is a good example of integrated learning.

❖ Preparing to Design Activities for the Classroom

The time to bring ideas into practice has come. This is your opportunity to use and apply all the information about multicultural education as well as all the ideas presented in the previous chapters. This is the most exciting part of your journey into multicultural education. Your desire to create the best learning environment for children, your professional knowledge, and your sense of commitment to the young will guide you as you design and create your program.

Ideas in Action

We have already defined the ideal multicultural classroom and taken inventory to find out what there is and what is needed to create the environment conducive to learning about diversity. Now it is time to think about appropriate activities that will transform ideas into action.

What Are Our Goals?

A primary goal of education for diversity is teaching children to be productive members of a culturally eclectic society. An appropriate classroom environment, where considerations for multiculturalism are followed, constitutes an ideal place for children to develop the appropriate social cognition. Social cognition will allow the child to perceive life from the perspectives of others. Perspective-taking, or the ability to see and understand one's position and the positions of others, is developed by growing up in a supportive environment (Berns 1994). Early childhood classrooms must become supportive environments in order to promote learning about diversity. It is important that the classroom activities lead children in discovering diversity as a normal part of life and, at the same time, adhere to the principles of cognitive development. In the next section, we will examine what cognitive and developmental characteristics teachers must consider as they prepare the classroom experiences. We will also examine the steps in lesson planning that will help us achieve instructional goals.

❖ Planning for Multiple Perspective Learning

No teaching is defined as developmentally appropriate if it is not providing the children with an *accurate* (meaning correct and legitimate views about our contemporary society) social knowledge and a *valid* (meaning applicable to our

---

IN ACTION . . . *Favorite Games*

▌ Do you remember your favorite games when you were a child?

▌ Can you name some of the songs and rhymes you used with the games?

▌ Which ones of them are still used by children today?

pluralistic social reality) assortment of interaction skills. Both are acquired and developed through the quality experiences the child encounters. But what are the attributes that characterize those activities or encounters? What is the framework that will help the professional to organize them?

Defining the Elements of Developmentally Appropriate Learning Encounters

The whole philosophy of developmentally appropriate practice (DAP) is based on the belief that the child follows a process of growth and development that defines what the child needs to learn in order to evolve. Education for diversity is solidly founded in this DAP principle. Its aim is not to expose children to the pluralistic society because "it is fun," but because they need it.

An Environment for Active Learning

Piaget's research on how children learn revealed that knowledge building is a process resulting from the dynamic interaction of the child with the environment. Piaget also found that the child's active learning depends on the stage of the child's cognitive development (DeVries & Kohlberg 1987). Both the concept of active learning and the existence of cognitive stages are relevant for designing classroom activities. He defined four cognitive stages (see Figure 9.8), spanning birth to adolescence.

Active learning in children occurs when the concepts about the world are formed by the child's direct experiences, or "hands on" learning. Because of the need for appropriate active learning, teachers need to carefully structure the

Figure 9.8 Piaget's stages of cognitive development

Sensorimotor Stage (Birth–2 years)*: Learning occurs mostly via the senses and via motor activity, which facilitates the child's interactions with the environment.

Preoperational (2–7 years): Learning happens through the senses and via language, which gives the child access to communicate interests and ideas and to inquire. Play is used as a means to "play out," or represent, actions from reality.

Concrete Operations (7–11 years): Learning occurs as a result of reasoning and direct experiences. Child still requires direct experiences (hands-on).

Formal Operations (11–15+): Learning is based on reasoning of abstract ideas and suppositions about reality.

*Ages do not indicate rigid age-periods but rather when the particular reasoning ability is most characteristically observed.

child's "learning encounters." The term refers to the child's experiences that occur in the environment *purposefully* set and organized by the teacher (Forman & Kuschner 1983). Learning encounters are emphasized in a program that is based on DAP. The classroom where the child is able "to encounter" denotes an active involvement and obvious participation of the environment with the child. This requires that the activities be of interest to children, so as to promote the acquisition of meaningful knowledge.

An organized environment is an integral part of multicultural education where the classroom is prepared to facilitate experiences based on diversity. Quality experiences should include specific traits.

WORKING GLOSSARY

▮ **Multiple Perspectives Learning**—process of discovering reality through more than one point of view.

Characteristics of learning experiences for children

▌ active involvement

▌ child participation

▌ age-appropriateness

▌ cognitive appropriateness

▌ developmentally relevant to the child

▌ holistic learning

A Framework for Planning

The possibilities for learning encounters in a multicultural classroom are endless. Translating many opportunities into action requires a child-appropriate framework for planning. This framework is referred to by Bredekamp and Rosegrant (1992) as "the cycle of learning and teaching." The cycle, consisting of four major levels, represents a practical and meaningful approach for implementing what Bredekamp and Rosegrant call a "mindful curriculum." This kind of curriculum "enables children to make sense of what they are learning and to connect their experiences in ways that lead to rich conceptual development" (Bredekamp & Rosegrant 1992, p. 29). A mindful curriculum should be meaningful, integrated, and based on the realities of the classroom. This is also the most appropriate curriculum for teaching about diversity issues.

The four levels of the cycle of learning are: awareness, exploration, inquiry, and utilization (Figure 9.9). Like building blocks, the experiences at each level are built upon the previous ones. This kind of planning and teaching strategy is considered to be constructivist in nature. Let us examine more closely how the circle of learning

and teaching can be used to set up your classroom scenario.

The learning process described in the cycle has two distinctive levels. The first level consists of the **awareness** and **exploration** phases. At this stage, the child is presented with what is new or different. The novelty or the "intrigue" of the new experience triggers the child's interest to learn more about it.

Awareness: The child becomes familiarized, apprised of the existence of an idea or an issue. Questions to guide the teacher's planning in this phase are

▌ How can the child become cognizant about this issue/idea?

▌ In what ways can the environment be set up to engage the child's interest?

Exploration: The child begins to search for the elements that define the issue or idea that captured his/her attention. In the process, the child will process information according to his/her own experiences. The child is actively using his/her cultural baggage to filter what is meaningful. Questions to guide the teacher's planning are

▌ How can I facilitate, support the students' investigation?

▌ What activities, materials can help the children in the process?

▌ What questions should I ask the students to verify their progress, understanding?

Level two is more advanced in nature and not frequently experienced by the children in the

WORKING GLOSSARY

▌ **Learning Encounter**—activity especially designed to lead the child into the active self-discovery of a given set of ideas/skills or knowledge (Forman & Kuschner 1983).

Figure 9.9 Cycle of learning and teaching

	WHAT CHILDREN DO	WHAT TEACHERS DO
Awareness	Experience	Create the environment
	Acquire an interest	Provide opportunities by introducing new objects, events, people
	Recognize broad parameters	Invite interest by posing problem or question
	Attend	Respond to child's interest or shared experience
	Perceive	Show interest, enthusiasm
Exploration	Observe	Facilitate
	Explore materials	Support and enhance exploration
	Collect information	Provide opportunities for active exploration
	Discover	Extend play
	Create	Describe child's activity
	Figure out components	Ask open-ended questions—"What else could you do?"
	Construct own understanding	Respect child's thinking and rule systems
	Apply own rules	Allow for constructive error
	Create personal meaning	
	Represent own meaning	
Inquiry	Examine	Help children refine understanding
	Investigate	Guide children, focus attention
	Propose explanations	Ask more focused questions—"What else works like this?"
	Focus	"What happens if . . . ?"
	Compare own thinking with that of others	Provide information when requested—"How do you spell . . . ?"
	Generalize	Help children make connections
	Relate to prior learning	
	Adjust to conventional rule systems	
Utilization	Use the learning in many ways; learning becomes functional	Create vehicles for application in real world
	Represent learning in various ways	Help children apply learning to new situations
	Apply learning to new situations	Provide meaningful situations in which to use learning
	Formulate new hypotheses and repeat cycle	

Source: Bredekamp & Rosegrant 1992.

classroom. In level two, the child, who already has acquired an individual understanding and is cognizant about the issues or concept, begins to reformulate the existing knowledge. During this reformulation, children discover the views of others, as well as the ways to apply the acquired knowledge. This is what happens when the child enters into the **inquiry** and **utilization** phases.

> **Inquiry:** Child begins to reexamine and compare the acquired knowledge. The child begins to consider his/her own beliefs while comparing them to the beliefs held by others. The outcome of this process is a refined view of the issue or concept where common points are ascertained. Questions to guide our planning are

- What are the additional experiences that will help the child see the idea from the point of view of others?

- What questions can I pose to the child that will help him/her focus on other aspects of the topic?

- What other areas, information, resources would he/she need to examine?

> **Utilization:** The child begins to bring things into a functional reality. Activities and opportunities are offered to help the child apply what has been learned. This validation of knowledge occurs as the child finds its usefulness in daily life. Questions that will help us plan this phase are

- What opportunities can I create in the classroom for the child to apply/demonstrate what was learned?

- What real-life situations can I use to illustrate the applicability of the knowledge learned?

A learning cycle implies a series of events that will lead to the reinitiation of the process. Once a concept has been learned by a child, it can be applied to other contexts leading the child to ex-

amine new ideas. In teaching about diversity, leading the child to examine the perspectives of others will create endless situations where the cycle of learning will be repeated over and over again. As that happens, you will see how the children's consciousness about diversity grows and becomes more concrete.

Using the Cycle of Learning: An Example

Remember Barbara? Well, she has been working very hard preparing to teach about diversity. She decided to try the cycle of learning using a topic she observed made the children uncomfortable. Let us see how she applied it in the example below.

Group: *Kindergarten*
Problem/issue: *Learning that my peers' families can be different from my own*

I. Awareness/What they seem to know
   1. Read and discuss the story *All kinds of families* (Simon 1976).
   2. Draw our families and display them on our "classroom mural."
   3. Have posters about families displayed around the classroom. Ask the children to bring pictures of their families and display them in the classroom.
   4. Include family sets in the block area.

II. Exploration/Investigating
   1. Make paper bag puppets of our families. Have the children present "families."
   2. Prepare family trees. Make a list of terms used to describe family relationships.
   3. Invite family members to the classroom to talk about their families.
   4. Have "persona dolls" talk about their families (single parent, foster).
   5. Include pictures of different families in the literacy area.
   6. Find and learn "lullabies" and "canciones de cuna" (baby music).

7. Have a grandparent or any other relative come to sing to the students.

8. Use play dough or paints to make the family of our best friend. Present it during circle time.

9. Make a graph about the sizes of families; members.

10. Prepare a chart about things families do. Search for pictures in old magazines. Do a Venn diagram to see the things in common/different about children's families.

11. Include baby and toddler items from other countries like India and Haiti in the housekeeping area. Observe reactions/ask questions.

12. Talk about the roles and tasks done by family members. Make stories about what we do at home. Role-play some of those stories. Share the story *Too many tamales* (Gary Soto); *The terrible thing that happened at our house* (Marge Blaine).

III. Inquiry/Self-investigation
1. Bring "family prop boxes." Have the children examine the contents. Ask them to infer what families they represent. Draw or make with play dough the family members they think each box represents. Guide children to describe their inferences. (Why do you think there are _____ in this family? How did you discover that?)

2. Using pasta, make families based on the characters in favorite stories. Discuss and compare them with the families of the children. Ask: "Why do you think we have families?"

3. Read stories about grandparents (i.e., *Song and dance man* by Karen Ackerman; *Grandfather's lovesong* by Reeve Lindbergh). Discuss other relatives in our families.

IV. Utilization/Applying what we know
1. Read and discuss *First pink light* (Eloise Greenfield). Have children talk about what keeps families strong even when they live apart or when a parent works until late at night. Discuss how children can help parents (What can I do at home?). Role-play some of the suggestions.

2. Display pictures of families from other countries (can be made into a book and placed in the literacy area). Add and read stories like *Jafta's father, Jafta's mother* (South African families).

3. Add/eliminate family figures to the manipulatives in the block and manipulatives areas.

4. Make game cards showing different family configurations as well as configurations of other kinds of groups. Ask the children to identify what cards depict a family configuration.

5. Have children create their own "persona doll" story. Have the "dolls" tell the class about their families.

6. Make a collective chart about "things in common and things that make families different." Refer to it whenever needed.

7. Have the children make a picture vocabulary depicting the different family configurations. Reinforce the terminology that defines them. Keep it available as a reference.

8. Take children on a field trip to observe how many families they see. Have them take a small note pad to jot down their findings.

Sources for Planning the Content and the Experiences

Developmentally appropriate content is characterized by being child-centered and integrated (Morrison 1995). The content in early childhood is derived from the children's interests and needs. It can also originate from what the teacher considers to be relevant for the children. The content identified by the teacher usually targets the needs and aims of families, the school, and the community in relationship to the children. Issues relevant to the community need to be targeted because children are members of and interact with the communities in which they live. Meaningful issues identified by the particular groups of which the children are members, and of the society at large, should be integrated into the instructional content, as well. A content based on the interests of the child, the needs of society, and the concerns of the teacher is considered child-centered and integrated (Figure 9.10).

An appropriate content presents topics as parts of a whole, not in isolation. When examining a theme, the child is led to view it holistically by providing opportunities to examine the theme from all angles and never in isolation. This integrated approach facilitates valid learning that occurs when the child knows how an idea relates and applies to a general context (Figure 9.11). This same rule applies to selecting topics for teaching about diversity.

There are two things that are important for teachers who are trying to define the content of the multicultural curriculum.

1. First, accurately observe the actions and the interactions of children in the learning areas.
2. Second, become a proactive teacher and bring the multicultural issues into the classroom. Throw away your "color-blindness" and seek ways to prevent the behaviors and beliefs that act against diversity and equity. Discard any misleading and inaccurate views about children and consider them individuals capable

---

Figure 9.10 Sources of DAP content in multicultural settings

DAP Content = Child interests + Needs +

Social goals + Teacher concerns

---

of facing situations when appropriately presented.

We also can define the content when we are alert to:

▐ comments made about other children in the class because of their race, language, or disability; about other children in the school; about adults and staff members; about story or TV characters; about stories read; pictures; visitors.

▐ use of pejorative words and terms to describe, allude to others; use of intentional namecalling.

▐ nonverbal expressions (puzzled faces, frowns, nuances) made in a response to a person, incidents, stories.

▐ open rejection or showing being upset about others.

▐ fear, distress when in front of other people (Derman-Sparks 1989; Thompson 1993; Robles de Meléndez 1994).

Creating Your Own Curriculum Using Thematic Teaching

Thematic teaching is a DAP strategy that facilitates integrated teaching. Introduced by Dewey and Kilpatrick (Katz & Chard 1989) in the early part of the twentieth century, it was recently popularized with the introduction of the whole-language philosophy. Thematic teaching is also an appropriate way to develop a classroom curriculum for diversity. Theme-teaching is defined as "a student-centered, coherent, and holistic approach to learning through the study of broad themes rather than compartmentalized subject areas" (Gamberg, Kwak, Hutchings, & Altheim 1988, p. 5). Developed around the topics that are of interest to children, theme studies present an opportunity to create a curriculum that addresses the reality of the classroom. Free of the rigidity of subject-based teaching, the flexible nature of theme studies allows teachers to incorporate

Figure 9.11 Web of integrated topics

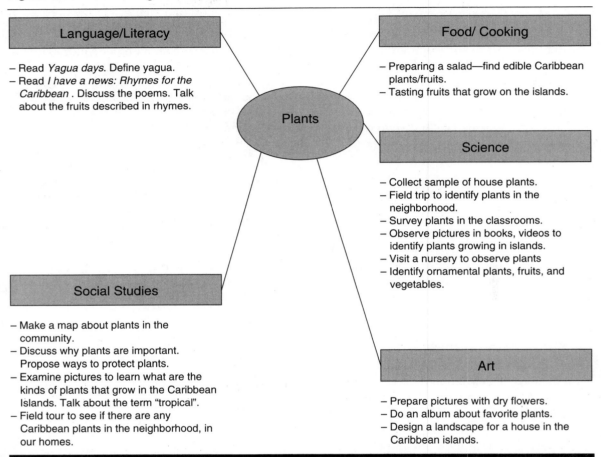

issues as they arise in the classroom (Gamberg et al. 1988). Several other characteristics define the appropriateness of theme-teaching.

1. Learning a topic is undertaken because of its value and pertinence. A theme is not casually included, but rather it is chosen for what it offers to children.
2. It emphasizes development and acquisition of ideas, not the accumulation of facts.

3. It places balanced attention on both the content and the process. It relies on systematic instruction to guide the child in the development of relevant skills.
4. Theme-teaching encourages social interaction. Children work together on topics of common interest.
5. It is an active process where the child takes the responsibility in finding sources, examining information, and arriving at conclusions

IN ACTION . . . *Formulating the Content*

❚ What additional details should teachers observe that may serve as a basis for the multicultural instructional content?

(Gamberg et al. 1988, pp. 11–13; Katz & Chard 1989).

Theme-based studies take the form of projects. Also called the project approach (originally called the project method by Dewey and Kilpatrick), theme-based studies are actual active investigations. The approach also offers an opportunity to have more than one topic "investigated" at a same time. Theme-teaching, or project work, in early childhood education for diversity is centered on four goals: knowledge, skills, dispositions, and feelings (Katz & Chard 1993). According to Katz and Chard, in an early childhood classroom each of these goals indicates different types of learning.

1. **Knowledge:** describes concepts, ideas, facts, information (for example, learning correct names to designate ethnic groups, significance of a given cultural celebration)
2. **Skills:** specific discrete units of behavior like social skills, thinking skills (for example, acquiring the ability to participate in a group, to make friends)
3. **Dispositions:** describes the patterns or habits of mind that characterize the individual's ways of responding to experiences (for example, curiosity, desire to learn about others, desire to share with others, unbiased responses)
4. **Feelings:** indicates the emotional or affective stances exhibited during and because of a given circumstance (for example, a positive attitude, tolerance, acceptance of others)

Areas of study in thematic teaching originate from the children's interests. However, topics can also be introduced by the teacher when they are based on the children's needs identified through the teacher's observations. Topics chosen by the teacher should guide the children to recognize the universal cultural traits shared with other groups first. Emphasizing what makes us alike reduces the possibilities of children distancing themselves even farther from the group. Consider, for example, a classroom where there are children of different Caribbean ethnicities who are the subject of namecalling by their classmates probably because their peers have limited exposure to members of those cultures. The teacher who observes such a confrontation is presented with an opportunity to introduce a very relevant and timely project. Possible topics that offer an initial awareness about Caribbean children could be "colors" and "decorations." Both topics depict universal concepts found in every culture that permit children to discover and establish the similarities among people. A description of the possible areas of investigation appears in Figure 9.12.

Selecting Topics for Teaching

According to some educators, it is advisable to observe the following rules when selecting topics for classroom exploration (Gamberg et al. 1988; Katz & Chard 1989):

❚ The topic is based on things of direct interest to the child. It leads to information or skills

Figure 9.12 Sample concept web

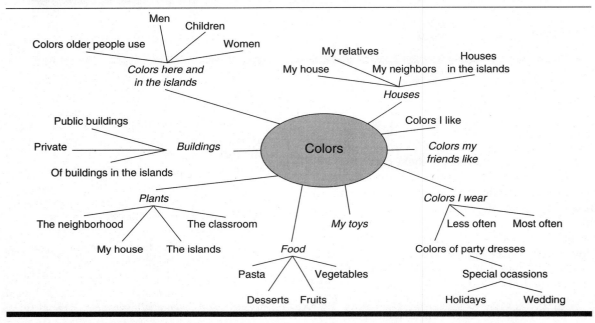

readily applicable to the child's reality. Teachers can generate the appropriate topics based on their knowledge of individuals and groups in their classrooms, and based on classroom observations.

∎ The chosen topics are feasible to investigate and allow for the child's involvement for a minimum of one week.

∎ Topics should be interdisciplinary in nature. Integration into several areas should be possible.

∎ Children work on topics for which there are sufficient resources at the school. Appropriate concrete and print materials are available for the investigation of the topic.

∎ The investigation of a topic will provide for the acquisition and enhancement of knowledge, feelings, and dispositions.

∎ Opportunities for parent, family, and community collaboration are possible through the investigation.

∎ Outcomes will have validity and usefulness in the child's current and future life.

Sample Frameworks for Theme Projects

The interest and awareness about diversity has led many educators to research and develop sample frameworks for theme study. Many of them are appropriate for teaching young children. We will limit our discussion to a few models we consider most appropriate.

Developed by Anderson, Nicklas, and Crawford (1994), the model presented in *Global Understandings: A Framework for Teaching and Learning* represents the framework recommended by the Association for Supervision and Curriculum Development (ASCD). It is a model that provides children with an understanding and an appreciation of the cultural interrelatedness characteristic of our world. Particularly applicable to the primary level and with a global focus, it emphasizes the value of the culturally diverse nature of our global society (Figure 9.13). The attention given in the ASCD model to diversity and multiculturalness provides valuable ways to approach and introduce the child to the virtual replica of the world's groups found in many cities around the nation. Several basic messages describe the main emphases developed throughout the lessons: (1) "You are a HUMAN BEING; (2) Your home is PLANET EARTH; (3) You are a CITIZEN of [*your*

nation-state], a multicultural society; (4) You live in an INTERRELATED WORLD" (pp. 5–6).

Intended to serve as "a guide for developing experiences for young people" (Anderson, Nicklas, & Crawford 1994, p. 4), the ASCD framework offers teachers a cross-curricular and interdisciplinary planning pattern. A valuable aspect of the model is the strong emphasis it gives to the development and acquisition of thinking and caring skills. For each message there is a set of corresponding thinking and caring outcomes. Sample integrated units are included showing how to convey the basic messages. Essential to the framework is the belief that students are not just to think about the diversity concepts, but that

Figure 9.13 ASCD model sample planning web

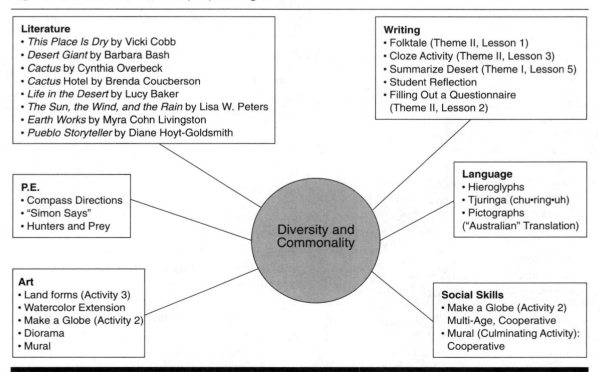

Source: Anderson, Nicklas & Crawford 1994 (p. 59).

"Students must act on the concepts" (p. 7). This proactive stance is the most positive attribute of the model. Another valuable set of ideas is found in the model proposed by Leslie Crawford (1993). Structured for the purpose of developing literacy, Crawford uses children's literature to introduce and examine multicultural themes. It is her belief that well selected multicultural literature provides a source (1) for helping the child understand the concept of cultural heritage, self, and others; (2) for contrasting cultural perspectives; and (3) for learning decision-making and social action skills. Crawford further contends that literature also fulfills the goals for multicultural education, both for the children of diverse cultural backgrounds and for those in the mainstream. Although, and as said before, the model targets literacy, it can be easily used for developing integrated project experiences. Crawford's model uses the format for teaching and learning proposed by Goodman and Burke (Crawford 1993), where lessons are structured around four basic actions: initiating (introduction), interacting (development), applying (utilization), and expanding (extensions). This format resembles the Bredekamp and Rosegrant (1992) model examined earlier. A specific "multicultural focus" guides the whole planning process and is included for each topic. A sample of Crawford's model is shown in Figure 9.14.

A group specific curriculum framework, developed around the concept of islanders, has also been proposed by Robles de Meléndez (1992; 1993). This model provides sample ways to create experiences aimed to help children develop an appreciation and an understanding about a particular cultural group (Appendix G). Rationale for the curriculum emerged from two facts: (1) the islanders are an underrepresented minority across the curriculum that infrequently defines them in common and real life settings; and (2) the islanders constitute a cultural entity de-

mographically significant in the United States. Using social studies as a key organizer, Robles de Meléndez suggests a series of themes, all leading to develop an understanding about this ethnic group. Focus is on similarities and it serves as a way of discovering and establishing the aspects that make identity of the islanders so unique. The model for the curriculum is founded on a developmental framework in which the tenets of education for diversity were incorporated (Figure 9.15).

Some Suggestions for Planning

We know that creating a totally new curriculum based on the ideas of diversity is a difficult task that will not be accomplished overnight. We also recognize that the progress for some of you may be slow if you are required to follow a state or a district curriculum. Whatever the reason for impeding change, we ask you to recognize that in order to implement an optimum program you must focus on what is most valuable for children. This belief is central for guiding you in the design, implementation, and modification of an effective and relevant program for your students. As you begin to develop your multicultural education program, there are some points to remember that will facilitate the transition from what you do now to teaching from multiple perspectives. These points are equally helpful in following any prescribed curriculum.

Points to consider when planning for multicultural teaching

▪ Begin by reviewing your present content to determine what was successful and what felt comfortable.

▪ Go through your lesson plan book and identify the topics developed in class.

▪ Find in your curriculum *where* you could add or expand the children's views by including

Figure 9.14 Crawford's model

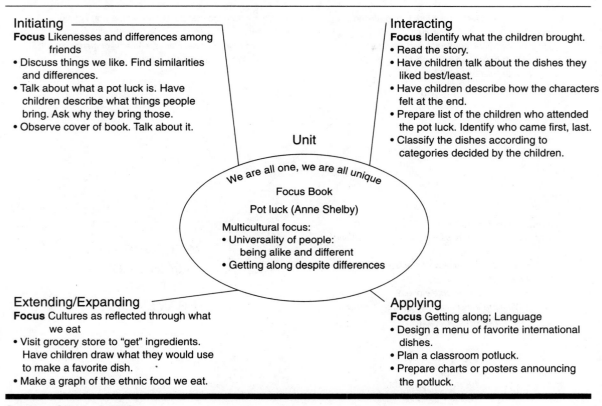

Initiating
Focus Likenesses and differences among friends
- Discuss things we like. Find similarities and differences.
- Talk about what a pot luck is. Have children describe what things people bring. Ask why they bring those.
- Observe cover of book. Talk about it.

Interacting
Focus Identify what the children brought.
- Read the story.
- Have children talk about the dishes they liked best/least.
- Have children describe how the characters felt at the end.
- Prepare list of the children who attended the pot luck. Identify who came first, last.
- Classify the dishes according to categories decided by the children.

Unit

We are all one, we are all unique

Focus Book

Pot luck (Anne Shelby)

Multicultural focus:
- Universality of people: being alike and different
- Getting along despite differences

Extending/Expanding
Focus Cultures as reflected through what we eat
- Visit grocery store to "get" ingredients. Have children draw what they would use to make a favorite dish.
- Make a graph of the ethnic food we eat.

Applying
Focus Getting along; Language
- Design a menu of favorite international dishes.
- Plan a classroom potluck.
- Prepare charts or posters announcing the potluck.

Source: Crawford 1993.

Figure 9.15 Framework for the "Children of the islands curriculum"

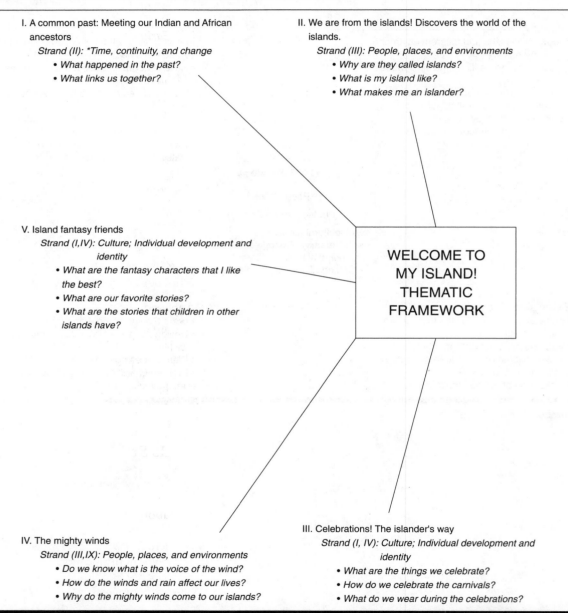

I. A common past: Meeting our Indian and African ancestors
  *Strand (II): *Time, continuity, and change*
    • *What happened in the past?*
    • *What links us together?*

II. We are from the islands! Discovers the world of the islands.
  Strand (III): People, places, and environments
    • *Why are they called islands?*
    • *What is my island like?*
    • *What makes me an islander?*

V. Island fantasy friends
  Strand (I,IV): Culture; Individual development and identity
    • *What are the fantasy characters that I like the best?*
    • *What are our favorite stories?*
    • *What are the stories that children in other islands have?*

WELCOME TO MY ISLAND! THEMATIC FRAMEWORK

IV. The mighty winds
  Strand (III,IX): People, places, and environments
    • *Do we know what is the voice of the wind?*
    • *How do the winds and rain affect our lives?*
    • *Why do the mighty winds come to our islands?*

III. Celebrations! The islander's way
  Strand (I, IV): Culture; Individual development and identity
    • *What are the things we celebrate?*
    • *How do we celebrate the carnivals?*
    • *What do we wear during the celebrations?*

*Indicates social studies curricular strand.

another perspective. Determine *what* other perspective you can add. Begin with only one additional perspective; then, as you gain confidence, add others.

▪ Adopt a flexible thematic teaching approach. It facilitates the integration of topics and views. It also helps to guide children into examining things they like or in which they have shown an interest.

▪ When including a second perspective, think about the ways in which it relates to the children's own cultural experiences. Remind yourself to always center your selections first on what is connected to the lives of your students.

▪ Include as many concrete experiences as possible. Children need things to do, things to touch and manipulate, if they are to construct new knowledge. In dealing with views and perceptions about others, present common daily-life situations where they can see the meaningfulness and the impact of the behavior (Figure 9.16).

▪ Make sure the experiences will offer accurate portrayals and not the stereotypes. Avoid what is exotic and include what defines the current realities (Derman-Sparks 1989). When presenting the folklore and traditional dresses or customs, clarify that they describe what happens during a holiday or a festivity.

▪ If uncertain about a detail from a particular group, postpone the experience until you have clarified it. Remember that children see you as an authority.

▪ Present perspectives in time frames that define the here/now first and then move into the then/now. Bring in ideas in terms of place (here/there) where there are elements children can relate to, such as common climate, topography, etc. (Figure 9.17).

Several reference sources can help teachers in selecting the curriculum content. It is advisable to have a copy of (as referred to by Barbara) "the green and white book," *Developmentally Appropriate Practices in Early Childhood Programs Serving Children from Birth Through Age 8* (Bredekamp 1987) that includes the guide to DAP teaching. *The Anti-bias Curriculum: Tools for Empowering Young Children* (Derman-Sparks 1989) is another relevant source to consult. *Words Can Hurt. Beginning a Program of Anti-bias Education* by Barbara Thompson (1993) and *The Global Child* by (Cech 1991) are two helpful sources describing a variety of activities teachers can use as they launch their multicultural programs. Teachers can also include among their references, books listing sources of multicultural literature as well as materials from journals like *Childhood Education, Teaching Tolerance, Children Our Concern, Dimensions,* and *Young Children.* When using activities from manuals or books, you are advised to adapt or modify them in accordance with the realities of *your* students.

As you get yourself ready to design and experience your curriculum, make sure that you keep good notes during your implementation. Prepare yourself to jot down the reactions and comments children make after and during the activities. This will be your source for future adaptations and improvements.

❖ The Stage Is Set!

Barbara looked around her classroom and realized she was almost ready to begin. She also began thinking about finding ways to work with the parents and families of her students. As an experienced teacher, she knows that without the parental involvement and collaboration, her program will be only partially successful. We will help Barbara achieve this goal in the next chapter.

Figure 9.16 Sharing common daily classroom situations

Yo comparto con mis amigos.

Objetivo: Describir las formas que puede compartir en la escuela.

Source: Camera Mundi *Este es mi mundo*, 1986.

Figure 9.17 Sample activity sheets promoting multiple perspectives with a here/there framework–comparing children's activities in Puerto Rico and India

Objetivo: Establecer semejanzas y diferencias entre las actividades que realizan los niños en Puerto Rico y en India.

❖ Things to Do . . .

1. Visit a local teacher materials store and examine its multicultural materials. Make a wish list of those you would like to have. Use the multicultural evaluation guidelines presented in this chapter to verify if they are developmentally appropriate. If you find any that are not DAP, describe what made them inappropriate.

2. Select two topics that you commonly teach in your classroom. Interview the media specialist or the librarian in your school and find ten resources for each topic that will help you develop two new perspectives about them. Use the form below.

   Topic: _____
   Perspectives: (Describe how each one offers an additional view and how they apply to the topic)
   Resources: _____

3. Select three learning centers found in classrooms for children of the age level of your preference. Assess them and determine what needs to be added or replaced. Make a plan of the things you would incorporate to make them suitable for learning about diversity.

4. Using the wheel of diversity, visit your local library and see what books are available for each area.

5. Select an area of diversity and prepare your own "persona doll" story. Share it with your colleagues.

6. Visit a local ethnic store and see which of its items you could include in your learning centers. List them and describe the learning areas where you would include them.

7. Examine the sample curriculum content that appears below. Determine **where** and **what** you would incorporate to transform it into a content for learning about diversity. Do the same with your own current curriculum.

Grade: 1st

Topics:

1. Who am I
2. Helping the family
3. The neighborhood
4. Community helpers
5. Going to the zoo

❖ Children's Literature Corner

Ackerman, K. (1988). *Song and dance man.* New York: Scholastic Books.

Bryan, A. (1991). *All night, all day: A child's first book of African-American Spirituals.* New York: Atheneum.

Cohen, M. (1986). *Will I have a friend?* New York: Macmillan.

Greenfield, E. (1988). *Under the Sunday Tree.* New York: Harper & Row.

Simon, N. (1976). *All kinds of families.* Morton Grove, IL: Albert Whitman & Company.

Stanek, M. (1990). *I speak English for my mother.* Chicago: Albert Whitman & Company.

Stein, S. (1979). *The adopted one.* New York: Walker.

Surat, M. M. (1983). *Angel child, dragon child.* New York: Scholastic Books.

Taylor, S. (1980). *Danny loves a holiday.* New York: E. P. Dutton.

Williams, V. (1982). *A chair for my mother.* New York: Scholastic Books.

❖ References

Allport, G. (1958). *The nature of prejudice.* Garden City, NJ: Doubleday.

Anderson, C. C., Nicklas, S. K., & Crawford, A. R. (1994). *Global understandings: A framework for teaching and learning.* Alexandria, VA: Association for Supervision and Curriculum Development.

Armstrong, T. (1994). *Multiple intelligences in the classroom.* Alexandria, VA: Association for Supervision and Curriculum Development.

Banks, J. (1988). Multicultural education (2nd ed.). Newton, MA: Allyn & Bacon.

Berns, R. M. (1994). *Topical child development.* Albany, NY: Delmar.

Berry, C. F., & Mindes, G. (1993). *Theme based curriculum goals activities and planning guides for 4's and 5's.* Glenview, IL: Goodyear Books.

Bredekamp, S. (ed.). (1987). *Developmentally appropriate practice in early childhood programs serving children from birth through age 8.* Washington, DC: National Association for the Education of Young Children.

Bredekamp, S., & Rosegrant, T. (eds.). (1992). *Reaching potentials: Appropriate curriculum and assessment for young children.* (vol. I). Washington, DC: National Association for the Education of Young Children.

Brewer, J. (1992). *Introduction to early childhood education. Preschool through the primary grades.* Boston, MA: Allyn & Bacon.

Bucher, K., & Fravel Jr., M. (1991). Local history comes alive with postcards. *Social Education 3, 3* (January–February) (pp. 18–20).

Camera Mundi. (1986). *Este es mi mundo.* Cagelas, PR: Camera Mundi.

Cech, M. (1991): *Globalchild. Multicultural resources for young children.* Menlo Park, CA: Addison-Wesley.

Cropley, A. (1992). *More ways than one. Fostering creativity.* Norwood, NJ: Ablex.

Crawford, L. (1993). *Language and literacy in multicultural classrooms.* Boston, MA: Allyn & Bacon.

Davidman, L., & Davidman, P. T. (1994). *Teaching with a multicultural perspective.* New York: Longman.

Delacre, L. (1989). *Arroz con leche: Popular songs and rhymes from Latin America.* New York: Scholastic Books.

DeVries, R., & Kohlberg, L. (1987). *Constructivist early education: Overview and comparison with other programs.* Washington, DC: National Association for the Education of Young Children.

Derman-Sparks, L., & A.B.C. Task Force (1989). *Antibias curriculum. Tools for empowering young children.* Washington, DC: National Association for the Education of Young Children.

Forman, G., & Kuschner, D. (1983). *The child's construction of knowledge. Piaget for teaching children.* Washington, DC: National Association for the Education of Young Children.

Gamberg, R., Kwak, W., Hutchings, M., & Altheim, J., with Edwards, G. (1988). *Learning and loving it. Theme studies in the classroom.* Portsmouth, NH: Heinemann.

Gómez, A. (1992). *Crafts of many cultures. Thirty authentic craft projects from around the world.* New York: Scholastic Books.

Haines, J. B., & Gerber, L. L. (1992). *Leading young children to music.* New York: Merrill/Macmillan.

Hernandez, H. (1989). *Multicultural education: A teacher's guide to content and process.* New York: Merrill.

Jalongo, M. R. (1992). Children's play: A resource for multicultural education. In E. Vold (ed.). *Multicultural education in early childhood education.* Washington, DC: National Association for the Education of Young Children.

Katz, L., & Chard, S. (1989). *Engaging children's minds. The project approach.* Norwood, NJ: Ablex.

Kendall, F. (1983). *Diversity in the classroom. A multicultural approach to the education of young children.* New York: Teachers College Press.

King, E. (1990). *Teaching ethnic and gender awareness.* Dubuque, IA: Kendall/Hunt.

King, E. W., Chipman, M., & Cruz-Janzen, M. (1994). *Educating young children in a diverse society.* Needham Heights, MA: Allyn & Bacon.

Kwolek Kobus, D. (1992). Multicultural/global education: An educational agenda for the rights of children, *Social education* 56 (pp. 224–227).

Lemlech, J. (1994). *Curriculum and instructional methods for the elementary and middle school* (3d ed.) New York: Macmillan.

Matsumoto-Grah, K. (1992). Checklist for Diversity. In D. Byrnes and G. Kiger (eds.). *Common bonds.* Wheaton, MD: Association for Childhood Education International.

McCracken, J. (1993). *Valuing diversity. The primary years.* Washington, DC: National Association for the Education of Young Children.

Morris, J. (1983). Classroom methods and materials. In O. Saracho & B. Spodek (eds.). *Understanding the multicultural experience in early childhood education.* Washington, DC: National Association for the Education of Young Children.

Morrison, G. S. (1995). *Early childhood education today.* (6th ed.). Englewood Cliffs, NY: Merrill.

National Association for the Education of Young Children. (1991). *Accreditation criteria for programs serving children from birth through age 8.* Washington, DC: NAEYC.

Neugebauer, B. (1992). *Alike and different. Exploring our humanity with children* (rev. ed.). Washington, DC: National Association for the Education of Young Children.

Nieto, S. (1992). *Affirming diversity: The sociopolitical context of multicultural education.* New York: Longman.

Norton, D. (1995). *Through the eyes of a child. An introduction to children's literature.* Englewood Cliffs, NJ: Merrill.

Ornstein, A. C., & Hunkins, F. (1993). *Curriculum Foundations, principles, and theory* (2nd ed.). Boston, MA: Allyn & Bacon.

Pecks, N., & Shores, E. (1994). Checklist for diversity in early childhood education and care. Little Rock, AR: Southern Early Childhood Association.

Raymond, P. (1992). 1991 Mini-grant winner. Oral history: A bridge to children's literature experience. *Childhood Education* 68, 4 (Summer) (pp. 224-L–224-P).

Robles de Meléndez, W. (1992). *Creating the multicultural environment.* Paper presented at the annual conference of the Florida Department of Education. Tampa, FL.

Robles de Meléndez, W. (1993). *Vocesillas de los niños de las islas: Un modelo multicultural para el nivel pre-k/2 (Voices of the children of the islands: A multicultural model for the k-2 level).* Paper presented at the 1993 Annual Conference of the National Association for the Education of Young Children. Anaheim, CA.

Robles de Meléndez, W., & Henry, A. (1994, Oct.). Using constructivism to develop literacy skills. Paper presented at Florida Reading Association Annual Conference. Orlando, FL.

Rosales, L. (1992). Listen to the heart. Unpublished manuscript.

Taylor, A., & Vlastos, G. (1983). *School zones. Learning environments for children.* New York: Van Nostrand Reinhold.

Thompson, B. J. (1993). *Words can hurt: Beginning a program of anti-bias education.* Menlo Park, CA: Addison-Wesley.

Watkins, K., & Durant Jr., L. (1992). *Complete early childhood behavior management guide.* West Nyack, New York: The Center for Applied Research in Education.

York, S. (1991). *Roots and wings. Affirming diversity in early childhood programs.* St. Paul, MN: Redleaf Press.

"All men [individuals] know their children mean more than life."

Euripides (426 B.C.)

A World of Resources: Involving Parents, Friends, and the Community

In this chapter we will:

- identify activities that involve the family and the community with the classroom
- describe the roles of families and the community in a multicultural program
- explain the importance of working with families and the community of early childhood students
- identify ways in which teachers can develop family support for their multicultural programs

Key concepts:

- families
- involvement
- collaborative efforts
- community resources

❖ Working Together: The Essence of a Child's Success

The old adage, "No man is an island," reminds us that all of us need and depend on each other. The same is true of schools and families. Sociologist James Coleman (1991) asserts that when parents work together with their children's teachers, there are positive emotional and intellectual gains. This partnership becomes even more important in a modern society, where family pat-terns and routines have drastically changed, forc-ing parents and children to depend more and more on the schools (Figure 10.1).

Not only have families changed as we saw in Chapter 3, but the neighborhood, the surrogate "family," has also become different. Today, many American neighborhoods are experiencing high population mobility, which lessens the possibility of establishing any stable, long-lasting relation-ships (Garbarino & Garbarino 1992). Serious eco-nomic pressures have caused the deterioration of

FIGURE 10.1 Living arrangements of children under 18 according to the 1989 statistics

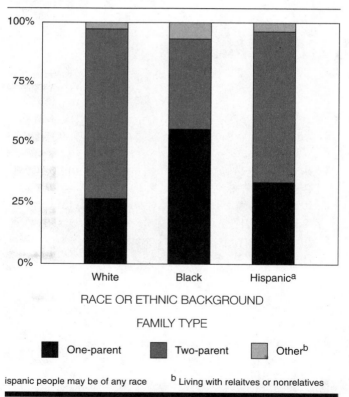

RACE OR ETHNIC BACKGROUND

FAMILY TYPE

■ One-parent   ■ Two-parent   ▩ Other[b]

ispanic people may be of any race   [b] Living with relaitves or nonrelatives

Source: National Commission on Children 1991 (p. 18).

Including parents and family members in early childhood multicultural programs ensures success. We believe that. Do you agree?

many neighborhoods, forcing their character to change (Children's Defense Fund 1992). These events have eroded the social relationships and changed the old practices in our neighborhoods. More impersonal and less caring, they are no longer the safe havens our children and families need. One of the results of this transformation has been that the schools have taken over more of the social responsibilities that parents and neighbors used to have.

The transformation of the American family and the neighborhood have resulted in the need for closer collaboration in the educational arena among the key players—schools, families, relatives, and the community. The purpose of this alliance is perceived as a way of solving problems of students in schools that also impact the society at large. Offering children a better and more responsive education has become a priority in America because it has been recognized that without an effective education system the future of our society will remain in jeopardy. Educators recognize that one of the keys to the successful schooling experience can be found in the close collaboration between teachers and families. This is also a premise for developmentally appropriate practices (DAP) that recommend creating classrooms where the child's needs are being met; where the child's individuality as a cultural entity is respected and strengthened; and where all efforts are made to enable the child to become a successful person. This kind of a DAP environment cannot be established without the joint efforts of teachers and families.

The need for collaboration among teachers and families of young children is most critical because the parents and the family are the child's first and most influential educators. Early childhood edu-

IN ACTION . . . *Results of a Parent Questionnaire*

Many people contend that families are no longer spending enough time together. Some see this as a problem and as a possible cause for the many problems faced by families. Trying to elicit how parents felt about this issue, the National Commission on Children conducted a survey that had the following results.

I/WE

. . . . . SPEND A RIGHT AMOUNT ------------ 39%

. . . . . NEED A LOT MORE -------------------- 30%

. . . . . NEED A LITTLE MORE ----------------- 29%

. . . . . WOULD LIKE LESS ---------------------- 2%

▌ If you had answered the questionnaire, what would have been your answer?

▌ Analyzing these results, in general, how do parents feel about the time spent with their families?

▌ What are the teaching implications found in these answers?

Source: National Commission on Children. (1991). *Beyond rhetoric. A new American agenda for children and families.* Washington, DC: The National Commission on Children.

cators need to develop a close involvement with families and parents in order to jointly build a common foundation that will brighten the children's future. Failure to bring parents closer to their children's school causes even the best of interventions to fail (Swick 1991).

Creating the atmosphere for learning both in the classroom and at home is a necessary component of effective education. Goals 2000, which define the national standards of education, speak to such learning environments for our children. Educator Ernest Boyer eloquently explained this idea in his interpretation of what "ready to learn," addressed in Goal 1, actually means.

> HOME IS THE FIRST CLASSROOM [capitalized in the original]. Parents are the first school and most essential teacher . . . [We] recommend that preschool PTAs be organized to give support to parents and build a bridge between home and school (Boyer 1991, p. 33).

Our classrooms can become the best kind of bridge between home and school. To build the bridge, educators need to reaffirm their commitment to children and in doing so do it for families as well. The social web that teachers and families can form together will nurture the child's proper development.

❖ Involving Everyone in the Family

Even the best classroom cannot foster the children's development in an appropriate manner without considering the nature and the structure of the families. The first task of early childhood educators is to discover the families of the children they teach. Learning about the families, who they are and what problems and issues they face, provides ways to initiate appropriate actions. This is especially important when dealing with families from diverse cultural backgrounds.

A Family Is. . . .

Nothing has become more widely discussed and debated in the social sciences than the concept of the family. Actually, social researchers are still trying to find an agreeable way to define a family.

As they come face to face with the reality of American families, early childhood teachers everywhere continue their search for a way to view and envision the variety of family patterns in their classrooms. What is a family of today? Do families still resemble those we knew when we were growing up? Is our notion about the happy family of decades ago still valid? After thinking about these questions, most of us realize that the family as a social unit has changed in recent years. The various configurations of today's families make it impossible to define a universal model of a family. This is why according to the United Nations, we no longer depict this institution in the singular, *family*, but in the plural, *families* (1993). The assertion made by the United Nations as it celebrated the International Year of the Family (1994), reaffirms the need for the new paradigm to be reflected in

---

WORKING GLOSSARY

▌ **Family Involvement**—activities and programs planned for the purpose of establishing effective ways to encourage the participation of all the family members. The underlying purpose of the program is to improve the opportunities for the proper development of the child.

school programs. In response to the new structure of families, we need to consider all the members of the unit, as well as any other significant social configurations surrounding the child. Early childhood programs must make efforts to include in their activities all those individuals who directly, or indirectly, show concern and affection and interact in a responsive and responsible way with the child. This new view of family involvement, which is actually ecological, is what schools are beginning to develop. The expanded view, of who impacts and who is responsible for what occurs to the child, has made room for many more possible social combinations. But the question is, "What are the other tenets making family involvement different from what parental involvement was?"

Defining Family Involvement

A review of the literature shows that family involvement is characterized by the following beliefs and areas of service (Garbarino & Garbarino 1992; Berger 1995; Swick 1991; Children's Defense Fund 1992; Dowling & Osborne 1994):

▌ A holistic vision of those who are the sources of influence in the lives of children.

▌ Consideration of the entire family as the target client for services.

▌ An inclusivist approach that considers *all* individuals (including the extended family and those without blood relationship) in the family unit as important when deciding on an intervention strategy (Figure 10.2).

FIGURE 10.2 Families have a myriad of structures

Cross-Cultural Configuration of Families

NUCLEAR: The unit where parents and children live together. It is the more commonly found unit in countries where life expectancy is high. Includes such configurations as:
—Biological
—Social (cohabitation)
—One-parent
—Adoptive
—In vitro

EXTENDED: A combination of several family members who together form an extended family. It does not imply size. It can be, i.e., a grandparent and grandchild living together. Includes configurations such as:
—Three generations
—Kinship
—Tribal

REORGANIZED: A unit that happens through marriage, remarriage, or cohabitation of persons who had children by former partners. Some of the causes are
—Remarriage (step-parenthood)
—Community living due to migration, exile, economics
—Same gender

Source: United Nations 1994.

▌ A systems perspective to deal with the reality of the child and where the school looks into all the elements that may effect an influence.

▌ A realization that any attempts to plan and establish services without the whole family would prove unsuccessful.

Diversity, the Defining Character of Families in Our Country

Today's families reflect the ethnographic and demographic diversity of our country. These social trends are also found in the early childhood classrooms. For example, it is probable that the families of children in your classroom belong not only to some of the ethnicities and possess the cultural factors we discussed earlier, but also reflect some of the new family configurations.

The different family structures depicted in Figure 10.2 are the best example of the assortment of combinations found today. It is important for the classroom teacher to realize and accept the existence of this diversity. In addition to this, educators and other professionals should care about the ability of these familial and quasi-familial configurations to be the best niche for nurturing the development of the child.

Acceptance of the diversity of family models in your classroom is essential for the success of your multicultural program. Learning to live with diversity begins by accepting that today's family is a multifaceted structure.

Collaboration: Also a Goal of Education for Diversity

Real education for diversity cannot exist without including and considering families as a fundamental element in the lives of children. The process of teaching and learning is enriched by bringing parents and entire families into the classroom as our partners. One of the main objectives of multicultural education is to have parents sharing with teachers the miracle of the children's learning. The proper development of any program about diversity must include the issues

---

FOCUS ON CLASSROOM PRACTICES

FAMILIES IN THE CLASSROOM

Learning about the family configurations in our classroom is an important step. The first days of school present a particularly opportune occasion to do so. For instance, as family members come to bring the children, you might want to try a more personal registration form for those very first days. Instead of just having a list where they will sign in the child, have a piece of butcher paper (size 14" × 17") or poster board and a basket with color markers. As they come in, ask family members to draw their families. Having your own family drawing conspicuously displayed will help to encourage family members to share theirs. Make sure each work is labeled with the child's name. The result will be a graphic depiction of the family configurations. Take time to carefully examine each one and make notes about the patterns in your classroom. Of course, display them in your classroom for children and family members to enjoy. They will draw many good discussions and will be a good starter for a thematic study you could title "This is how we are."

IN ACTION . . .   *What is Your Family Like?*

▪ Looking back at the types of family configurations in Figure 10.2, how many of those are found among your relatives? In your neighborhood? In your classroom?

and needs of the families. Combining the ideas and concerns of parents and families improves the quality of the service provided to the child, and increases the responsiveness of the program to the child's needs. Quality and responsiveness are vital elements that must be considered by teachers as they transform their teaching.

What Does Collaboration Mean?
Collaboration, termed by some as the "buzzword" of today, reflects the quest to remedy the inequalities and sparse existence of social programs and services (Kagan & Rivera 1991). In schools, collaboration calls for the concerted efforts of educators, families, and communities. A kind of joint work ambition, collaboration is based on "a vision of better society" (National Commission on Children 1991). A better society, where equity exists for all individuals regardless of their characteristics, is the principle on which education for diversity is founded.

FOCUS ON CLASSROOM PRACTICES

WELCOMING FAMILIES

Nothing makes a better start for positive relationships with families than making them feel important and welcome in the classrooms. Professionals know that showing our sincere respect and interest for them and their children will open many doors. Here are two simple tips to make families feel welcome in our classroom especially during the beginning of the year.

▪ During the first days of school, have a basket of simple treats right next to the sign-in sheet. A simple sign reading "Have a good and sweet day" could be placed next to the treats. Fruits (grapes and bananas are especially good), cookies, and hard candies are always favorite items. Even those family members who rush in and out will enjoy taking a sweet bite as they leave their children.

▪ Send welcome notes. A simple message presented in a creative and colorful manner is another way of reaffirming our desire to work together with the children's families. If some families speak languages other than English, write the message in both languages. Your school or the school district probably has resource people to help you with the translation. To make families remember your note, try rolling or attaching a lollipop to the note. They will certainly remember the detail!

We envision a nation of strong and stable families, where every child has an equal opportunity to reach his or her full potential, and where public policies and personal values give highest priority to healthy, whole children (National Commission on Children 1991, p. xxxv).

Educators Sharon Kagan and Ann Rivera define collaboration as "those efforts that unite and empower individuals and organizations to accomplish collectively what they could not accomplish individually" (1991, p. 52). Applying their definition to what multicultural educators advocate, we see that it implies the need for establishing collaborative efforts (Figure 10.3). Multicultural programs cannot exist without the support and constant sharing with the families of the children served. Attempts to do so would be fruitless. Pretending to separate our classrooms from the families can only produce fragmented, if not isolated, views of the children's realities. When our programs are linked with the chil-

dren's realities, the programs acquire a sense of valid connectedness. This sense is what "helps provide the rationale, motivation, and social action necessary for educational reform [multicultural education]" (McGee-Banks 1993, p. 334).

Consider the Community as Your Partner, Too
Collaboration also includes the community. Now more than ever, we find public agencies and the private sector willing to offer their support to schools. Consider them as partners and as a part of your team for multicultural education. Together, families and communities form what Goodlad describes as "the necessary coalition of contributing groups" (cited by McGee-Banks 1993, p. 334). Whether it is through services, enhancement of existing resources, or sharing their expertise, schools can find a myriad of resources right there in their communities (Mannan & Blackwell 1992).

FIGURE 10.3 Collaboration begins by finding what families can and want to do in our classroom

Can you help us in our classroom?

Our class wants to count you among its collaborators. Please tell us in what ways you would like to participate. Just enter check marks to indicate your preferences. Any kind of collaboration is always welcome!

_____ 1. I can serve as a room parent. I am available during: (please indicate weekdays and times)

_____ .

_____ 2. I can help prepare materials for the class.

_____ 3. I can help organize activities.

_____ 4. I can help collect materials for the students.

_____ 5. I can accompany a group during field trips.

_____ 6. I can share my knowledge about (please indicate) _____ .

_____ 7. I can serve as an interpreter of _____ (indicate language).

_____ 8. I can be a member of the PTA.

_____ 9. I cannot volunteer in the classroom; however, this is what I can do at home: (for example, cutting pictures, making crafts, evaluating materials, calling other parents, typing, and recording songs and music)_____ .

IN ACTION . . . *Community Support*

■ Have you considered the community agencies that could support your program? Make a list of possible groups to contact. Use the local phone directory and look for the agencies you think may be willing to help. Begin a list of "Sources for My Program."

❖ At Home: Where the Self Begins, Where We Become

To properly appraise the important role of families and the need for their involvement, we need to examine how relevant they are in a child's life. We also need to see how they become our best resource for multicultural education. To begin this task, let us read Barbara's journal comments about her class.

> Twenty-one five-year-olds! All of them have names that signify something to their families. I know I'll learn them quickly, but I wonder if I'll be able to discover the real child behind each long or short name. I wonder if I'll be able to "read" the stories they bring to the classroom. Their files tell me little about them, and none of it means much until I meet and work with their families.

Do you agree with Barbara? We do. Barbara is right. It is impossible to know what each child brings into our classroom from a list of unfamiliar names or a stack of official files. It is equally hard to anticipate the children's needs. The secret to who they really are rests with their families. Good multicultural early childhood educators know that and strive to work closely with the children's families. As they join hands with parents, they come to know their students. They also discover new directions for their curriculum.

All of us are products of our families and our home environments. In Chapter 3 you saw how your family and relatives influence your ways and behaviors. You examined their roles in trans-

mitting ideas and beliefs to the young. From our families, we even learned the gestures and nuances that characterize each of us.

When you try to "read" a child, you come to understand that the key to deciphering some of the behaviors and attitudes lies in the family. The more we know about the values, culture, and ways of the families, the better equipped we are to provide a setting that is responsive to the children's needs.

Adopting Positive Attitudes About Our Students' Families

The early childhood professional is characterized by an open and tolerant attitude. This attitude is what will facilitate achieving success in the endeavors that await. We believe that you are such an individual. You identified yourself as a person who believes in equity and in the rights of all when you decided to teach about diversity. You also affirmed yourself as a positive person, capable of making changes and, more so, a person who believes in children. This positive attitude should also extend to the families of your children. We ask you to set aside your own notions of *what families should be like*, or *how they should act*. By putting aside your personal biases, you will see your children's realities clearly, without blurring them with your value judgments.

Working with families of different ethnic and cultural backgrounds brings the early childhood teacher in contact with value systems not necessarily consistent with those held by the educator.

FOCUS ON CLASSROOM PRACTICES

SURNAMES, LIKE LOOKS, CAN BE DECEIVING

Have you ever attempted to use your students' surnames to identify their families' cultural backgrounds? Or, have you tried to use them to learn who is a non-English speaker? We hope your answer is "NO" to both questions because nothing could prove more deceiving than that. Because today we have a more open level of acceptance for social interaction, which has resulted in more frequent interethnic marriages, chances are a family surname might not necessarily reflect that a person belongs to a specific cultural or language group. Also, it is important to remember that many families might not necessarily be recent immigrants but possibly second and third generations or groups who historically came to inhabit a given region. In both cases, it is possible to find that the child and his/her family are proficient English language speakers. Unfortunately, there are occasions where children have been assigned to special groups because they are presumed to be non-English proficient. So the moral here is that because the child's name is Pérez; Takeshita, and Singh, never assume he/she cannot speak English. (Also, do not assume that they speak the languages of the ethnicities they belong to!) Always wait until you meet the child and the family. Decisions should always be made on concrete evidence and never on assumptions or stereotypes.

We base many of our opinions on our particular value systems. Our perceptions and reactions are many times the hardest roadblock to overcome.

Because we all rely on our own values when meeting and communicating with others, it is important to realize that a difference in ideas will affect our communication and interaction with the family members of our students. Sadly, unawareness about the interference of our own ideas often hinders even the best intended efforts. To say that the solution lies in teachers becoming more aware of their attitudes is overly simplistic (Turnbull & Turnbull 1990). Although evidence exists that attitudes are modified over time, Rogers says that it is more important to have "a willingness to look at and understand your own perceptions,

---

IN ACTION . . . *Family Influences*

- Have you ever thought about where you learned some of the gestures and phrases you use, or where you acquired the tastes you have? Try to identify one of them, and explain its origin.
- Observe the children at the housekeeping area. What adult-like behaviors do they show while role-playing at the center?

FOCUS ON CLASSROOM PRACTICES

LEARNING ABOUT THE FAMILIES IN OUR CLASSROOM

The more we know about the families in our classroom, the better prepared we will be to effectively work together. Because culture influences how we raise our families, learning about rearing patterns opens doors to our understanding of the family's and the child's behaviors. A favorite unit in most early childhood classrooms is learning about ourselves when we were babies. An important theme because it helps children to explore the concepts of time, change, and cause and effects, it is also a source of cultural data for teachers. There are three aspects in particular that we find yield interesting details about rearing practices: food, nursery rhymes and songs, and infant toys.

1. *Food:* A thematic unit entitled "What we used to eat as babies" could offer good opportunities to explore the variety and kinds of food considered appropriate for infants. Ask families to share what they used to serve the child during the first year of life. You may want to ask families to share the child's favorite food and the one he/she dislikes most.
2. *Nursery Rhymes/Songs:* A unit on "Our favorite baby songs and rhymes" could lead to many creative experiences. For example, the opportunity to compare how babies react to music and rhymes and how the class reacts now (concept of change) presents an excellent way to explore traditions and movement.
3. *Toys:* One of cultures' common denominators is toys. Exploring what the class enjoyed during infancy gives children an opportunity to discover how their preferences have changed. A unit titled "Toys we used to like" can also provide chances to explore materials used to build toys and could introduce children to view toys in a nonsexist way.

If you work in a community of high cultural diversity, do not be surprised to find that families have more in common than you expected. Remember that not all families are recent immigrants and that social status and the level of ethnic identity also influences their behaviors.

attitudes, and values, and to reflect on how they may be affecting your family-professional interactions" (cited by Turnbull & Turnbull 1990, p. 147).

A successful program requires people to believe in those they work with. An affirmation of our belief in those we work with establishes the emotional tone of the program. This was the experience of a parenting model developed in the Midwest (Fox, Anderson, Fox, & Rodríguez 1991). In the Stop Think Ask Respond (STAR) parenting model, the opening session was used to "establish[ed] a nonthreatening, realistic atmosphere . . . through statements of a positive philosophy of parenting [that we] developed at the center" (Fox et al. 1991, p. 56). The staff openly shared their positions about parents with statements such as: "Parenting is important and underrated," and "There is no one best way to parent." The parents responded positively, knowing they were not going to be admonished or chastised.

This example relates directly to our goals. Just like the STAR model, teachers of multicultural education need to reaffirm their positive, non-judgmental position about the family. This reaffirmation needs to be shared with the students' families through visible signs such as statements posted in the classroom and, more importantly, through modeling.

Developing a Philosophy About Families

What will be your philosophy about families? What affirmations will you share with them? Take time to outline your beliefs about the family. Have them posted in a place where parents and families can see them. We will share what Barbara wrote on the chart that she posted on the classroom door and from which she made flyers to send home.

"All families are important in this classroom."

"Families are the child's richest source of nurturance."

"Families want the best for their children."

"All families and family members can help in this classroom."

"Here, we learn about children through their families."

Planning to Learn More About the Families in Your Classroom

Coleman (1991) states that knowledge about the families and planning for their participation have increased in importance as a result of continuous changes experienced by American families. He also points to the need to use a variety of ways to know and plan for parent participation. A list of those possible avenues is offered in this section. However, because families differ, it is most important to adapt the strategy to the needs of the particular family. The activities in which parents are expected to participate need to be feasible and tailored to the parents' schedules and other important commitments. Coleman recommends that in order to avoid problems that might limit our efforts for family participation, we must first have a realistic view of what these barriers might be. His suggestion is to make a list of possible obstacles consisting mainly of those that arise from family obligations and work schedules.

For example, ask yourself if you know:

▌ how many parents or heads of households are both employed and work full-time?

▌ how many parents have a day time/night time work shift?

▌ how many families have small children or an elderly family member they care for?

▌ how many families lack any means of transportation (or depend on public transportation)?

Learning about families is an ongoing process. You do not get to know everything about a family

---

IN ACTION . . . *Examining Our Position About Families*

▌ What can you say about the families in your classroom?

▌ What do you think about Barbara's affirmation of the family?

▌ What do you like about her statements?

▌ Which one of Barbara's statements do you believe is the most important?

▌ What is your philosophy regarding parents?

from the answers on a questionnaire or from a parent conference. However, we need to have some basic information to guide and direct our planning. Learning who the family members are can be done formally or informally. Formal sources include the following:

1. information included in the child's file
2. formal interviews
3. parent questionnaires, surveys, checklists administered by the school or district
4. interviews with other professionals, i.e., guidance counselor, social worker
5. reports of formal home visits.

Data obtained through formal sources is important because it includes the necessary documentation that supports specific details and facts about the child and the family. Analysis of the data provides the initial insight into the children's families particularly in terms of the home culture. Learning interesting things about the home cultures of the children will help readdress our lessons and make them more relevant.

Additional data can be collected through informal means. Actually, many relevant details can only be gathered through more informal methods. Some of those methods teachers can use are

1. Meeting and talking to parents/family members as they bring their children to school.
2. Holding unscheduled parent-teacher interviews.
3. Establishing periodic telephone contacts.
4. Doing informal interviews and surveys.
5. Inviting parents/family members to share morning "coffee/tea."
6. Using a "pony-bag" (a plastic bag where teachers periodically send a note asking about a particular detail about the family, i.e., things they like to eat, do together, and others).
7. Using a classroom "family sharing tree" (interesting details that identify each family

and that are shared on a weekly/monthly basis in the classroom).

Using Surveys and Checklists
There are many instruments teachers themselves can develop to use in acquiring more information about the families of their students. They can create their own surveys and checklists structured to the unique needs of their families. When deciding to use a teacher-made tool, there are some rules to remember.

Points to remember when designing an instrument
1. *Purpose:* To create a good instrument, first identify its purpose and goal. Knowing what information you want to obtain defines the questions to be asked.
2. *Missing data:* A way to begin learning about the families is to review the children's files and see what relevant data are missing. What is not included, and what you consider important, should be incorporated into your instruments. Among the information to be considered could be details such as nicknames used at home; the meaning of children's names for the family; the correct pronunciation of the child's name; holidays that are more important for the family, and so on.
3. *Data relevant for curricular planning:* Information that is relevant to the curriculum also needs to be included in the instrument. For example, data that will help teachers know more about the cultural ways of the family can clarify what should be emphasized in the classroom. Remember, the more we know about families, the better prepared we will be to organize our teaching.
4. *Family needs and interests:* When teachers are aware of the family's needs, issues, and interests, actions can be taken to provide the support or assistance at the classroom level. The information concerning the diversity

Snapshot 10.1
Families, Schools, and Communities Making a Difference in the Lives of Children

Programs for children have dramatically grown in the last decade. Let's sample a few that have made a difference in the lives of children.

- **The Walbridge Caring Communities Program (St. Louis, MO):** Housed at The Walbridge Elementary School, it serves as a hub for a network of local agencies providing coordinated services to families. The program offers a variety of services to families, which include cultural awareness, after-school services, substance abuse treatment, a parenting program, and case management. The goal of the program is to build a community, to link families to available services, and to create a formal and informal support for families (National Association of State Boards of Education 1991, p. 39).

- **Family Literacy Program (Pompano Beach, FL):** Developed through a grant from the Toyota Foundation, the program services the ethnically diverse community attending Charles Drew Elementary School. The school population, mainly comprised of African Americans, Haitians, and Hispanics, services both the four-year-olds and their parents. Selected on a voluntary basis, parents attend school along with their children. The program offerings include English for Speakers of Other Languages (ESOL) classes, tutoring for those wanting to take the General Equivalency Diploma (GED), and parenting sessions.

- **The Redlands Christian Migrant Association (RCMA) Child Development Program (Florida):** Serving rural children in Florida, the RCMA is an organization composed of farm worker parents, produce growers, and concerned professionals and citizens. The RCMA was established in 1965 in the Redlands agricultural area in South Florida. Today they offer services throughout the state of Florida. Offering services to children from birth to age four, they believe that parents and families want and are capable of helping their children. Central to the existence of the program is the fact that almost the entire staff and all the program center directors are former farm workers. The continued success of the program is the best acknowledgment of what families and parents can do. Having an active voice in the program's decision-making process, farm workers and individuals from various cultural groups represent the majority of the membership of the State Board of Directors.

variables that characterize particular families is most important for establishing an effective classroom curriculum. This knowledge also establishes a foundation for a sound collaboration between the school and the family.

A teacher-made instrument is not only to be used for "writing in" answers. It can also be used as a guide during a parent interview. Instruments should not be too lengthy and they need to be written in clear and simple language and format. Some sample instruments are included in Figure 10.4.

Knowing enough about a specific culture is always a concern for teachers working with children whose families' cultures differ from the teachers' own. A good way to initiate positive interaction is by finding out more about the culture from the families. What one wants to know about a culture is difficult to decide.

Another very helpful tool is the set of questions developed by Saville-Troike (1978). Teachers can use it as a guide when trying to learn more about the culture of the family. Relevant in any setting, it is definitely useful when working in communities where the population is especially diverse. The questions provide a way to profile the cultural life of an individual. The insights offered through each question yield a portrait of what being a part of a given ethnic group actually means to the individual or family. Answers prove especially helpful because they provide the opportunity to depict the family in a nonstereotyped way. Questions are categorized by different areas that are commonly impacted by culture. Very comprehensive in nature, the questions cover points including the life cycle, roles, religion, communication, and food and can be utilized selectively to obtain information from the family whenever teachers consider that a particular aspect requires more clarification (Figure 10.5).

Since the nature of the questions leads to very culturally subjective responses, Saville-Troike

(1978) warns that there are no correct or incorrect answers. Teachers must remember that when talking about culture, the interpretation one gives to an incident or phenomenon is subject to the view held in one's own cultural milieu. Valuable as a data-gathering instrument, the responses should be used to deepen our knowledge about the families in our classroom. It is also a tool to further our understanding about the community we serve.

Saville-Troike (1978) suggests that educators use this set of questions as a way

- *to reflect on one's culture.* By answering some of the questions, teachers can clarify some of their own views about cultures. Through this introspection, teachers can appreciate and understand the similarities and differences found in the views held by their students and families.

- *to serve as a guide for observations.* Because of their comprehensiveness, questions can be used to guide teachers' observations in the classroom or in any other setting. For instance, questions regarding "communication" can help teachers identify the appropriate and acceptable patterns in a family's or child's culture.

Recording What We Know About Families: The Family Folder

So much information can be gathered about the families of your students! Throughout the school year you will learn many interesting details that are worth saving. Usually, teachers keep this information in the child's portfolio where it is often lost amid all the work samples and drawings. We recommend that teachers keep a separate file for family information. Like the children's portfolios, the family folder is open to families to incorporate samples of activities done or pictures and information about important family events. An

FIGURE 10.4 Survey of the family

SURVEY OF THE FAMILY—PART A

Sample Letter to the Family

Dear Parent/Family Members:

In this classroom we believe families are an important part of the child's life. We also believe that to create a good program for your child we need to know more about your family. For that reason we are asking you to share some information about your family by answering this questionnaire. Answering this questionnaire is optional; however, it will help us to better know your family and your child. As we learn more about the students and families, we will discover more ways to make your child succeed in school. Please know that all information will be kept confidential and that it will be used only for planning purposes. Thanks!

Sincerely,

(classroom teacher)

Sample *Questionnaire*

Dear family of _____ (child's name):

Please read each question carefully and write your answer in the space provided.

1. Who are the members of your family?
2. Does your family use any language other than English? Is the child encouraged to use that language?
3. Who is the family member we should contact in case of an emergency? Please give name and relationship to the child.
4. What is the family's favorite TV program?
5. Does the family have pets?
6. What are some of the activities that your family enjoys doing together?
7. What are the holidays that your family celebrates?
8. Are there any religious or cultural traditions your family considers very important?
9. What expectations does your family have of this school/classroom?
10. We would like to know in what ways we can collaborate with you. From the list below, please check all those areas that represent areas of **interest** or **concerns** for your family. If the point is of interest, write an *I;* if a concern, write a *C.*

_____Understanding my child

_____Learning more about my child's behavior

_____Planning activities at home for my child

_____Locating good materials for my child

_____Learning more about my child's development

_____Dealing with nutrition (appropriate feeding)

_____Obtaining after-school care services

_____Dealing with health problems in the family

_____Locating health services for the child

_____Learning more about what the community offers for my child (for example: parks, library, and others)

_____Obtaining information about housing, food stamps, county services

_____Other: (please comment)

FIGURE 10.4 continued

SURVEY OF THE FAMILY—PART B

Name of the child _____ Age _____ Gender: F _____ M _____

Directions to the teacher:
(This part is to be administered in the classroom. After a motivational experience, have the child draw his/her family. Provide crayons and/or markers.) Once the child has finished, ask the following questions:

1. Can you tell me what this drawing shows?
2. Can you tell me who are the people in your drawing?
3. Are you in this drawing? Show me where.
4. What is the family doing in this drawing?
5. Can you tell me what you like most about your family?

on-going project,it serves as another way to bring families into our classroom. Confidentiality of the information kept in the folder is essential. Early childhood teachers need to guarantee families that the data saved in the folders are to be used only to plan and design activities for both children and their families. Information can also be kept in a large envelope within the portfolio. Information that teachers might want to save include the following:

▌ data about the family (surveys, checklists)
▌ written communications from and between the family and teacher
▌ photographs of home, school, and classroom activities
▌ notes from telephone conferences
▌ family referrals
▌ samples of projects done by families
▌ participation in classroom activities.

In some ways, the family folder lays the ground for the development of the individual family service plan (IFSP), a strategy used in programs serving exceptional students and now gaining popularity in early education programs. The IFSP was initially introduced as a result of the statements established in Part H of the Education of the Handicapped Act Amendments (P.L. 99-457). In the opinion of Vincent (in Paciorek & Munro 1994), programs for the culturally diverse child are significantly improved when they assume a family-centered approach where the family is also included in the services offered.

Maintaining Confidentiality
"Ideals: I-2.I-To develop relationships of mutual trust with the families we serve."
Principles:P-2.9-We shall maintain confidentiality and shall respect the family's right to privacy, refraining from disclosure of confidential information and intrusion into family life."
NAEYC Code of Ethical Conduct (1989)

Developing and achieving a sense of trust among families and early educators is essential to a successful program. It is important to remember that families will trust us when they see that they are respected as individuals. They will also believe in teachers when they find that we are safeguarding the information we know about them and their children. Because early childhood teachers gather

FIGURE 10.5 Culture questionnaire

Selected sections from Saville-Troike's questions about culture

▌ Family
   a. Who is in the 'family'? Who among these (or others) lives in one house?
   b. What is the line of authority in the family?
   c. What are the rights and responsibilities of each family member? Do children have an obligation to work to help the family?
   d. What are the functions and obligations of the family to the larger social unit? To the school? To its individual members?
   e. How close together does the family appear to be? Is there a degree of solidarity among its members?

▌ The life cycle
   a. How do they refer to or define the different stages, periods, or transitions in life? (i.e., before X was born, after the divorce, etc.)
   b. What are the attitudes, behaviors, and expectations held by the family members during different life stages?
   c. What behaviors are deemed acceptable or inappropriate for children? Are they in conflict with the expectations of the school?
   d. How is language related to the life cycle?

▌ Roles
   a. What roles exist in the family or group? Who holds those roles? Do they consider education an important requirement to hold any of those roles?
   b. What knowledge or perception does the child or the family have about the roles found in their cultural group?
   c. Does the group consider the use of language as an important characteristic or social marking of roles?
   d. Do expectations about children's attainment differ according to class status? Are expectations realistic?

▌ Interpersonal relationships
   a. How do people greet each other? What are the forms of address used between people? Are there differences because of status held (age, position)?
   b. What are the expectations held for interaction between girls and boys? Do these differ from what is expected in school?
   c. When and how is consideration or deference shown? What are the social courtesies expected by and from the family?
   d. What constitutes an insult or an offense? How are these expressed?
   e. Who is allowed to disagree and with whom? When are individuals allowed to disagree?

▌ Communication
   a. What are the languages and language varieties used by the family? In the community? When? Who uses what? For what purposes? Are children expected to know these varieties?
   b. Which varieties of the language are written? Is there a widespread knowledge of the written form? Does the family use it?
   c. How does the family define "speaking well"? How does it relate to age, gender, social context?
   d. What is the acceptable speech behavior? What roles, attitudes, personal characteristics are commonly associated with particular ways of speaking?
   e. What is the current level of functionality of the native language in the house? In the community?
   f. What are the gestures or postures considered socially objectionable? What are their meanings? What meaning is ascribed to direct eye contact? To eye contact avoidance?
   g. What are some of the terms or words that are socially unacceptable? Why?
   h. Who is allowed to talk to whom? Under what circumstances? What topics are acceptable for discussion?

▌ Food
   a. What do the family members eat? How often?
   b. What foods are 'favorites, taboos, typical'?
   c. What rules are observed during meals regarding age and sex roles within the family (order of serving, seating, appropriate verbal formulas)? What social rules are individuals expected to observe during meals? What utensils are used during meals?
   d. What social obligations are there in regard to food preparation? In regard to food giving, reciprocity, and honoring people?

FIGURE 10.5 continued

   e. What medicinal uses are made of some categories of food?

   f. What rules exist regarding food handling, offering, or discarding?

▮ Dress and personal appearance

   a. What type of clothing is considered 'typical'?

   b. What clothes are worn for special occasions? What seasonal differences are considered appropriate?

   c. How does dress differ for age, gender, and social class?

   d. What restrictions are imposed for modesty?

   e. How is beauty or attractiveness defined? What characteristics are most valued?

   f. What are the acceptable verbal compliments?

   g. What symbolic value, if any, is given to color of dress?

▮ Education

   a. What are the family's ideas about the purpose of education?

   b. What methods of teaching are used at home (for example, direct verbal instruction, modeling, proverbs, didactic stories)?

   c. Do teaching methods vary according to class, setting, or depending on what is taught?

   d. Is it acceptable for the child to ask questions or volunteer information?

   e. What is accepted as a positive response by teachers to students? By students to teachers?

   f. How many years are children expected to normally attend school? Does it differ by gender?

▮ Work and play

   a. What range of behaviors are considered as "work" and as "play"?

   b. What kind of work is considered prestigious, and why?

   c. Do they hold any stereotypes regarding the occupations of particular groups?

   d. What is the purpose of "play"? Who is allowed to participate?

Source: Adapted from Saville-Troike 1978 (pp. 19–34).

IN ACTION . . . *The Family Folder*

▮ What other items would you include in a *family folder*?

▮ Who would be allowed to read the family folder?

▮ How would you ensure that the child's next teacher understands the information in the folder?

▮ How would you involve the parents and the child in the management of the folder?

▮ Regarding the issue of confidentiality, what do you suggest to protect the contents of the family folder?

a lot of details about the families they work with, it is necessary to emphasize the need for guaranteeing confidentiality. In fact, this is essential to establishing a relationship of mutual trust between the family and the teacher.

There are two relevant points that underscore confidentiality. First, families are not required to give information about what happens inside the family unit. Actually, it is their option to do so. Second, we must remember that any information a family member gives to the teacher furthers the understanding of the child and the child's reality. Even the simplest detail that families offer must be used professionally and treated confidentially. Professionals need to remember that among what defines ethical practices in early childhood

is protecting the data we learn about children. Section II of the NAEYC Code of Ethical Conduct and Statement of Commitment (1989) specifically addresses responsibilities and practices with families.

❖ The School Neighborhood and the Community

Planning a multicultural program cannot take place devoid of the community. The community has relevant qualities and characteristics that are just as important for the children's learning as the knowledge about the families.

FOCUS ON CLASSROOM PRACTICES

SHARING THE CODE OF ETHICS WITH FAMILIES

The purpose of the NAEYC Code of Ethics is to help early childhood teachers define their work professionally. It also serves as a tool for parents to understand that what we do for children and for parents is guided by ethical beliefs. For that reason, the Code should be shared with parents and other professionals. It will help underline our commitment to work together. There are many ways to share the code. Some suggestions are listed here.

- Display it permanently on the classroom bulletin board. A good place is by the door or next to the sign-up sheet.
- Share copies during parent meetings and conferences. This is a good opportunity to discuss some of its vital points.
- Leave copies or segments as part of home visits.
- Share segments. Include a section in the classroom newsletter. It will probably be more effective for it brings attention to a specific point at a time.
- Have copies available as part of the school registration/information packet. Available as a brochure and reasonably priced ($10.00 for a set of 100), they can be ordered from NAEYC (Telephone 1-800-424-2460). The brochure is available in English (brochure #503), as well as in Spanish (brochure #504).

According to Garbarino, Galambos, Plantz, and Kostelny (1992), the neighborhood is the child's territory that plays a leading role in the child's process of socialization. The neighborhood is the playground where the child is initiated into the community life (Garbarino et al. 1992). What a neighborhood or a community offers to the child and to the family will affect their experiences and their abilities to cope with life. The characteristics that define a community even affect the internal life of its families. Factors in the neighborhood that directly influence the lives of the family are

▌ neighborhood safety
▌ recreational facilities
▌ health and social services
▌ schools
▌ economic conditions
▌ opportunities to develop supportive relationships (Garbarino et al. 1992, p. 202).

Profiling the Community

The success of our school programs is influenced by the level of awareness we have about the nature and the characteristics of the community. Discovering the cultures of our communities helps teachers obtain an accurate portrayal of the communities' expectations. This knowledge facilitates the planning of activities that will propel the collaboration between the school and the community. The fact that many educators commute to their work places and are not members of the local culture and/or ethnic groups makes the need to learn about the community in which the families and the children live even more important.

Learning about the community can be accomplished through a variety of ways. You can begin by checking the school reports where general data are found. You may "tour" the community with a local resident who can point out the various rele-

vant places. Another way to learn is by going on a field-visit on your own. When visiting the community, observe the following:

▌ physical appearance (general impression)
▌ types of residential areas (public housing, private developments)
▌ available recreational areas and kind of recreation offered (parks, playgrounds, stadiums, theaters, community centers)
▌ public and private services (hospitals, libraries, churches, banks, public service agencies, transportation, police, fire station, other educational institutions)
▌ existence of religious institutions and types of denominations
▌ types of businesses (grocery stores, crafts shops, repair shops, etc.)
▌ languages used in signs, advertisements, and in anything posted or on the walls
▌ decorations, symbols found throughout the community
▌ activities people do (engaged in during your observation).

You can also gather information about the community by finding the answers to the following questions:

▌ What is defined as the perimeter/part of the community?
▌ How do children define their community?
▌ How do residents describe their community?
▌ What social classes are found in the community?
▌ What specific services are available for families?
▌ What community agencies are found in the community?
▌ What issues or problems are present in the community?

Many communities have their own newsletter and newspapers, usually available in local stores. Reading them can give us an idea about "what is happening" and what is considered socially important. Local news publications will also tell you about the community organizations, activities they sponsor, and who their leaders are.

Using What We Know About Families

The discovery process in which we have been engaged will show you how much diversity exists among the families of our students and in the communities in which they live. We also find many incredible resources among the families and in the neighborhoods. Despite what you might have heard about the community, or the families of school X, families want to help their children and are willing to do so. Many times family members are just waiting for the teacher to give them the opportunity to share what they know and who they are.

The ways in which families can collaborate in our classrooms are identified by analyzing the information collected by the schools and teachers. This provides an accurate picture of the various families' interests, traits, concerns, and talents that will serve as a foundation for the parent/teacher partnership. As you begin to examine your surveys, checklists, and notes, you will be faced with selecting what is truly important. Look for the following points when examining your data.

▮ **Family configurations:** What are the different family patterns (single parent, extended, etc.)?

▮ **Social class:** What particular social and economic characteristics define the families of your students?

▮ **Expectations:** What do families expect from you and the school?

▮ **Diversity:** What elements of diversity are descriptive of the families (language, exceptionalities, ethnicities, religion)?

▮ **Concerns/issues:** What are the problems and situations faced by parents?

▮ **Possible resources for the classroom:** What abilities and characteristics of the families can become a resource for the class? Include those parents who expressed a desire to help.

Information highlighted through such an analysis will help you refocus your efforts and decide on more effective ways to link families to your classroom. Knowing who our families are will help make our curriculum more sensitive and realistic for the students.

❖ Communication: The Road to Positive Relationships

Good communication is the key to any successful relationship. Stone (1987) states that teachers are in a position to establish the foundation for a productive and lasting relationship the very first time parents come to the school. Everything we say from the very first time we meet the families counts! What can we do to develop good

---

IN ACTION . . . *A Visit to Your Own Neighborhood*

Take time to visit your own neighborhood. Using the guidelines mentioned in this section, describe what you discovered about your own community.

FOCUS ON CLASSROOM PRACTICES

IDENTIFYING CLASSROOM COLLABORATORS

The first source of classroom collaborators is found among the families themselves. Doing a simple survey early in the year will help to identify them. Here is a sample survey you can use to create one that better fits your classroom needs.

1. Would you like to collaborate as a volunteer in our classroom?

   _____ Yes, I am interested in collaborating.

   _____ No, I am unable to help at this time.

2. If you answered "yes," how would you like to collaborate with our classroom? Please enter a check mark (√) to indicate how:

   _____I can help as a classroom volunteer. Please call me to discuss times and days.

   _____I can prepare materials at home.

   _____I can help by serving in the PTA.

Once you get your surveys back, remember to tabulate the answers. An easy way to make good use of what you discovered is to classify answers according to the following categories:

1. in-classroom volunteers (those interested in coming to the classroom)
2. resources (those interested in doing things from home and those who can collaborate for specific activities like craft-making, music and dancing, speakers, etc.)
3. translators (important if you have children and families who speak languages other than English!)
4. storytellers (essential for they add interest to literacy activities)
5. community services/network (those who can provide information or help with community agencies)

IN ACTION . . . *Data Analysis*

Review the important points to remember during your data analysis.

▌ Indicate which ones you consider particularly important.

▌ Which ones may be more difficult to document?

▌ What would you add to the list?

Families enjoy learning about what happens in the classroom.

communication with them? To begin, we must be open-minded and assume a nonjudgmental attitude regarding the family members. This will contribute to the establishment of a successful and effective multicultural program.

Communication is a process that involves sending and receiving messages. Good communication begins when the messages are not just received but are actually understood by the receiver. There are many times in our schools when we fail to complete this process. For example, parents receive our notes and letters; however, there are instances when they do not grasp our intentions. The chance of this happening is much greater when working with families with ethnic and language differences than with families of the mainstream culture. Therefore, it is important to verify that the messages we send are received and understood by the recipients. In a study done with parents of handicapped children, Harry (1992) found that in the case of parents with different cultural backgrounds, written communication was usually received, but failed to convey any messages. Harry found that miscommunication was not just restricted to what was written. She found that even during personal interviews, the school personnel failed to communicate effectively with parents. Three important points influencing communication with the culturally different are derived from Harry's study.

IN ACTION . . . *Parent-Teacher Relationships*

In the following quote, educator James Hymes describes how parent-teacher relationships can become positive or negative.

"Show your interest in a child, and parents are on your side. Be casual, off-handed, be cold toward the child and parents can never work closely with you. . . . To praise the child is to praise the parent. To criticize the child is to hit the parent. The two are two, but the two are one".

▌ Do you agree with what Hymes says? Why?

▌ How else could you express this relationship?

▌ How do your personal experiences support or deny his premise?

Source: Berger, E. (1995). *Parents as partners in education. Families and schools working together.* Englewood Cliffs, NJ: Merrill (p. 124).

1. Language used in written communications should be explicit and free of professional jargon. Even when letters are written in the parents' native language, professional jargon should be avoided. If any terms are used, they should be explained.
2. A bureaucratic tone might fail to convey the message. The tone of written communication should be personal and not intimidating. The message should indicate the school's desire and concern for the child and the parent.
3. Communication should not be limited to what is sent in writing. Opportunities for participation in open conversations should be encouraged. A person whom parents can trust should serve as a liaison during meetings.

Bringing Attitudes into the Classroom

Attitudes, as much as anything else, define who and what we are. They influence our actions, the way we look at the world, and the way we perceive others. It is the same for the parents and families of the children we serve. They, too, come into our classrooms with a myriad of experiences that shape the way they see us and the school. For instance, think about the attitudes of the parents who have had little or no experience with the American school system, or consider the feelings of the family that has experienced discrimination. Imagine the mindset of those facing harsh economic burdens. All of these individuals and groups need a truly supportive environment. The road to successful collaboration can begin the first time these family members come to school and find themselves accepted. Berger (1995) reminds teachers that what parents need to find in our schools is a setting that welcomes them and their children as they are. Rather than finding another agency that will only look at their problems, schools need to exhibit a supportive attitude characteristic of a collaborative partnership.

Opening Doors to Collaboration with Parents and Families

Positive communication in diverse settings is built when teachers show their honest desire to help

Snapshot 10.2
What Comes First? Compliance or Communication?

A study done by Harry with parents of exceptional students of culturally different origins revealed that many schools often seek and achieve compliance with the law while failing to establish positive communication with parents. In her study, Harry examined the incidents and perceptions of a group of Puerto Rican parents of handicapped children with the educational system. She found that communication styles due to language differences, not the experiences and expectations between parents and schools, were found to be the leading cause of miscommunication. While parents wanted to trust the school, the impersonal approach followed by the school personnel only served to widen the distance between both groups. Harry documented various instances where use of educational jargon and the bureaucratic tone, even when written communications were in the parents' language, failed to convey the urgency or importance of the situation. In one of the cases studied, a parent realized after a year that her son had been placed in an exceptional student self-contained classroom. Although the parent had received a letter, she was unable to comprehend its meaning. When the parent visited the school, she received oversimplified information about what the school intended to do with her son. Told by a social worker that the boy was going to receive "extra help in English and math," and not that the boy was being assigned to a self-contained classroom for exceptional students, the parent accepted the school's decision. Her trust in the school made her accept the decision without knowing the implications of her child's placement. A year later, during a meeting with the teacher, the parent discovered not only what the self-contained classroom was, but also that her child was classified as emotionally handicapped in accordance with P.L. 94.142.

Harry found that to develop an appropriate level of communication with culturally different parents, schools need to use a more personal tone, as well as a more open-ended type of communication. Although compliance with the law is important, it should not be done at the expense of the clients, especially when they are not being properly informed.

Source: Harry, B. (1992). *Cultural diversity, families and the special education system. Communication and empowerment.* New York: Teachers College Press.

families. Our frank intent to collaborate with them and the children, accompanied with a friendly smile, opens doors to many opportunities. Those opportunities also arise when we invite the families for a closer look at our classrooms. But, how will they know they are welcome and that their help is wanted in our schools? This is where skillful communication works like magic.

Effective communication requires a combination of one- and two-way methods. One-way communication happens when parents receive letters, handbooks, memorandums, or printed materials aimed at informing them *about* the school plans. On the other hand, two-way communication occurs when schools and families *interact by sharing* views and ideas. In two-way situations, each part gains from each other's knowledge and experience (Berger 1995). Teachers working in multicultural settings will find many opportunities to share ideas and communicate with families. Let's examine some of the strategies we can use to establish better communication.

Sharing Ideas in Writing

Perhaps one of the things that parents value most is being informed about the events and activities in their children's schools. Good and appropriate written communication is important to keep parents well apprised of what occurs in the school. It can be either periodic or incidental. Whether formal or informal, written communication sent home should be clear and simple. Newsletters, reports, and notes with curriculum information are examples of periodic communication. Forms of incidental communication include notes, letters, and flyers about special events. Here are a few points to guide your written communications.

▪ Use simple and clear language. In settings where there is a language difference, write your messages in that language, if possible. When writing in a language other than English, ask someone fluent in the language to edit your materials. Remember, you represent the school!

▪ Avoid use of figurative language with parents who have limited English language proficiency. Figurative language is usually culturally based and not easily understood by those who do not share that culture. Remember that sometimes it is difficult for a non-native speaker to grasp the meanings of metaphors and analogies (Lee 1995).

▪ Communications should be attractive and appealing to the reader. For newsletters, Berger (1995) recommends using colorful paper and clear headlines, having samples of children's work including practical suggestions for the families.

▪ Communications should have something relevant to tell. Make sure that the message will be important to the reader.

▪ Include topics that relate to the families' cultures. Try to incorporate ideas or points that recognize the value of the cultural groups in your classroom.

▪ When writing notes or letters, always have something positive to say about the child.

Classroom News

Families enjoy receiving materials that are both informative and fun to read. A good practice that enhances a constant flow of communication is to have a classroom newsletter. Simple and not difficult to prepare, teachers can send home one-page weekly or bi-monthly newsbriefs. Find an appealing name, which can be suggested by your class, and get ready to become an editor. If your students' families are linguistically diverse, having a bilingual edition is a great help. A parent can volunteer to serve as a translator if you do not have the mastery of the other language. The next step is to select your content. For example, teachers can include notes about topics studied, a list of songs learned, highlights about children's accomplishments, and a schedule of upcoming events. When working with a multicultural curriculum, having this kind of communication is important because it allows parents to learn and know what is happening in the classroom.

Another useful technique is regularly sending a list of suggested activities for parents to do at home with their children. This not only allows families to participate in extending the curriculum into the home, but it also provides parents with good activities to share with their children. Including a section for parents to provide feedback about the activities they like the most is a way to invite their participation.

Planning Meetings and Conversations

Nothing takes the place of personal interactions. What is shared through personal contacts carries a totally different meaning from any other kind of communication. The opportunity to share an actual moment in time with another person enhances the quality of the experience. You probably know of many instances where the impression you had about someone drastically changed after meeting the individual in person. Whether face-to-face or by telephone, personal contact should be established with families and parents. Personal interaction requires attention to such communication elements as the tone of the voice, the voice inflections, and the body language. All convey messages that can never be transmitted by a letter or a note. Results from research done by Miller, Wackman, Nunnaly, and Miller (cited by Berger 1995) confirm that in an interpersonal communication there are many more things "said" through our gestures and movements and our tone of voice than by words alone. "Oral, verbal messages (the spoken word) account for only 7 percent of the input; vocal and tonal messages (the way in which the word is spoken) account for 38 percent; visual messages account for 55 percent" (p. 161).

Conversations need to be carefully planned because they provide the perfect opportunities to initiate real partnerships. There are several factors to consider if one wants to have effective interactions. The first thing to understand is that the impression you leave on a parent is not solely conveyed through your words, but also through the context in which they are placed and through the manner in which they are spoken. The place and time chosen for a conversation also play an important part in creating effective communication. Working with families that have cultures and languages different from ours requires even more careful planning. We must always remember that in some cases, the parents' views of education may be very different from ours. Their perceptions and knowledge about the philosophical concepts and systemic issues of education are grounded in their cultural heritage. That by itself establishes how they will approach and react toward "a meeting with the teacher." Try to be sensitive to this by just considering how you would feel in a setting where your values and ideas might be distinctively dissimilar from those of the school.

When planning to talk with parents, consider the following:

▪ Select a pleasant environment. If the conversation takes place in the classroom, have adult seats available.

▪ When having a telephone conversation, make sure the time you plan to call is convenient. Know in advance how much time you have. However, avoid long telephone conversations. A series of short, specific ones are usually more productive than very long ones.

▪ Whether on the telephone or in person, always treat parents with respect and courtesy. Even if your values and ideas are not in harmony with those they have, show your professionalism by respecting their ways.

■ Be aware of your own body gestures and avoid any nuances that might send a distorting message. For instance, if the parent or adult dresses in a different way or wears a particular personal decoration, avoid staring at it.

■ Keep yourself focused on the conversation. Avoid looking around the place, for it sends the message of "I'm not interested."

■ If meeting the parent/family for the first time, introduce yourself in a friendly manner. Avoid giving the impression of being the "know it all" kind of person (Eliason & Jenkins 1993). Show you are a professional through your work with children, and not by presenting yourself as the "power person."

■ To maximize your meeting, it is important to send a note in advance describing in simple terms the purpose of the meeting. Providing a brief description is especially convenient for those families that are linguistically different, for it prepares them to have a more productive conversation (Lee 1995). Some parents have said that before coming to school, they would ask a friend or check in a dictionary how to say given words and phrases. A note sent in advance explaining the objective of the meeting will avoid misinterpretations. For some cultures, being called by the teacher means the child has misbehaved. Some parents have reported punishing their children in advance because of what they "might have done" (Robles de Meléndez 1992).

■ Keep your conversation friendly and professional. Avoid asking very personal questions about the family. Some cultures might find it offensive to ask certain personal details. Accept what they are disclosing. Remember that by establishing a positive relationship, families will continue sharing other ideas.

■ When meeting parents from other cultures, always refer to them as "Ms.____, Mrs.____, or Mr.____" and never by their first name. In many cultures, people would feel offended if called their first name by someone who is not a close friend or relative. Using a title will not only show your respect, but it will serve to establish a professional tone. If elders are present, show deference and acknowledge their presence.

■ With families that are culturally different, do not address your conversation to the mother alone if the husband, or the father, is also present. In some cultures like Hispanic American and Middle Eastern, males play a strong role in the family. Acknowledge their participation and input.

■ Talk in a courteous, not patronizing way. Talking slowly and clearly can be done without falling into a patronizing tone.

■ Avoid showing your knowledge using "teacher jargon." Talk in simple and clear terms.

■ Be patient. Do not rush to say a lot because you have limited time. Also, be patient with parents who are linguistically different and for whom communicating in English is difficult. Most cultural groups show a lot of patience toward Americans when they try to communicate in their languages. Think about yourself trying to speak in their language!

■ When parents or relatives are not fluent in English, have an interpreter. If you use interpreters, give them a summary or a description of the purposes of the meeting. This will help them to become aware of "the content and context of a conference in advance" (Lee 1995, p. 6).

■ If parents speak a language different from English, try to learn a few words in that language. It is always a good opener and it also demonstrates that you are interested in learning more about them and their child.

▪ When parents are accompanied by other family members, relatives, or friends, acknowledge their presence. Find out who they are and what their relationship is to the family. Many cultural groups include relatives and some close friends among those responsible for the well-being of the child (Lynch & Hanson 1992).

▪ Be a good listener. Don't monopolize the conversation. Remember that all of us have very busy lives and that time is very precious to everyone. Select topics that can be feasibly discussed in the time you have.

▪ Show you care and want to help their children. Be positive and show your warm feelings. Always have something positive to say about the child. Share an anecdote or a sample of the child's work.

▪ Try to end your conversations with a positive outlook.

Using Modern Technology to Enhance Collaboration

We already know that one of the most important features of the twenty-first century will be technology. Because technology is also an important part of our current world, we need to consider using it as a part of our communication system. James Coleman (1991) recommends educators include modern technology among the ways to reach parents and families. The multicultural teacher can do no less. What technology to use will depend upon the resources available in the schools.

Telephone answering machines are among today's commonly used effective technology-based communication tools. Many people have these "personal electronic secretaries," or "voice mail," to keep them informed and organized. Answering machines enable teachers to establish information lines parents can access at any time. Details about activities, descriptions of the classroom events, or things children need to bring to school can be recorded in advance (Eliason & Jenkins 1993). For example, families appreciate voice mail suggestions for possible activities during weekends and holidays. Having information in the languages spoken by the students' families is an excellent way to link them to the classroom.

In many places, schools operate a homework hot line. Daily assignments taped by teachers can then be easily accessed by parents. There are some schools that also have bilingual specialists available for consultations during specific evening hours. Many times these specialists are parents and community members who donate their time. This service helps parents clarify their children's homework, which benefits the child. Children whose parents work evening hours can call to verify and check on the next day's assignments.

If available, include electronic mail among your communication tools. Many schools now have messages offered regularly to parents through e-mail. This opens another channel of interaction particularly suitable for working family members with full schedules.

❖ Ideas for Planning Activities with Families

What you know about the families and children in your classroom will serve to help you plan a wide variety of activities. The innumerable differences families exhibit become your best source of ideas for learning experiences. Families can literally "energize" the whole school program.

Curriculum Activities

Consider first how families can enhance the curriculum. Examine your projected curriculum experiences and identify those areas where families can help with demonstrations, telling stories, teaching a song or a dance, bringing specific resources, or serving as speakers. For instance, parents and family members can help by demonstrating how to use a given ethnic instrument or how to wear a typical piece of clothing. Make a list of the instances where their collaboration is needed. If told in advance, families are usually willing to share their knowledge and their resources. Notes can be sent home asking for help for specific topics children will study. An example of these kinds of notes appears here (Figure 10.6).

Keeping a file of resources that parents have and are willing to share is a convenient way to know what is available to support your curriculum. Include the parents as resources as well by creating a "special resources (parents/materials)" file. To facilitate identification, include a note about those areas of diversity they represent (i.e., cultures, exceptionalities). Even if you no longer teach their child, parents can always be contacted to share their knowledge with your current class. They will feel flattered to serve as your "special resources."

Parents and families are also a valuable resource when planning the curriculum. Their participation is one of those required components of developmentally appropriate teaching. Considering them as partners while developing units and experiences can bring in fresh and relevant ideas. Parents and family members can provide valuable suggestions when trying to determine how to address a topic from a variety of perspectives. They can also be considered a source of support and affirmation for your activities.

Support and Social Activities

Activities can provide opportunities for parents and families to interact with the school and with other families. This way they can learn more about other families and build their sense of identification with the school. The list of possible activities can be as long as our creativity allows. Here are some suggestions.

1. **Family of the month/week:** Prepare a display presenting the special characteristics and uniqueness of families. All families have something special and particular that you can highlight. You can either use a bulletin board or the classroom door to exhibit your display. Make sure it is located in a prominent place.

2. **Families get-together:** Times can be arranged to have families come to the classroom to be together and to get to know each other (Berger 1995). The traditional pot-luck meal is still a good idea when parents are able to come in during evenings or on a Saturday. Parents can bring something to share with others. Ask them to write the names of their dishes so that everyone can remember them. Early morning coffee can be organized for families that work. Mid-day or afternoon refreshments and cookies are other activities for those whose schedules are more flexible.

3. **The classroom mural family album:** A mural album of activities carried out by families and their children can be prepared and displayed in the classroom. Things to include are important events, celebrations, and participation in classroom activities. Parents can share pictures, and children can also make drawings of the special times spent with their families.

4. **Classroom "experts":** Identify those areas where families are definite experts. For example, a family can become your expert for craftmaking or for learning typical dances. Recognition of their qualities affirms their importance.

5. **Family/parent networks:** With the collaboration of families in your classroom, you can organize a support network. Families who are new to the neighborhood, or those with limited English language skills, can benefit from the support that other parents may offer. A list with names and telephone

FIGURE 10.6 Notes (bilingual) can be sent to parents to ask for their participation in the classroom

---

Can you help us? Our class needs your help!

Soon our class will be studying _____. Can you share some of your ideas? We know that sharing what you know will benefit our students. Please let us know how you can help by completing the included form.

Thanks!

I can:

____ bring the following: _____
____ demonstrate a dance or a song.
____ talk about my experiences.
____ describe some of the traditions.
____ other: _____

(Spanish Translation)

¿Nos puede ayudar? ¡Nuestro salón necesita su colaboración!

Estimada familia:

Muy pronto estaremos estudiando _____. Es posible que ustedes sepan mucho sobre este tema. Sabemos que al compartir algo de lo que ustedes saben nuestros niños aprenderán mucho más. Contamos con su ayuda. Si puede colaborar, déjenoslo saber completando el volante que incluímos.

¡Gracias!

La familia de (nombre del estudiante) _____ puede:

____ traer lo siguiente: _____
____ demostrar un baile o enseñarles una canción.
____ hablar sobre nuestras experiencias.
____ leer algún cuento sobre el tema.
____ describir algunas de las tradiciones y costumbres.
____ demostrar como preparar algún plato típico.
____ Otros: _____

numbers of the support person can be made available to those in need (Berger 1995).

6. **Storytellers' club:** Invite families and family members to share their stories. They can also read stories from their cultural groups. A pool of volunteer storytellers can add variety to your classroom activities while reinforcing to parents that their collaboration is wanted.

7. **Special multicultural events committee:** Families are the best source of ideas about what and how to celebrate cultural events. Invite families from different cultural backgrounds to form a committee. Together they will advise how to appropriately celebrate those special dates.

8. **Meetings:** Good topics that are of interest to the families are always attractive. Periodic meetings can bring families together to discuss and share ideas while learning about other views.

9. **Welcome committee:** Parents of different cultural groups can form a "welcome" group for other parents. They can prepare handouts with key places in the community, recreational services, and other important information that any newcomer always appreciates. This is a particularly effective resource for families of recent immigrants who need to cope with their new reality.

10. **Educational packets:** With the help of the teacher, a group of volunteers can prepare home-learning materials. Parents and volunteers can duplicate materials to be sent home and prepare calendars of activities. With the guidance of the teacher, parents can locate resources in the school library or even develop their own set of references.

11. **Special projects:** All classrooms have special projects where parents and community volunteers are the essential resources. Call on the parents whenever you and your class plan to begin a project. They are the best way to design experiential activities that

will define the actual and not the idealized ways of cultures.

Counting on the Community as a Resource

A teacher's list of resources would not be complete without the resources of the community. McGee-Banks (1993) recommends knowing well what services and resources are available in our community if you want to count on their support. She further suggests answering the following questions, which we adapted for your use.

1. Are there any local arts (drama, dance, music, storytelling) organizations in this community? Are there any at the county level?
2. Are there any local museums? What services or programs do they offer?
3. Is there a local library?
4. Are there any programs and activities offered for young children by social and civic organizations like: Boys and Girls Clubs, the Optimist Club, Boy and Girl Scouts, YMCA, YWCA, the Kiwanis Club, local religious groups, ethnic clubs, sports clubs, and others?
5. Do any civil rights organizations (like Urban League, Anti-Defamation League, NAACP, Alliance of Jews and Christians) offer programs for young children?
6. What social and family support agencies are available in the community?
7. Is there a senior-citizens action group?

A definite advantage of using community resources is the awareness children develop about the people in their community. This is especially important for children engaged in programs focused on diversity. By being involved with the community, children will not only develop an awareness of multiculturalism through direct experiences, but also through the many opportunities they have to develop classroom activities using community resources. This is known as social action-based teaching.

Opportunities for social action-based teaching are created through an active link with the community. Community leaders can help with suggestions of possible experiences appropriate for young children. For example, taking action to clean the yard of an elderly person, working in the garden of a handicapped person, preparing crafts to give as a welcome present to the children moving into the neighborhood, or painting a park fence are some of the activities that provide concrete ways to demonstrate that we care about others despite their diversity.

Establishing contacts with community-based organizations is a way to gain access to unlimited ideas and experiences for your classroom. A note or a call to learn what services are offered will open the door to a world of resources right there in your community.

❖ What Lies Ahead?

Working with the families of children in our classroom is an experience that offers many possibilities. Linking families and schools to work and respect each other is a way to gain equity for all, an important goal of multicultural education. If our classroom doors are truly open, the future of children will be brighter. We would like to end this chapter with some advice: Building positive relationships with parents and families takes time. So be patient and work toward productive relations with those who are your partners in educating the child in your classroom. And, yes, you can!

❖ Before We End, a Word to the Reader

Caminante, no hay camino. Se hace camino al andar.
[Traveler, there is no road. You blaze it as you go.]
Antonio Machado

We could not conclude this work without saying to our readers: "Congratulations on your determination to explore how to create multicultural classrooms for young children!" Now that you are familiar with the basic knowledge about multiculturalism and have the working tools for teaching about diversity, the rest of the challenge lies ahead. This is your opportunity to become a change-agent for educational reform on behalf of young children. It is also the chance to put into practice your own ideas regarding diversity and education. This is, in fact, your best opportunity to demonstrate your personal and professional commitment to equality for young children.

Multicultural early childhood teaching is still in its infancy. Although there are examples and ideas that tell us how it should be done, additional efforts are still required to give it its definitive shape. The challenge sometimes looks insurmountable. However, the beliefs that brought you here and your determination to provide an empowering environment for young children will let you conquer the obstacles. We have faith in your ability to create culturally empowering classrooms for all our children. We know you will succeed because early childhood teachers are people who have the courage to dare because they believe in children. That's why we believe in you!

❖ Things to Do . . .

1. What do you think are some of the main problems faced by families today? Write a brief paper about what you believe are the most urgent issues.
2. All of us have a notion of what a family is. How does your own concept differ from the views of families of your students?
3. We learn about others when we interact. Plan to interview two families of different social and ethnic backgrounds. Ask them about their views concerning children. Compare their responses and find how similar and different they are.

4. We all have different perspectives of appropriate family/parent involvement in schools. Ask five of your colleagues about their views. Then ask five parents and compare their responses.
5. Many schools have successfully involved the families into their programs. Interview 3–4 of the teachers and administrators from those schools. List their successful strategies.
6. Every classroom is different. Based on the nature of your own school and classroom, prepare a list of ten possible ways to involve the families. Share the list with a colleague.
7. Many organizations in your community can become a source of support and information for your program. Locate at least five in your community and list them.

❖ Organizations and Advocates for Parents and Families

Many national groups are working for the cause of children and families. You might want to contact them for information and services. Addresses of selected groups are included here.

American Home Economics Association
2010 Massachusetts Avenue, NW
Washington, DC 20036-1028

Center on Families, Communities, Schools and Children's Learning
605 Commonwealth Avenue
Boston, Massachusetts 02215

Child Welfare League, Inc.
67 Irving Place
New York, New York 10003

The Children's Defense Fund
122 C Street
Washington, DC 20001

Family Resource Coalition
230 North Michigan Avenue
Chicago, Illinois 60601

The Home and School Institute
1201 16th Street, NW
Washington, DC 20036

National Black Child Development Institute
1463 Rhode Island Avenue, NW
Washington, DC 20005

National Coalition of Hispanic Health and Human Services Organizations
1501 16th Street, NW
Washington, DC 20036

National Congress of Parents and Teachers (the National PTA)
700 N Rush Street
Chicago, Illinois 60611

National Families in Action
2296 Henderson Mill Road
Suite 204
Atlanta, Georgia 30345

National Head Start Association
1220 King Street, Suite 200
Arlington, Virginia 22314

❖ Children's Literature Corner

Cowen-Fletcher, J. (1993). *Mama Zooms.* New York: Scholastic Books.

Dorros, A. (1991). *Abuela.* New York: Dutton.

Lomas Garza, C. (1990). *Family pictures.* San Francisco: Children's Book Press.

Munoz, P. (1994). *One hundred is a family.* New York: Hyperion Books.

Ringold, F. (1991). *Tar beach.* New York: Crown Press.

Ryland, C. (1982). *When I was young in the mountains.* New York: Dutton.

——— (1985). *The relatives came.* New York: Dutton.

Strickland, D., & Strickland, M. (1994). *Families: Poems celebrating the African-American experience.* PA: Boyds Mills Press.

❖ References

Berger, E. (1995). *Parents as partners in education. Families and schools working together.* Englewood Cliffs, NJ: Merrill.

Boyer, E. (1991). *Ready to learn. A mandate for the nation.* Princeton, NJ: The Carnegie Foundation for the Advancement of Teaching.

Coleman, J. (1991). *Planing for parent participation in schools for young children.* Bloomington, IL: ERIC Digest.

Children's Defense Fund (1992). *The state of America's children 1992.* Washington, DC: Children's Defense Fund.

Dowling, E., & Osborne, E. (1993). *The family and the school. A joint system approach with children* (2nd ed.). London, UK: Routledge.

Eliason, C., & Jenkins, L. (1993). *A practical guide to early childhood education curriculum.* New York: Merrill.

Fox, R., Anderson, W., Fox, B., & Rodriguez, A. (1991). STAR parenting: A model for helping parents effectively deal with behavioral difficulties. *Young Children.* 46, 2 (pp. 54–60).

Garbarino, J., & Garbarino, A. (1992). In conclusion: The issue is human quality. (Chapter 11). In J. Garbarino. *Children and families and the social environment* (2nd ed.). New York: Aldine de Gruyter.

Garbarino, J., Galambos, N., Plantz, M., & Kostelny, K. (1992). The territory of childhood. (Chapter 8). In J. Garbarino. *Children and families and the social environment* (2nd ed.). New York: Aldine de Gruyter.

Harry, B. (1992). *Cultural diversity, families and the special education system. Communication and empowerment.* New York: Teachers College Press.

Kagan, S., & Rivera, A. (1991). Collaboration in early care and education: What can and should we expect? *Young Children.* 47,1 (pp. 51–56).

Lee, F. Y. (1995, March). Asian parents as partners. *Young Children.* 50, 3 (pp. 4–9).

Lynch, E. W., & Hanson, M. J. (1992). *Developing cross-cultural competence. A guide for working with young children and their families.* Baltimore, MD: Paul Brooks.

Mannan, G., & Blackwell, J. (1992, April). *Parent involvement: Reality behind the rhetoric.* Paper presented at the Annual Conference of the Association for Childhood Education International. Chicago, IL.

McGee-Banks, S. (1993). Parents and teachers: Partners in school reform (Chapter 17). In J. Banks (ed.). *Multicultural education. Issues and perspectives.* (2nd ed.). Boston, MA: Allyn & Bacon.

National Association for the Education of Young Children (1989). *Code of ethical behavior and statement of commitment.* Brochure #503. Washington, DC: NAEYC.

National Association of State Boards of Education (1991). *Caring communities: Supporting young children and families.* A report of the National Task Force on School Readiness. Alexandria, VA: NASBE.

National Commission on Children (1991). *Beyond rhetoric. A new American agenda for children and families. Final Report of the National Commission on Children.* Washington, DC: NCC.

Robles de Meléndez, W. (1992, July). *Creating the multicultural environment.* Paper presented at the Conference of the Florida Department of Education: Tampa, FL.

Saville-Troike, M. (1978). *A guide to culture in the classroom.* Rosslyn, VA: National Clearing House for Bilingual Education.

Stone, J. (1987). *Parent-teacher relationships.* Washington, DC: National Association for the Education of Young Children.

Swick, K. (1991). *Teacher-parent partnerships to enhance school success in early childhood education.* Washington, DC: National Education Association. ED (pp. 339–516).

Turnbull, A., & Turnbull, H. R. (1990). *Families, professionals and exceptionality: A special partnership* (2nd ed.). New York: Merrill.

United Nations (1993). *U.N. Year of the Family.* New York: U.N. Department of Public Information.

United Nations (1994). Changing family structure. *1994 International Year of the Family.* New York: U.N. Department of Public Information.

Vincent, L. (1994). Implementing individualized family service planning in urban, culturally diverse early intervention settings. In K. Paciorek & J. Munro. *Early childhood education 1993/1994. Annual Editions.* Guilford, CT: Dushkin.

Appendices

Appendix A
List of Multicultural Children's Books

The books on this list are a sample of the many books available. You may want to check your local library or bookstore for additional titles. The books are classified according to the basic elements of diversity and are appropriate for the early childhood level.

❖ Ethnicity

African Americans

Aardema, V. (1975). *Why mosquitoes buzz in people's ears.* New York: Dial.

Aardema, V. (1981). *Bringing the rain to Kapiti Plain.* New York: Dial.

Aardema, V. (1994). *The crocodile and the ostrich.* New York: Scholastic.

Adler, D. (1994). *A picture book of Sojourner Truth.* New York: Holiday House.

Alexander, L. (1992). *The fortune tellers.* New York: E. P. Dutton.

Angelou, M. (1987). *Now Sheba sings the song.* New York: Penguin.

Bryan, A. (1982). *I'm going to sing: Black American spirituals* (vol. 2). New York: Atheneum.

Cameron, A. (1987). *Julian's glorious summer.* New York: Random House.

Clark, C. (1970). *Black cowboy: The story of Nat Love.* New York: Putnam.

Cowen-Fletcher, J. (1994). *It takes a village.* New York: Scholastic Books.

Dragonwagon, C. (1990). *Home place.* New York: Macmillan.

Dupre, R. (1993). *The wishing chair.* Minneapolis, MN: Carolrhoda.

Feelings, M. (1974). *Jambo means hello.* New York: Dial.

Feelings, T. (1993). *Soul looks back in wonder.* New York: Dial.

Flournoy, V. (1985). *The patchwork quilt.* New York: Dial.

Flournoy, V. (1995). *Tanya's reunion.* New York: Dial.

Golenbock, P. (1990). *Teammates.* San Diego: Harcourt Brace Jovanovich.

Hadithi, M., & Kennaway, A. (1984). *The greedy zebra.* London: Hodder & Stoughton.

Hamanaka, S. (1994). *All the colors of the earth.* New York: Morrow.

Hamilton, V. (1985). *The people could fly: American black folktales.* New York: Knopf.

Hamilton, V. (1989). *The bells of Christmas.* San Diego: Harcourt Brace Jovanovich.

Hamilton, V. (1995). *Her stories: African American folktales, fairy tales, and true tales.* New York: Scholastic Books.

Havill, J. (1986). *Jamaica's find.* Boston, MA: Houghton Mifflin.

Hudson, W. (1993). *Pass it on: African-American poetry for children.* New York: Scholastic Books.

Johnson, D. (1994). *Seminole diary: Remembrances of a slave.* New York: Macmillan.

Johnson, J. (1993). *Lift every voice and sing.* New York: Walker.

Lewin, H. (1983). *Jafta's father.* Minneapolis, MN: Carolrhoda.

Lewin, H. (1983). *Jafta's mother.* Minneapolis, MN: Carolrhoda.

Lewin, H. (1983). *Jafta-the town.* Minneapolis, MN: Carolrhoda.

Lewin, H. (1983). *Jafta: The journey*. Minneapolis, MN: Carolrhoda.

Lewin, H. (1994) *Jafta: The homecoming*. New York: Knopf.

Livingston-Cohn, M. (1994). *Keep on singing: A ballad of Marian Anderson*. New York: Holiday House.

Medearis, A. (1991). *Dancing with the Indians*. New York: Holiday House.

Mendez, P. (1989). *The black snowman*. New York: Scholastic Books.

Mennem, I., and Daly, N. (1990). *Somewhere in Africa*. New York: E. P. Dutton.

Miller, W. (1994). *Zora Thurston and the chinaberry tree*. New York: Lee & Low.

Musgrove, M. (1988). *Ashanti to Zulu: African traditions*. New York: E. P. Dutton.

Sokoni, M. (1993). *Mcheshi goes to the market*. Nairobi, Kenya: Jacaranda.

Steptoe, J. (1987). *Mufaro's beautiful daughters*. New York: Lothrop, Lee & Shepard.

Thomas, J. (1993). *Brown honey in broomwheat tea*. New York: HarperCollins.

Wanyama, M. (1992). *Mcheshi goes to the game park*. Nairobi, Kenya: Jacaranda.

Asian Americans

Battles, E. (1978). *What does the rooster say, Yoshio?* Morton Grove, IL: Whitman.

Chiemruom, S. (1992). *Dara's Cambodian new year*. New York: Half Moon.

Coerr, E. (1988). *Chang's paper pony*. New York: HarperCollins.

English, K. (1995). *Neeny coming, Neeny going*. New York: Bridgewater.

Friedman, I. (1984). *How my parents learned to eat*. Boston, MA: Houghton Mifflin.

Garland, S. (1993). *The lotus seed*. San Diego: Harcourt Brace Jovanovich.

Girard, L. (1989). *We adopted you, Benjamin Koo*. Morton Grove, IL: Whitman.

Keller, H. (1994). *Grandfather's dream*. New York: Greenwillow.

Lee, J. (1987). *Ba-Nam*. New York: Henry Holt & Company.

Melmed, L. (1993). *The first song ever sung*. New York: Lee, Lothrop & Shepard.

Miho, S. N. (1995). *The last dragon*. New York: Clarion.

Sakade, F. (1994). *Japanese children's favorite stories*. Rutland, VT: Charles E. Tuttle.

Sakai, K. (1990). *Sachiko means happiness*. San Francisco: Children's Book Company.

Say, A. (1994). *Grandfather's journey*. Boston, MA: Houghton Mifflin.

Say, L. (1990). *El chino*. Boston, MA: Houghton Mifflin.

Surat, M. (1983). *Angel child, dragon child*. Milwaukee, WI: Raintree.

Tuyet, T. (1987). *The little weaver of Thai Yen village*. San Francisco: Children's Book Press.

Uchida, Y. (1981). *A jar of dreams*. New York: Atheneum.

Uchida, Y. (1994). *The bracelet*. New York: Philomel.

Yashima, T. (1955). *Crow boy*. New York: Viking.

Yep, L. (1992). *The ghost fox*. New York: Scholastic Books.

Yep, L. (1993). *Tiger woman*. New York: Bridgewater.

Caribbean

Agard, J. (1989). *Calypso alphabet*. New York: Holt.

Belpre, P. (1973). *Once in Puerto Rico*. New York: Warner.

Binch, C. (1994). *Gregory Cool*. New York: Dial.

Buffet, J., & Savanna, J. (1988). *The jolly mon*. San Diego: Harcourt Brace Jovanovich.

Crespo, G. (1993). *How the sea began. A Taino Myth*. New York: Clarion.

Delacre, L. (1989). *Arroz con leche: Popular songs and rhymes from Latin America*. New York: Scholastic Books. [Includes traditions of Spanish Caribbeans]

Garcia, R. (1987). *My Aunt'a Otilia's spirits*. Chicago: Children's Press.

González, L. (1994). *The bossy gallito.* New York: Scholastic Books.

Hernandez, R., Villarini, A., & Robles, W. (1991). *Aventuras de nuestra historia.* [Adventures of our history (PR)]. San Juan, PR: Santillana.

Hubley, J., & Hubley, P. (1985). *A trip to Jamaica.* New York: Lerner.

Lessac, F. (1994). *Caribbean alphabet.* New York: Tambourine.

Lloyd, E. (1979). *Nini at carnival.* New York: HarperCollins.

Lye, K. (1988). *Take a trip to Jamaica.* New York: Franklin Watts.

Mohr, N. (1990). *Felita.* New York: Dial.

Presilla, M. (1994). *Feliz Nochebuena, Feliz Navidad.* Christmas feast of the Hispanic Caribbean. New York: Holt.

Robles, W. (1990). *Los Indios de Boriquén (The Indians of Boriquén).* Naguabo, PR: Producciones Anisa.

Robles, W. (1991). *La sirena que no sabía nadar (The mermaid who could not swim).* Naguabo, PR: Producciones Anisa.

Wolkstein, D. (1978). *Horse and toad. A folktale from Haiti.* New York: Scholastic Books.

Zapater, B. (1992). *Three king's day.* IL: Modern Curriculum Press.

Native Americans

Aliki. (1976). *Corn is maize: The gift of the Indians.* New York: Crowell.

Arnold, G. (1992). *The ancient cliff dwellers of Mesa Verde.* New York: Clarion.

Baker, O. (1981). *Where the buffalos began.* New York: Puffin.

Baylor, B. (1972). *When clay sings.* New York: Scribner's.

Bouchard, D. (1995). *If you're not from the prairie.* New York: Atheneum.

Casler, L. (1994). *The boy who dreamed of an acorn.* New York: Philomel.

Cherry, L. (1992). *Year of impossible goodbyes.* Boston: Houghton Mifflin.

De Paola, T. (1983). *The legend of the bluebonnet.* New York: Putnam.

Esbensen, B. (ed.). (1988). *The star maiden.* New York: Macmillan.

Gates, F. (1994). *Owl eyes.* New York: Lothrop.

Goble, P. (1984). *Buffalo woman.* New York: Aladdin Books.

Goble, P. (1985). *The great race of the birds and animals.* New York: Aladdin Books.

Goble, P. (1988). *Iktomi and the boulder.* New York: Orchard Books.

Goble, P. (1993). *The lost children: The boys who were neglected.* New York: Bradbury.

Hayes, J. (1988). *Coyote and the butterflies.* New York: Scholastic Books.

Jeffers, S. (1991). *Brother Eagle, Sister Sky: A message from Chief Seattle.* New York: Dial.

Kendall, R. (1992). *Eskimo boy. Life in an Inupiaq Eskimo village.* New York: Scholastic Books.

Lyon, G. (1993). *Dreamplace.* New York: Orchard Books.

Martin, B., & Archambault, J. (1987). *Knots on a counting rope.* San Diego: Holt, Rinehart & Winston.

Medearis, A. (1991). *Dancing with the Indians.* New York: Holiday House.

Murphy, C. R. (1993) *The prince and the Salmon People.* New York: Rizzoli.

Oughton, J. (1992). *How the stars fell into the sky: A Navajo legend.* Boston, MA: Houghton Mifflin.

Oughton J. (1994). *The magic weaver of rugs: A tale of the Navajo.* Boston, MA: Houghton Mifflin.

Petersen, P. (1993). *Inunguak the little Greenlander.* New York: Lothrop.

Prusski, J. (1988). *Bring back the deer.* San Diego: Harcourt Brace Jovanovich.

Roth, S. (1990). *The story of light.* New York: Morrow.

Swamp, J. (1995). *"Giving thanks" a Native American good morning message*. New York: Lee & Low Books.

Hispanic Americans

Atkinson, M. (1979). *Maria Teresa*. Carrboro, NC: Lollipop Power.

Baylor, B. (1963). *Amigo*. New York: Aladdin.

Behrens, J. (1978). *Fiesta!* Chicago: Children's Press.

Belting, N. (1992). *Moon was tired of walking in the air*. Boston, MA: Houghton Mifflin.

Brown, T. (1986). *Hello, amigos!* San Diego: Holt, Rinehart & Winston.

Delacre, L. (1989). *Arroz con leche: Popular songs and rhymes from Latin America*. New York: Scholastic Books.

Delacre, L. (1990). *Vegigante masquerader*. New York: Scholastic Books.

Delacre, L. (1993). *Las Navidades. Popular Christmas songs from Latin America*. New York: Scholastic Books.

Ets, M. H., & Labastida, A. (1959). *Nine days to Christmas*. New York: Viking.

Garcia, M. (1987). *The adventures of Connie and Diego: Las aventuras de Connie Y Diego*. San Francisco: Children's Book Press.

Griego, M. (1981). *Tortillitas para mama and other Spanish nursery rhymes*. San Diego: Holt, Rinehart & Winston.

Hayes, J. (1993). *Antonio's lucky day*. New York: Scholastic Books.

Herrera, J. (1995). *Calling the doves/El canto de las palomas*. San Francisco: Children's Book Press.

Hinojosa, F. (1984). *The old lady who ate people*. New York: Little, Brown & Company.

Lattimore, D. (1987). *The flame of peace: A tale of the Aztecs*. New York: Harper & Row.

López de Mariscal, B. (1995). *The harvest birds/Los pájaros de la cosecha*. San Francisco: Children's Book Press.

Mohr, N. (1986). *Going home*. New York: Dial.

Palacios, A. (1994). *A Christmas surprise for Chabelita*. New York: Bridgewater.

Pico, F. (1994). *The red comb*. New York: Bridgewater.

Schon, I. (1983). *Dona Blanca and other Hispanic nursery rhymes and games*. New York: Denison.

Soto, G. (1992). *Neighborhood odes*. New York: Harcourt Brace Jovanovich.

Soto, G. (1993). *Too many tamales*. New York: Putnam.

❖ Gender

Blumberg, R. (1993). *Bloomers!* New York: Bradbury.

Bonsall, C. (1980). *The case of the double cross*. New York: HarperCollins.

Butterworth, N. (1992). *My dad is awesome*. Cambridge, MA: Candlewick Press.

Feller-Bauer, C. (1981). *My mom travels a lot*. New York: Puffin.

Hoban, L. A. (1976). *Arthur's pen pal*. New York: HarperCollins.

Hoban, R. (1969). *Best friends for Frances*. New York: HarperCollins.

Lyon, G. B. (1994). *Mama is a miner*. New York: Orchard Books.

Waxman, S. (1989). *What is a girl?/What is a boy?* New York: Harper & Row.

Williams, V. (1982). *A chair for my mother*. New York: Greenwillow.

Zolotow, C. (1972). *William's doll*. New York: Harper & Row.

❖ Age/Intergenerational

Bang, M. (1985). *The paper crane*. New York: Mulberry.

Berger, B. (1984). *Grandfather twilight*. New York: Philomel Books.

Bryan, A. (1989). *Turtle knows your name*. New York: Macmillan.

Caines, J. (1980). *Window wishing*. New York: HarperCollins.

DePaola, T. (1973). *Nana upstairs, Nana downstairs.* New York: Putnam.

Gary, L. M. (1993). *Miss Tizzy.* New York: Simon & Schuster.

Gary, L. (1993). *Dear Willie Rudd.* New York: Simon & Schuster.

Greenfield, E. (1980). *Grandma's joy.* New York: Putnam.

Hallinan, P. K. (1988). *We're now good friends, my grandpa and I.* Nashville, TN: Ideal's Childrens Books.

Lindbergh, R. (1993). *Grandfather's lovesong.* New York: Viking.

Miles, M. (1972). *Annie and the old one.* New York: Little, Brown & Company.

Orr, C. (1990). *My grandpa and the sea.* Minneapolis, MN: Carolrhoda.

Patent, D. H. (1989). *Grandfather's nose: Why we look alike and different.* New York: Franklin Watts.

Say, L. (1995). *Stranger in the mirror.* Boston, MA: Houghton Mifflin.

Schecter, B. (1989). *Grandma remembers.* New York: Harper & Row.

Shihah, N. (1994). *Sitti's secret.* New York: Four Winds.

Stolz, M. (1988). *Storm in the night.* New York: HarperCollins.

Tews, S. (1993). *The gingerbread doll.* New York: Clarion.

Wahl, J. (1993). *"I remember!" Cried Grandma Pinky.* New York: Bridgewater.

Zolotow, C. (1974). *My grandson Lew.* New York: Harper & Row.

❖ Disability

Brown, T. (1984). *Someone special, just like you.* New York: Holt, Rinehart & Winston.

Carrick, C. (1985). *Stay away from Simon!* New York: Clarion.

Clifton, L. (1980). *My friend Jacob.* New York: E. P. Dutton.

Coerr, E. (1994). *Sadako.* New York: Putnam.

Corn, A. (1977). *Monocular Mac.* Reston, VA: National Association for Visual Impairments.

De Paola, T. (1981). *First one foot, now the other.* New York: Putnam.

Fleming, V. (1993). *Be good to Eddie Lee.* New York: Philomel Books.

Grollman, S. (1977). *More time to grow.* New York: Beacon.

Hesse, K. (1993). *Lester's dog.* New York: Crown.

Lichtfield, A. (1976). *A button in her ear.* Niles, IL: Whitman.

Lichtfield, A. (1980). *Words in our hands.* Niles, IL: Whitman.

Petterson, J. (1977). *I have a sister, my sister is deaf.* New York: Harper & Row.

Powers, M. (1986). *Our teacher's in a wheelchair.* Niles, IL: Whitman.

Sobol, H. (1977). *My brother Steven is retarded.* New York: Macmillan.

Stein, S. B. (1974). *About handicaps.* New York: Walker.

Wolf, B. (1974). *Don't feel sorry for Paul.* New York: Harper & Row.

❖ Social Class

Bunting, E. (1989). *How many days to America?* New York: Clarion.

Hagen, B. (1979). *Tight times.* New York: Puffin.

Harshman, M. (1993). *Uncle James.* Freeport, ME: Cobblehill.

Ho, M. (1991). *The clay marble.* New York: Farrar, Strauss & Giroux.

Lasker, J. (1980). *Nick joins in.* Niles, IL: Whitman.

Ryland, C. (1985). *When I was young in the mountains.* New York: E. P. Dutton.

Simon, N. (1976). *Why am I different?* Niles, IL: Whitman.

Wolde, G. (1979). *Betsy and Peter are different.* New York: Random House.

❖ Differences/General Cultural Diversity

Barnabas, Kindersley, A., and UNICEF. (1995). *Children just like me*. London: Dorling Kindersley.

Brandenberg, A. (1993). *Communication*. New York: Greenwillow Books.

Bunting, E. (1991). *A turkey for Thanksgiving*. New York: Clarion.

Celsi, T. (1992). *Squanto and the first Thanksgiving*. Austin, TX: First Steck Vaughn Edition.

Cohn, A. (1993) (comp.). *From sea to shining sea: A treasury of American folklore and folk songs*. New York: Atheneum.

Coles, R. (1995). *The story of Ruby Bridges*. New York: Scholastic Books.

Duncan, A. (1994). *The National Civil Rights Museum celebrates everyday people*. New York: Bridgewater.

Freeman, D. (1968). *Corduroy*. New York: Puffin.

Gray, N. (1991). *A country far away*. New York: Orchard Books.

Hopkins, L. (1994). *Hand in hand: An American history through poetry*. New York: Simon & Schuster.

Intrater, R. (1992). *Two eyes, a nose, and a mouth*. New York: Scholastic Books.

Jaffrey, M. (1994). *Market days. From market to market around the world*. New York: Bridgewater.

Jordon, M. (1989). *Losing Uncle Tim*. Niles, IL: Whitman.

Klamath County YMCA Family Preschool. (1993). *The land of many colors*. New York: Scholastic Books.

Kraus, R. (1971). *Leo the late bloomer*. New York: Scholastic Books.

Kraus, R. (1991). *How spider saved Thanksgiving*. New York: Scholastic Books.

Kroll, S. (1994). *By the dawn's early light: The story of the Star-Spangled Banner*. New York: Scholastic Books.

Lester, J. (1994). *John Henry*. New York: Dial.

Levine, E. (1992). *If your name was changed at Ellis Island*. New York: Scholastic Books.

Lionni, L. (1967). *Frederick*. New York: Pantheon.

Maestro, B. (1994). *Coming to America. The story of immigration*. New York: Scholastic Books.

Manushkin, F. (1992). *The matzah that papa brought home*. New York: Scholastic Books.

Manushkin, F. (1993). *Latkes and applesauce. A Hannukah story*. New York: Scholastic Books.

Mendez, P. (1989). *The black snowman*. New York: Scholastic Books.

Moorman, M. (1993). *Light the lights! A story about celebrating Hannukah & Christmas*. New York: Scholastic Books.

Morris, A. (1989). *Hats, hats, hats*. New York: Lothrop.

Moss, M. (1994). *Mel's diner*. New York: Bridgewater.

Nelson, V. M. (1993). *Mayfield crossing*. New York: Putnam.

Panzer, N. (1994). *Celebrate America in poetry and art*. Washington, DC: National Museum of Art and the Smithsonian Institution.

Randall, R. (1994). *"Thanksgiving fun": Great things to make and do*. New York: Larousse Kingfisher Chambers.

Raphael, E., & Bolognese, D. (1991). *The story of the first Thanksgiving*. New York: Scholastic Books.

Rascal, A. (1993). *Oregon's journey*. New York: Bridgewater.

Ray, L. (1994). *Shaker boy*. New York: Browndeer.

Speregen, D., & Newberger, S. (1993). *Arielle and the Hannukah surprise*. New York: Scholastic Books.

Spier, P. (1980). *People*. New York: The Trumpet Club.

Stock, C. (1993). *Thanksgiving treat*. New York: Aladdin.

United Nations and Jim Henson Publishing. (1995). *My wish for tomorrow*. New York: Tambourine Books.

Vincent, G. (1982). *Ernest and Celestine*. New York: Greenwillow.

Appendix B
Web of Possibilities Using Multicultural Literature*

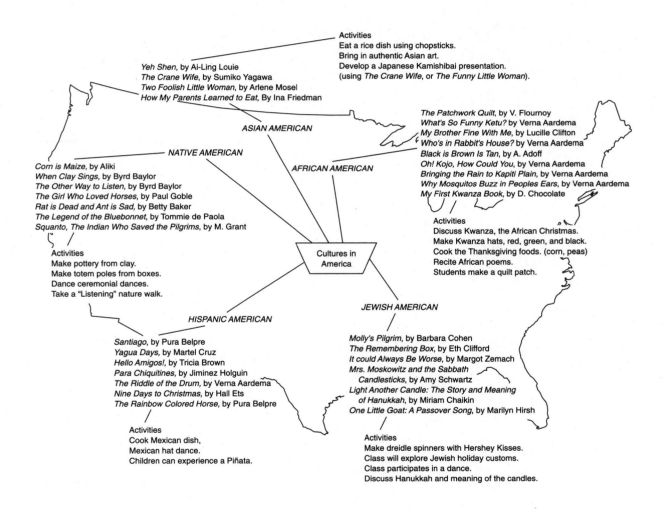

Activities
Eat a rice dish using chopsticks.
Bring in authentic Asian art.
Develop a Japanese Kamishibai presentation.
(using *The Crane Wife*, or *The Funny Little Woman*).

Yeh Shen, by Ai-Ling Louie
The Crane Wife, by Sumiko Yagawa
Two Foolish Little Woman, by Arlene Mosel
How My Parents Learned to Eat, By Ina Friedman

ASIAN AMERICAN

NATIVE AMERICAN

AFRICAN AMERICAN

Corn is Maize, by Aliki
When Clay Sings, by Byrd Baylor
The Other Way to Listen, by Byrd Baylor
The Girl Who Loved Horses, by Paul Goble
Rat is Dead and Ant is Sad, by Betty Baker
The Legend of the Bluebonnet, by Tommie de Paola
Squanto, The Indian Who Saved the Pilgrims, by M. Grant

The Patchwork Quilt, by V. Flournoy
What's So Funny Ketu? by Verna Aardema
My Brother Fine With Me, by Lucille Clifton
Who's in Rabbit's House? by Verna Aardema
Black is Brown Is Tan, by A. Adoff
Oh! Kojo, How Could You, by Verna Aardema
Bringing the Rain to Kapiti Plain, by Verna Aardema
Why Mosquitos Buzz in Peoples Ears, by Verna Aardema
My First Kwanza Book, by D. Chocolate

Activities
Make pottery from clay.
Make totem poles from boxes.
Dance ceremonial dances.
Take a "Listening" nature walk.

Cultures in America

Activities
Discuss Kwanza, the African Christmas.
Make Kwanza hats, red, green, and black.
Cook the Thanksgiving foods. (corn, peas)
Recite African poems.
Students make a quilt patch.

HISPANIC AMERICAN

JEWISH AMERICAN

Santiago, by Pura Belpre
Yagua Days, by Martel Cruz
Hello Amigos!, by Tricia Brown
Para Chiquitines, by Jiminez Holguin
The Riddle of the Drum, by Verna Aardema
Nine Days to Christmas, by Hall Ets
The Rainbow Colored Horse, by Pura Belpre

Molly's Pilgrim, by Barbara Cohen
The Remembering Box, by Eth Clifford
It could Always Be Worse, by Margot Zemach
*Mrs. Moskowitz and the Sabbath
  Candlesticks*, by Amy Schwartz
*Light Another Candle: The Story and Meaning
  of Hanukkah*, by Miriam Chaikin
One Little Goat: A Passover Song, by Marilyn Hirsh

Activities
Cook Mexican dish,
Mexican hat dance.
Children can experience a Piñata.

Activities
Make dreidle spinners with Hershey Kisses.
Class will explore Jewish holiday customs.
Class participates in a dance.
Discuss Hanukkah and meaning of the candles.

*Prepared by Pam O'Kell (Elementary School Teacher,
Brevard County, Florida)

Appendix C
Developing Multicultural Awareness: Sample Activities

Workshop Activity: A Year to Celebrate Cultural Diversity

Background

Have you ever thought about the many festivities that are probably taking place around the world? Probably now at some point on our planet a group of people are celebrating their culture. You and your students can join in their celebration if you decide to adopt the transformational curricular approach (Banks & Banks 1993). In multicultural education, a transformational approach (T-approach) for curriculum development implies a significant change in the structure and nature of the content area. A thorough revision of the scope, goals, and materials of a program is done to have students experience the concepts and topics from the point of view of different cultural groups (Hernández 1989). The result is a realistic, more current curriculum that will empower children with an honest vision about the essence of the society they live in.

Suggestions for Action

Concerted efforts must be taken by schools to follow the transformational approach. However, early childhood educators can initiate this approach by examining the holidays that are observed by the school. Holiday activities are fundamentally ways to manifest cultural values and ideas. Because of the very nature of celebrations, they serve to motivate and interest children.

They also open the door to a more culturally responsive curriculum. During this workshop session you will apply some of the principles of the T-approach using the holidays as main focus.

Into Action . . .

1. Begin by listing the cultures present in your classroom. Include also those found in the school and community. Keep this list handy, for it will help you balance the focus of activities.

   My classroom has the following ethnicities/cultures:

   _____

2. Review the list of official/observed school holidays. Check if they reflect the ethnic makeup of your children; of the community.

   Official holidays observed at my school are:

   _____

3. Now, ask people from different cultures what their main holidays are. Also, check in the encyclopedia or ask the librarian. Select those that represent activities of cultural groups in your class. Add any others not listed here.

Holidays Chosen	*Holidays Added*

4. Enter the cultural festivities into your calendar. Select a month of your choice and design a plan to incorporate these celebrations as part of that month's activities.

Let's Cook, Let's Think! A DAP Experience in Diversity for Ages 4–6: The Many Ways of . . . Pasta!*

Introduction

Who isn't turned on by food? Almost everybody is, which is why cooking and food experiences are an excellent resource in the classroom. Besides the obvious integration of academic areas, cooking can become a tool for multicultural education. In this example, you will use pasta to guide children in discovering how one object can hold a variety of forms and yet maintain the same identity.

Goal: To help children see that people can have a variety of characteristics while being all the same

Concepts: differences, similarities, people

Developmental areas targeted:

1. cognitive—observing, predicting, comparing, evaluating
2. language—describing, acquiring vocabulary, listening
3. motor—pouring, stirring, sorting
4. social—working in groups, waiting for turn, sharing utensils

Academic areas: Social studies, math, health

Materials:

- different types of pasta (macaroni, ziti, lasagna, linguini, rotini, etc.) If possible, select those with different colors.
- paper plates
- pot (to boil pasta)
- sauce or sour cream (to prepare salad)

Suggested Activities:

1. Have children sit in a circle. Place all the pasta in a box or any other container and have children guess what it is. Use some of these clues to guide them:
   - What I have here are different sizes, shapes, and colors.
   - Although they can be placed in groups according to their shapes and sizes, they all belong to one group.
   - You can find them dressed differently.
   - They can have many purposes.
   - They are all made of the same things.

   After they have guessed/attempted to guess, have one child open the box and show it to the class. Review the clues and discuss each idea with the group. Clarify any of the concepts presented through the clues.

2. Give each child a paper plate and pass around the pasta. Have each child get a handful. Invite children to observe and feel the pasta. Have them talk about it. Discuss how they can be similar (texture, materials they are made of) and different (shapes, sizes, color).

3. Have children discuss how they are used and say which ones they have tried.

4. Discuss the names assigned to pasta. Have labels to identify the different types. Introduce the relationship to people who, like pasta, also have different names. Have them select the ones they like best. Emphasize resemblance with people (there are some people we prefer to be with).

5. Establish all the relationships with people. Use the different characteristics they listed (color, size, shape, names) to define how people whom we find in the community may, like pasta, look different and still be wonderful to be with.

6. Cook the pasta. Have children observe how it looks after cooking. Give each child a piece to smell, touch, and taste. Highlight once

---

*Adapted from an idea in the unit *Apples, apples* in King, Chipman, and Cruz–Janzen (1994).

again the concept of people (still the same despite the changes).

7. Mix the pasta with sauce or sour cream and have the class enjoy it. Have a great diversity pasta snack!

Extensions:

▮ Place uncooked pasta in the art center for children to make art designs.

▮ Have some pasta boxes in the housekeeping area.

▮ Paste pasta samples on cardboard and place them in the writing corner. (Who knows what children will have to say about it!)

▮ Language Experience Approach (LEA) Make a poster about the "pasta family." Ask children to describe and discuss what they did.

Appendix D
Sample Lesson Plan Using "The Black Snowman"

Sample Kindergarten Lesson Plan*

Grade Level: Kindergarten

General Theme: Cold and snowy weather

Other Themes: Developing awareness about stereotypes

Concepts: Winter, concept of what is good/bad, stereotypes, unfairness

Content Overview: This lesson plan is part of a unit directed to offer children from the central Florida area opportunities to see how the weather affects the environment and how they should dress in order to be warm. This lesson will also offer children an opportunity to examine a stereotype and how it leads to unfairness.

Language/Literacy General Objectives:

1. To help children expand their vocabulary (winter objects; words or phrases depicting dislike about others).
2. To be able to describe (compare and contrast) how Jacob felt at the beginning of the story and how he felt at the end.
3. To have children discuss whether Jacob was right in disliking the color black.
4. To have children identify other situations in which people show dislike about something or someone because of their beliefs.

Developed by Brenda K. Herman, kindergarten teacher at Hiawatha Elementary School, Orlando, Florida.

Materials:

- mittens
- scarf
- kente cloth
- slush (melted, dirty shaved ice)

Utilization of the Environment as an Experiential Resource

A. Blocks: Make a tenement building similar to the picture in the story. Emphasize height.
B. Cooking/food experience: Make pancakes. Prepare "arepas" (a type of fried bread made by some Afro–Caribbean groups). It is made with flour, water, salt, baking powder, and vegetable oil.
C. Dramatic play: Dance with the Snowman; get Peewee out of the burning building; pretend dance with the African warriors.
D. Literacy: Display pictures of tenement buildings in New York (I had just returned from a visit to New York); sample of a *kente* cloth from Africa. Include other books like *Felita* (Mohr 1988) and *Black is brown is tan* (Adoff).
E. Writing/author's corner: Provide paper, markers, crayons, tape recorder for those children who might want to record their story instead of writing it.
F. Math: Count collected canned goods that will be donated to the needy; establish criteria to

group the collected canned goods; group cans according to established criteria.

Note:

In the story, Jacob is an angry boy who hates the color black because people associate the word negatively. Jacob states that even the white knight is good and the black knight is bad. This part of the story opened up quite a discussion in my classroom and a White [sic] child stated that a white man can be dressed up in a black suit and still be nice. An African American child jumped up and said that a black man can be dressed up in a white suit and be bad. Almost in unison the class said "It's not how you are dressed up or what your skin is like that makes you good or bad, it's how nice you are [to others]."

Appendix E
Sample Lesson Plan Using the Bredekamp and Rosegrant Model (1992)*

Families

Age: 1st Grade*

Topic: Families

Awareness

I will begin to focus on the family by sharing with the students some things about my own family. I will show photographs and describe my family. Students will be encouraged to bring photographs that will be labeled and displayed. There will be a table set up for displaying books and pictures about families. Students will be encouraged to share comments and anecdotes about their families.

We will make a list of family words. We will list family members as the students in my class perceive family members, remembering extended family members.

Exploration

Print the poem "Family Fun" on a chart. Read it aloud to your class, pointing to each line as you read. Then have students read it aloud with you

as you point to each line. Ask students who have sisters to raise their hands. Do this for brothers, pets, oldest children, youngest children, and children who are "in the middle." Children who have no brothers or sisters can include themselves in both the oldest and the youngest child categories.

Family Fun

A family can have some fun,
Come rain or snow or summer sun.

You want to play a family game?
Then stand when something is the same.

I have a sister, yes, I do,
Now stand up if you have one, too.

I have a brother, yes, I do,
Now stand up if you have one, too.

I have a pet, oh yes, I do,
Now stand up if you have one, too.

I am the oldest one, it's true,
Now stand if you're the oldest, too.

I am the youngest one, it's true,
Now stand if you're the youngest, too.

I am the middle one, it's true,
Now stand if you're the middle one, too.

Students will enjoy reciting this delightful action poem about families again and again. They will also get to know more about each other and their families.

*Prepared by Lori McCracken, first grade teacher, Las Vegas, Nevada.

Inquiry

This writing activity includes sharing between children and parents. Give students a day or two to think about and talk with parents about three significant events in their lives. When students have identified three important events, have them draw a colorful picture to illustrate each event. Teacher can circulate and write dictated sentences on each of the student's pictures. Each student will choose the most important event. Students will share their picture and the event with the class. We will include their choice in a class book.

Utilization

We will brainstorm a list of rules that families might have and decisions families might make. Students will use stick puppets or hand puppets to act out these family situations. Students could role-play instead of using puppets.

Let's Celebrate . . . Me!

Age: 1st Grade

Topic: Five Senses

Awareness

▌ Read *My Five Senses* by Aliki

▌ Discuss the five senses and the sensory organs we use for each one.

▌ Game: "Which Senses?" i.e., When we play with a ball, what senses are we using? We you help your mom make dinner, what senses are you using?

▌ We will make popcorn. While it is popping we will discuss the senses we are using. What sense will be the last one we use? Taste!

▌ Sing "Mr. Popcorn."

Exploration

Students will rotate in small groups to five stations. Each rotation will last 15 minutes. The stations will be student directed except for the two stations marked with an asterisk (*) .

1. Smelling Station
   Cups with ten smells inside will be covered. Students will match the smell to the card with the correct name of the object. When finished, they will make spice pictures. They will trace a simple picture with glue. Sprinkle with different spices.

*2. Hearing Station
   Students will play telephone. One student whispers a message to the child sitting beside him/her. The message continues around the circle until everyone has passed it on. The last person says the "secret message" aloud. Did it start and end the same?

3. Touching Station
   Students put their hands in tube socks. There has been an object placed in each of the ten socks. Students try and figure out what is in each of the socks. Socks are labeled one through ten. Students write the number of the socks on a piece of paper. With their inventive spelling, they write what they think is in each of the socks.

*4. Tasting Station
   Students will be blindfolded and will have their noses pinched as they taste a small piece of apple and then raw potato. We will discuss the senses we really use when eating.

5. Seeing Station
   Students will be blindfolded and will try to put a simple puzzle together. They will manipulate clay and try to build a simple object.

Inquiry

We will have some special vistors during this part of the five senses unit. Students will be given the opportunity to meet, listen to, and question some handicapped people who come to speak. We will have a blind speaker and a speaker who is deaf. After speakers leave, we will discuss differences and likenesses in people around us. We will make braille names with popcorn glued on tagboard. We will also begin learning the sign language alphabet.

Utilization

We will take a field trip to the local discovery museum. Students will get the chance to put their five senses to work. This is a child-centered museum to visit and use. Students will be challenged to put all five senses to work during our visit there. After lunch in the courtyard, students will record in their journals the many ways they used their five senses at the museum.

Appendix F
Patterns for Persona Dolls

Appendix G
Learning About Islands

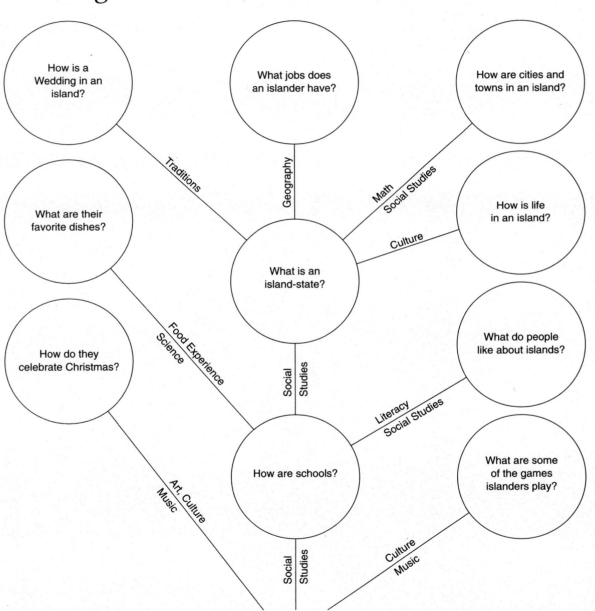

Appendix H
Island Stick Puppets

Ages: 4–6
Goal: To introduce children to common island animals (Caribbean, Bahamas).
Skills: To observe for details
        To compare objects based on similarities
        To work cooperatively with peers
Areas: Social Studies
        Science
        Art
        Literacy

Suggested Activities:

1. *Whole group activities*
Have children discuss the things they think are found on a Caribbean island. Observe pictures and posters about the region. Using a map of Central America or the Antilles, locate the island Caribbean region. With a wax pencil, draw a circle around them. Have children copy some of the names of the islands. If possible, invite a person from another Caribbean island to share with the class about their island-country.

2. *Small group activities*
Divide children in cooperative groups. Then, using a piece of ribbon or any other material, have children find out which islands are farther from, closer to, where they live. Start planning an imaginary trip to any other of the islands. Have children investigate the animal and plant life they would find.
Discuss with each group their findings. Guide children to make stick puppets to represent any of the animals they found. Children can write their own story and use the puppets to represent it. Have children dramatize their puppet story.

3. *Involving parents*
Ask parents to help children find what Caribbean foods are available at the grocery store. Have them select one item to taste and report to the class how they like it.

Appendix I
Planning for Cultural Diversity: Developing a Class Profile

Responsive and developmentally appropriate planning and teaching requires having a good knowledge about the children we teach. Teachers can prepare a class profile based on the elements of diversity. The form below could be used for creating your class profile.

CLASS PROFILE

Grade Level _____ Date: _____

Ages _____ Class size _____

Area: Urban ___ Suburban ___ Rural ____ How many girls? ___ Boys? ___

Social class structure	Ethnicities present	Main religious affiliations	Languages other than English

Family configurations present in my class	Exceptionalities present in my class	Comments, points to remember

Summary/highlights:

Appendix J
Creating the Multicultural Environment: Resources for the Classroom

❖ Videocassettes

Videos have become a powerful educational resource. Although for developmental reasons they are not as commonly used in early childhood classrooms, videos are another resource available for the multicultural curricula. They can be used to create a lending video library for parents. In schools with closed circuit systems, videos can also be shared with the entire school community. We have found several interesting titles that could help primary children to develop further awareness of multicultural issues. Titles marked with an asterisk* are available from Filmic Archives. The Cinema Center, Bostford, CT 06404. Telephone number: 1-800-366-1920.

On Diversity

*Fat Albert and the Gang Series. (1994). Included are the following titles:

> Everybody's Different and That's okay. 15 minutes
>
> Who Is an American? 15 minutes

*The Human Race Club Series. (1989). Includes six titles and particularly interesting are

> Prejudice and Discrimination. The Unforgettable Pen Pal. 28 minutes
>
> The Letter on Light Blue Stationery. 22 minutes

Cultural Celebrations (holidays)

*The series Holidays for Children (1994) includes 12 titles. They are close-captioned and each one is 30 minutes long.

▮ Traditional American Holidays
 Thanksgiving
 Arbor Day
 Valentine's Day
 Independence Day
 Halloween

▮ Hispanics
 Cinco de Mayo

▮ African American
 Kwanza

▮ Asian American
 Chinese New Year

▮ Religious celebrations
 Christmas
 Easter
 Hannukah/Passover
 Rosh Hashanah/Yom Kippur

*The series of grandmother Bubbe (1989) has two titles on Jewish holidays that include:

> Channuka at Bubbe's
>
> Passover at Bubbe's

Other Titles About Holidays

Children will enjoy these two videos about Thanksgiving:

> *Mouse on the Mayflower (1991)
>
> *Squanto and the First Thanksgiving (1993). 30 minutes

Multicultural Literature

Many well-known stories are also available on videocasettes. Videos can certainly add to the enjoyment of stories.

African American:

Joshua's Masai Mask. 9 minutes

Koi and the Kola Nuts. Rabbit Ears Collection

How the Leopard Got His Spots. Rabbit Ears Collection

Stories from the Black Tradition. A collection of stories to include: *A story, a story, Mufaro's Beautiful Daughters, Why Mosquitoes Buzz in People's Ears, The Village of Round and Square Houses,* and *Goggles.*

Follow the drinking gourd. (1992). 30 minutes

Asian American:

Peachboy

The boy who drew cats

Ye-Shen: A Cinderella story from China. (1985). 25 minutes

Native American:

Hawk, I'm your brother. (1989). 25 minutes

The song of Sacajawea. (1992). 30 minutes

❖ Classroom Materials

Nothing depicts children's beliefs better than their behavior in the classroom. To teach appropriate behavior, early childhood educators need different concrete materials in addition to their words and gestures. Materials are important tools that help us to design and build experiences for the child. This is especially true in a multicultural environment.

Teachers often obtain materials through parents, the school, and the community. There are also many commercially produced materials that can be purchased at most teacher supply stores. We have included the guidelines for an appropriate selection of materials. Listed in a checklist format, it will also serve as a guide of necessary classroom items. They represent basic materials for any typical early childhood classroom. For your convenience, names of distributors of multicultural materials have also been listed.

One word of advice: As you begin to select materials, use your "teachers' eyes." They will let you see resources where you would least expect to find them!

Guidelines for Selecting Basic Multicultural Materials for Any Typical Early Childhood Classroom

Grade/level: _____   Date: _____

Teacher: _____

Comments: _____

_____

_____

_____

_____

Type of Material	Guidelines for Responsive Selection of Materials	Enter a Check Mark (√) if Resources Comply with Guidelines
Visuals 1. posters 2. pictures 3. photographs of the class 4. cut-outs 5. classroom signs, labels	∎ Have posters, pictures of children from different ethnicities ∎ Include visuals about different disabilities ∎ Include visuals about people from different social statuses ∎ Avoid stereotypic pictures like ethnic people wearing only typical costumes or women doing only house chores ∎ Include pictures depicting intergenerational relationships	

Manipulatives
1. puzzles
  ∎ flags
  ∎ people
  ∎ countries
  ∎ places
  ∎ houses
2. ethnic items to include:
  ∎ cooking tools
  ∎ personal ornaments (bracelets, earrings, turbans, etc.)
  ∎ costumes
3. table games
4. objects for sorting, classifying
	∎ Look for accurate representations of flags, silhouette of countries
	∎ Avoid tokenism. Have more than one representation of a given culture, ethnicity
	∎ Avoid stereotypes. Include current ethnic costumes. Always include what people of cultures targeted commonly wear
	∎ Select cooking tools from various cultures
	∎ Include ethnic items for sorting (beans; pasta; food labels of canned ethnic food, boxes, etc.)	

Guidelines *continued*

Type of Material	Guidelines for Responsive Selection of Materials	Enter a Check Mark (√) if Resources Comply with Guidelines

Art supplies
1. paint
  ▪ fingerpaint
  ▪ tempera
  ▪ water colors
2. markers
3. crayons and color pencils
4. modeling clay
5. templates
  ▪ people
  ▪ alphabet
  ▪ holiday symbols
6. paper
  ▪ butcher paper
  ▪ construction paper
  ▪ brown paper bags
7. yarn
8. paper plates (different colors)
	▪ Include paint, markers, crayons, and modeling clay with a variety of skin colors
	▪ Select or prepare templates that include people with disabilities (i.e., child in wheelchair)
	▪ Include shapes of senior citizens
	▪ Include holiday symbols representing those of class and others
	▪ Have different shades of paper for art projects
	▪ Have yarn in a variety of colors (for hair color, skin color)	

Music/Movement 1. musical instruments 2. recorded music (tapes, records, compact discs) 3. charts with lyrics 4. materials to create ethnic musical instruments 5. dancing/movement outfits	▪ Include ethnic instruments or pictures of those if not easy to obtain ▪ Include music from a variety of cultures. Include familiar pieces played with ethnic instruments ▪ Include ethnic music for different family events (birthdays, weddings, births, etc.) ▪ Have a variety of items used for ethnic dances, games ▪ Display lyrics in various languages ▪ Include both familiar and new vocal music in other languages ▪ Have a variety of instrumental music ▪ Avoid stereotypic music, i.e., only loud music (like only "rap," "merengues," or "salsa") to depict given cultures ▪ Whenever possible, include names of composers of ethnic music	

Guidelines *continued*

Type of Material	Guidelines for Responsive Selection of Materials	Enter a Check Mark (√) if Resources Comply with Guidelines
Media Products (Before purchasing or checking out, always consider the developmental age level of the class) 1. videocassette programs 2. computer programs 3. films 4. filmstrips 5. transparencies	▮ Always preview before sharing programs with class. You will avoid surprises ▮ Avoid making selections on the title alone. They are not always descriptive of its content ▮ Avoid programs that stereotype cultures, people ▮ Evaluate the language used. Look for terms, words that might present biases ▮ Look for accuracy of information, images	

❖ Where to Obtain Learning Resources

The following companies and organizations offer a variety of multicultural materials including children's books, games, and teacher guides.

Afro-Am Education Materials. 819 S. Wabash Avenue, Chicago, IL 60605. Telephone: 312-922-1147

Arte Público Press. University of Houston 4800 Calhoun, M.D. Library, Room 2, Houston, TX 77204. (Good resources about Hispanic Americans)

Bellerophon Books. 122 Helena Avenue, Santa Barbara, CA 93101. (Books about Native Americans and American colonial times including coloring books. Includes series about distinguished women in American and European history)

Bridgewater Books. An imprint of Troll. 375 Hudson Street, New York, NY 10014. Telephone: 800-526-0275. (An excellent selection of multicultural literature for children)

Camera-Mundi Inc. Educational Materials. Amatista #8, Villa Blanca, Caguas, PR 00625. (Materials, music about Hispanic Caribbean cultures for early childhood education)

Carolrhoda Books, Inc. 242 First Avenue N., Minneapolis, MN 55401. (Good collection of ethnic books)

Creative Concepts for Children. P.O. Box 8697, Scottsdale, AZ 85252-8697. Telephone: 602-483-9274

Children's Book and Music Center. 2500 Santa Monica Blvd., Santa Monica, CA 90406-1130. Telephone: 800-443-1856

Children's Book Press. 6400 Hollis St. Emeryville, CA 94608. (Excellent collection of ethnic books)

China Books and Periodicals. 2929 24th Street, San Francisco, CA 94110

Children's Press. Subs. of Grolier, Inc. 5440 N. Cumberland Avenue, Chicago, IL 60656

Cobblestone Publishing, Inc. 7 School Street, Peterborough, NH 03458-1454. Telephone: 800-821-0115. (Publishes excellent magazine series on cultural and historical topics)

Council on Interracial Books for Children. 1841 Broadway, New York, NY 10023. Telephone: 212-757-5339 (Information and guidelines about culturally appropriate materials)

Generations Together. 121 University Place, Suite 300, Pittsburgh, PA 15260. (Offers a variety of materials to promote intergenerational understanding)

Gryphon House, Inc. 3706 Otis Street. P.O. Box 275 Mt. Rainier, MD 20704. Telephone: 800-638-0928. (Good source of nonsexist, multicultural classroom materials and literature)

National Geographic Society. 1145 17th St. NW, Washington, DC 20036. (Materials about people of diverse cultural backgrounds. Excellent resources about Native American groups)

Identity Toys Inc. 2821 N. 4th Street, Milwaukee, WI 53212. Telephone: 800-272-0287. (A variety of children's books, toys, games, and puzzles about African American topics)

Lakeshore Learning Materials. 2695 E. Dominguez St., Carson, CA 90749. Telephone: 800-421-5354. (Good source for multicultural classroom materials)

Harambee/Just Us Books, Inc. 301 Main Street, Suite 22-24, Orange, NJ 0750. (Good collection of African American children's literature. Also publishes *Harambee*, a newspaper for upper elementary students and a good reference for teachers)

People of Every Stripe! P.O. Box 12505, Portland, OR 97212. Telephone: 503-282-0612. (Durable persona dolls representing all the characteristics of diversity)

Redleaf Press. A division of Resources for Child Caring. 450 N. Syndicate Suite 5, St. Paul, Minnesota 55104-4125. Telephone: 800-423-8309. (A variety of reference books for teachers, children's books, videos, and audiocassettes)

Reading Rainbow. GPN University of Nebraska-Lincoln, P.O. Box 80669, Lincoln, NE 68501-0669. Telephone: 800-228-4630. (Excellent videocassette collection of PBS's multicultural literature TV series. Teacher's guide available)

Scholastic, Inc. 730 Broadway, New York, NY 10003. (Good source for multicultural children's books and teacher reference materials)

Smithsonian Institution. Washington, DC 20560. Telephone: 202-357-2700. (Excellent resource on American ethnic groups and the arts. The exhibits at the National Museum of African Art and the National Museum of American History are impressive. Information on ethnic groups and educational materials is available through their education department)

Social Studies School Service. 10200 Jefferson Boulevard, Room P3. P.O. Box 802, Culver City, CA 90232-0802. Telephone: 800-421-4246. E-Mail: SSSService@AOL.com

UAHC Press. Division of American Hebrew Congregations. 838 Fifth Avenue, New York, NY 10021

Appendix K

Checklist for Diversity in Early Childhood Education and Care (SECA)

CHECKLIST FOR DIVERSITY IN EARLY CHILDHOOD EDUCATION AND CARE

How do we support diversity in early childhood classrooms? Genuine diversity begins with respect for each and every individual and grows with adults' understanding that culture is a powerful part of children's development. In early childhood settings, this means that each and every child and family feels respected and valued.

This checklist includes features of the culturally diverse, developmentally appropriate early childhood classroom. It can help you think through the fundamental issues of diversity in early childhood education and care. Remember that some of these features may be appropriate for very young children but not for primary-grade children, and vice versa. Few programs have all of these features, but all early childhood programs can and should have some of these features and demonstrate that they are working toward the others.

INTERACTIONS IN THE CLASSROOM

☐ •Are children encouraged to talk with each other?

☐ Are there times when children can tell imaginative and true stories of their own experiences?

☐ Are children encouraged to listen to everyone's ideas as they work on projects in groups?

☐ Do they have opportunities throughout the day to work and play in pairs and small groups as well as in mixed-age groups and alone?

☐ Does the teacher help children who do not speak English to participate in conversations?

☐ •Does the teacher really listen to the children?

☐ Does she respond to children's specific ideas and questions instead of making general comments like "good idea" or "we'll get to that later"?

☐ Does the teacher pay attention to and use different communication styles?

☐ Does she sit at the children's eye level?

☐ •Does the teacher intervene when children hurt each other's feelings?

☐ Does she help children figure out reasons for conflicts and support their problem-solving, rather than simply discouraging insults?

☐ •Does the teacher observe rather than lead the activity in the room much of the time?

FAMILY INVOLVEMENT

☐ •Does the teacher see family members as resources?

☐ Are family members encouraged to visit classrooms at any time?

☐ Does the teacher solicit family participation?

☐ Does she make arrangements as necessary to accommodate all family members, including persons with disabilities and extended family members?

☐ •Does the teacher consider children's home cultures in planning center or school events?

☐ Do working parents receive enough notice of assignments and special activities to allow them to fully participate?

☐ Are announcements, newsletters, etc., spoken and written in families' home languages?

☐ Are activities inexpensive enough for all to participate?

☐ •Are activities, materials, and resources in the classroom open-ended about the nature of families, instead of suggesting, for instance, that every family has "a mommy and a daddy"?

COMMUNITY INVOLVEMENT

☐ •Do children have many informal opportunities to meet parents and other community members who work in various capacities? For example, do they meet the father who is a blind executive, or the merchant who is Vietnamese?

☐ •Do teachers encourage visitors to talk with individual children and with small groups as well as with whole classes?

☐ •Do centers and schools recognize that all people are important, instead of occasionally celebrating a few well-known persons such as Martin Luther King, Jr.? Do they recognize persons in children's own families who contribute to the community?

☐ •Does the center or school use senior citizens as resources? What about high school students?

☐ •Are children able to take field trips to various nearby locations so that they can learn about their own community?

PHYSICAL ENVIRONMENT

- [ ] •Does the classroom seem to be the children's place or the teacher's place?
- [ ] Are children's creative artworks displayed throughout the room?
- [ ] Is a bulletin board available to the children as a work space for notes and plans and for works in progress?
- [ ] Are there "mailboxes" where children can leave private messages for each other and for teachers?
- [ ] Is there a show-and-tell display area? Are photographs and artifacts of the children's families evident?
- [ ] Does the teacher continually replace or rearrange materials in classroom centers to support children's changing interests? For example, does the dramatic play center lend itself to a fishing pier as well as the traditional "housekeeping"?
- [ ] •Do materials in the room reflect the cultural diversity of the children and of the world?
- [ ] Do dolls and other toys reflect different ethnic backgrounds and physical abilities?
- [ ] Is there a large quantity and wide variety of classic and contemporary picture and story books?
- [ ] Are high-quality, culturally diverse children's periodicals, such as *Cricket*, *Spider*, and *Ladybug*, available?
- [ ] •Does the teacher demonstrate the world's variety of languages in her classroom?
- [ ] Do labels in the classroom reflect children's home languages? Are some labels in Braille?

CURRICULUM

- [ ] •Does the curriculum incorporate each child's personal experiences?
- [ ] Does the curriculum reflect that different individuals view and interpret the world differently?
- [ ] Are children able to suggest topics for exploration?
- [ ] Does the teacher suggest that children pursue interesting ideas through different forms and media? For example, would the teacher suggest that a child experiment with creating a self-portrait in crayon, pencil, and then collage? Would he invite a preschooler to expand a block construction, or a second-grader to write a second draft of a story, adding more details?
- [ ] •Does the teacher recognize and support children's different learning styles?
- [ ] Does the school honor all children's efforts instead of focusing on academic "stars"?
- [ ] •Does the teacher pay attention to individual children's interests and provide opportunities for them to pursue those interests?
- [ ] Does the teacher frequently group children according to their interests, instead of grouping them by ability?
- [ ] •Does the teacher discourage bias? For example, does he support a girl's interest in science or math?
- [ ] •Do children have many opportunities to express themselves and explore ideas through art, music, and plays?
- [ ] •Do children have many opportunities to write notes, letters, lists, diaries, stories, and songs?
- [ ] Does the teacher treat children's writings seriously by "publishing" some and sharing it with other classes, families, etc.?
- [ ] •Does the program measure each child's accomplishments in comparison to that child's earlier work through the use of portfolios?

Glossary

Bias—"any attitude, belief, or feeling that results in and helps to justify unfair treatment of an individual because of his or her identity".

Checklist—an assessment instrument, usually consisting of "go" or "no go" choices used in an educational setting to collect factual data about student behaviors, physical arrangements, use of materials and activities, and student achievement, among others, that are objectively observed in the classroom.

Classroom Environment—the overall result of the arrangement and disposition of materials and equipment within a given learning setting. It is designed to promote the physical, cognitive, and social–emotional development of young learners; the sum of all the parts that comprises a teaching/learning setting. It includes the space, the social and emotional atmosphere, the cognitive, and the creative opportunities.

Content—the topics, concepts, and themes selected for children to experience in the classroom.

Culture—the way of life of a social group, including all of its materials and nonmaterial products that are transmitted from one generation to the next.

Cultural Pluralism—a social state based on the premise that all newcomers have a right to maintain their languages and cultures while combining with others to form a new society reflective of all our differences.

Cultural Schema—information that defines how to behave in a particular culture. Information in schemes represents the way the particular cultural group interprets reality.

Development—process of continuous change observed over time and experienced by all human beings.

Developmental Milestones—significant events children will exhibit at different periods of life. They describe typical characteristics of a child at a certain time during childhood like the onset of talking, walking, and reading.

Early Childhood Curriculum—the formal and informal experiences through which young children are empowered to continue the process of knowledge acquisition and development.

Eclectic—a combination of two or more ideas or approaches to produce a new vision, solve a problem, achieve a goal, or define a position.

Educational Equity—establishing the same educational resources and opportunities for all children, despite their diverse characteristics.

Equality—when all individuals in a society are provided with equal access to the same opportunities and resources.

Family Configurations—the variety of forms depicting the combination of individuals found in a family.

Family Involvement—activities and programs planned for the purpose of establishing effective ways to encourage the participation of all the family members. The underlying purpose of the program is to improve the opportunities for the proper development of the child.

Family Rituals—practices depicting rites and ceremonies performed by families across cultures with the intent to signify and mark a particular event.

Family Structure—the composition and associated roles of family members.

Goal—a statement that defines the intent and aspirations of a program or of an activity.

Immigrants—individuals from a country or a nation who settle in another country for various reasons. For example, Jamaicans came from their native country to establish themselves in the USA.

Learning Encounter—activity especially designed to lead the child into the active self-discovery of a given set of ideas/skills or knowledge.

Material Culture—those overt or tangible aspects that are easily observed in a culture. They include ways of decoration, what people eat, manners, and what they wear.

Migrants—individuals who relocate to a different geographical region of one country or cross borders of other countries on a regular basis for a specific reason. For example, farm workers move seasonally from one state to another to pick oranges.

Multicultural Content—the "what" children experience, which is defined by its significance, validity, interest, and usefulness.

Multicultural Early Childhood Educator—a teacher with a professional commitment to offer children ages 0-8 specially designed developmental experiences where both the child's immediate multicultural realities and those of our nation are considered and valued. This educator tailors the curriculum to the developmental and cultural needs of children for the purpose of helping them learn to interact and succeed in the American multicultural society.

Multicultural Education—a process of comprehensive and basic education for all students. It challenges racism and other forms of discrimination in schools and society and accepts and affirms the pluralism (ethnic, racial, linguistic, religious, economic, gender, exceptionalities) that students, their communities, and teachers represent.

Multicultural Literature—the collection of literature depicting ethnic groups and other elements of diversity.

Multiple Perspectives Learning—process of discovering reality through more than one point of view.

Multiculturalism—a philosophical position and movement that assumes that the gender, ethnic, racial, and cultural diversity of a pluralistic society should be reflected in all of the institutionalized structures of educational institutions, including the staff, the norms, and values, the curriculum, and the student body.

Non-European Americans—a broad category that includes all those who are, or whose ancestors were originally, from any part of the world other than Europe.

Nonmaterial Culture—represents those things not overtly seen but discovered through interaction with people of a specific culture. Nonmaterial aspects include ideas, values, ethics, beliefs, and behaviors.

Nontraditional Family—those with configurations different from the two-parent model.

Objective—a statement that establishes the specific purposes for an activity or exercise. It describes the nature and the level of knowledge the student will derive from the experience.

Planning—process through which actions are taken and decisions are made to accomplish a chosen goal and the directions and procedures for implementation are selected and organized.

Process—ways and procedures used by teachers to deliver the curriculum content.

Socialization—the process through which individuals learn the accepted patterns of behavior and interactions in the context of the society to which they belong. During the process, adults pass on to the young the group's social concepts that will mold them in consonance with their patterns.

Stereotype—"an oversimplified generalization about a particular group, race, or sex, which usually carries derogatory implication".

Survey—an oral or written assessment instrument designed to get specific answers from a designated constituency. Similar to a questionnaire, a survey usually consists of a list of open- or closed-ended statements designed to elicit information about targeted points or issues.

Traditional Family—typically represented by being a two-parent family.

Index

A

Acculturation, 88
ACEI (Association for Childhood Education International), 211, 232, 292
Action map, 237
Activities, 273–318
  sample, 365–67
  with families, 349
Activity levels, influenced by culture, 125
Activity sheets, sample, 314–15
Addams, Jane, 158, 162–63
African Americans
  and diversity, 63
  and racial awareness, 136
  and slavery, 27
  as Civil War soldiers, 13
  education history, 159–60
  history of, 165
  population percent, 20
American Revolution, 154
Americans with Disabilities Act, 168
Amish, 63
Anti-bias approach, 203, 249. *See also* Derman-Sparks, Louise
Anti-Bias Curriculum (A.B.C.) Task Force, 36
Art, 285–88
Art materials, 287
  and cultures, 287
ASDC (Association for Supervision and Curriculum Development), 32, 309
  model planning web, 309
Asians, and family, 85
Assessment tools. *See also* Baruth and Manning's Assessment Criteria

designing, 232
  in school districts, 231–32
Assessment web, 218
Association for Childhood Education International (ACEI), 211, 232, 292
Association for Supervision and Curriculum Development (ASCD), 32, 309
Atlanta Compromise, 162
Attitudes, into classroom, 344
Awareness
  multicultural, 365–67
  phase of learning process, 301
  sample less plan, 371–73

B

Bank Street College of Education, 169
Bank Street models, 181
Banks' Levels of Integration, 184–85, 249
  additive approach, 186, 188
  contributions approach, 184–86
  social action approach, 189, 192, 193
  transformation approach, 186, 189
Banks' profile of multiculturalism, 231
Banks, James S., 37, 164, 169, 170, 182–83, 241, 280
Baruth and Manning's Assessment Criteria, 229
Bethune, Mary McLeod, 159
Bias, defined, 281
Bilingual Education Act of 1974, 168

Bilingual kindergarten programs, 195
Biological inheritance, 120
Birth weight, 118
Breathwaite, Elizabeth, 292
Bredekamp and Rosegrant Model, sample lesson plan, 371–73
Bronfenbrenner, Urie, 79, 121
Bronfenbrenner ecological model, 122
Brown vs. Board of Education (1954), 28, 67, 166, 168
Brown, Esther, 166
Bruner, Jerome, 45

C

Calderón de la Barca, Pedro, 45
Cambodia, 23
Caribbean ethnicity, 64
Carnegie, Dale, 14
Carroll, Lewis, 51
Cary, Miles A., 158, 163
Castro, Fidel, 16
Central Intelligence Agency (CIA), 23
Central Pacific Railroad, and Chinese immigrants, 13, 15
Cermak, 14
Chapter I programs, 195
Chard, Sylvia, 225
Checklist, defined, 230
Checklists, family, 332
Cheney State College, 159, 161
Child development, 109–44
  by age, 114–16
  defined, 110–13
  Piaget's levels of, 113–16, 297
Childrearing, 84

Children, as labor force, 15–16
Children's literature recommendations
   child development, 143
   classroom designs, 206
   community, 354
   culture, 71–72
   families, 106
   multicultural education history, 175–76
   planning, 271
   program implementation, 238
   resources, 316
   social diversity, 39
Children at-risk programs, 195
Chinese immigration, 13, 15
Cicero, Marcus Tillius, 153
Civil Rights Act (1875), 165
Civil Rights Act (1964), 29, 168
Civil War, 13, 14
Clark, Kenneth, 137
Class profile, 381
Classroom
   and curriculum design, 209–39
   as mirror of family, 94
   as reflection of society, 70
   materials, 384–87
   news project, 346
   physical design, 253
Classroom applications of theory
   celebrations, 52
   classroom quilt, 130
   code of ethics, 339
   collaborators, 342
   concept development model, 246
   conceptual scheme, 222–23
   contribution, 187
   diversity, 10, 59
   dressing visual environment, 255
   early childhood content selection, 194
   ethnicity in perspective, 224
   families in classroom, 325, 326, 330, 339

family cookbook, 97
family origins, 18
finding help for environment assessment, 256
group investigation model, 201
holiday time line, 85
human relations approach, 197–98
immigrants, 16
inequality as a concept, 156–57
language diversity, 139
NCSS performance expectations, 226
planning for whole child, 258
prop boxes, 132
surnames, 329
Taba's model, 247
Tyler's curricular model, 245
universal milestones, 119
Classroom environment
   creative, 278
   defined, 253, 275
   flexible space, 278
   guidelines for multicultural, 280–81
   instructional materials, 279–80
   interest areas, 279
   physical, 275
   social-emotional, 276
Classroom teaching, and diversity, 278
Cold War, 16
Coleman, James, 168, 320, 349
Coleman Report, 168
Collaboration, 325–27
   and modern technology, 349
   defined, 326
   with parents and families, 344
Comenius, John Amos, 155
Communication, 341–49
   vs. compliance, 345
   defined, 343
   nonverbal, 118
   planning meetings, 347
Communist countries, 19

Community
   and schools, 339
   as resource, 352
   profile, 340
Comprehensive Child Development Program (CCDP), 173
Concept web, 308
Confidentiality in surveys, 336
Congress on Racial Equality (CORE), 167
Content, defined, 223
Content infusion, 268
Conversations, 347–48
Coppin, Fanny Jackson, 158–60
Cordero, Rafael, 158–59
CORE (Congress on Racial Equality), 167
Courtesy words, 141
Covert culture, 47–48
Crawford, Leslie, 310
Crawford model, and literature, 311
Cultural composition, of classroom, 199
Cultural diversity, 57
   analyzed, 57
   and the American way, 61
   social factors of, 58
Cultural identity
   defined, 58
   ecological, 58
   elements of, 55
   national, 58
   racio-ethnic, 58
   regional, 58
   universal, 58
Cultural origin, defined, 8
Cultural pluralism, defined, 8
Cultural plurality, 9
Cultural relevancy, 260
Cultural schema, 51–54
   and behavior, 51–52
   defined, 53
Cultural values, and family, 100
Cultural viewpoints, 70
Culturally different, teaching, 193
Culturally mixed marriage, 91

Culture, 43–73. *See also* Cultural
    identity
  and behavior patterns, 46
  and children, 48
  and development, 120
  and family, 79, 83
  and identity, 47
  and interactions, 46
  and social groups, 45
  and subcultures, 47
  as contributor to identity, 119
  as dynamic process, 69
  defined, 6, 44
  stability and change in, 69–70
  types of, 47
Curriculum
  and families, 349
  appraisal of existing, 199
  bridge elements, 194
  early childhood, defined, 223
  early multicultural, 169–70
  emergent, 221
  establishing goals in, 199
  framework, 312
  integrated, 225
  models, 181–204. *See also specific
    models*
  process, defined, 223–24
  programs, assessment, 219
  tourist approach, 204
  transformative, 245
Curriculum content
  child-centered, 220–21
  early childhood, 220
  synthesis perspective, 221
Curriculum design
  elements of, 375
  for multicultural education,
    248–49
*Curriculum Guidelines for Multi-
    ethnic Education*, 169

D

Dance, 293
DAP (developmentally appro-
    priate practice), 34, 117, 121,
    234, 244, 300, 305, 313, 366

Dara, Chiemruom, 139
Delacre, Lulu, 139
Derman-Sparks, Louise, 137, 182,
    184, 203, 280, 281, 283,
    305. *See also* Anti-bias
    approach
Design activities, for class-
    room, 299
Development. *See also* Child devel-
    opment
  and individuality, 117–18
  and influence of teachers, 131
  and nonverbal communi-
    cation, 118
  intellectual, 113
  social-emotional, 131
  traits of, 112–13
Developmental areas, wheel,
    259
Developmental instructional mate-
    rials, 282
Developmental milestones,
    119, 128
Developmental planning, and in-
    dividual needs, 123
Developmentally appropriate
    goals, 261
Developmentally appropriate
    practice. *See* DAP
Disabilities, 141, 198
  children's perceptions of, 141
Diversity
  and collaboration, 325
  and families, 325, 341
  checking classroom environ-
    ment, 236
  elements of, 60
  infusing perspective on, 270
  language, 139
  social directions caused
    by, 61
Dolls, and multicultural experi-
    ence, 284. *See also* Persona
    dolls
Dorros, Arthur, 139
DuBois, W. E. B., 136, 167
Dupont, E. I., 14

E

Early childhood programs, 223
Eclectic, defined, 246
Ecological levels, 124
Ecological view of develop-
    ment, 121
Education of All Handicapped Act
    of 1975 (EHA), 168, 174. *See
    also* IDEA
Education, as family function
Educational equality, 149–50, 154
Educational equality, milestones
    of, 168
Educational models, 181–206
Educational reform, 180
Egyptian immigrants, 99
EHA (Education of All Handi-
    capped Act of 1975), 168, 174.
    See also IDEA
Eight Year Study model, 245
El Salvador, 25
Elders, valuing, 198
Emancipation Proclamantion, 13,
    161, 165
Emile (Rousseau), 155
Emotional readiness, of mother,
    118
Environment. *See also* Classroom
    environment
  as shaping force in develop-
    ment, 121
  as source of awareness, 136–37
  forces in, 124
  multicultural, 383
  teaching, 252
Equal opportunity, as classroom
    philosophy, 1
Equal Opportunity Act of 1964, 29
Equality, 148–54
  defined, 154
  early efforts in education, 152–53
  in education, 149–50
  in 18th c., 155
  in modern history, 154
  in the Americas, 158–63
  history of idea of, 148
Erikson, Erik, 128–29

ESOL programs, 195
ESOL teachers, 256
Ethnic characteristics, awareness of, 135
Ethnic diversity, 1
Ethnic feelings, intensity of, 65
Ethnic music, 293
Ethnic perception, with non-European Americans, 64
Ethnicity
    Caribbean, 64
    defined, 62
    how received, 63
Ethnographics, changing in U.S., 6
Ethnography, 54, 56
European Americans, 20–23
    and dolls, 284
    and family, 85
    defined, 22, 33
    descent, 20
European immigrants, 15
Even Start programs, 195
Exceptional children, teaching, 193
Expectations, setting, 259–60
Exploration phase of learning process, 301
    sample lesson plan, 371–73
Extended family, 341

F

Family, 75–107
    and communication, 84–85
    and cultural differences, 87
    and diversity, 76, 86
    and employment of women, 92–94
    and teachers, 88
    aspirations, 100
    children's definitions of, 80
    children's views of, 83
    components of, 87
    configurations, 86, 341
    defined, 76–79
    entitlement by society, 96–98
    evolution and change, 92–94
    extended, 341
    functions of, 80–82

history of change, 92
importance of, 94
in crisis, 87
involvement, defined, 323–24
learning in classroom, 331
models, 90
pluralistic view of, 94
positive attitudes toward, 328
records, 334
rituals, 98, 100
roles, 82–83
sense of belonging in, 81
single-parent, 341
social interaction in, 85
structures, 324
survey, 335–38
tasks, 80–81
transformation of, 93
Family diversity, implications for teachers, 90–92
Family folders, 334, 338
Family Literacy Program, 333
Family map, 88–89
Farmer, James, 167
Folk songs, 293
Follow Through Project, 168, 173, 174
Foods, ethnic, 4, 132, 337
Ford, Clyde, 67
Freire, Paulo, 203
French Revolution, 154–55

G

Games and play, 297–99
Gender
    and Eastern European culture, 131
    and Hispanic culture, 131
    awareness, in children, 131
    perception of differences, 131
    stereotypes at play and in classroom, 133–35
Gender roles, and parents, 134
General educational goals, 257
Genetic code, and development, 118

German-Americans, 95
Gibson, Eleanor, 129
Goal, defined, 257
Gómez, Aurelia, 287
Grant, Carl, 183. *See also* Sleeter *and* Grant Typology
Great Plains Indians, 15
Greenfield, Eloise, 304
Group investigation model, 201
Groups, 45, 55

H

Hampton Normal and Agricultural Institute, 162
Hawaiians, 30
Head Start Program, 168, 169, 171–74, 195
Hernández, Hilda, 37, 229, 280
Hernández's Teacher Survey, 229
Heterogeneity, defined, 33
High scope model, 181
Hispanics
    and childrearing, 84
    defined, 23
    groups inside, 25
Hmong, of Southeast Asia, 23
Holidays, 383
Home environment, and development, 118, 120
Home Start Program, 168
Homeless children, 198
Hoover, Herbert, 170
Hull House, 162–63
Human relations approach, to curriculum, 195–96, 202

I

IDEA (Individuals with Disabilities Act), 174. *See also* EHA
Identity, finding , 57
Immigrants, and immigration, 11–19
    Chinese, 13
    defined, 11
    Eastern European, 19
    economic, 15

Immigrants, (*continued*)
  illegal, 19
  Irish, 13
  Latin American, 19
  Mexico, 19
  non-European, 19
  Oriental, 13
  Pennsylvania families, 17
  Western Europeans, 16
Immigration history
  17th c., 9
  18th c., 9, 13
  1850s, 13
  1880s, 14
  19th c., 13
  20th c., 15
  1960s, 93
  Chinese in 19th c., 13
  European, 15
  Great Migration of 1618–1623, 12
Indentured servants, 13
Individuality
  and cultural differences, 129
  and self-esteem, 128–29
  as character of development, 117–18
  inside diversity, 128
Individuals with Disabilities Act (IDEA), 174. *See also* EHA
Inequality, concept of, 156
Integrated topics, web, 308

J

Japanese-American Relocation Camps, 163
Jenkins, Ella, 297
Jim Crow laws, 28
Journals, 290, 292
Judaism, and diversity, 63

K

Kagan, Sharon, 327
Katz, Lillian, 225
Kendall, Frances, 151, 182, 184, 204, 283, 298

goals for multicultural education, 205, 250
  model, 249
Kennedy, John F., 168
Kennedy, Robert, 168
Kilpatrick, William, 225
Kindergarten, 303, 369–70
King, Martin Luther, Jr., 28, 167, 168
Konner, Melvin, 83
Ku Klux Klan, 28
Kung culture, 83
Kutner, Bernard, 137

L

Language, 123
  acceptable by group, 124
  diversity, 139
Learning cycle, 302, 303
Learning encounter, defined, 301
Learning resources, source list, 387, 388
Lesson plan, sample, 369–70
Life Among the Paiutes (Winnemucca), 159
Life events, as themes in curriculum, 297
Lincoln, Abraham, 165
Literacy area, in classroom environment, 288–93
Literacy-based approach to education, 153
Literature
  and multiculturalism, 288–93
  Crawford model, 311
  multicultural web, 363
  sample lesson plans, 369–73
Living arrangements, statistics, 320
London, Jonathan, 139

M

Machado, Antonio, 353
Magazines, 290

Mann, Horace, 159
Marshall, Thurgood, 28
Material vs. nonmaterial culture, 47, 49
Matsumoto-Grah, Karen, 282
Mayer, Gina, 80
Mayer, Mercer, 80
McCarren-Walter Act, 16
McCracken, Lori, 371
Meisel's model for early childhood assessment, 181
Melting pot, 61
  vs. multiculturalism, 31
Miami, as immigration center, 23
Middle Eastern groups, 26, 33
  and family, 85
Miel, Alice, 137
Migrant Program, 168
Migrants, defined, 11
Million Men March, 29
Models, guidelines for examining, 182
Monocultural classroom, 251–52
Morgan, J. P., 14
Morris, Jeanne, 282
Movement, 293
Multicultural classroom setting, 278
Multicultural activities, action-oriented, 68
Multicultural awareness, sample activities, 365–67
Multicultural children's books, 357–62. *See also* Children's literature recommendations *and* Literature
  age/intergenerational, 360–61
  Asian Americans, 358
  Caribbean, 358
  differences/diversity, 362
  disability, 361
  ethnicity, 357–58
  gender, 360
  Hispanic Americans, 360

Multicultural children's books,
(*continued*)
Native Americans,
359–60
social class, 361
Multicultural content,
defined, 268
Multicultural early childhood
educator, defined, 213
Multicultural education, 145–206
advocates of, 37
and individuality, 128
beginnings of, 147–57
classroom implementation of,
179–206
curricular approach, 198
defined, 150
goals for, 182
history of, 164–75
ideas into action, 241–72
models, 181–206
Roman contributions to, 154
time line, 151–52
Multicultural environment, resources, 383
Multicultural literature. *See also*
Literature
defined, 288
evaluation criteria, 290
web, 363
Multicultural resources, inexpensive, 284
Multicultural society, classroom
design, 274
Multicultural teaching, 180,
209–40
content selection, 266–72
early childhood, 212–13
organizing, 243
planning, 214, 242
Multiculturalism, defined, 8
vs. melting pot, 31
Multiethnic studies, 169
Multiple perspective learning, defined, 299–300
Multiracial class materials, 254
Music, 293, 296

N
NAACP (National Association for
the Advancement of Colored
People), 28, 166, 167
Naming of children, 101–104
National Association of Early
Childhood Specialists, 226,
227, 261, 265
National Association for the Education of Young Children
(NAEYC), 32, 34, 211, 226, 232,
254, 261–62, 265, 336
National Association for the Ad-
vancement of Colored People
(NAACP), 28, 166, 167
National Council for the Social
Studies (NCSS), 32, 264–65
National Geographic, 292
National Origins Act, 16
Native Americans
and alcoholism, 26
and English colonization, 12
and family, 85
and gambling, 26
and reservations, 15
and rising population, 20
and tourism, 26
defined, 22
school for, 159
visit to family, 53
NCSS (National Council for
the Social Studies), 32,
264–65
Needs assessment, 217
Neighborhood safety, 340
Newspapers, 290, 292
Nieto, Sonia, 37, 280
Non-European Americans
and future, 35, 36
as victims, 69
defined, 21, 22, 33, 34
origin, 20
population, 30
Non-Hispanic teachers, 125
Nonmaterial culture, 49
Nonquota immigrants, 16
Nonsexist class materials, 254

Nonstereotypic class materials, 254
Noori, Kathryn, 140

O
Objective, defined, 257
Operation Wetback, 166
Organizations for parents and
families, 354
Ornaments, in transformation ap-
proach, 189–90
Overt culture, 47–48

P
Pacific Islanders, 30
Palmer, Hap, 297
Parent-teacher relationships, 344
Parks, Rosa, 28, 166–67
Patet Lao forces, 23
Patterns of life, 51
Peabody, Elizabeth, 159
Pearl Harbor, 163
Perceptions of disability, 141
Persona dolls, 293, 297, 375
Pestalozzi, Johann, 157
Physical characteristics, and race,
65–66
Physical differences, aware-
ness, 135
Physical environment, of class-
room, 275
Physical scenario, changing, 252
Piaget, Jean, 113–16, 297
Planning
defined, 246
framework, 301
matrix, 267
web, 291, 308, 309
Plato, 152–53
Play, survey of, 338
Play, theory of, 298
Plessy vs. Fergusson, 165, 166
Pluricultural program, 207. *See also*
Multicultural education *and*
Multicultural teaching
Post-Civil War Era, 27
Poston Relocation Center, 163–64

Pregnancy, stress during, 118
Prejudice, 68, 138. *See also* Race
Prenatal experience, and development, 120
Preterm birth, 118
Prior knowledge, and classroom setting, 260
Process, defined, 223
Project Follow Through, 168, 173, 174
Project Head Start, 168
Prosocial skills, 141–42
Protagoras, 148
Puerto Rican teachers, 125

Q

Quintilian, Marcus Fabius, 153, 154

R

Race
  awareness, 135–41
  defined, 64
  social implications of, 66
Raffi, 297
Raymond, Patricia, 292
Reconstructionist, educational approach, 200
Redlands Christian Migrant Association (RCMA), 333
Refugees, 198
Relevant knowledge, vs. trivial, 260
Resources, 319–55, 383
  family, 323–25
  parents, 321–23
Reunification Act of 1965, 23
Rivera, Ann, 327
Rockefeller, John D., 14
Rousseau, Jean Jacques, 155, 157
Russo-Japanese War (1905), 15

S

Samoans, 30
School for the Poor, 158
School neighborhood, 339–40

School-Parent environment, 219
Scott, Elisha, 166
SECA (Southern Early Childhood Association), 232, 389–91
Self as social entity, 137–38
Self-investigation, 304
Shapiro, Laura, 133
Single-group studies, in curriculum, 196
Sino-Japanese War (1895), 15
Slavery
  abolition of, 27
  history of, 160
  in New World, 13
Sleeter and Grant Typology, 192–96, 202, 203, 249
Sleeter, Christine, 168, 182–83
Social activities, with families, 350–52
Social Contract (Rousseau), 155
Socialization, 123–26
Social learning, 126–27
Social scientists, 45, 127
Southern Early Childhood Association (SECA), 230, 232, 389–91
Special education programs, 195
STAR model (Stop Think Ask Respond), 330
Stereotypes, 67, 68
  defined, 281
Stereotypical content, avoiding, 269
Student attitude assessment, sample, 232
Surnames, 104, 329
Surveys, 332
  and confidentiality, 336
  defined, 230
  family, 335–38

T

Taba, Late Hilda, 204
Taba model, 247
Takei, George, 163, 164
Taus, Kay, 293
Teaching. *See also* Multicultural education

blueprint, 242, 267
cycle, 302
envirnoment, 213
models, evaluation of, 183
thematic, 191, 305
topics for, 307
Theme projects, 308
Token diversity, avoiding, 283
Tuskegee Institute, 159

U

United States, as multicultural country, 4
U.S. Census Bureau, 20
U.S. Supreme Court, 67, 165, 168
Universality, as character of development, 113, 118

V

Vanderbilt, Cornelius, 14
Vietnam War, 16, 168
Voting Rights Act, 168

W

Walbridge Caring Communities Program, 333
War on Poverty, 168, 171
Washington, Booker T., 158–62
Western Expansion, post-Civil War, 14
White House Conference on Children, 170
Whole child, concept of, 257–58
Winnemucca, Sarah, 158–59
Wollstonecraft, Mary, 158
Women's rights, history of, 158
World Magazine, 292
World War I, 15
World War II, 163

Z

Zangwill, Israel, 61